Imagining the Forest

Imagining the Forest // Narratives of
Michigan and the Upper Midwest

John Knott

THE UNIVERSITY OF MICHIGAN PRESS

Ann Arbor

Published in the United States of America by
The University of Michigan Press
Manufactured in the United States of America
⊗ Printed on acid-free paper

2015   2014   2013   2012   4 3 2 1

A CIP catalog record for this book is available from the British Library.

Library of Congress Cataloging-in-Publication Data

Knott, John R. (John Ray), 1937–
        Imagining the forest : narratives of Michigan and the Upper
    Midwest / John Knott.
            p. cm.
        Includes bibliographical references and index.
        ISBN 978-0-472-07164-7 (acid-free paper) — ISBN 978-0-472-05164-9
    (pbk. : acid-free paper) — ISBN 978-0-472-02807-8 (e-book)
        1. Michigan—In literature.   2. Middle West—In literature.
    3. Forests in literature.   4. Forestry in literature.   5. Nature in
    literature.   6. Forests and forestry—Michigan—History.   7. Natural
    history—Michigan.   8. Great Lakes Region (North America)—
    Description and travel.   I. Title.
    PS283.M5K58   2012
    810.9'358774—dc23

                                                        2011023782

For Robert Henshaw Knott, 1942–2010

Acknowledgments

This book grew out of more than fifteen years of teaching courses that explored ways in which Americans have imagined and continue to imagine their relationships to their natural environments. Various writing projects have deepened my interest in the literature of place, most recently editing a collection of essays and photographs for The Nature Conservancy illustrating their work in Michigan. My thanks to Helen Taylor, the dynamic director of the Michigan Conservancy, for persuading me to take on a job that helped me discover the rich natural heritage of my adopted state, often in the company of Conservancy biologists.

Any project of this nature depends on the resources of many libraries and the help of those who tend their collections. I have benefited from the excellent libraries of the University of Michigan, including the Hatcher Graduate Library, the Shapiro Undergraduate Library, the William L. Clements Library, and particularly the Bentley Historical Library, whose staff proved exceptionally helpful. Librarians at the Library of Michigan in Lansing and the Clarke Historical Library in Mount Pleasant were quick to respond to inquiries and offer advice. I am grateful to the staff of the English Department of the University of Michigan, especially Donna Johnston and Jane Johnson, for support of many kinds. I owe special thanks to the Mellon Foundation for timely and generous support in the form of a Mellon Emeritus Fellowship.

Various individuals with many years of experience dealing with the science and politics of forests and the issues involved in managing them were patient with my inquiries about matters on which I needed expert guidance, including Burt Barnes, Bill Rockwell, Ann Woiwode, Marvin Roberson, Donald Waller, Lee Frelich, Dennis Albert, Robert Sprague, Robert Evans, Lisa Klaus, Doug Cornett, Don Henson, Brian Carlson, and Kathrine Dixon. Knute Nadelhoffer generously offered the hospitality of the University of Michigan's Biological Station, as well as advice. Stan Latender proved a helpful guide to the Menominee Logging Camp Museum.

University colleagues offered advice and comments on portions of the work in progress or otherwise provided help, including Susan Scott Parrish, Margaret Noori, Gregg Crane, June Howard, Robert Grese, Keith Taylor, Virginia Murphy, David Cave, and Lincoln Faller. I also benefited from the comments of my anthropologist daughter, Catherine Henshaw Knott, and my grandson Daniel Tucker. My research assistant for the later stages of the project, Carolyn Dekker, provided valuable help in tracking down elusive sources.

I have tried to indicate through my notes how much I profited from the work of many scholars of Michigan and midwestern forests and forest policy, environmental and conservation history, forestry science, and ecology, among other subjects. I could not have ventured into some of the areas that I did without the foundation they provided. Any errors I may have made, and any opinions expressed, are my own responsibility.

My editor at the University of Michigan Press, Tom Dwyer, has been an enthusiastic supporter and a consistent source of good advice. I benefited from the expertise of Alexa Ducsay, who shepherded the book through production, and Christina Milton, who oversaw the copyediting. I am grateful to the two anonymous readers for the press for comments that prompted revisions that strengthened the book.

I am grateful to "The Detroit News Archive" for permission to use a photograph of The Lumberman's monument; to the University of Minnesota Press for permission to use an illustration by Francis Lee Jaques from *Canoe Country* by Florence Page Jaques (copyright 1938 by the University of Minnesota Press, renewed 1966); to American Forests, and Daniel C. Smith in particular, for permission to use an advertisement from *American Forests and Forest Life* (April, 1928); to the Archives of Michigan for permission to use maps from Rolland H. Maybee, *Michigan's White Pine Era* (Lansing: Michigan Historical Commission, 1960); to the Clarke Historical Library, Central Michigan University, for permission to use a photograph of a logging crew. The coda first appeared in a slightly different form in the *Michigan Quarterly Review,* as "Boundary Crossings in Michigan's Upper Peninsula." It is reprinted here by permission.

I am deeply grateful, as always, for the patience, support, and good advice of my wife Anne Percy Knott, and for her eagle-eyed editing.

The dedication is an act of homage to my late brother Bob Knott, longtime faculty member at Wake Forest University and gifted teacher, art historian, artist, and musician, who loved taking his granddaughters for walks in the woods.

Contents

Introduction

Landscapes are culture before they are nature;
constructs of the imagination projected onto
wood and water and rock.

—SIMON SCHAMA, *Landscape and Memory*

We all . . . apprehend the land imperfectly, even when
we go to the trouble to wander in it. Our perceptions
are colored by preconception and desire.

—BARRY LOPEZ, *Arctic Dreams*

An impressive white pine, now some seventy feet high, grows in a four-story, open courtyard at the center of the Michigan Historical Museum complex in the state capital, Lansing. Not only is the white pine (*Pinus strobilis*) Michigan's state tree; its history over the last two centuries is interwoven with that of the state and offers dramatic evidence of the evolution of cultural attitudes toward Michigan's forests from the beginnings of European settlement to the present. Its continuing appeal can be seen in book and song titles (*White Pine Whispers, Where Once the Tall Pines Stood,* "Under the Whispering Pines") and in the streams of visitors to rare old-growth stands, especially the readily accessible Hartwick Pines State Park near Grayling in Michigan's Lower Peninsula. As the largest and longest-lived tree in the northern forest, the white pine came to symbolize the north woods of the upper Midwest. To lumbermen in the East looking for new sources of timber, the abundant stands of white pine in Michigan, and in Wisconsin and Minnesota as well, represented "green gold," prime lumber in high demand as waves of settlers surged into the Midwest and beyond into the plains states.

The Apostle Islands Indian Pageant presented at Bayfield, Wisconsin, in 1924 and 1925, which purported to represent three hundred years of the history of the Chequamegon Bay area, included a scene titled "The Dance of the Spirits of the Vanished Pines." Program notes describe the scene as the dream of an Ojibwa medicine man representing the loss of "millions of magnificent pines" in the logging boom of the last half of the nineteenth century. They explain that the pines were cut down to provide houses for those who succeeded the Ojibwa as "proprietors" of the "beautiful northland" and that the dream presents the spirits of the pines "as they appear in a dance of vanished memories."[1] This "dream" transforms the destruction of the forests on which the Ojibwa depended into a nostalgic and sentimentalized vision of a world whose loss is assumed to be an inevitable consequence of progress. The pageant omits any reference to the roles of the lumberjacks, mill owners, and others responsible for the extension of white civilization, largely skipping over a crucial period in the human and environmental history of the area. It appealed primarily to tourists drawn from cities to the south, presenting a broad historical drama dominated by recognizable European figures, with stereotyped Indians cast in secondary roles.[2]

To those who thought of themselves as the Anishnabeg (including those we know as Ojibwa, Ottawa, Potawatomi, and in Wisconsin the Menominee), the white pine (*zhingwaak*), along with other culturally important trees such as the white cedar (*giizhik*) and paper birch (*wiigwass*), had various medicinal and practical uses. It was a major constituent of the woodland environment that sustained their lives and shaped their identity. A poem written about a century before the pageant presented in Bayfield by Jane Johnston, the daughter of an Ojibwa mother and an Irish father who became the wife of Henry Rowe Schoolcraft, gives pines a real rather than a ghostly presence. In the poem Johnston was trying to recapture the excitement she had experienced on seeing a stand of white pines in Ontario as she and her father made their way home to northern Michigan from a trip to Ireland and England in 1810, when she was ten years old.

The pine! The pine! I eager cried,
The pine, my father! See it stand,
As first that cherished tree I spied,
Returning to my native land.
The pine! the pine! oh lovely scene!
The pine, that is forever green.

The pine symbolizes not only the homeland that Johnston had missed in her travels but the Ojibwa culture of her mother in which the pine, along with plants and animals generally, was understood as possessing its own spirit or *manito*. Writing her poem in Ojibwe ("Shing wauk! Shing wauk!"), then translating it into English, was one means of expressing her attachment to a way of life that as an adult she had seen transformed by white settlement and commerce. The poem conveys her personal sense of a spiritual connection with the pine, which she imagines as welcoming her "with a friend's delight." Johnston's translation reflects the influence of her reading of English romantic verse, with its own sense of an animate natural world, on her effort to express her strong emotional response to the familiar sight of pine trees.[3] As an adult, she had become adept at moving between the two worlds to which she belonged.

Jane Johnston may have been nostalgic for an Ojibwa culture that she saw as fading, but the pines themselves were still a prominent feature of the northern Michigan landscape in which she had grown up, near Sault Ste. Marie in the eastern Upper Peninsula. Subsequent evocations of Michigan's pines are colored by nostalgia for the trees themselves. Writers of fiction and historians who have told the story of Michigan's "Big Cut," the logging boom that stripped the state of virtually all of its stands of white (and red) pine and subsequently of most of its old-growth hardwoods, have been drawn to images of devastated forestlands, especially landscapes dominated by stumps. In Jim Harrison's *True North* (2004) giant pine stumps serve as a powerful image of the destructiveness of the white pine era in Michigan's Upper Peninsula. The novel begins in the 1960s with narrator David Burkett, obsessed with the crimes of his grandfather and great-grandfather against the land and its people, haunting the Kingston Plains south of Grand Marais and finding in the thousands of acres of waist- and chest-high stumps emblems of loss and the rapacity of his family and other lumber barons: "Maybe to try to imagine the trees was like asking a contemporary Lakota to imagine a million buffalo. There was an eerie sense of the gray stumps as ghost trees."[4]

The landscape of the Kingston Plains is indeed an eerie one, where the intense fires that followed the late-nineteenth-century logging of the area burned off the topsoil to the extent that even now little vegetation other than mosses and lichens has emerged. The "ghost trees" that the stumps conjure up for Harrison suggest both the scale of the native forest, with its stands of towering white pines, and the unlikelihood that anything similar will return. For Harrison the stumps symbolize a larger pattern of conquest in America. He imagines the logging of the pines as a kind of warfare, driven by greed disguised as piety, in which the exploitation of natural resources was thought to be a response to a divine mandate to extend the reach of civilization. The victims of this warfare include not only the Ojibwa but the thousands of loggers and miners, many of them recent emigrants from Europe, who were maimed or lost their lives in accidents. Harrison's interwoven stories of their descendants, hanging on in a marginal economy and nursing grudges against members of David's family and others like them, register the lasting human damage done by the men who built the companies that exploited the natural resources, copper and iron ore as well as timber, that gave the Upper Peninsula its boom times.

In *True North* David Burkett comes to see his family as representative of the "alpha predators" who took pride in their ability to cut "all the virgin timber in the state of Michigan" (280) and then mythologized its destruction. Harrison engages in the work of demythologizing, telling the story of the pine forests by tracing the decline of a family, from the great-grandfather and grandfather, who invoke God and flout the law in their accumulation of wealth and power; to the feckless and dissolute father, who sells off the lands they acquired to finance his vices, the most corrosive of which is his sexual appetite for teenage girls; to the narrator, who immerses himself for twenty years in the ultimately hopeless project of writing an economic and social history that will exorcise his family's guilt by exposing it, hoping to heal his psychic wounds and free himself from this history in the process. David negotiates his own relationship with the landscape, and tries to distance himself from his family heritage, by living in a primitive cabin and seeking a form of peace in fishing and rowing. His favorite refuge is the hollow interior of an immense pine stump on the Kingston Plains, the closest thing that he can find to a church in which he can believe.

Like William Faulkner tracing the decline of the "Big Woods" of Mississippi river bottoms in "The Bear" and its sequel "Delta Autumn," Harrison focuses on loss and guilt. He uses the device of a journal of a 1920 trip to France to introduce a comparison between "the massive carnage of the natural world" visible in the blasted forests of World War I battlefields and the "shredded" landscapes around Ontonagon (253) in the western Upper Peninsula. Belleau Wood recalls the journal writer's father's reminiscences of the horrific Peshtigo fire on the Wisconsin border, the most infamous of the "holocaust" fires that swept through heavily logged areas of the upper Midwest and burned with such intensity that they destroyed whole towns and hundreds of people unable to escape the firestorms. The accumulated logging debris (slash), in combination with dry and windy late summer weather (in 1871, 1881, 1891, and the early twentieth century), created ideal conditions for such fires, which roared through large sections of the cutover lands.

The story of these wildfires, still the most destructive ever recorded in the United States, has been told many times.[5] Ernest Hemingway's description of the "burned-over country" around Seney in the first part of his "Big Two-Hearted River" recalls their devastating effect ("Even the surface had been burned off the ground") and mirrors the psychic damage caused by his protagonist Nick Adams's experience in World War I. Yet Hemingway's narrative also suggests possibilities for regeneration, in the "islands of dark pine trees" rising out of the pine plain and in the river itself, where Nick begins his own tentative recovery through the fly-fishing that is the ostensible reason for his trip.[6] Harrison shows David beginning to recover as well, released from his obsession and his resentment of his father by publishing a long, moralizing newspaper essay that sums up what he is finally able to say about his family history. He rediscovers the sensuous pleasures of the landscape and realizes that his quest for solitude was a form of romantic self-indulgence, an epiphany he arrives at as he meditates beside a stump on the Kingston Plains.

For much of *True North* David tries to imagine the Upper Peninsula as it would have appeared when seen "through the eyes of Schoolcraft or Agassiz before the landscape was fatally violated" (207). Through David, Harrison taps into a kind of nostalgia, and a history, that we need to recognize if we are to understand our own perceptions of the "pristine" forests that existed in Michigan and the upper Midwest prior to European settlement and the motivation for contemporary efforts to preserve, restore, shape, or exploit them. We need to ask how these forests have been imagined over time, how they have evolved in the cultural imagination, and what preconceptions and desires have colored our perceptions of them, as well as how their composition has evolved. And we need to consider how the interplay between our perceptions of forests and the ways in which they have changed physically has affected how and why we value them.

The race to log Michigan's white pines, the lingering human and environmental consequences of which Harrison explores in his fiction, offers the most revealing example of changing cultural attitudes, as well as of the physical transformation of Michigan's forests, but pines represent only one element in the mosaic of these forests. In the northern Lower Peninsula and the Upper Peninsula, where stands of white pine are mainly found, they coexist with other conifers and northern hardwoods, depending on the habitat: in mesic, deciduous areas with hemlock, white spruce, red and sugar maple, beech, yellow birch, and basswood; in drier, sandier areas with jack and red pines, various oaks, paper birch, aspen, and red maple; and in wet, coniferous-boreal forests with black and white spruces, balsam fir, tamarack, northern cedar, balsam poplar, yellow birch, and red maple. The southern Lower Peninsula is dominated by hardwood forests: beech and maple mixed with other hardwoods, including basswood, tulip poplar, black cherry, and elms, in wetter, mesic habitats; and oaks and hickories mixed with hardwoods, including black walnut, white ash, and sassafras, in drier ones. At the time of the first waves of European settlement in the early nineteenth century, the extensive forests in the south were interrupted by prairies and savannas, now greatly diminished.[7]

Whatever their composition, we give our forests meaning with the metaphors we choose to represent them and the stories we learn to tell about them, in other words with the changing ways in which we see them. The first European visitors to the eastern shores of North America emphasized its astounding natural abundance, including vast and diverse forests. Early promoters, eager to encourage more migration from Europe, expanded on this optimistic view, favoring metaphors of the New World as garden or paradise. Yet this story of the promise of America coexisted with another one, which emphasized the dangers and uncertainties of an unfamiliar land. As has often been noted, the English settlers who arrived on Cape Cod in the early seventeenth century were culturally conditioned to see the North American forest as a hostile wilderness. It recalled for them the dark forest of European tradition, thought to be evil as well as dangerous, and also the inhospitable, desert wildernesses of the Old Testament. In the words of the poet Michael Wigglesworth, the immense, forested country was "A waste and howling wilderness, / Where none inhabited / But hellish fiends and brutish men / That Devils worshiped."[8] A "waste" place because this apparent wilderness was not domesticated, or productive in ways that Wigglesworth could understand; "howling" because, like the howling of the wolves that was frequently heard at night, it radiated danger.

In writing from the colonial period well into the nineteenth century, "wilderness" was commonly described as "howling." Wolves, the subject of numerous legends and folktales about attacks on humans, had come to be regarded as demonic. The human inhabitants of the howling wilderness were seen by the early settlers as dangerous, perhaps evil "savages" whom it was their duty to Christianize. The nonconformists who fled religious persecution in England saw themselves as latter-day Israelites sent by God to claim a new promised land, and they were determined to domesticate it. In fact, the landscape of southern New England had already been altered by tribes whose members regularly burned wooded areas to improve conditions for hunting and to create fields for agriculture, moving on to establish new fields when the soil in the old ones was depleted. The European newcomers did not find unbroken forest but rather a patchwork that included open areas and parklike woods shaped by Indian fires, and they sometimes established their homesteads on abandoned Indian fields.[9]

By the early nineteenth century an antithetical way of looking at the American wilderness, influenced by European romanticism, was beginning to take root. The idea that divine truth could be found in nature as well as the Bible was not new (nature was commonly regarded as the second of God's two books), but a focus on the value of wilderness and the sense in which it could be a manifestation of the sublime was. The categories of the sublime and picturesque, along with that of the beautiful, had been popularized by late-eighteenth-century English writing on the aesthetic dimensions of natural landscapes.[10] Henry David Thoreau played the most crucial role in redefining the American understanding of wilderness and wildness and in arguing that transcendental truths could be found in natural facts. He discovered in the forests and swamps of the landscape around Concord, Massachusetts, metaphors for the spiritually and intellectually energizing effects of contact with wild nature: "When I would recreate myself, I seek the darkest wood, the thickest and most interminable and, to the citizen, most dismal swamp. I enter a swamp as a sacred place, a *sanctum sanctorum*. There is the strength, the marrow, of Nature."[11] For the Thoreau of "Walking," the late essay in which he distilled his mature views of wildness, "The most alive is the wildest. Not yet subdued to man, its presence refreshes him."[12] Yet Thoreau's provocative view of nature as representing an "absolute freedom and wildness," which he opposed to civic culture and conventional ways of thinking, would have its greatest influence much later, on such iconoclastic defenders of wildness as John Muir at the end of the nineteenth century and Edward Abbey and Gary Snyder in the latter half of the twentieth.[13]

Another metaphor, the popular one of the forest as temple, is more representative of a shift in thinking about the forest in nineteenth-century

America that interests me here. The belief that forests, in particular sacred groves, were the dwelling places of gods goes back to European prehistory and can be found in Greek and Roman writing. The columns of Greek temples, as well as the architecture of Gothic cathedrals, invited analogies with forests. Christianity appropriated elements of the pagan veneration of the forest in the decoration of churches and in an iconographic tradition associating crosses and churches with woodlands.[14] William Cullen Bryant's "A Forest Hymn," which appeared in 1825 and became one of his best-known poems, belongs to a rich tradition of imagining the forest as sacred space. Bryant begins by asserting that "The groves were God's first temples" and describes the elements that make the forest sacred for him: tall trunks that look like "venerable columns," a high canopy forming a "verdant roof," darkness, soft winds. The silence and solitude that Bryant finds in the forest give it a "tranquility" that makes it seem fit for meditation and worship, a "shrine" where he feels the power of "sacred influences." He sees a reminder of his own mortality and of the "eternity" visible in God's works in the ongoing "miracle" of creation around him, with new life springing from decay. Everything in the forest—the grandeur of the "mighty" oak, the beauty of the "delicate" woodland wildflower—becomes a sign of God's presence. Bryant's romantic sensibility transforms the forest into a place of spiritual and moral renewal and an emblem of the "beautiful order" of God's works. His "Hymn" helped to establish in America habits of imagining impressive stands of trees, particularly old-growth forests, as sacred and of describing them as cathedral-like, habits that have become so pervasive that they continue to influence travel writing. The metaphor of the forest as cathedral can still carry an emotional charge, even when it has become a cliché. The fact that a stand of old-growth white pines in northwestern Connecticut protected by The Nature Conservancy was known as Cathedral Pines raised the stakes in the debate about how to respond to the devastation of these pines by a violent windstorm.[15]

These two central metaphors, the forest as howling wilderness and the forest as temple or cathedral, underwent metamorphoses as attitudes toward forests changed and other metaphors became popular (the forest as "playground"). Like the early settlers, loggers saw the forest as wilderness, though less as a place of danger than as an antagonist that challenged their abilities and determination. Lumberjacks had to perform what now seem Herculean tasks in order to fell tall pines and haul giant logs in the winter woods, then contend with the force of spring rivers and with the logjams that inevitably formed to get them to sawmills. It was not until the early 1920s that a more positive view of wilderness began to get wider attention, as Aldo Leopold and others lobbied the U.S. Forest Service to set aside wilderness areas within national forests. Like Thoreau, they came to regard wild nature as something to value rather than something to fear or seek to dominate. They saw wilderness areas as a way to preserve opportunities for primitive recreation and to protect natural forests and other undisturbed landscapes from the incursions of automobile tourism and the roads necessary to support it. Additional reasons for valuing wilderness were advanced as the campaign for designating wilderness areas gathered strength, including scientific ones. With the growing public awareness of ecology as a science in the 1960s, forests came to be regarded as ecosystems whose natural processes should be protected. Wilderness areas preserved from human disturbance could serve as laboratories, providing a standard by which forest health could be measured, and they could offer habitats for a variety of plant and animal species, some of which would be classified as threatened or endangered under the Endangered Species Act of 1973.

Imagining forests as sacred spaces served the aims of those intent on seeing areas designated as wilderness and on protecting old-growth forest generally. The image of the forest as cathedral came to be less obviously associated with divinity than it was for Bryant, but it might suggest beauty or peacefulness or a quiet that invites solitude and reflection, all aspects of the forest's appeal for Bryant that would become more important in subsequent arguments for preservation. A public that by the 1920s was becoming more interested in the use of state and national forests as places for outdoor recreation than as sources of timber came to associate forests with aesthetic and spiritual values as well as with recreational ones. One of my concerns is to show how these values have been expressed over time in various forms of writing, including a vital tradition of nature writing influenced by Thoreau, John Muir, and John Burroughs among others, and how they have become a part of public discourse about the management of forests. The fact that Aldo Leopold associated ecological health with beauty and that other scientists have been motivated by humanistic as well as scientific values in arguing for protecting natural areas attests to the breadth of their appeal, as well as to their persistence. The agencies that develop forest plans for state and national forests, recognizing public concerns, typically address aesthetic, spiritual, and social, as well as economic and scientific, values in the planning process, though with uneven efforts to accommodate them in the final plans and their implementation.

The values associated with forests, including aesthetic and spiritual ones, mutated as cultural contexts changed. Caroline Kirkland, writing in the 1830s, found southeastern Michigan forests and oak openings "picturesque," invoking the accepted standard of scenic beauty. In the 1890s John Muir would find "beauty" in the forests of the Sierra Nevada under all conditions, even when they were set into violent motion by a windstorm or showed the aftereffects of such a storm, and was more inclined to find them sublime than picturesque. Aldo Leopold, writing roughly a century after Kirkland, would devalue the merely "pretty" and point the way to finding beauty in the workings of natural processes. The sense of the forest as restorative would evolve along with aesthetic standards, with the emphasis on its curative and health-giving powers waning and recognition of its role as a source of spiritual and psychological regeneration increasing. William Murray lured visitors to the Adirondacks in 1869 with a testimonial to the power of restful sleep and the fragrance of pine and balsam and cedar to cure consumption; travel literature distributed by Michigan railroad companies in the 1920s and 1930s touted the healing effects of the woods and waters of Michigan at resorts served by the railroads. The kind of restoration that Wendell Berry finds in the remnant of the "old forest" on his Kentucky farm to which he periodically retreats, a "high, restful sanctuary" where he can experience a sense of timelessness and harmony with what he describes as the ongoing work of creation, is more typical of modern accounts of the restorative power and spiritual appeal of forests.[16]

Perceptions such as Berry's depend on a temporary withdrawal from the demands of daily life in society, and they are of course not unique to our own time. One can find an attraction to similar kinds of experience in accounts of forests from at least the early nineteenth century forward. One of the most intriguing themes that can be found in such accounts is the importance of silence, typically understood as the absence of human sounds. Depending on the writer and the circumstances, the forest can suggest timelessness, peace, or the sacred character of a place, or a combination of these qualities. It can encourage a heightened sensuous alertness, and it can clear mental space for meditation. Silence becomes progressively more important as an index of the quality of human experience of forests as the "noise" of industrial society intensifies, with automobiles and then jet engines and more recently off-road vehicles (ORVs) becoming emblematic of the intrusions that threaten to transform this experience. As silence has become more elusive, appreciation for it has grown, as have efforts to preserve it, at least in some places.

The values that have come to be associated with the modern ideal of wilderness and with forests generally, including ecological ones, need to be understood in relation to others that reflect a view of the forest primarily as an antagonist (when wilderness was seen as an oppressive presence) or as an economic resource to be exploited. A fundamental opposition between these two basic orientations runs through the interrelated stories that I tell, an opposition that grew as the effects of massive logging became apparent. It is embedded in Thoreau's provocative assertion that it is the poet rather than the lumberman who makes the "truest" use of the pine ("It is the living spirit of the tree, and not its spirit of turpentine, with which I sympathize, and which heals my cuts").[17] Yet a viewpoint such as Thoreau's had little practical effect when logging was in the ascendant, in New England and then in the Lake States. In the later nineteenth century, at the height of the logging boom in Michigan, it was difficult to challenge an industry that was driving the economy and providing lumber essential for the development of the plains states, even if the lumber companies that supplied it were stripping virtually all of the state's old-growth forest without regard for what was left behind.

The creation by Congress in 1891 of a system of forest reserves, precursors of the national forests, launched a national effort to prevent a "timber famine" by guaranteeing a sustainable supply of timber, with the added goal of protecting watersheds. The movement to conserve natural resources implied continuing to use them productively, as Gifford Pinchot made clear when he became the first chief of the new U.S. Forest Service in 1905 and began aggressively marketing timber and grazing rights in the national forests. Pinchot articulated and put in practice the policy of multiple use of resources ("wise use," as he put it) that guided the Forest Service from its beginnings. This would later be codified in the Multiple-Use Sustained-Yield Act of 1960, which defined the uses to be supported as timber production, protection of watersheds, grazing, recreation, and wildlife habitat, all supported by tradition and prior law.[18] Arguments about how to interpret and prioritize these uses have continued and seem unlikely to diminish.

The conflict that developed between Pinchot and his former friend John Muir over the management of forests and other natural areas is often characterized as one between conservation and preservation. With his passionate descriptions of Sierra landscapes and his appeals for the creation of national parks, Muir became the most prominent national spokesman for a new movement for preservation, an important outgrowth of which was the campaign to create wilderness areas that led eventually to the passage of the Wilderness Act of 1964. Conflicts about the management of public forests in the upper Midwest, reflecting differing views of how these forests should be valued, can be seen as part of an ongoing national debate with its roots in arguments that first claimed wide public attention in the early twentieth century but reflect attitudes that had taken shape earlier. The texts and phenomena that I consider reveal the persistent tension between utilitarian views of forests, reflecting the assumption that nature should serve human needs, and others that value forests for their own sake, whether for aesthetic, spiritual, ecological, or other noneconomic reasons.

Yet if this tension has persisted it has also diminished at times, in ways that suggest that the opposing attitudes are not so absolute as they sometimes seem. Many of the same pioneering settlers who cut down and burned great numbers of trees to establish their farms would look back nostalgically to the "grand old forest" that they had feared and struggled with but had gradually come to appreciate, regretting its loss. Lumberjacks who complained about the hard conditions of their work developed their own kind of nostalgia for the freedoms and elemental nature of the life they had led in the woods and on the rivers. Early sportsmen who took pride in their hunting prowess were often avid students of natural history, and present hunters and fishermen can be found among the most vigorous advocates of protecting natural habitats. Attitudes toward forests can be complicated, and the fundamental opposition that I have sketched assumes new forms as technologies and interests change. The managers who supervise current efforts to chart the future of public forests struggle to find a balance that will satisfy competing and sometimes starkly opposed interests. On the one hand, they work to nurture the ecological health of forests; on the other, they use the mandate of multiple use to justify such actions as authorizing a higher level of timber cutting for economic reasons and extending the network of snowmobile and ORV trails in response to social pressures.

While I focus primarily on Michigan and the upper Midwest in the chapters that follow, the texts I discuss illustrate broad shifts in cultural attitudes toward forests that reflect national trends. Chapters focus on important stages in the evolution of these attitudes. They follow a chronological progression, although individual chapters may range forward and back to explore how particular attitudes and practices have developed. Thus the chapter on the explosion of public demand for recreational use of forests in the early twentieth century ("The Forest as Playground") considers the development of the most prominent of these uses in the nineteenth century and carries strands of the story into the present. The arc of the book's narrative takes the reader from Anishnabeg understandings of the forest (as a physical and spiritual home and the major source of their livelihood) and the formative struggles of early European settlers to make space for themselves in a forest "wilderness" to our present concern with shaping our forests through ostensibly rational and inclusive kinds of planning.

A preliminary chapter examines images of presettlement forests, particularly of what we have come to think of as the north woods, presented to the public by Schoolcraft, by a member of Louis Agassiz's expedition, and by other early explorers, juxtaposing accounts of their travels with Henry Wadsworth Longfellow's idealized version of Ojibwa life in Michigan's Upper Peninsula in his hugely popular poem *The Song of Hiawatha*. I am concerned both with the popular image of the Ojibwa and their environment established by Longfellow's poem and the way this influenced perceptions of the Upper Peninsula and with what we know about the actual life of the Ojibwa, especially their physical and spiritual uses of the forest. Images of presettlement forests, whether they derive from early narratives of exploration and reconstructions of Anishnabeg life or from recent studies of nineteenth-century surveyors' notes, are important to an understanding of what our forests were and what they have become. And of whether and to what degree it might be possible to restore them to their presettlement state.

A chapter on the experience of the early settlers who followed the Jesuits and fur traders into the upper Midwest considers their view of the forest as a threatening place that had to be made safe and hospitable for humans (other than the "savages" whose natural home it was) and as an adversary that stood in the way of the progress of civilization, understood as bringing with it civic and religious order as well as a flourishing agriculture. These pioneering settlers regarded themselves as engaged in a continuing struggle with nature, carving out clearings in the wilderness in order to establish the farms and towns that would enable them to thrive. To create clearings was to let in light and win a sense of freedom from the dark, enclosing woods. When they pushed westward across southern Michigan into regions marked by parklike oak openings, these settlers found a more welcoming landscape, one that travelers celebrated as combining wildness with the illusion of art and that James Fenimore Cooper made the symbolic center of a novel (*The Oak Openings*) set in southwestern Michigan at the time of the War of 1812. Cooper's novel and settlers' memoirs suggest how both oak openings and the old forest became objects of nostalgia when they were almost gone and how expressions of nostalgia could coexist with celebrations of progress.

I devote three chapters to the most important event in the recent forest history of the Lake States, the rise of commercial logging in the mid–nineteenth century, which focused initially on the abundant white pine, the source of the finest lumber. The first of these chapters deals with the culture of the lumberjacks themselves and how it came to be understood. I am interested in how these lumberjacks shaped their own identity through songs they adapted to local circumstances as these songs passed from Maine to the Lake States and from camp to camp and through stories in which they magnified their exploits in the retelling, some about local heroes and others about the legendary Paul Bunyan. I am concerned as well with the changing and sometimes contradictory ways in which the lumberjacks were viewed by others. One of the paradoxes of writing about lumberjacks is that writers could find romance in their daily lives in the forest and at the same time recognize the destructiveness and waste of their lumbering practices. When public opinion turned against the excesses of the logging era, it was primarily the bosses who were blamed, for greed and unscrupulous practices, while the early lumberjacks themselves often emerged as folk heroes.

In another chapter I treat Stewart Edward White, little known now but widely read in the early decades of the twentieth century, as exemplifying the best of popular fiction about logging. His two novels and a related book of stories about logging in Michigan in the late nineteenth and early twentieth centuries, along with others that extend the story of logging to California and then to Alaska, represent loggers as embodying another version of the pioneer spirit. White portrays logging as an epic enterprise in which victory consists of getting out "the cut," heroically overcoming whatever obstacles nature and human enemies may present. Yet the protagonists of his Michigan novels, however quick to justify intensive logging as necessary for the progress of civilization and to authorize lawlessness if necessary to complete their river drives, reveal a strong attraction to the forest. White himself was a student of natural history and an energetic outdoorsman who became a conservation activist and an advocate for national forests and parks. He dealt with the seeming contradiction between his protagonists' natural admiration for forests and their commitment to cutting whatever prime timber they could by carefully separating manliness from sentiment in his treatment of gender roles, giving aesthetic responses that his protagonists seem incapable of articulating to the women they eventually marry. Part of the interest of his fiction lies in the sometimes unacknowledged tensions between the imperatives of logging and romantic representations of the forest.

In a chapter on the aftermath of the logging era, I use several novels from the 1920s and 1930s that dramatize the human and environmental costs of the profligate logging of the late nineteenth century to show how the images of lumber bosses and their companies were transformed in the public imagination. The most important of these for my purposes, Harold Titus's influential *Timber* (1922), challenges the heroic image of logging offered by White. Titus focuses on the problem of what to do with the vast cutover lands, marked by the expanses of pine stumps and slash left by logging. He helped to establish what became the common practice of comparing these cutover lands with the devastated battlefields of World War I. The primary reason for the influence of Titus's novel when it appeared, however, was the way it used his heroine's vision of a restored pine forest that could produce timber "forever" by means of sustainable logging practices to advance the agenda of forestry scientists. This vision offered an alternative to failed attempts to farm the cutover lands based on planting trees as a crop, simplifying the structure of the restored forest to make it more efficient. It would be challenged in time by ecologists who would argue that sustaining the health of forests depends on respect for their natural complexity.

As the forests of the upper Midwest began to recover and holdings of state and federal forestland mushroomed, a surge of public interest in recreational uses of public forests challenged the priority that foresters gave to timber production. In a chapter on forest recreation I consider the evolution of the principal recreational activities and how they altered perceptions of forests and forced debate about how they should be used, exposing tensions not only between recreational users and those who managed the forests but also among users with different recreational aims. Questions about priorities arose as different groups of users lobbied for their interests. What priority should be given to the Forest Service's traditional mission of supplying timber for the mills that sustained local economies? To the wishes of hunters and others interested in maintaining habitat for wildlife? To those of automobile tourists concerned with road access and scenic beauty (and to those who saw the automobile as the chief threat to primitive recreation and the survival of wilderness)? To the interests of hikers and nature photographers? To those of snowmobile and ORV users pressing for greater access when motorized recreation in the forests intensified later in the century? The need to justify and support particular visions of the forest contributed to the development of game laws, urged by sportsmen, and to the articulation of aesthetic and spiritual values associated with forests by nature writers among others. Without the growth of public demand that forests be protected, and managed in ways that serve perceived recreational needs, we would not have the laws, infrastructure, or mechanisms for developing forest policy that we do.

A major advance in the scientific understanding of forests with the rise of ecological forestry in the 1970s and the passage of environmental laws that reflected this new understanding forced a more radical rethinking of forest policy. In a chapter on the forest as ecosystem, more accurately a collection of ecosystems, I explore the shift from controversies over preserving and sustaining old growth (initially in the Pacific Northwest) to a broader emphasis on protecting functioning ecosystems generally. I discuss Aldo Leopold as a bridging figure who influenced the development of ecological forestry and also played a critical role in providing a rationale for the wilderness movement. Leopold advanced the case for preserving forest and other wilderness initially made by John Muir by developing a compelling "land ethic," distinguishing between regarding land as "a commodity belonging to us" and considering it as part of "a community to which we belong," a "biotic community."[19] Like Muir, Leopold offered an alternative to Pinchot's doctrine of "wise use" of natural resources and showed that he could make the case for preservation to a wide public, on emotional as well as rational grounds. I include Sigurd Olson, the primary interpreter and advocate of the north woods of Minnesota, and philosopher and nature writer Kathleen Dean Moore in the line of those who have articulated values important to a holistic view of forests, Moore chiefly for her persuasive illustration of the compatibility of ecological and humanistic values in a personal essay that draws on Leopold.

My final chapter focuses on the language of current forest plans and the complex processes by means of which they are developed, the interplay between planners and representatives of contesting interest groups, and questions about how forest plans are implemented. I am interested in how positions on key issues reflect differing visions of the forest and in how the language used by the agencies (in the plans themselves and in responses to public comments on them) reflects the difficulties of trying to balance competing interests and at the same time satisfy mandates to sustain and enhance biological diversity. A central question that underlies forest plans and related documents, as well as the debates surrounding them, is how much management, and what kinds, forests need. To what extent can and should we design our forests through active management? I discuss two wilderness areas in Michigan's western Upper Peninsula, the Porcupine Mountains Wilderness State Park and the Sylvania Wilderness Area in the Ottawa National Forest, as successful efforts to realize the wilderness ideal through minimal management. They offer examples of the resilience of forests and at the same time, like other northern forests, show evidence of threats (including invasive species, excessive browsing by deer, and the potentially far-reaching effects of global warming) that are introducing new kinds of uncertainty about the future shape and condition of these and other forests, however we try to influence their development.

In a coda I introduce related novels by Philip Caputo (*Indian Country*) and Jim Harrison (*Returning to Earth*) that comment obliquely on many of the themes of the book and explore contemporary modes of living with the forest in Michigan's Upper Peninsula. Considering these novels serves as a way to return the larger story that I tell to Ojibwa beliefs in a spirit world of *manitos* by showing how Caputo and Harrison give these beliefs a critical role in the redemption of their protagonists and use them to suggest possibilities for harmony with the natural world that depend upon alternative ways of imagining our relationship to it. These fictional imaginings of interactions with the forests and other landscapes of the Upper Peninsula offer a counterpoint to the elaborate dance of forest planners and administrators and their critics and, while they cannot substitute for it, suggest that there may be truths that elude the bureaucratic and political language of the official documents.

1 // What Was Here Before

The narratives of Schoolcraft and Agassiz, the source of David Burkett's vision of the primitive forests of Michigan in Jim Harrison's *True North*, provide useful starting points for attempting to understand how early explorers and European settlers perceived the landscapes they found. What *did* Schoolcraft and Agassiz see in their nineteenth-century travels? Henry Rowe Schoolcraft's narrative of his trip along the western shore of Lake Huron and the southern shore of Lake Superior as a member of the 1820 expedition led by Lewis Cass, governor of the Michigan Territory, offers the best record of his reactions to Michigan landscapes.[1] The Cass expedition included soldiers, voyageurs, and Indians, making up a party of forty in three large canoes. Its primary purpose was to promote white settlement and economic development by implementing federal Indian policy in the Northwest Territory and surveying the trading activity of the rival British.[2] As the expedition geologist, Schoolcraft gave much of his attention to geological formations and the potential availability of minerals, but his narrative also reveals aesthetic and emotional responses to the changing landscapes he observed. When the expedition proceeded north along the Lake Huron shore toward Mackinac Island, he saw the patchwork of cultivated fields and deciduous forests near Detroit gradually yield to denser forests of pine and hemlock mixed with birch and poplar. Later he responded enthusiastically to the rugged shoreline of Lake Superior, with its rocky headlands and seemingly endless forest, which came into view when he emerged into Superior from the St. Marys River, now the site of the Soo Locks.

Schoolcraft shows the characteristic nineteenth-century preoccupation with the picturesque and the sublime, complaining of the lack of "bold or sublime" features on the Lake Huron shore but delighting in "the picturesque views of northern scenes" that he found at Sault Ste. Marie, where he was struck by the contrast between the "snowy whiteness" of the rapids of the St. Marys River and "the deep green foliage of the hemlock, spruce, and pine." The high shores of Lake Superior in the distance added drama (95). In the wave-sculpted, sandstone bluffs of the Pictured Rocks on Superior's southern shore, Schoolcraft discovered battlements and towers comparable to those Sir Walter Scott saw in the mountain scenery of "The Lady of the Lake," betraying a fondness for architectural metaphor that he shared with others of his time, as well as a typical need to validate American scenery by describing it as rivaling European landmarks.[3] If America lacked monuments and ruins of the sort that in Europe embodied a rich human history, it had natural formations such as the eroded sandstone of the Pictured Rocks that offered their own record of the passage of time.[4] Schoolcraft was determined to do justice to this "grand" and "picturesque" scenery, which he characterized as unparalleled in America and compared to that of the Hebrides and "the romantic Isles of the Sicilian coast" (107–8).

Schoolcraft's romantic sensibility, nurtured by Scott's immensely popular works, emerges most clearly when he attempts to render scenes that he found particularly remarkable, but much of the detail of the narrative reflects his geologist's eye and his eager curiosity about fresh and unspoiled territory, uninhabited except for the Chippewa (an English corruption of Ojibwa, now used in legal descriptions of the tribe) his party encountered on Lake Superior and in villages or the rare fur-trading outpost. A canoe journey up the Ontonagon River to investigate a legendary mass of copper, culminating in a strenuous hike led by an Indian guide, yielded a more intimate and disturbing view of the forest. The scene that Schoolcraft found at the site of the partially submerged copper boulder, with rocks overhanging the roaring stream and fallen trees strewn along its high banks, presented what he perceived as "a mixed character of wildness, ruin, and sterility." The sense of alienation and shock that he conveys anticipates Thoreau's description of his experience of discovering a stark and forbidding landscape of a different sort near the summit of Mount Katahdin in *The Maine Woods*. Like Thoreau, Schoolcraft found an alien scene.

> One cannot help fancying that he has gone to the ends of the earth, and beyond the boundaries appointed for the residence of

man. Every object tells us that it is a region alike unfavourable to the productions of the animal and vegetable kingdom; and we shudder in casting our eyes over the frightful wreck of trees, and the confused groups of falling-in banks and shattered stones. Yet we have only to ascend these bluffs to behold hills more rugged and elevated; and dark hemlock forests, and yawning gulfs more dreary, and more forbidding to the eye. (123–24)

It was one thing to admire the native forest from a canoe, quite another to trek through it and try to imagine a continuous human presence in a place that seemed so inhospitable to civilization. Seen up close, the forest could appear disorderly, resistant to metaphors that would place it in a familiar aesthetic frame. When he climbs the bluffs that close in the river, Schoolcraft seems overwhelmed by dark hemlock forests that in their immensity and ruggedness evoke the terror sometimes associated with the sublime.

Schoolcraft's recollection of this occasion was no doubt influenced by the difficulty of making his way to the scene of the boulder and his shock on returning to the boats and not finding Cass, who had abandoned the hike and became lost on his way back to the river. His narrative also reflects the fact that he was writing primarily for a cultivated eastern audience, dramatizing his emotional reactions in ways that he thought would appeal to his readers. His companion, David Bates Douglass, who did not bother to revise his own account of the expedition when he discovered that Schoolcraft had rushed to get his into print, registered none of the dread of the forest that Schoolcraft expresses.[5] Nor did Bela Hubbard, who found the view of the Ontonagon in the vicinity of the boulder, with its overhanging cliffs, "most wild and romantic."[6] Another observer, the geologist Charles Whittlesey, described a very different emotional response to the forested landscape he found along the Ontonagon River, closer to the Superior shore, on a sunny fall day three decades after Schoolcraft's visit.

The sides and the bottom of the valley of the Ontonagon were brilliant in the mellow sunlight, mottled with yellow and green; the golden tops of the sugar [maple] tree mingled with the dark summits of the pine and the balsam. The rough gorges that enter the valley on both sides were now concealed by the dense foliage of the trees, partly gorgeous and partly somber, made yet richer by the contrast, so that the surface of the wood as seen from our elevation, in fact from the waving top of a trim balsam which I ascended, lay like a beautifully worked and colored carpet ready for our feet.[7]

Whittlesey saw dense foliage and a rugged landscape with a mind-set that differed from Schoolcraft's, more attentive to the visual composition of the forest he surveyed from his high perch and primed to experience a sense of wonder at the intricate beauty of the scene. Both were trying to frame an unfamiliar, wild landscape in a way that would register its emotional impact. The differing reactions they convey mark the range of possible emotional responses, from wonder to something close to terror.

Louis Agassiz was a celebrated European scientist who had just been appointed Professor of Geology and Zoology at Harvard University when he led an expedition to Lake Superior in 1848, eager to begin his study of the natural history of his newly adopted country. His party included Harvard students, European naturalists, and a few "scientific gentlemen," one of whom, J. Elliot Cabot, wrote a lively narrative of the trip that complements Agassiz's scientific observations. The expedition was supported by a group of twelve voyageurs, a mix of French Canadians and Indians. Agassiz superintended the collection of specimens and with the aid of a portable blackboard that he insisted on bringing along gave periodic lectures on what they were seeing, faithfully summarized by Cabot. Like the Cass expedition three decades earlier, they encountered largely uninhabited country, in their case on the north shore of Superior where the transition to boreal forest was more apparent. This shore was marked by Indian lodges and mining camps, many unoccupied, and by Hudson's Bay Company posts with adjacent Indian villages at Michipicoten, the Pic, and Fort William.

Cabot, like Schoolcraft, calls attention to the grandeur and the "picturesque" qualities of the rugged shoreline, but he shows more self-consciousness about journeying into "the wilderness." He was fascinated by the primitive songs of the voyageurs, far removed from the *chansons* of Paris (as Agassiz observed), and by the exotic appearance of the Indians who approached them in canoes offering fish, reminding him of pictures of South Sea islanders. Cabot gives more particulars of the hazards of wilderness travel than Schoolcraft, including the clouds of blackflies that attack him and his companions during their forays away from the shoreline, yet he shows none of Schoolcraft's anxiety in the presence of an encompassing forest and the "ruin" of fallen trees. Although he comments on the impenetrability of cedar swamps and describes making his way through dense spruce woods littered with fallen birches, he gives no sense of being daunted by the obstacles he encounters on two longer excursions upriver and overland to notable waterfalls. Cabot shows a sharp eye for botanical detail, no doubt instructed in this by "the Professor," describing not only the varying composition of the forest but such vegetation as lichens, blueberries, Labrador tea, and carpets of moss in which he claims to sink up to his waist. Despite a growing awareness of the hardships of wilderness life, reinforced by seeing abandoned cabins whose furnishings testify to its loneliness and privation, he finds much to marvel at, including cliff faces striped with lichen, continuous forest, and an abundance of sturgeon and other fish (also remarked on by Schoolcraft). Cabot describes one sturgeon that Agassiz asks him to sketch as four to five feet long.

Cabot's wonder, apparent at many points in his narrative, is especially pronounced in his reflections on the quiet that he experiences in the forest: "Our little point was as silent as a piece of the primeval earth" (109). The occasional cry of a loon or song of a white-throated sparrow has for him "a wild and lonely character," giving him a feeling of entering a world startlingly remote from the civilized one of Boston from which he came: "It is like being transported to the early ages of the earth, when the mosses had just begun to cover the primeval rock, and the animals had not yet ventured into the new world" (124). Cabot's imaginative leap, stimulated by the strangeness of his surroundings and his awareness that he was standing on bedrock some five hundred million years old, suggests a desire to experience a much earlier natural order unmarred by either a native or a European presence, even by that of the animals. In the solitude and silence of the place, he experiences the illusion of having entered a timeless world outside the flow of history.

Cabot's sense of the wildness of the place is inseparable from his fascination with the primeval. The northern forest was alluring not only because it offered rich opportunities for the study of natural history that Agassiz encouraged but because he could perceive it as ancient and truly primitive, seemingly unaltered from its original state. Whereas the common tendency today is to describe the presettlement forest as "pristine" or "virgin," nineteenth-century observers were likelier to call it "primeval." Like Cabot on the shore of Superior, they imagined themselves connecting with a distant era through what they assumed to be an unchanging forest. Modern biologists would challenge the notion that a forest remains constant over time, having abandoned the model of a climax forest in favor of one that explains ecosystems as continually evolving in response to natural and human disturbances.[8] The northern forests that Cabot and Schoolcraft encountered had changed radically since the withdrawal of the last glaciers approximately twelve thousand years earlier, from spruce after the ice receded to pine or oak as the climate reached its maximum warmth and then to the hemlock-hardwood forest of today's upper Midwest about three thousand years ago.[9]

The popular image of the presettlement forest of Michigan's Upper Peninsula and the Lake Superior shore in the later nineteenth century actually owed more to Henry Wadsworth Longfellow's *The Song of Hiawatha* (1855) than to either Agassiz or Schoolcraft. Longfellow offered a poetic vision of the indigenous Ojibwa in their natural environment roughly two centuries before the expeditions of Schoolcraft and Agassiz and other nineteenth-century explorers, at the point of first contact with Jesuit missionaries in the seventeenth century. His rendering of Ojibwa stories became the most popular American poem of the nineteenth century and generated pageants and staged readings that continued to be performed into the early twentieth century.[10] The famous opening of his *Evangeline* offers a romanticized version of the northern forest that could be as easily associated with the Upper Peninsula as with the coastal Nova Scotia of that poem, neither of which Longfellow had in fact seen: "This is the forest primeval. The murmuring pines and the hemlocks, / Bearded with moss, and in garments green, indistinct in the twilight."[11] For the subject matter of *The Song of Hiawatha,* Longfellow drew heavily on the Ojibwa legends that Schoolcraft had adapted for genteel audiences in his *Algic Researches* (1839), with his half-Ojibwa wife Jane Johnston acting as translator. Longfellow conflated Schoolcraft's Manabozho with the historical Iroquois leader Hiawatha to create a godlike hero and benefactor of the Ojibwa who has none of the trickster qualities of the mythic figure whose exploits Schoolcraft had described. He forged a coherent narrative by selecting and elaborating on legends retold by Schoolcraft and by inventing such pivotal episodes as the marriage of Hiawatha and Minnehaha and the dramatic departure of Hiawatha with the coming of the Jesuits. Longfellow found a convenient literary model in the Finnish *Kalevala,* an early-nineteenth-century epic based on stories and songs of the folk, drawing also on George Catlin's images of plains Indians and Catlin's writings about his experience with them and mingling Ojibwa and Dakota traditions in his rendering of Ojibwa life.[12]

Longfellow idealized the Indians he portrayed, locating them in a pre-contact past before the changes that by the time he wrote in the mid–nineteenth century had transformed many Ojibwa cultural practices. He presents a timeless idyll of Indian life, one that turns dark with the arrival of the famine and fever that kill Hiawatha's Dakota wife Minnehaha and abruptly collides with history in the final two sections portraying the appearance of the Jesuits and the departure of Hiawatha. Longfellow embraced the widespread notion of the vanishing Indian, a favorite tragic theme of nineteenth-century writers. He regarded the dispersal of the Ojibwa as a necessary consequence of the westward march of white civilization; Hiawatha counsels the tribe to welcome the "Black-Robe chief" and listen to the "truth" of his Christian message.[13] Yet the poem ends on a strongly elegiac note, with Hiawatha's followers scattered to the west "Like the withered leaves of Autumn" and Hiawatha himself paddling away into a fiery sunset in his birchbark canoe, seeming to rise and fall in the distance as he merges with Lake Superior.

Whatever its simplifications, Longfellow's poem established the Upper Peninsula of Michigan as "Hiawatha land" and created an enduring image of the northern forest and Lake Superior, the "shining Big-Sea-Water" (Gitche Gumee) of the poem.[14] In the 1930s and 1940s the Upper Peninsula was actively promoted as Hiawatha land, through such vehicles as a magazine called *The Hiawathan;* travel literature from the American Automobile Association (AAA), which describes "The Land of Hiawatha" as retaining a beauty and charm "unsullied by the modern age"; and a large pictorial map published by the Upper Peninsula Development Bureau in 1935 to encourage travel to its resorts.[15] At the top of the map a woodland Indian in a birchbark canoe paddles away into Lake Superior under a banner inscribed "Land of Hiawatha." The association persists in the Upper Peninsula today in Hiawatha festivals of various kinds and in a fifty-foot, fiberglass statue representing a stereotypical Indian with an eagle-feather headdress, cradling a peace pipe, that towers over Hiawatha Park in Ironwood. One can find numerous place-names based on *The Song of Hiawatha,* including Hiawatha Township in Schoolcraft County and Gitche Gumee Landing at the mouth of the Ontonagon River. The U.S. Park Service quotes Longfellow in descriptions of the Pictured Rocks National Lakeshore, a place that figures in the poem.

The Song of Hiawatha fixed in the popular imagination the idea of a primitive, indigenous people living in harmony and intimacy with a natural world in which everything (bear and loon and pine tree) has its own

The Upper Peninsula as Hiawatha land. (Courtesy of the Bentley Historical Library, University of Michigan.)

spirit (*manito*). Longfellow's Hiawatha grows up hearing the "whispering" of the pine and the "lapping of the waters," and the forest offers itself (the birch's bark, the cedar's branches, the tamarack's roots, the fir's resin) for his canoe: "All the forest's life was in it, / All its mystery and magic" (158, 184). This sense of reciprocity between humans and their natural environment extends to scenes from daily life that Longfellow shows following his account of the marriage of Hiawatha and Minnehaha. We see a peaceful and contented people hunting, fishing, making maple sugar, gathering wild rice, and harvesting Indian corn as seasonal rhythms dictate. Hiawatha carries out the injunction of his father Mudjekeewis ("Cleanse the earth from all that harms it, / Clear the fishing-grounds and rivers, / Slay all monsters and magicians" [167]), becoming the cultural hero whose feats, such as bringing about the origin of corn by defeating Mondamin in wrestling, explain the traditional way of life enjoyed by the Ojibwa.[16] Longfellow was able to dramatize this life in ways that would appeal to an audience eager for new and exotic versions of the primitive, minimizing aspects that might be disturbing, such as the violence of intertribal warfare, and avoiding any reference to the contemporary history of the treatment of native tribes.

The popularity of *The Song of Hiawatha* also reflected readers' responsiveness to a new kind of national romance, which offered a way of assimilating the Indian to the American story of expansion as a benign and ultimately obliging people, and to the evocation of an unspoiled natural world. Longfellow's generalized northern landscape functions chiefly as a romantic backdrop for the primitive life that he represents through his story of Hiawatha and his people.

> Ye who love the haunts of Nature,
> Love the sunshine of the meadow,
> Love the shadow of the forest,
> Love the wind among the branches,
> And the rain-shower and the snow-storm,
> And the rushing of great rivers
> Through the palisades of pine-trees. . . .
> Listen to these wild traditions,
> To this song of Hiawatha!
>
> (142–43)

Longfellow offered his educated audience a beguiling sense of the aesthetic appeal of a natural world that seems to be dedicated to pleasing and nurturing humans. Cabot, who found "wildness" in the solitude and comparative quiet of the northern forest, describes a more detailed and varied landscape than Longfellow represents, with swamps, different forest types, and open areas that offered relief from sometimes difficult hiking through the woods. In fact, the presettlement forest of the Upper Peninsula was a complex patchwork that included openings created by natural disturbances, swampy areas with cedars and tamaracks, a mix of evergreens and northern hardwoods in varying stages of succession, and sandy plains with scrubby growth known as pine barrens.[17] The pine stands, though dense and towering to the point of shutting out the sky and discouraging undergrowth, were localized and are thought to have constituted no more than 15 percent of the total forested land.

In their different ways Longfellow's mythologized version of Ojibwa life and the primeval forest and the narratives of Schoolcraft and Agassiz's companion Cabot contributed to the myth of a pristine world with inexhaustible natural resources. Harrison's David Burkett presents an acute case of nostalgia for this world, as refracted by the narratives of Schoolcraft and of Agassiz's expedition, compounded by guilt and anger over his family's part in ruining it. We may experience our own sense of loss, and related nostalgia, when we see pockets of woods give way to development in suburbs where streets assume the names of the trees they have displaced (Oak Hollow, Maple Road) or when we experience something closer to presettlement forests in places such as The Nature Conservancy's Nan Weston Preserve in Southeast Michigan, with its beech-maple woods and flush of spring ephemerals, or when we visit the Porcupine Mountains State Wilderness Park in the western Upper Peninsula, with its thousands of acres of old-growth hemlock and northern hardwoods. Nostalgia for a lost ideal—particularly as this reflects longing for contact with a purer, more intact natural world—remains a powerful force that helps to explain the desire to foster and preserve old-growth forest and restore largely vanished landscapes such as oak savannas. We are no longer likely to describe forests as "primeval" but still like to call them "pristine," despite reminders from biologists that the natural world is always changing and should never have been thought of as "virgin."[18] It is easy to dismiss such nostalgia as naive, but this is to ignore its role in arousing emotions that can lead to the informed, intimate engagement with natural environments that many urban dwellers have found increasingly satisfying. The more aware we are of the complexity of forest ecosystems and the importance of biodiversity to forest health the deeper this engagement is likely to be, but it begins in and is sustained by the kind of emotional attachment that reflects aesthetic and spiritual values, as well as ecological understanding. To explore how we arrived at our current ways of imagining and interacting with forests we need to have some awareness of the collision of European ways of thinking and feeling about the forest with those of the indigenous peoples who had inherited attitudes toward the forest that reached back for millennia.

The federal Land Ordinance of 1785 mandated that the Western Territory between the Appalachians and the Mississippi River be divided into townships of thirty-six square miles each, subdivided into a grid of square-mile sections according to a plan devised by Thomas Jefferson, enabling the federal government to transfer this land to private ownership through Land Office sales. This grid was a product of Enlightenment rationality that served as a way of making unknown lands legible and asserting a form of mastery over them. Once such lands were mapped and subdivided they could be bought and sold.[19] The surveyors who imposed the Jeffersonian grid on the irregular terrain they found left field notes describing landscape features, including witness trees marking property corners. These notes have made it possible to form a reasonably accurate picture of the composition of Michigan forests and other landscape types in the early nineteenth century, now accessible in graphic form in the maps of an excellent atlas drawing on the work of staff of the Michigan Natural Features Inventory with the Land Office surveys.[20]

The evidence for how indigenous tribes lived with these forests is more elusive, but anthropologists and historians have been able to reconstruct a culture that evolved from that of the Paleo-Indians who colonized the upper Midwest after the retreat of the last glaciers to that of late Woodland Indians at the time of the first European contact in the seventeenth century. The Ojibwa, whose stories as adapted by Schoolcraft served as the basis for Longfellow's vision of the Indian in *The Song of Hiawatha,* lived in nomadic bands, moving their villages as the seasons changed. In the spring they located near rivers where they could catch spawning fish, in a place where they had access to a sugar bush for making the maple sugar they used as a sweetener and preservative for fruits. In the late spring they would relocate to a summer camp or village where the women tended crops that included corn, beans, and squash while the men hunted and fished. By the late summer and fall they would be harvesting wild rice and hunting waterfowl, moving the village as necessary. For the winter they would move inland, to customary hunting and trapping territory.

To the Ojibwa the forest was not "wilderness" but part of a familiar and sacred natural world that supplied their needs. Their shelters were constructed of poles covered with sheets of bark lashed with cord made from nettle fiber or the inner bark of basswood, comparable to the cord they used for seines and gill nets. Each tree had its functions, many of them medicinal. Needles from the white pine made a smudge used to cure headaches. Leaves of the northern white cedar made a tea rich enough in vitamin C to be effective against scurvy and could also be used for incense;

it was respected for sacred as well as practical uses. Paper birch had multiple uses, including sheathing for lodges and skin for canoes, baskets, scrolls used for picture writing, tinder, and medicine. Bark, needles or leaves, fiber, roots, and resin, as well as the wood and nuts and fruit of trees, all had their functions, discovered and passed down over centuries of living in natural environments that changed relatively little until the arrival of European settlers.[21] Trees provided the Ojibwa with dyes, oils and gums, the wooden ladles and bowls used for eating, the bows and arrows and snares used for hunting large and small game, and the canoes essential for navigating lakes and streams and transporting people and supplies over longer distances. The forest sustained the animals (including black bear cubs that found refuge in white pines and eagles that nested in them), many of which were hunted or trapped. It provided nuts and berries and other fruits to be gathered. As Ignatia Broker of the White Earth reservation in Minnesota describes the forest in her account of the transformation of Ojibwa life with the coming of white settlement, it was a "gift" that would always "give shelter and life to the Anishnabe and their Animal Brothers."[22] She captures the emotional and spiritual bond of the Ojibwa with the forest by describing the murmuring of the trees when their branches brush together (the *si-si-gwa-d*) as a peaceful and welcoming sound when her village moves away from a river and into the pine forest to escape the advance of logging; it becomes for her the sound of weeping when the Ojibwa leave the forest and are assimilated into white culture.[23] In both instances her interpretation of the sound made by the branches moved by the wind implies a sense of intimate connection with the forest.

Winter brought isolation and sometimes famine to the Ojibwa, but it was also a time for storytelling. Stories, passed down orally, reinforced beliefs that informed a worldview in which the Ojibwa saw themselves as sharing the earth with the animals and plants and recognized the importance of respecting them. They accepted the reality of *manitos,* spirits or essences associated with animals and plants, natural forces, and particular places.[24] Believing in a supernatural world with which they continually interacted, as well as in the visible world, meant that the Ojibwa attempted to ensure the cooperation of the animals they hunted and to propitiate the spirits of those they killed. To do otherwise would have been to risk the balance by which they maintained their way of life. They made offerings and observed traditional ceremonies intended to bring about success (of the harvest, for example) by earning the goodwill of the *manitos* on whose power they regarded themselves as depending for their survival (the sun, the thunder and lightning). They sought visions of their own personal *manitos*, animals or birds, whose power they believed could protect them. The Midewiwin, a society of specially trained priests or shamans, with their ritual songs and dances, were the principal custodians of tribal knowledge and traditional ceremonies. These Mide, as they were known, also served as healers who preserved the knowledge of herbs and plants and the ritual elements of healing ceremonies through which they sought to restore the harmony with creation necessary for mental, as well as physical, health. One implication of this view of a natural world dominated by *manitos* was that it could seem mysterious and unpredictable. Another was that the Ojibwa, and the Ottawa, whose beliefs and ceremonies resembled their own, were careful not to deplete the resources on which they relied for their subsistence. They practiced their own forms of conservation, characteristically taking only what they needed and avoiding practices that would compromise their future well-being.[25]

Longfellow's hugely popular poem offered a mythologized version of events in the lives of Ojibwa on the southern shore of Lake Superior, one that he described as "purely in the realm of Fancy."[26] A historical perspective would reveal the turbulence and dislocations caused by the attacks of the Iroquois on the Ojibwa and other Algonquian tribes around the Great Lakes, including those that occupied parts of what would become the state of Michigan, and patterns of settlement and resettlement, as well as cultural changes, beginning with the earliest European contact in the seventeenth century.[27] *The Song of Hiawatha* reproduces the seasonal rhythms followed by the Ojibwa and offers enough detail to suggest the outlines of daily life. Longfellow's descriptions of their northern environment clearly reflect his own aesthetic sensibility. One can imagine readers who shared this aesthetic responding to the emotional appeal of "singing pines" and "moaning hemlocks" (over Minnehaha's grave), as well as to the repeated use of words such as *mystery, mystical,* and *magic,* which had the effect of distancing the Ojibwa world from their own and giving it an exotic appeal. Longfellow incorporates *manitos,* and the creator Gitche Manito, into his narrative but tends to give them dramatic roles (as "Evil Spirits," for example, or the mountain Manito who lets Pau-Puk-Keewis into the interior of the Pictured Rocks) rather than emphasizing their pervasiveness in the natural world. The Mide (Longfellow's "Medas") become "the Medicine-men," seen as coequal with the "Wabenos" (magicians) and "Jossakeeds" (prophets) rather than as the most important and influential priestly society. All of these elders collaborate in ceremonies, such as those designed to cure Hiawatha of his disabling grief for his friend Chibiabos (a brother of Manabozho in Anishnabeg mythology), that involve herbs and drums and the chanting of "mystic songs" (235–36). Longfellow's insistence on the mystical character of their rites (he has previously described the Ojibwa as painting on bark and deerskin "Figures mystical and awful" that each suggest some "magic song" [230]), as well as on "the mystery and the magic" of the forest, has the effect of magnifying the difference between the lost world of the presettlement Ojibwa and that of his readers. He effectively played on the nostalgia of these readers for the primal world of the vanishing Indian by mystifying that world.

When Longfellow published *The Song of Hiawatha* in 1855, the disjunction between his vision and the actual condition of the Ojibwa (and the Ottawa and the Potawatomi, who also inhabited the area that became Michigan) could hardly have been more striking. Their involvement in the fur trade and successive dealings with French, British, and finally American traders had made the Ojibwa dependent on European trade goods (guns, traps, axes, kettles) and had undermined traditional crafts such as making pottery vessels for eating and drinking, as well as customary means of subsistence. They had been pressured to abandon their spiritual beliefs in favor of Christianity. The economic incentive to accumulate furs for trade eroded their habits of conservation (by causing them to trap more beaver than they would have otherwise, for example) and disrupted the cyclic routine of their lives. This routine was further altered by the demands of warfare in which they supported first the French against the British and then the British against the Americans, moving their camps to follow the campaigns of armies rather than the rhythms of a life of subsisting on the land.

The Americans would eventually succeed in taking control of most of the traditional Indian lands through a combination of coercion and bribery. The three dominant tribes progressively ceded these lands through a series of treaties beginning in 1785 and culminating in the Treaty of 1855, which effectively dispersed the Ojibwa nation.[28] This treaty completed the transition to a system of private property from one in which communal lands were used by particular tribal groups according to custom by giving individual allotments of land to members of the tribe. They were then expected to farm their land in the manner of the European settlers and required to pay taxes on it, a concept alien to their culture. Many found themselves unable to pay these taxes and either sold their land to speculators or lost title to it through fraud or default. Some found work as lumberjacks or market hunters, becoming part of an economy that was rapidly depleting the forests and the once abundant wildlife that had sustained them before contact with Europeans transformed their lives.[29]

When European settlers began to radiate out from Detroit in the early nineteenth century, in growing numbers as more arrived after the completion of the Erie Canal in 1825, the lives of the Indians they encountered (Ojibwa in the southeast, Ottawa in the watershed of the Grand River, and Potawatomi across the southern part of what would become Michigan in 1837) were much changed from those of the bands that inhabited the area prior to European contact. They were under increasing pressure to cede their lands and integrate themselves into American society and, after 1830 when Indian removal became federal policy, they also had to deal with efforts to remove them to "Indian Territory" west of the Mississippi River. The Potawatomi, a more agricultural people than the nomadic Ojibwa and Ottawa, had settled in semipermanent villages and enjoyed a greater degree of tribal organization. They ceded their land in the southeast in 1807 and moved to central and southwestern lower Michigan, where they settled in small villages with a loss of tribal cooperation.[30] The European settlers who moved west to clear the "wilderness" for farms mainly found scattered remnants of bands that were unlikely to pose the kind of threat many of them feared, at least after the defeat of the British and their Indian allies in the War of 1812. Indians might cause alarm when they showed up unexpectedly at a settler's cabin demanding food or drink, but they were more nuisance than threat.

The primitive society living in harmony with the forest that Longfellow would idealize in *The Song of Hiawatha,* one that had probably existed in the vicinity of Lake Superior since the fifteenth century, was greatly compromised by European influences by the early years of the nineteenth century and would deteriorate further as pressure from the federal government led to more land cessions and the incursions of individual settlers began to transform the forested landscape.[31] These settlers brought a mentality according to which the forests and the "savages" who still inhabited them were hindrances to the progress of civilization, which they saw themselves as advancing. They would learn that the forests they saw as constituting a "wilderness" to be attacked with their axes had their uses, and could even be a source of pleasure, but they would never see them as part of a spirit-haunted world to which they belonged. Their coming inaugurated a more materialistic, fundamentally different way of understanding the natural environment.

2 // Clearings

In July of 1831 Alexis de Tocqueville traveled from Detroit to Saginaw, described by those he consulted as the last outpost of civilization, because he wanted to experience the American forest in its wildest form. He and his companion, Gustave de Beaumont, posed as prospective land buyers but were in fact driven by curiosity. Disregarding warnings about Saginaw's remoteness and the difficulty of finding their way, they set out on horseback and engaged two Indian guides when they were beyond the village of Pontiac and the scattered clearings of individual settlers, facing "fifteen leagues of wilderness." Tocqueville, accustomed to European woods where he was never out of earshot of human activity, saw himself as entering a region of solitude and "a silence so profound, a stillness so complete, that the soul feels penetrated by a sort of religious terror." The dense forest appeared to him as an "ocean of leaves" in which one could easily feel isolated and lost.[1] Whereas the Indian guides seemed comfortable in the woods and sure of their direction, Tocqueville felt as though he had entered a labyrinth. The frightening aspects of the forest were magnified by what he perceived as a chaos of undergrowth and broken and uprooted trees in various stages of decay, radically different from the managed European forests to which he was accustomed. Having to force their way through obstructions while they were simultaneously contending with hordes of mosquitoes compounded the hardships of the journey and made Tocqueville and his companion Beaumont anxious to be done with it. As they pressed on at night, over the objections of their guides, the forest took on an even more alarming appearance with branches and fallen trees assuming fantastic shapes.

Yet if Tocqueville was unsettled by his encounter with such a forest, he was also awed by it. The canopy, unlike the tangled forest floor, seemed to him "immense" and "indestructible," with tall oaks and pines straight as ships' masts rising to form a vault of spreading branches that created deep shade. He saw "majestic order" above, "confusion" below. In Tocqueville's description of his wilderness experience one can see a tension between visceral reactions to what was alarming or disorienting in the forest and a readiness to find in it evidence of a divinely ordered natural world. Like others influenced by European romanticism, he was predisposed to see the wilderness as sublime.[2] His romanticism manifests itself more fully after he has emerged from the forest and reached the security of the settlement at Saginaw, where he and Beaumont are taken in by the surveyor Eleazer Jewett.[3] When Tocqueville glides through the forest in a dugout canoe on the Saginaw River the evening after his arrival, he falls into a reverie under the influence of the "serenity" of the calm scene: "The wilds were surely just the same as when our fathers saw them six thousand years ago: a flowering solitude, delightful and scented: a magnificent dwelling, a living palace, but to which its master had not yet reached" (371). Such a characterization assumes an unchanging, "primeval" forest when in fact it was a dynamic ecosystem. It also assumes that these "wilds" were created for human use and that the wilds would eventually be mastered. Tocqueville's architectural metaphors transform the forest in his imagination from a disorienting wilderness into a potential "dwelling" for settlers, one characterized by natural splendor but not, apparently, by the disruption that settlement would bring. In his visionary moment he ignores the consequences of clearing the forest to make room for those who would domesticate it.

The responsiveness to the aesthetic appeal of the forest that Tocqueville displays here is the other side of the fearfulness and sense of isolation he had felt when engulfed by "wilderness." Solitude is no longer a source of anxiety but a state associated with a profound calm in which he can respond to the sensuous delights of the forest, seen from a vantage point outside it. The geologist and explorer Bela Hubbard describes a similar appreciation of what he calls "the wild and primeval forest" in the account in his 1887 memoir of a geological expedition on the Shiawassee River not far from Saginaw in 1837. Below the last white clearings along the river Hubbard and his party experience "the sense of awe inspired by a forest solitude that has never echoed to the woodman's axe."[4] The fact that Hubbard was writing toward the end of a century that had seen the massive exploitation of Michigan's forests, as well as the emergence of a language of aesthetic and emotional responsiveness to wild nature, helps to explain how he could rhapsodize over the solitude of the "grand, old, untutored forest" and what he could see as its "boundlessness" and "sublimity."

It is not coincidental that Tocqueville's celebration of the "charm" of the forested landscape comes after he describes his safe arrival in the settlement at Saginaw. He has come through his unsettling adventure in the wilderness and returned to civilization, in the form of a cluster of log houses in a clearing bounded on three sides by forest and on the fourth by the river, with a prairie extending beyond it. The small settlement's heterogeneous population of thirty (Americans, French Canadians, Indians, and a few persons of mixed blood) represented the advance guard of a civilization that Tocqueville expected to transform the American wilderness: "In but few years these impenetrable forests will have fallen. The noise of civilization and of industry will break the silence of the Saginaw" (372). His attitude illustrates the early stages of an ecological nostalgia that would become more pronounced as the forest diminished.[5] He could begin to be comfortable with wild nature when he had one foot in civilization, and he could appreciate such wildness more fully because he recognized its impending loss.

As a European observer conscious of the drastic shrinkage of the forests on his own home ground, Tocqueville was struck by the obliviousness of the American pioneers to the destructiveness with which they "fell[ed] the forests and drain[ed] the marshes" (329), displacing the original inhabitants of the continent in the process. Yet this did not mean that he questioned the "triumphant march" of civilization and what he was confident would be the ultimate mastery of the forest by the new settlers or the disappearance of the Indian, whose apparent inability to adapt to the new civilization seemed to him proof that God intended the race to be destroyed. Hubbard, despite questioning the management of Indian affairs by the federal government, assumed that western as well as eastern tribes were destined "to fade before the Anglo-Saxon" (192). Both expressed an attitude that was shared by many, including Francis Parkman, who linked the demise of the Indian to that of the forest in his chronicles of the warfare of French and English in the mid–eighteenth century: "He will not learn the arts of civilization, and he and his forest must perish together."[6]

When Tocqueville wrote, the clearings of individual settlers still seemed precarious, mere footholds in the wilderness. He described the characteristic dwelling of the pioneer as "an ark in the middle of an ocean of leaves," with the "everlasting forest" a hundred paces away (341). The clearings around the crude log cabins appeared to him "half-wild," with wheat growing amid weeds and the trunks of felled trees, giving the impression of a place "where man is still maintaining an unequal fight against nature" (338). He regarded Pontiac, with twenty attractive houses and shops and a clearing that pushed the forest back farther than at Saginaw, as a village on the way to becoming a town. Detroit, where he and Beaumont had arrived after crossing Lake Erie by steamer, was already a flourishing town of two to three thousand. Yet outside of a few villages and towns the forest still seemed an overwhelming presence. Tocqueville was impressed by the difficulties the pioneering settler faced in carving out space for himself and his family in this encompassing forest and by the austerity of the life they lived, laboring to raise the food they needed while coping with recurrent bouts of "forest fever" (malaria, commonly called ague).

One can get a more concrete and detailed sense of the challenges faced by the early pioneers from memoirs, typically from the late nineteenth century, that recall the process of clearing land and gradually developing successful farms. In one of the fullest of these, *The Bark Covered House,* William Nowlin recounts his family's journey from Putnam County, New York, in 1833 to a property near the village that would become Dearborn, Michigan. This property in what was still regarded as wilderness represented his father's hope for a better life for his family on land that promised to be more productive than the rocky terrain of upstate New York. Nowlin senior would have found this western land neatly divided into 36-square-mile townships as a result of the land survey mandated by Congress, with the townships subdivided into 640-acre sections. He owned 80 acres when he moved his family to Michigan and subsequently bought another 80, giving him a quarter section (160 acres).

Mrs. Nowlin dreaded the move, and twelve-year-old William viewed the prospect of relocating to Michigan with alarm, imagining it as a terrifying place of bears, wolves, and Indians. His attitude mirrored the popular conception of wilderness at the time. In the collection of stories that make up his well-known *Legends of the West* (1833) James Hall describes the apprehensions of one of his protagonists as he travels through the wild country near the Ohio River: "For the bear, the wolf, and the panther, still lurked in these solitudes, and the more dangerous Indian still claimed them as his heritage."[7] Whatever his own apprehensions, once in Michigan young William joined his father in the hard work of clearing land and cutting logs for a crude cabin, roofed with bark, which they managed to put up with the help of neighbors who had preceded them. Three years later they would build a second, more substantial cabin roofed with split oak shakes. For his father, as for other early settlers, the forest was an adversary that had to be pushed back before the rich soil could be cultivated. With his young son's help he cleared two acres around the cabin, creating a log and brush fence and rolling logs into piles to be burned, using handspikes and when necessary a neighbor's team of oxen. The initial planting was a difficult business of raking the available soil in spaces between stumps and logs with an improvised harrow and using an ax to make holes for seeds in spots where the roots were thick. The forest did not give up easily; it would be years before most fields were fully cleared. Establishing a farm that would sustain a family meant acquiring a few cows and pigs, making maple sugar, and shooting deer and turkeys for meat while continuing to work at improving and extending the clearings to make possible more planting of food crops.

One of the strongest story lines in Nowlin's narrative of his family's new life in Michigan traces their progress in opening up the forest and expanding their cultivated land. He recalls their relief at seeing the sun earlier in the morning when he and his father connected the two large clearings they had gradually extended. They were convinced the sun shone brighter in Michigan than in "York state," perhaps because "the dark gloom of the forest had shaded us so long and was now removed."[8] Another early Michigan settler, R. C. Kedzie, wrote of feeling smothered by the omnipresent woods and gasping to "drink in the open sky."[9] The larger the space open to the light the greater the sense of controlling their environment, and escaping the threats associated with the gloomy forest, settlers were likely to feel. Nowlin writes that when he and his father finally had cleared a sixty-acre strip of land extending across the original property and the adjacent eighty acres his father had bought, "the light of civilization" dawned on them, as if they found assurance of victory over the wilderness at this decisive moment. They had "cleared up" what only a few years before had been "the lair of the wolf and the hunting ground of the red man" (136) and could finally feel themselves safe, since they were now less likely to be troubled by Indians paying unexpected visits or a bear raiding the pigpen at night. When their clearings had grown to such a degree, settlers could believe that they had tipped the balance in their struggle with nature and were no longer living in a wilderness but in settled country, with neighbors they could actually see from their property.

The interplay of forest and expanding clearings that Nowlin describes

THE BARK COVERED HOUSE—1834.

The Bark Covered House, 1834. (Courtesy of the Bentley Historical Library, University of Michigan.)

marks his family's gradual progression from a wilderness to a pastoral mode of existence. It also suggests why clearings were so appealing. They signaled not only emergence from the hardest phase of the struggle to claim land from the forest for agriculture but also emotional relief from the forest's gloom and the sense of confinement associated with it. To let the sun in was liberating. The new sense of openness and light suggested a future in which they could prosper and also find a sense of community with their increasingly visible neighbors. Jens Jensen, one of the landscape gardeners who pioneered the "prairie style" of landscaping in the Chicago area in the early twentieth century, liked to intersperse woodland plantings with openings: "I always have a clearing in every garden I design—a clearing that lets in the smiling and healing rays of the sun. A sunlit clearing invites hope."[10] Jensen was talking about a different kind of hope, of course, but his justification of his landscaping practice suggests the persistence of the emotional and aesthetic appeal of open spaces in a wooded setting.

In retrospect, at least, Nowlin came to appreciate the cost of all their chopping and burning. In one elegiac chapter he registers a growing consciousness of the loss involved in transforming the forest, observing that "the grand old forest was melting away" (134). Nostalgia for the old forest became a commonplace theme in settlers' reminiscences and a way of memorializing a past that was beginning to be mythologized. Kedzie offered a dramatic lament of his own, mingled with a sense of guilt that others shared or at least felt it necessary to declare: "Those grand old forests! I look back with remorse upon their pitiless destruction."[11] If such settlers saw the forest as an antagonist and an obstacle to their plans for agricultural self-sufficiency when they were busy with their axes, they came to regard it differently when their future was more secure and their lives more comfortable. When Nowlin was no longer oppressed by the "deep gloom" of the forest or laboring to escape it, he could begin to notice and take pleasure in what he found appealing about the forested landscape.

Looking back on his early years in Michigan, Nowlin writes appreciatively of the "beautiful workmanship of nature" in tall trunks and "high arching boughs" and of his enjoyment of the glistening of the woods after an ice storm (134–35). He remembers particular "venerable" trees, including an elm and a swamp white oak both measuring five to six feet in diameter, and seems to regret having helped to cut down the ancient elm. His father had decided to let the oak remain as "the monarch of the clearing" (142). Nowlin imagines the history of this oak from colonial times, prompted by the memory of finding arrowheads and stone hatchets around it. The fact that the oak had been cut down by the time he came to write his memoir would have heightened his nostalgia for a past he saw it as representing. By praising the "majesty" of this old oak and portraying it as having outlasted the changing cast of characters it would have witnessed (from Indians to fur traders and voyageurs to surveyors and the loggers who followed them), he granted it the kind of dignity that came to be associated with memorable old white pines, about which similar stories would be told. Nowlin's ability to cut down hundreds if not thousands of trees and yet pay homage to individual trees and the natural beauty he came to see in the forest illustrates a paradox that one encounters frequently in the literature of settlement and sometimes in the literature of commercial logging as well. Pragmatic settlers who threw themselves into the work of clearing the forest could display a romantic sensibility when they attempted to characterize it, particularly when they were removed in time from the struggles of the early pioneering days.

It was, of course, necessary to cut down vast numbers of trees to clear enough land for waves of settlers to support themselves by farming and, later, to satisfy the voracious appetite for lumber to build towns in Michigan and the prairie states. Nowlin asserts in his preface that he wrote his book to perpetuate the memory of the first generation of pioneers, including his mother and father. He wanted to honor the virtues and accomplishments of the "enduring" and "self-sacrificing" Michigan pioneer, seeing his father as representative of the type: "He had gone into the forest, built him a house, cleared up a farm, and lived where a white man had never lived before" (203). With the passage of time these pioneers assumed heroic dimensions. At the dedication of a log cabin at the beginning of the twentieth century General B. M. McCutcheon characterized Michigan's pioneers as living "in a very narrow and contracted sphere, hemmed in by forests, cut off from contact with the outer world" and praised "the heroic men and women who here battled with the savage forest, and perhaps with savage beasts."[12]

In his 1881 memoir Henry Little of Kalamazoo County assimilated these pioneers into an even grander narrative, echoing William Bradford's famous characterization of the Cape Cod, which he found in 1620 to be a "desolate wilderness, full of wild beasts and wild men," as well as biblical promises to the Israelites to make the waste places of Zion like Eden.[13] Little saw the pioneers as creating a garden in the wilderness, like their New England forebears, submitting to "hardships and privations" while "converting a waste wilderness, previously the abode of wild beasts and wild men, into fruitful fields and gardens, so that it became a land of corn and wine and of the finest wheat . . . a land of milk and honey."[14] This mythologizing of the achievement of the pioneers coexisted with the other kind of story, which acknowledged the losses involved in making space for these fields and gardens in the "grand old forest." After describing how pioneers burned the trees they felled, L. D. Watkins, writing in 1900, called this "the first act in the great tragedy of subduing the forest."[15] Many of those who participated in the work of clearing and later honored the "noble" accomplishments of the pioneers who made homes for their families in Michigan developed an aesthetic appreciation for the forest they had helped to destroy. They had to find ways of reconciling their contributions to the progress of civilization, and the mastery of the "wilderness" this necessitated, with romantic impulses to celebrate the grandeur of the presettlement forest and a felt need to express regret for its loss.

Nowlin came to recognize the great waste involved in the kind of clearing he and his father did, at one point speculating that they burned the equivalent of five thousand cords of wood simply to get rid of it. Pioneers such as the Nowlins used wood to build their cabins and fences, to construct plank or log (corduroy) roads over marshy ground, and to feed constantly burning household fires that seem extravagant by modern standards, with four- and five-foot logs hauled into outsize fireplaces used for cooking as well as heat. Yet the supply of wood they generated with their clearing far exceeded what they could use, and few had access to markets for it, at least until the arrival of the railroads with their demands for fuel. The early settlers became proficient in burning the prodigious amounts of wood that remained in their newly created fields, sometimes holding "logging bees" to help each other with the work of moving it into piles to be burned. They also learned techniques that facilitated burning, including jampiling (felling groups of trees in such a way that their tops joined at the center) and windrowing. The latter involved creating a windrow of fallen trees by cutting all the trees in a line halfway through and then felling the end tree and watching it bring down the rest with a gigantic, rolling crash. Either technique would leave a mass of timber ready for burning when sufficiently dry. The ashes would be used to fertilize the newly cleared field or collected for sale to a nearby ashery, which could convert them to potash.[16]

If the forest initially seemed a formidable barrier to the progress of civilization, requiring large expenditures of labor before land could be made fit for raising crops, it would subsequently be seen as a resource, providing not only a seemingly inexhaustible source of fuel and building material but game, nuts and berries, maple sugar, honey, and forage for cattle and pigs.[17] The forest supplied many of the basic needs of settlers, but it also came to be valued for more than economic or utilitarian reasons. Once their farms were well established, settlers could begin to enjoy what remained of the forest they had once feared and combated. The southern Michigan forest at the time of European settlement, now visible only in a few remnants of something recalling the original forest found in preserves, presented a scene of tall trunks rising as much as sixty feet to the first branch, with some trees three to four feet or more in diameter.[18] Nowlin describes the pleasure he took in listening to birdsong in the early morning and in roaming the woods hunting deer and wild turkey and sometimes bear as a young man, occasionally losing his way but finding it again by using familiar trees as landmarks.

For Nowlin and others like him the forest gradually became a more familiar and welcoming place, valued as a bountiful source of game, wild foods, dyes, and medicinal plants but also appreciated for its own sake. Settlers in time learned to feel at home there, as the forest became part of the fabric of their lives, a landscape whose signs they could read and whose seasons they could enjoy.[19] It also became a convenient place for public gatherings. These might be religious meetings of a kind described by Tocqueville, with people coming from fifty miles away to camp out for several days and gather in what he characterized as a "rustic church" in the woods, where a preacher would speak from an improvised pulpit to the faithful arrayed on the trunks of trees cut down to serve as seats (344). Or they might be political meetings of the sort recalled by Caroline Kirkland, with a hastily erected stage facing an amphitheater with seats that consisted of rough benches, in a beautiful grove "in all the wildness of nature" with oaks and maples forming a canopy that shaded the gathering.[20] These "grove meetings," as they came to be called, had social as well as political or religious functions, drawing together members of a widely scattered community of settlers who might linger to enjoy each other's company, as Kirkland describes them doing in her account of the feasting and revelry in the woods that follow the political meeting she observes.

Kirkland offers an example of a more detached and sophisticated commentator on the process of developing settlements in the Michigan wilderness, one who resembles the eastern and foreign travelers who offered romantic impressions of the West in some respects but radically differs from them in others. She was a well-educated easterner who became a professional writer celebrated for her sketches of western life based on her experience of the Michigan frontier. In 1835 she moved with her husband William from upstate New York to Detroit so that he could take up a position as the head of a women's seminary, then moved sixty miles west to the village of Pinckney where William Kirkland had bought eight hundred acres of land with the hope of developing the fledgling settlement there. The experiment eventually proved disillusioning for the Kirklands, for cultural and intellectual as well as financial reasons, and in 1843 they removed themselves to New York City where he became a newspaper editor and contributor to magazines and she continued to publish the essays and western sketches that she had begun to write in Michigan. After her husband's premature death in 1846, Kirkland, now the sole support of her family, pursued a literary career in earnest. Her work has enjoyed a revival primarily because of the original, satiric voice of her first book on her Michigan experience, *A New Home, Who'll Follow?* (1839), and her successful career as a professional woman writer.[21] Kirkland's *A New Home* earned her an instant literary reputation as a frank observer of the rough conditions of frontier life and its crude social ways and simultaneously succeeded in outraging her Pinckney neighbors. Renaming Pinckney Montague, changing names, and writing under a pseudonym (Mrs. Mary Clavers) did not fool them. Kirkland's ability to satirize her own genteel expectations as well as the incivilities of her new neighbors may have amused her eastern admirers, but it complicated her life in Pinckney and caused her to moderate her satire and broaden her focus in two subsequent books on the West, *Forest Life* (1844) and *Western Clearings* (1846), the latter a collection of pieces first published in magazines.

Kirkland's unusual situation, writing primarily for an eastern audience while making a life for her family in a frontier village, positioned her to offer a witty critique of what she saw as overly romantic accounts of the West by such popular writers of travel narratives as James Hall and Charles Fenno Hoffman. She alludes to their descriptions of picturesque western scenery "touched by the glowing pencil of fantasy," including Hoffman's accounts of riding through inviting oak openings, before describing a typical mud-hole that swallowed her family's carriage on their journey from Detroit to Pinckney.[22] In a similar vein she shows her narrator, Mrs. Clavers, disabused of visions of life in the woods derived from reading François-Auguste-René de Chateaubriand's popular romance of the New World, *Atala,* by her experience of living in a cramped, one-room log cabin with her husband and children. Kirkland prided herself on showing the "real woods" as opposed to Chateaubriand's fantasies. The realism that impressed her contemporaries worked by rendering a series of shocks to her narrator's refined sensibility and capturing the social peculiarities of her frontier neighbors, made more convincing and amusing by her skillful use of dialect.

Yet Kirkland was capable of delighting in western scenery herself, expressing her responses through her narrator. In *A New Home* Mrs. Clavers, once acclimated to her surroundings, describes her great pleasure in riding with a friend through lovely woodlands in which she finds ferns and wild strawberries and can see dazzling lakes "through the arched vistas of the deep woods" (86). She labors over a garden where she cultivates flowers, as well as the vegetables her family needs, but finds recreation and escape in the woods, where she can indulge her romantic musings: "Many a dreamy hour have I wandered in this delicious solitude" (150). Kirkland's narrator never seems fully comfortable in the woods in the ways that

Nowlin and others of the early settlers come to be, and she continues to filter her impressions through a literary sensibility, but her favorable reactions to her natural environment contribute to her efforts to establish frontier Michigan as a place with claims to scenic beauty, as well as hazards for the traveler.

Mrs. Clavers embodies another aspect of Kirkland's response to the landscapes of her new home, one that contrasts with her satiric observations on the traveler's lot, an aesthetic sense that becomes more pronounced in some of the sketches of *Forest Life* and distinguishes her from settlers who are so immersed in the work of clearing that they cannot recognize what they are destroying. In *Forest Life* Kirkland spends a chapter criticizing the settler's habit of regarding trees simply as something to be removed, making a plea for preserving "the fine remnants of the original forest that still remain to us."[23] She blames settlers for linking the advancement of civilization with "the total extirpation of the forest" and excoriates a particular one from Ohio for girdling a favorite oak of hers, a "relic of primeval grandeur," to increase the size of his potato patch (1:43, 46). Such failings were symptomatic of a more general failure of settlers to care for "the beautiful" that was one of the disillusioning aspects of life on the frontier for Kirkland. It took Nowlin and others involved in the work of clearing, as Kirkland was not, much longer to acknowledge the value of this "original" forest.

Kirkland's sharp eye for the inconveniences of daily life and the foibles and moral failings of those she found on the frontier, including indolent settlers and devious land speculators, has given her a deserved reputation as an early practitioner of realism. She was also, however, an acute observer of her natural environment and one capable of responding to the aesthetic appeal of inviting woodlands, scattered lakes, and wet prairies with their springs and wild grasses, all part of the charm of scenery that she found "quietly beautiful" (*Forest Life*, 1:134). The contrasts between newly settled areas and "the untouched forest" sharpened her sense of the "wild freshness" of a nature not yet radically transformed by humans: "Immense trees give an air of solitary grandeur to the landscape and the absence of every thing like fence or dividing line of any sort, inspires ideas of immensity,—of solitude,—which make the sudden apparition of man and the traces of his busy hands produce a feeling akin to surprise" (1:172–73). Kirkland's descriptions of her rambles through the countryside in *Forest Life* suggest that the attraction of the landscape lay partly in its variety, with wheatfields as well as prairies and oak openings contrasting with frequent stretches of woods, but the woods held a particular fascination for her as the place where the contrast with village life was complete. The forest offered a "primeval solitude and silence" (1.176) where one could get away from the hectic activity of carving farms out of the woods, buying and selling parcels of land, and struggling to establish towns.

Kirkland's responsiveness to distinctive Michigan landscapes makes her sensibility seem more akin to those of Hoffman and Hall than her dismissal of their renderings of the West would suggest. While she makes a point of revealing unattractive aspects of life on the frontier that they ignore through her commentary on the condition of the roads and on what pass for amenities available to travelers, she shows a similar eye for picturesque scenery. Kirkland qualifies her responses to the natural environment, however, by continuing to call attention to the trying conditions of frontier life and to suggest how easy it can be to romanticize them. She begins *Forest Life* by offering a dream vision of an Arcadian countryside allegedly made possible by a magic mirror and then showing the mirror broken and herself returned to the reality of tumbledown log cabins and the patched and mended farm wagon in which she travels.

Kirkland's contemporary Charles Lanman, by contrast, indulges romantic fantasies, based on recollections of his experience of the Michigan woods growing up on his father's farm near Monroe, which he presents without irony. Lanman had established himself in New York and later Washington, D.C., as a writer and painter, a friend of William Cullen Bryant and Asher Durand, with a knack for writing popular essays and accounts of his travels that appealed to the public taste for the picturesque. In an essay he calls "Dream of the Wilderness" and prefaces with an epigraph from Bryant ("And I was in the wilderness alone") he imagines himself wandering at sunset in a forest where the trees seem "like the columns of a vast temple" and coming on a series of picturesque scenes, including an Indian village where hunters are returning with game, deer bedded down for the night, and delicate wildflowers in the moonlight.[24] Lanman's "dream" seems to have been prompted by a childhood hunting experience of getting lost at night in a Southeast Michigan forest of "great oaks, and hickories, and walnut trees" and coming on an encampment of sleeping Indians where he lay down and slept himself, despite his fears, and then was fed and taken home in the morning by his surprised hosts. Lanman embellishes his adventure by heightening the mysteriousness of the forest, describing it as casting a spell and himself as "alone and lost in that silent wilderness."[25] Early in the same collection he invites the reader to see the forest as a sacred space: "[C]ome with me into the woods, and we will hold silent and holy communion with the visible forms of Nature."[26] While Lanman shows that the "wilderness" of the forest could be frightening, he presents it as fundamentally benign, a place that prompted meditation on the beauty of nature and the benevolence of God.

Unlike Lanman, Kirkland complains about mosquitoes and details the hardships of settlers' lives, including poverty and accidental death caused by a mistake in felling a tree, more fully and sympathetically in *Forest Life* than in *A New Home*. She gives the most romantic responses to the landscape in *Forest Life* to a fictional couple she calls the Sibthorpes, English émigrés whose story she tells through the device of a series of letters to friends in England. Mr. Sibthorpe dwells on the repose and sense of freedom he finds in the forest, with the sighing of wind in the leaves and the "masses of deep shade," seeing it as forming a "natural Coliseum" that rivals Italian relics (2:69). Mrs. Sibthorpe rhapsodizes about the pleasure she finds in the solitude of the forest and finds inspiring natural architecture all about her: "If we want pillars and arches, and corridors and cloisters, we have them all close at hand, built by mighty Nature, and ready to put to shame man's puny efforts at imitation. This architecture never tires" (2:80). She counters the anticipated skepticism of her fashionable correspondent by defending her romantic enthusiasm. In the couple's letters Kirkland offers an exaggerated version of responses to the landscape that have something in common with her own, presenting them through sympathetic characters whose enthusiasms may at times seem mannered, but she never dismisses or satirizes them as she does those of Hoffman and Hall.

In one of the pieces she collected in *Western Clearings* Kirkland describes an autumn interlude "when every winding valley, every softly swelling upland, in the picturesque 'openings,' is clothed in such colours as no mortal pencil can imitate, blended together with such magical effect, that it is as if the most magnificent of all sunsets had fallen suddenly from heaven to earth, and lay, unchanged, on forest, hill, and river."[27] Such straining for language fit to describe a transcendent natural scene reflects a chauvinism about American scenery common at the time, as well as the character of Kirkland's aesthetic response to particular Michigan landscapes that she found inviting. Like Hoffman, she felt compelled to champion American landscapes against more famous European ones, in her case with a marked defensiveness about the alleged tameness of the scenery of her adopted home ("I know of no feature of rural beauty in which our green peninsula is found wanting").[28] She saw Michigan's oak openings as offering something that Europe could not claim.

> We can at least boast some features unique and peculiar in our landscape—our "openings" and our wide savannas are not to be found in Switzerland, I am sure. These—as to the picturesque which we are wild about—bear something like the same proportion to the Alps that the fair, blue-eyed, rosy-cheeked and tidy daughter of our good farmers, does to the Italian improvisatrice with her wild black eyes and her soul of fire.[29]

Kirkland's surprising analogy invests oak openings with a sense of moral stability and enduring appeal; they are more "comfortable" to live with than the flashier but more unreliable European epitome of the picturesque.

The oak openings that attracted Kirkland, now called oak savannas (or oak barrens in drier environments), were well known to settlers who ventured into the interior of southern Michigan. The openings fascinated observers such as Hoffman who reported on their travels in the West. They can be thought of as clearings of a different sort, encouraged in some cases by sandy soils but sustained by periodic fires set by lightning or by Indians who wanted to create conditions favorable to hunting or agriculture. The openings suggest the possibility of release from the modest initial clearings of the early settlers into a more expansive landscape, one still defined by the surrounding woods (and the small groves of trees that dotted them). The great majority of those that existed in the early nineteenth century have disappeared, victims of development or a policy of fire suppression that allowed trees to colonize them. Oak openings were neither forest nor prairie but something in between, open spaces with clusters of trees that constituted a separate ecosystem with its own family of plants.[30] The partial recovery of this distinctive midwestern landscape, in the environs of Chicago and Toledo among other places, is one of the success stories of the contemporary ecological restoration movement.[31] An official highway sign that greets motorists driving south from Michigan to Ohio on U.S. 23 announces "Entering Oak Openings Region," as if reclaiming the presettlement landscape for purposes of tourism.

For settlers the openings offered relief from the density of the enveloping forest, seemingly hospitable land through which they could drive their wagons at a time when roads were few and poor. They could begin farming in the openings without the arduous work of clearing to which they were accustomed if they were willing to settle for typically sandier soils that were less fertile than what they could reclaim from the forest. A promotional pamphlet aimed at prospective settlers sketches a mixed landscape of forest and prairies alternating with oak openings "extending as far as the eye can reach, like lofty parks" with soils that are highly productive with only "the careless tillage of a new country."[32] Federal surveyors had reported in 1818 that nearly half of the interior of Michigan was "open oak woodland," stirring excitement in settlers who had been hesitant to venture beyond Detroit.[33] Speculators and promoters took notice, and the movement westward accelerated.

In his account of an 1836 trip to Michigan, land speculator John M. Gordon described the openings as being like orchards, with white oaks and bur oaks (about the size of pear trees) at intervals of thirty or forty feet with grass underneath. Like other early observers, Gordon found the oak opening particularly inviting: "It [the oak opening] assumes the appearance of a grove carefully kept near a gentleman's residence and it is difficult to divest yourself of the impression that you are approaching a stately mansion through a stately forest. It thus has the charm of inviting the traveler still on, and if he has a lively sensibility to the softer beauty of natural scenery he may wander from rise of moon to set of sun in these arcadian regions in groves of Oaks."[34] The appeal of oak openings had to do with the sense that such landscapes were more civilized, as if shaped for human habitation and enjoyment by a well-to-do landowner. Analogies to orchards, stately groves, and particularly parks reflect an attraction to a landscape that was more hospitable than the forest, free of obstructions and hidden dangers, and that seemed to be artfully ordered in a fashion perceived by some as more English or European than American. Orchards, moreover, had special meaning for settlers as a symbol of mastery over the wilderness and evidence of lasting settlement. Thus a landscape that seemed to resemble an orchard would have been a highly encouraging sign.[35] Yet, as Gordon's description of his reaction suggests, the fact that the openings constituted a "natural" landscape gave them a romantic aura. He conveys a sense of wonder at having wandered into "arcadian regions," an idealized middle landscape recalling the mythical Arcadia of Virgilian pastoral, poised between the wilderness of the forest and the domesticated space of a town.

In *A Winter in the West* Charles Fenno Hoffman, the object of Kirkland's criticism in *A New Home*, characterized Michigan and other western lands for a wider and more literary audience through a series of letters describing his travels, alone and on horseback, on a circuit that took him from Pennsylvania through Ohio, Michigan, and Illinois and then down the Mississippi River and back to Virginia. Hoffman was a young member of the Knickerbocker group of New York writers, which included such notables as Washington Irving and James Fenimore Cooper, who became the editor of a succession of literary monthlies. He consciously sought out the picturesque in his travels through what he thought of as the "romantic West." Hoffman admired the wilder scenes he found in the mountains of western Virginia and the bluffs and ravines of the upper Mississippi but delighted especially in gentler landscapes that seemed more accommodating to a human presence, such as the "Arcadian" scene of groves opening on meadows that he found between the Kalamazoo and St. Joseph rivers of western Michigan. He imagined the meadows carpeted with summer wildflowers, although it was December when he saw them.

Hoffman first encountered oak openings after traveling through swampy country west of Detroit and then coming out of dense woods at a sudden turning in the path.

> Imagine yourself emerging from a New Jersey swamp, and coming at one bound upon one of the English parks which Puckler Muskaw so admirably describes. Clumps of the noblest oaks, with not a twig of underwood, extending over a gently undulating grassy surface as far as the eye can reach; here clustered together in a grove of tall stems supporting one broad canopy of interlacing branches, and there rearing their gigantic trunks in solitary grandeur from the plain. The feeling of solitude I had while in the deep woods deserted me the moment I came upon this beautiful scene, and I rode on for hours, unable without an effort to divest myself of the idea that I was in a cultivated country.[36]

The groves of oaks that Hoffman found scattered across the plain onto which he emerged could serve as a reminder of the forest, preserving a sense of its grandeur, without the oppressiveness he felt in his solitary travels through the "deep woods." Hoffmann emphasizes his sense of wonder, marveling at the beauty and expansiveness of this surprisingly open landscape. The fact that he relished the illusion of coming on a "cultivated" landscape in his journey through the western wilderness suggests other reasons for the appeal of oak openings. They implied a sense of human presence, thus offering relief from the isolating effects of the forest. And they were unexpected, an aspect of the native American landscape that was both wild and not wild, suggesting the European aesthetic ideal of the varied, parklike landscape favored for the grounds of great houses without actually being cultivated in the sense in which Hoffman understood the word. They were all the more charming for seeming to be accidental, an American form of pastoral sprung from the wilderness.

Hoffman was astute enough to realize that oak openings were not a purely natural landscape type but rather one shaped to some extent by deliberately set fires. He believed these were annual fires started by settlers to improve the supply of wild grass, apparently not recognizing the long-standing native practice of setting fires (or the effects of lightning in sparking fires), which had more to do with the process of shaping the openings. Kirkland, by contrast, was aware of speculation that the fires were set by Indians to aid their hunting. Hoffman was oblivious to the irony that a landscape largely created and maintained by "savage" tribes became for cultivated travelers an echo of a European upper-class ideal. He describes a scene from a little later in his travels across southern Michigan that offers a revealing glimpse of such a fire as it sweeps across prairies and through woods and at the same time shows how Hoffman played to the expectations of his audience. He recounts his anxious efforts to observe the fire and yet avoid being engulfed by it, self-consciously comparing himself as he rides nervously back and forth to a figure in one of Sir Walter Scott's popular novels (Andrew Fairservice trying to avoid the bullets of Rob Roy's followers). When he eventually takes refuge on a little peninsula isolated by the windings of a stream, he finds himself next to a "grim-looking savage" who calmly surveys his anxious activity with folded arms. Hoffman excitedly describes his new companion's native dress, complete with tomahawk and scalping knife, and recounts how he gazed in fascination and delight at this "noble apparition," confessing that he was "carried away" completely by his encounter. The fact that his companion proved friendly and was able to communicate the origin of his alarming battle scars, despite their lack of a common language, no doubt colored Hoffman's recollection of the scene. The story of his encounter with what he could not help seeing as a "theatrical" figure, under the dramatic circumstances created by the fire, gives the landscape itself a feeling of wildness that would have enhanced its appeal to his readers.

Hoffman in fact found stretches of the southern Michigan landscape monotonous and looked forward to a time when cultivation would give it more variety. He complains that the December landscape could be "dreary," but his imagination continued to be sparked by scenes he found picturesque such as lakes with high banks and irregular wooded promontories. Oak openings pleased him for a different reason, because they gave an impression of artful regularity. When he encountered his first bur oak opening in western Michigan, he found it to be like a pear orchard in the shape and size of the trees, "standing at regular intervals . . . as if planted by some gardener."[37] Whereas the picturesque charmed by means of its wild irregularity, the "novel beauty" of oak openings appealed by giving the appearance of a man-made order. Hoffman was as conscious as a land speculator of the promise of actual cultivation in such relatively open and fertile land, suggesting that it would produce twenty-five bushels of wheat an acre in its first year as opposed to ten on unsettled land in New York. He was also sensitive to the commercial promise of railroads and canals that would open up the country. At the same time, paradoxically, he could celebrate the beauty of Michigan's still relatively unmarred landscape of dense forests (nature's "unviolated sanctuary"), numerous "limpid lakes," expansive meadows, and oak openings. Like many others at this time, he regarded the freshness and wildness of American landscapes as a counterweight to Europe's more historically layered ones, with their many ruins: "I confess that a hoary oak is to me more an object of veneration than a mouldering column" (1:195).

The best-known writer to describe Michigan's oak openings was James Fenimore Cooper in his late novel *The Oak Openings,* published in 1848 after Cooper had made two visits to the Kalamazoo area of western Michigan in connection with landholdings there but set at the beginning of the War of 1812. Cooper treated "the Openings" as a definable region distinct from the forest and prairie and intimately known by the native inhabitants, mainly Potawatomi and Ottawa, who claimed it as their hunting ground. For Cooper's protagonist, the bee hunter Ben Boden, the uncultivated openings represent a way of life opposed to that of the settlements. Boden is one of a small group of white adventurers, forerunners of subsequent waves of settlers, who have begun to penetrate the area but so far have made little impact on it. The Kalamazoo River, the principal means of access to the openings, has only a few shanties and wigwams along its banks. To white settlers, still concentrated around Detroit, the area is "wilderness."

Cooper's initial description of the openings resembles those of travelers who preceded him. He finds suggestions of civilization in the irregularly spaced oaks separated by verdant grasses "that bear no small affinity to artificial lawns."[38] Like Hoffman, whose *A Winter in the West* he would have known, Cooper compares the bur oaks that dominated western Michigan openings to pear trees. He strikes a careful balance between nature and culture in his descriptions, noting that the region is "in one sense, wild" while offering "some of the most pleasing features of civilization" (10). The distribution of the trees sometimes suggests to him the regularity of an orchard, yet elsewhere the trees appear scattered, "with much of that air of negligence that one is apt to see in grounds, where art is made to assume the character of nature" (10). Cooper implies that nature here plays the role of artist, with the kind of negligence that appeals to a refined sensibility. The fact that the scene is "wild" is critical to its appeal, but such wildness does not admit any sense of unruliness or disorder.[39]

The sense of nature blending with "seeming civilization" is most pronounced in Cooper's descriptions of Prairie Round, a prominent landmark for Hoffman and also for Gordon. Cooper describes this large prairie, surrounding a wood with a lake at its center, as "like a well-kept park" (307). The terrain, with its undulating plain marked by copses of native trees, so reminds Cooper of a domesticated landscape that he imagines himself looking upon the site of an old settlement from which all human traces have disappeared, finding a pleasing refinement in what he sees as the artistry of nature: "There were the glades, vistas, irregular lawns and woods, shaped with the pleasing outlines of the free hand of nature, as if consummate art had been endeavoring to imitate our great mistress in one of her graceful moods" (309).

Cooper was conditioned by eighteenth-century aesthetics and a seven-year stay in Europe to see the landscape of Prairie Round as resembling a European park. He shared the contemporary attraction to the picturesque, which could blend at one extreme with the beautiful and at the other with the sublime.[40] For him oak openings would have combined qualities of the beautiful and the picturesque. It has been said that *The Oak Openings* is the most Europeanized of Cooper's novels about the American wilderness in its emphasis on the artistry and "finish" of nature and a tendency to formality in its landscapes.[41] Yet Cooper does not let us forget that the openings are beguiling because they offer the illusion of civilization rather than the evidence of human design seen in the landscapes of parks or gardens. He observes that finding new grasses and flowers on Prairie Round in the late summer is "in some degree accidental," contingent on a recent fire whose cause he does not try to identify. As

Cooper was aware, the state of all the openings was similarly dependent on fire to hold off the natural advance of trees and undergrowth and to stimulate new growth. Acknowledging the role of fire introduces an element of unpredictability into the apparent artistry of the landscape and enables Cooper to preserve a sense of its wildness without losing the appearance of an underlying order that made it seem hospitable.

Oak openings served Cooper's dramatic purposes as stages for key scenes that advance the action of his fiction.[42] The narrative moves from his initial description of the openings into the first of these scenes, a chance meeting among Boden, the white adventurer Gershom, the Chippewa Pigeonswing, and the Potawatomi Elksfoot. Cooper describes the place itself as a grassy glade "Far in the wilderness" (17), abounding in the fresh grass and blooming white clover that spring up after a fire and make it a suitable place for Boden to practice his art of lining bees to their hives. Such openings function as meeting places and, along with the prairies onto which the woods occasionally open, spaces that enable Boden to pursue the solitary life in the woods that he seeks. Cooper locates Boden's shanty in an opening on the banks of the Kalamazoo River, "a most beautiful grove of the burr-oak" (28) where sunlight streams through the trees and one finds "wild but verdant" grass. It seems entirely fitting that Boden and his bride Margery are married by Parson Amen in another of "the venerable Oak Openings," before an altar "of nature's own erecting": "[T]he good missionary stood within the shade of a burr oak, in the centre of those park-like Openings, every object looking fresh, and smiling, and beautiful. The sward was green, and short as that of a well-tended lawn . . . while charming vistas stretched through the trees, much as if art had been summoned in aid of the great mistress who had designed the landscape" (350–51). The scene has the features that Cooper typically associates with oak openings but seems particularly idyllic because of the dramatic circumstances, and also distinctively American: "No gothic structure . . . could have been half so appropriate" (351).

Cooper's openings constitute a version of pastoral, offering a sense of refuge from the forest with which they are contrasted and reflecting his desire to see wilderness as compatible with domesticated, settled space.[43] Yet these engaging, seemingly natural clearings are also associated with vulnerability at the historical moment that Cooper chose for the novel. He derived much of his drama from the tension between their apparent tranquility and the impending or actual violence that disrupts it. The conjunction of wonder at the natural beauty of the openings and the violence that shatters their peacefulness makes them symbolic of a vision of arcadian life in the wilderness that is doomed by the forces that inevitably destroy it.[44] The settlers' clearings that Tocqueville describes appear fragile against the backdrop of the surrounding forest, but they belong to a time when the threat of violence from Indians who remain in the area has receded. The action of Cooper's novel takes place two decades earlier at a particularly fraught time, when the hostility of the Potawatomi to anticipated white settlement in western Michigan was inflamed by the renewal of war between Americans and the Potawatomis' British patrons.

Cooper's fictional treatment of Michigan's oak openings suggests a particular kind of pastoral dynamic in which the disruptions we see are all the more shocking because the openings imply a sense of security in the ease and delight they offer along with a deceptive sense of freedom from the uncertainties and dangers of life in the forest. As the novel progresses, descriptive passages become charged with suspense. The natural amphitheater near Boden's shanty in which the Potawatomi chiefs gather resembles the oak openings in its aesthetic appeal, with a rivulet running through a "wood-circled arena, of velvet-like grass and rural beauty" (256). Yet the juxtaposition of this pastoral setting with the stalking, "half naked" forms of the chiefs gives the scene a "wild and supernatural aspect" that anticipates the violence that will unfold there later, when the naive Parson Amen is executed and his companion, Corporal Flint, subjected to an especially horrific form of torture.

One can see a similar dynamic operating in the scenes surrounding a pivotal council of chiefs at Prairie Round called by Scalping Peter, a Potawatomi famed for scalping his enemies who is alternately Boden's adversary and his protector. When Boden sets out toward Prairie Round with his party to give the chiefs a demonstration of his bee-hunting skills, Cooper makes the early morning scene especially alluring, "a picture of rural tranquility and peace," while reminding the reader of the political turmoil of the war between Britain and America and the presence of "savages" in the immediate vicinity (304). The lyricism of Cooper's description of openings bathed in sunlight, with birds singing in greater numbers than usual, has ominous undertones for the reader by now conditioned to expect disruption of idyllic interludes. Cooper modulates into an extended description of Prairie Round itself, which epitomizes the loveliness of the openings. He describes the waiting Indians as embellishing the scene, implying that their presence enhances its picturesque beauty, but then ratchets up the suspense by making the reader aware that Boden's life depends on his ability to dazzle the chiefs by demonstrating his seemingly magical rapport with the bees.

The dynamic of the pastoral ideal disrupted by violence is best exemplified in *The Oak Openings* by the burning of Boden's shanty by the Potawatomi in the expectation of trapping the whites inside. The howling of Boden's dog Hive, left behind when Boden and the others make a last-minute escape by canoe and set afire by the collapse of the burning roof, registers the horror of the scene. Cooper characteristically couples this scene of devastation with a description of the profound tranquility of the openings immediately before Scalping Peter arrives to urge Boden to flee.

> The whole of the landscape was bathed in the light of a clear, warm, summer's day. These are the times when the earth truly seems a sanctuary, in spots remote from the haunts of men, and least exposed to his abuses. The bees hum around the flowers, the birds carol on the boughs and from amid their leafy arbors, while even the leaping and shining waters appear to be instinct with the life that extols the glory of God. (420)

We see Boden and Margery entirely relaxed, enjoying a Sabbath repose in their apparent sanctuary "beneath the shade of the oaks, near the spring," when Scalping Peter appears with his urgent warning.

The destruction of Boden's haven and his precarious escape with Margery and a few others mark the collapse of his ideal of a life of coexistence with the native inhabitants of the area. The danger associated with the forest, their natural habitat, suddenly manifests itself. The promise of the parklike openings themselves, with their suggestion of peaceful domesticity and aesthetic delight amid the wilderness, is revealed to be deceptive. Cooper makes this promise seem deeply ironic at the moment before Peter appears: "[T]he Openings seemed so rural and so much like pictures of civilization, that apprehension had been entirely forgotten in present enjoyment" (421). His presentation of the oak openings in the novel is ultimately elegiac, reflecting his attraction to a frontier landscape that offered the prospect of order and refinement in a still wild country yet was subject to the violence of historical processes, in this case the vengeance of native inhabitants of the forest encouraged by their alliance with the British. The epilogue that Cooper offers in his concluding chapter reflects his sense of a larger and more inexorable historical force represented by advancing white settlement that would largely eliminate the openings, along with the simple pastoral life that Boden embodies for much of the novel.

In his epilogue Cooper represents himself as visiting Prairie Round and meeting the central characters of the novel thirty-six years after the events of the story, showing the "prairie" (actually an undulating oak savanna) transformed into a neat agricultural landscape sprinkled with barns and farmhouses. With its pious justification of the advance of civilization as evidence of the workings of divine providence and its celebration of Scalping Peter's metamorphosis into "a civilized man and a Christian" (490), the epilogue drains the novel of dramatic tension and confirms what critics have branded the extreme conservatism of Cooper's late work.[45] Its didacticism invites this kind of criticism and seems a crude, nationalistic endorsement of the blessings of progress and an effort to justify the displacement of the native inhabitants and the transformation of the landscape of forest and openings as ordained by divine providence. Speaking for the native inhabitants, Scalping Peter now accepts white expansionism as God's will. Boden in his old age has become a gentleman farmer and patriarch (General Boden) who tends his beehives and supervises the harvest, and Pigeonswing is a dependent who has compromised his dress and behavior sufficiently to bring himself "within the habits of conventional decency" (498). The source of wonder is no longer the landscape but a huge threshing machine adapted to the needs of "a gigantic country" (495), a machine that makes possible a vision of a great commercial network by means of which flour milled from the wheat of Prairie Round will eventually make its way to Europe.

Cooper's account of the triumph of Christianity and white settlement, with the flourishing agriculture that makes westward expansion possible, can be seen as the logical extension of themes that run through the novel.[46] If the oak openings appeal primarily because of their resemblance to parks or orchards, then the domestication of the countryside might seem to be the realization of a future that they imply. Prairie Round has become fenced and cultivated fields "of the most surpassing fertility," producing great crops of wheat. Yet the island of woods at the heart of the former prairie remains ("an old-fashioned virgin forest"), with the lake at the center of the woods serving as a link with a more challenging and dangerous past. In describing the approach to Kalamazoo, Cooper registers the changes in the openings and accepts these as necessary, "incident to the passage of civilized men."

As the periodical fires had now ceased for many years, under-
brush was growing in lieu of the natural grass, and in so much
those groves are less attractive than formerly; but one easily com-
prehends the reason, and can picture to himself the aspect that
these pleasant woods must have worn in times of old. (492)

Cooper allows a suggestion of nostalgia for the old landscape of the openings, despite embracing the new prosperity of the countryside and its
promise for the future. His fictional treatment of Michigan's oak openings
presents a particularly striking version of the paradoxical embrace of
progress and of the aesthetic and emotional appeal of the countryside that
the original settlers transformed. Cooper's ecological nostalgia is not so
much for the "grand old forest" whose loss Nowlin and others came to regret as for the openings that offered the sense of a welcoming landscape
and the promise of relief from the forest's gloom. These openings, with
their pleasing alternation of meadow and grove, survive mainly in the
imagination and in the art of the novelist. The ability to lament what has
been lost while confidently embracing progress, with no apparent sense of
contradiction, belongs to a particular stage of American expansionism.
One of its exemplars, John James Audubon, deplored the loss of an earlier
America epitomized by the wild scenery of the banks of the Ohio River
and of the marshes along coastal rivers, with the vast flocks of birds they
nurtured, while accepting and even celebrating the advance of civilization.
He appealed to "our Irvings and our Coopers" to capture through their art
the "original state" of a country that was changing rapidly as its population expanded.[47]

The definition of the pioneer would be expanded as the wave of settlement spread through southern Michigan and began to move north as
roads were extended and new watersheds settled, including those of the
Saginaw River in the east and the Muskegon River in the west. Lumbermen who set in motion large-scale, commercial logging of Michigan's
abundant white pines and the lumberjacks who worked in the woods
came to be recognized as different kinds of pioneers. The lumberjacks engaged the wilderness in a new way, as an army of workers living in winter
camps deep in the woods, risking their lives felling giant pines and engaging in the dangerous work of loading and banking the logs, then managing the tumultuous spring river drives that delivered them to the mills.
Not that the settlers' work of clearing was without its own dangers.

Nowlin describes the risks of wielding axes in the woods, and Kirkland tells a story of a father crushed by a bee tree whose fall he miscalculates. The advent of logging, however, dramatically escalated the risks and gave rise to new kinds of stories of the struggles of humans with the nature they sought to master. The great surge of commercial logging in Michigan and the other Lake States, beginning in the mid–nineteenth century and lasting into the early twentieth, transformed ways of imagining the forest and generated a folklore and a literature that reflect a distinctive culture. The plundering of the pines and then the hardwoods had immense economic, social, and environmental ramifications, and its effects continue to be felt today in debates about the proper use and management of public forestland.

3 // The Culture of Logging

The Lumberman's Monument stands on a high bluff overlooking the Au Sable River in the Huron National Forest southwest of Oscoda, where the Au Sable enters Lake Huron. Three nine-foot bronze figures commemorate the golden age of Michigan logging in the second half of the nineteenth century. A landlooker (or timber cruiser) with his compass stands slightly forward and in the center of the group, flanked by a sawyer with his ax and crosscut saw and a riverman with his peavey (a long, iron-tipped pole with a movable iron hook). The monument, completed in 1931, was sculpted by Robert Aitken of New York and financed by families representing the early lumber industry in Michigan. The plaque at its base proclaims that it was "Erected to perpetuate the memory of the pioneer lumbermen of Michigan through whose labors was made possible the development of the prairie states." The inscription gives an emphatically positive spin to the plundering of Michigan's white pine by focusing on the lumber industry's role in the country's westward expansion. Michigan was in fact the leading lumber-producing state in the country at a time (from the 1870s to the 1890s) when settlers were pushing into the Great Plains and needed to import lumber for building, railroad ties and telegraph poles, and even fencing and plank sidewalks. The monument presents the "pioneer lumbermen" whose labor it celebrates as heroic figures: energetic, resolute, and looking fully capable of meeting the challenges of wresting giant white pines from the "wilderness" and driving them down rivers such as the Au Sable to the waiting sawmills.

It would be more accurate, however, to call these heroic figures (the sawyer and the riverman at least) lumberjacks or shanty boys rather than lumbermen, a term that was sometimes used of loggers in the nineteenth

ERECTED TO PERPETUATE THE MEMORY OF THE
PIONEER LUMBERMEN OF MICHIGAN THROUGH
WHOSE LABORS WAS MADE POSSIBLE THE
DEVELOPMENT OF THE PRAIRIE STATES

The Lumberman's Monument. (Courtesy of the *Detroit News*.)

century but came to be associated with the landowners and operators of lumber camps for whom they worked. In his dedicatory speech on July 16, 1932, William B. Mershon invoked many of the "lumber clans" whose representatives had provided the funding for the monument and vigorously defended the reputation of the "original lumbermen of Michigan," who included his father and grandfather. Mershon himself was a successful lumberman who became a well-known sportsman active in battles for conservation, particularly those involving fish and game regulation and state forest management.[1] On this occasion, celebrating a past in which his family had played a prominent role, he stressed the difficulties of the early logging days and insisted that few of the original lumbermen had made fortunes. Rather than the rascals or lumber barons they had come to be called by politicians, he argued, they were pioneers who often struggled to pay off bank notes and make their payrolls after river drives. Many of the "hardy old race" of entrepreneurs Mershon described started out by working in the woods themselves, but his speech makes it clear that he was more concerned with celebrating and justifying the business success of these owners than with praising the sawyers, river drivers, and all the others who did the physical work of getting pine logs to the mills.

One effect of Mershon's speech, and of calling the sculpture the Lumberman's Monument, was to associate those who built the lumber industry by acquiring land and creating companies with the labor of the lumberjacks themselves and the aura of romance they had acquired. The lumber clans that Mershon represented had responded to his vision of creating "a lasting memorial worthy of these heroic men who were often so unjustly criticized as destroyers of the forests when they were really the pioneers of an industry that was necessary for not only the building up of our own state but the settlement of the West." Mershon defended these men by arguing that "the forest was created for use" and the pioneer lumberman "provided for its wise use and received little recompense."[2] By focusing on "use," particularly in enabling the country's westward expansion, he sought to counter what had become a widespread public perception that the early lumbermen were interested only in enriching themselves, without regard for the future of the state's forests. Mershon and the other sponsors of the Lumberman's Monument were engaged in an act of rehabilitation. The monument was meant to call attention to the accomplishments of Michigan's early lumbermen and assure that they would be remembered.

The Lumberman's Monument and the circumstances surrounding its creation illustrate both the controversy and some of the mythology that came to surround the early lumbering era in Michigan. Whatever its origins and the intent of its sponsors, the monument functions today as a popular symbol of this era, appropriately situated in a wooded site that overlooks a state-designated natural river once filled with floating "cork" pine (the mature, buoyant white pine that was particularly valued) during spring logging drives but is now more likely to be populated by canoeists and trout fishermen. It stands next to the U.S. Forest Service's Lumberman's Monument Visitor Center, which tells the story of the lives of the early lumberjacks in the Au Sable Valley through dioramas and photographic exhibits inside and large-scale replicas outside (a rollway, a logjam, a floating wanigan of the sort that supplied river drivers). These reminders of the daily lives of the lumberjacks reflect a growing fascination with pioneer life, in Michigan often represented by exhibits recalling the emergence of the logging industry.

The best and most extensive representation of Michigan's major logging era can be found at Hartwick Pines State Park just north of Grayling (also on the Au Sable), which contains the largest stand of old-growth white pines in the Lower Peninsula. Its Visitor Center and related Logging Museum re-create the life of "shanty boys" in the primitive logging camps in which they spent the winter (with reconstructions of a bunkhouse, a combination cook shanty and mess hall, a blacksmith shop, a camp office, and a store) and display the history and material culture of logging. One can see a remarkable array of tools, from pike poles and saws to the measure with which the scaler estimated board feet in a log; the loggers' gear, including the "caulked" (spiked) boots they often wore to keep their footing, especially on river drives; a selection of iron log marks, comparable to cattle brands, with which owners stamped the ends of their logs to distinguish them from others with which they were mingled during the drives; and, outside, some of the heavy equipment necessary to move logs that were twelve to eighteen feet long and could be as much as five feet in diameter. This equipment included sleighs pulled by oxen, and later by workhorses, on which huge loads of logs were transported via iced roads to the rollways where they were piled in anticipation of the spring drive. After 1875 it also included Big Wheels about ten feet in diameter with which several logs at a time could be skidded without the need for the snow and ice that until then had confined logging to the winter months. The coming of railroads to the pineries beginning in the 1870s was a more significant development, since it was no longer necessary to rely exclusively on river drives to get the logs to mills, and consequently areas farther from rivers could be logged. Railroads made possible year-round logging and encouraged the logging of hardwoods, too heavy to float to mills. Main line railways such as the Michigan Central and the Flint and Pere Marquette were extended, and owners constructed shorter narrow-gauge railways to feed into these or to connect camps with mills.

The emergence of large-scale commercial logging in Michigan in the nineteenth century has been well charted, from its real beginnings in the early 1850s through its gradual decline in the late 1890s and the early twentieth century. The original boom in the Lower Peninsula led to the rise of Saginaw and Bay City in the east, serving the rich pinelands in the watershed of the Saginaw River, and of Muskegon and Manistee in the west at the mouths of the Muskegon and Manistee rivers. By the height of the boom in the mid-1870s there were sixteen hundred Michigan sawmills in operation, producing over a billion board feet of pine lumber a year. The focus of logging activity would gradually shift to the northern Lower Peninsula and then to the Upper Peninsula as major pine stands near navigable rivers, including the Grand and Pere Marquette in the west and the Au Sable and Cheboygan in the northeast, were depleted. In the Upper Peninsula lumber towns grew up first at the mouths of major rivers emptying into Lake Michigan (the Menominee, Escanaba, and Manistique) and then elsewhere when the advent of the logging railroads opened up new territory. A rail connection with Seney (near the Fox River) established in 1887 made Grand Marais on Lake Superior a logging center, and another center on the Superior shore emerged at Ontonagon at the mouth of the Ontonagon River. In the eastern Upper Peninsula the Tahquamenon and the Two Hearted became important logging rivers.

In both the Lower and Upper Peninsulas, attention turned to hardwoods (including beech, maple, oak, and hickory) when the pine stands were exhausted. Swamp forests in the Upper Peninsula yielded spruce, tamarack, and cedar for railroad ties and telegraph poles. Hemlock was valued for its bark, a source of tannin, and for use as mine timbers. Logging for pine (Norway, or red, pine as well as white) in the Upper Peninsula peaked in the mid-1890s, and by the early twentieth century the great wave was largely spent, although hardwood logging continued to prosper, with Michigan leading the nation in hardwood production from 1900 to 1910.[3] Eventually the old-growth hardwoods as well as the pine, both formerly thought to be inexhaustible, were largely depleted. Michigan was left with millions of acres of cutover land and a residual logging industry based primarily on pulpwood, for which aspen and birch could be used.[4] Because of the tangles of branches and other debris (called slash) left by logging operations, this land was highly susceptible to forest fires, some of which blew up and became uncontrollable in particularly dry years. The most intense

Michigan logging rivers. (Reprinted from Rolland H. Maybee, *Michigan's White Pine Era* [Lansing: Michigan Historical Commission, 1960].)

of these famously destructive firestorms degraded the soil by oxidizing organic matter built up over centuries, greatly retarding natural succession.

The story of Michigan's Big Cut is often expressed in figures: 161 billion board feet of pine and about 50 billion board feet of cedar, hemlock, and hardwoods produced between 1840 and 1900; 2.5 million acres burned in the fires of 1871 and over 1 million in the fires of 1881 in Michigan's Thumb region; and 92 percent of Michigan's original forest cut or destroyed by fire or clearing by 1929.[5] I am more interested in the stories that have been told about the rise and decline of logging, particularly of the white pine that was the focus of the early logging industry, and about the lives of the loggers themselves. To understand these stories and the culture of logging represented in the displays at Hartwick Pines and elsewhere one needs to have some awareness of the broader development of commercial logging in nineteenth-century America. Many of Michigan's loggers and the owners who employed them came from Maine and Canada's maritime provinces, especially New Brunswick, where the Miramichi rivaled Maine's Penobscot and Kennebec as a logging river. Most of the practices in Michigan's early logging camps and much of the folklore associated with them originated in the East, where the 1830s and 1840s were boom times for the logging industry.

The pattern of winter logging followed by spring drives commencing with the first high water was well established by the time significant commercial logging developed in Michigan. So was the organization of labor found in the camps. The camp boss or foreman was at the top of the hierarchy, and the "road monkey," responsible for establishing and maintaining roads (and clearing manure from icy sleigh tracks), was at the bottom. Skilled sawyers felled the trees, priding themselves on their ability to drop them exactly where they wanted, and then bucked them into logs; a filer sharpened the saws. Others were responsible for brushing out roads, still others for loading the logs on the sleighs and unloading them at the rollways. Teamsters managed the oxen and the horses that eventually replaced them; a blacksmith was necessary to keep the animals well shod. One of the most important people in the camp was the scaler, who estimated the board feet produced by the operation and thus determined how much cutting had to be done to satisfy the terms of the contract. An even more critical camp member was the cook, who with his assistants (cookees) had more to do with the morale of the men and their willingness to work at the camp than anyone else.

As early as the late seventeenth century the British had recognized the value of the abundant white pine they discovered along New England rivers. They found that the long, straight trunks, devoid of branches for as much as seventy-five to a hundred feet, made ideal masts and claimed for the Royal Navy all white pines two feet or more in diameter at the base and no more than three miles from a river. Enforcing their claim was another matter. It did not take long for others to realize that clear, workable white pine made prime lumber, and the rush to log it was on. The logger emerged as a distinct American type, with characteristic speech and dress (including a mackinaw and "stagged" pants raggedly cut off above the boot tops with an ax or knife) and a body of songs and stories featuring memorable characters and exploits. These exploits included not only remarkable deeds in the woods and on river drives but hard drinking, hard fighting, and wild carousing during the sprees in Bangor and other logging towns that followed the logging season.

By the 1850s, sensing the approaching depletion of the pine stands in the Northeast, loggers were "following the pine" to Michigan, where easterners had responded to reports of great pine stands in the Saginaw River basin by buying land in anticipation of another boom. Some had gone earlier to New York or Pennsylvania, where logging flourished for a time, but the largest migration was to Michigan. The loggers who headed to the upper Midwest, drawn by the prospect of plentiful work in the lumber camps, came from Ontario and Quebec as well as from Maine and the maritime provinces and, in later waves, from Ireland, Germany, Scandinavia, and eventually Eastern Europe. When Michigan's vast supply of pine began to give out, many moved on to northern Wisconsin or northeastern Minnesota, the other Lake States. The last big move was to the West Coast, where Michigan lumbermen (many of them transplants from New England) had been investing in forestland and where immense trees (redwoods, Douglas fir, and the sugar pines that are the closest relative of the white pines of the East and the upper Midwest) dictated changes in the familiar methods of logging. Washington and Oregon soon became the leading lumber-producing states. Pine lumbering was also taking hold in southern states and beginning to supply southern yellow pine to the prairie states through the vast Chicago market, but their heyday would come later.[6]

The exhibits at Hartwick Pines provide an introduction to this history. They are supplemented by a slide show produced by the Department of Natural Resources (DNR), which traces the development of the logging industry in Michigan but is more concerned with justifying the industry's current forest management practices. The exhibits, including the various tools and pieces of equipment, are chiefly valuable for the tangible ways in which they expose visitors to the culture of logging. They include historic pictures of the sort also found in popular books about logging: two sawyers with a crosscut saw dwarfed by the large white pine, several feet in diameter at breast height and perhaps 120 feet tall, they are about to fell; five grinning loggers sitting on the butt ends of massive logs with estimates of the board feet they contain marked on the ends; a stump field with scattered snags; a massive logjam on one of the many rivers used for drives; and the "commemorative load" for the 1893 Chicago World's Fair from Ewen on the Ontonagon River, showing a towering pyramid of 50 huge logs (estimated at 140 tons) on a sleigh ready to be pulled along an ice road by a team of two Percherons. Such photographic displays suggest the ability of the early loggers to perform tasks that seem inconceivable today. The photographs show loggers cutting pines of a size no longer found in Michigan outside of a few protected areas, with tools that look distinctly primitive beside modern chainsaws, and managing the hazardous job of moving massive logs to rollways on ice roads through hard labor and ingenuity. In others loggers risk their lives to find and dislodge the key log that will release a jam by means of skillful use of their peaveys, or dynamite in more difficult cases, or they run across the loosening jam to shore to avoid being crushed by logs that break free and accelerate in the current. The familiar photograph of the World's Fair load, ubiquitous in displays and books about early logging in Michigan, exaggerates the scale of the challenges the loggers took on and invites comparison with the mythical feats of Paul Bunyan. Pictures and displays of tools alike contribute to an image of the logger as heroic antagonist of nature.

Life in the logging camps could indeed be dangerous. Men were seriously injured or killed by limbs (known as widow makers) unexpectedly sheared off in the process of felling trees and by logs that slipped during the precarious business of loading them on sleighs or releasing them from rollways. Toploaders, who worked atop stacks of logs, were particularly vulnerable to serious injury or death. The logger's life was also hard, with days starting before dawn with the cook's cry of "Daylight in the swamp!" and lasting until dusk, six days a week, for wages averaging a dollar a day in the early decades of the industry. Those who worked on the spring drive earned more, given the greater danger of this work and the degree of skill it demanded. They might spend as much as a month working as long as daylight lasted, with those on the crew at the rear spending much of their time waist deep in frigid water getting stranded logs back into the river (known as sacking) and others working at the front of the drive keeping the logs moving or breaking up the jams that repeatedly formed.

Despite all the hardships and dangers, the loggers' life was remarkable for its camaraderie, another theme of the exhibits at Hartwick Pines. Guides to the Logging Museum show visitors, including groups of schoolchildren, the fiddle and mouth organ with which loggers provided music for Saturday night entertainment and tell them about the stag dancing in which the men partnered with each other to romp around the cleared mess hall floor. They distribute copies of a song popular in camps on the Manistee River operated by an owner notorious for skimping on food, Louis Sands, with the help of a camp boss named Jim McGee, sung to the tune of "O' Tannenbaum": "Who feeds us beans? Who feeds us tea? / Louis Sands and Jim McGee / Who thinks that meat's a luxury? / Louis Sands and Jim

Logging crew. (Courtesy of the Clarke Historical Library, Central Michigan University.)

McGee." Someone with a good voice would lead the singing of this and other favorite songs, and the rest would join in the chorus or sing along; he might also play an instrument and tell stories, orchestrating the evening's entertainment from his place on the bench known as the deacon's seat.

One gets little sense from the exhibits at Hartwick Pines of the underside of life in the camps, including the effects of isolation, the difficulties of coping with the harshness and unpredictability of winter weather, injuries, frequent disease, and unclean conditions. With many men living in relatively cramped quarters, without facilities for bathing and with wet socks drying over the central fire or stove, the smell must have been overwhelming to anyone who had not become accustomed to it. Lice and bedbugs were a fact of life, the subject of jokes. The men might boil their clothes and blankets on Sundays and mix tobacco in their bedding in the hope of coping with the infestation of "graybacks," as the lice and bedbugs were called, but they knew they were fighting a losing battle.[7] Although logging camps improved from their primitive beginnings over the course of the nineteenth century, with better buildings and better and more varied food as the camps grew to contain as many as a hundred men, crowded and unsanitary conditions persisted well into the twentieth century in camps in the Upper Peninsula as the focus of the industry shifted to hardwood and then pulpwood production.

Museums such as the one at Hartwick Pines appeal to the public's interest in the contrast between the pioneer era and our own times by re-creating a sense of a way of living, and working, notable for its austerity. We may be tempted to see such lives as more elemental and somehow more authentic than our own, buffered as we are from the kinds of challenges from the natural world the early loggers faced. It is easy to be nostalgic for the simpler life of the frontier when we don't have to live it. Songs and stories popular with loggers offer a better window on the ways in which they liked to think of their own lives than museum exhibits are likely to, capturing a sense of the camaraderie and spirit of adventure as well as of the hardships of life in the lumber camps. They also give a better indication of how lumberjacks mythologized a way of life that had its share of drudgery. One song popular in the Saginaw area that originated in Maine, "Once More A-Lumbering Go," begins:

> Come all you sons of freedom
> > That run the Saginaw stream,
> Come all you roving lumber boys,
> > And listen to my theme.
> We'll cross the Tittabawassee,
> > Where the mighty waters flow,
> And we'll range the wildwoods over
> > And once more a-lumbering go.[8]

The song goes on to contrast the dull life of farmers with the freedom of shanty boys roaming the woods with axes on their shoulders, making "many a tall and stately tree . . . come tumbling to the ground," then driving the logs to Saginaw where their girls await them. After a pleasurable summer they go "once more a-lumbering" and continue this seasonal pattern until they are ready to settle down with a farm and a "little wife."

We get no sense of hardship or danger or even real labor from the song, just the promise of the freedom and masculine adventure that the "lumber boys" will enjoy in the "wildwoods." A version popular in Maine contrasts their life in the winter camps, where they delight in making the woods resound with the music of their axes, with the shivering of city dwellers in the cold. Going "a-lumbering" offered escape from the routines of settled life and the promise of a unique kind of camaraderie to be found among like-minded men who took up the challenges of life in the camps. At least temporary escape, since many of those who worked as lumberjacks in the winter spent the rest of the year working on the family farm. Part of the appeal of such a song was that it kept alive the sense that a kind of frontier life was still possible despite the proliferation of farms and towns and the more commonplace existence they represented. The Maine version pictures a time when the pine will be gone and the lumberjacks will sow grain on land they have cleared, having to content themselves with reliving a more exciting past: "O! we'll tell our wild adventures o'er, and no more a lumbering go."[9] A poem by John Greenleaf Whittier praises the labors of Maine lumberjacks as hastening a future of "Golden wheat and golden maize-ears" and celebrates the masculine spirit with which they pursue their calling in a wild, wintry "North-land": "Up my comrades! up and doing! / Manhood's rugged play / Still renewing, bravely hewing / Through the world our way!"[10] Whittier's poem captures something of the sense of freedom and adventure conveyed by the songs but invests the lumberjacks' labor with a sense of high purpose. He was more interested in turning them into heroic figures than in catching the mood of the camps.

Another kind of song popular in Michigan camps and elsewhere presents the less appealing side of camp life, cataloging its deprivations and afflictions, from bad food to grueling work in harsh conditions. One of these, "A Shantyman's Life," complains of wintry winds and "swinging an ax from morning till night / In the midst of the forest so drear," the absence of whisky and "fair maids," wake-up calls at 4:00 a.m., and wet clothes and freezing conditions on spring drives.[11] This song ends with a resolve to give over roaming and live a quiet and sober life at home "With a smiling and charming little wife." One can imagine the loggers singing both kinds of songs with gusto, convincing themselves of the freedom of life in the woods by celebrating it and making their hardships more tolerable by belting out their complaints in song. Interestingly, both assume an eventual escape to a quiet and comfortable domestic existence outside the woods, as if to suggest that the shantyman's life is only a phase, a young man's game. In fact, many loggers returned to the camps season after season, and more than a few grew old in the work.

There were ballads and songs associated with particular camps and rivers, some of them telling stories of feats of daring or legendary fights such as that between Silver Jack Driscoll and Joe Fournier. Fighting, whether in the camps or more commonly in a lumber town saloon during the drinking bouts that followed a season in the woods, was the most extreme manifestation of a competitiveness that characterized all phases of the lumberjack's life, from trying to best rival crews or camps in productivity to trading tall tales, and a generally accepted measure of one's manhood. There were dialect songs that found humor in the language of Swedes or Norwegians or French Canadians and songs that recounted famous events in logging country. Another familiar kind of song tells stories of disappointment in love, with the absent sweetheart abandoning her shanty boy for a lover closer to hand, sometimes a hated "mossback" (farmer).

Some of the most popular songs related memorable tragedies in the woods or on the river. The song reported to be the most popular in the Michigan camps, "The Jam on Gerry's Rocks," was associated with rivers in Maine, Ontario, Wisconsin, and the western logging states, as well as in Michigan, in other versions.[12] It tells of the deaths of six Canadian boys and their young foreman Jack Monroe, "so tall, genteel, and brave," while breaking a jam on a fateful Sunday morning, turning more obviously sentimental as it describes finding Monroe's "crushed and bleeding" body washed up downstream and then the inconsolable grieving of his true love, Clara, who dies of a broken heart three months later and is buried with him under a solitary hemlock on the riverbank. Such songs wring out the pathos of untimely death by including graphic descriptions of bodies crushed by logs or falling trees and by dwelling on the anguish of the grieving lover or aging parent left behind. One effect of turning unexpected, violent death into stories that could be handed down and passed from camp to camp was to elevate and at the same time distance it. Jack Monroe and the "brave boys" who volunteered to help him break the jam become young heroes cut down in their prime, the stuff of legend rather than simply casualties of a notoriously hazardous occupation.

Songs and stories about the fabulous exploits of Paul Bunyan were another feature of life in logging camps in Michigan and elsewhere. These reflect the kind of heroic self-projection, along with the tendency to comedy and exaggeration, characteristic of tales of other folk heroes of the American frontier such as Davy Crockett and the riverboat man Mike Fink.[13] The Paul Bunyan who survives in the popular imagination today owes more to literary elaborations of the stories that began to appear in the early twentieth century than to the oral tradition of the lumber camps, preserved in songs and in recorded recollections of lumberjacks.[14] For the lumberjacks Paul Bunyan was a larger than life figure, at least seven feet tall and in some tellings much taller, with prodigious physical strength and uncommon ingenuity; his blue ox Babe was said to be seven ax handles wide between the tips of his horns, between his eyes in some accounts. The stories are typically located in an identifiable place not far from the camp in which they are told and begin realistically, then slip into the realm of the fabulous: Paul killing giant mosquitoes that attack his camp, the cook needing a cord of wood to start a fire in his enormous stove, Babe dragging a whole section of land (640 acres) to the landing, where the trees are sheared off like sheep's wool, and then dragging it back. One of the more elaborate examples of Paul's ingenuity has him dealing with a formidable logjam by placing Babe in the river immediately below it, then shooting him in the flank with a rifle. Babe, thinking he has been bitten by a fly, starts twitching his giant tail and creates a propeller effect that forces the river back and releases the pressure that has been holding the jam.

A favorite song set in the "good old days" immediately after the Civil War, "Round River Drive," preserves many of the favorite Paul Bunyan stories, including one of taking a hundred million feet off one "forty" shaped like a pyramid with pine on all sides. The song builds to an account of the spring drive, on which the men assume they will eventually reach a mill town but find themselves passing their camp again and again on what turns out to be the "Round River." A final stanza tells of finding the very camp, years later, on section 37 west of Grayling. Trying to outdo each other in telling Paul Bunyan yarns was another form of competition in which lumberjacks engaged, passing on and embellishing familiar stories of Paul's ingenuity and staggering appetite and Babe's incredible strength. If they knew they were indulging in ever more comic exaggerations, they were also transforming the drudgery and dangers of their occupation. Or, in the image of the Round River, finding a way to laugh at the seeming endlessness of the work of the river driver. However comic the stories might become, they had the effect of projecting the lumberjacks' own labors onto a giant screen and of embodying a fantasy of mastering the difficulties and the forces of nature with which they contended as easily as Paul and Babe did.[15]

Accounts of the early lumberjacks by observers and historians up through at least the mid–twentieth century tend to mythologize them, whatever they may offer in the way of details about their daily lives. As the white pine era faded and what logging there was became more mechanized, with transport by railroads replacing spring river drives and the living conditions of the loggers dramatically improved, some writers enveloped the remembered or imagined life of the camps in a nostalgic haze. George Angus Belding liked to transform the stories he heard from old lumberjacks into poetic narratives.

> I'm an old jack from the pine-wood track
> > By the banks of the Manistee;
> I've toiled with Swedes and tough half-breeds
> > And other jacks, wild and free. . . .
> I saw men meet with steel-shod feet
> > In the towns by the river tracks—
> The very least was a husky beast
> > Of the breed called Lumberjacks! . . .
> Now the timber's gone like an April dawn
> > And the loggers are long gone too—
> But in my dreams I drive wild streams
> > From the Saginaw to the Sault![16]

The rhythm and verse form of Belding's poem, and the spirit, recall the immensely popular verse of Robert Service based on the Klondike Gold Rush and that of Service's model, Rudyard Kipling. With a change of setting to the Yukon Territory this could almost be a Service poem about manly adventure and the struggle for survival in the rugged north, although the characteristically American phrase "wild and free" suggests release from conventional obligations and norms of behavior. Belding alludes to the potential for violence in the lumberjack's world with a reference to the caulked boots ("steel-shod feet") that men used as readily as their fists in their frequent fights, particularly in town after a season of hard work and deprivation in the woods, but he softens the violence and danger, as well as the hard labor, by making it part of an old man's dream of the reckless times of his youth.

After growing up in Presque Isle County in the northeastern Lower Peninsula at the turn of the century and working in lumber camps in Michigan and Wisconsin as a young man, Belding eventually became a municipal judge in Dearborn and set about recording the world of the early lumberjacks in verse, most of it collected in *Tales from the Presque Isle Woods* (1946). In an address to the Michigan Historical Society in 1948, Belding praised a late-nineteenth-century book by John W. Fitzmaurice for its sympathetic and detailed presentation of the life of the "shanty boy." Fitzmaurice was a sometime journalist who traveled to hundreds of Michigan and Wisconsin lumber camps in the early 1880s as a hospital agent selling tickets that guaranteed care for sick or injured lumberjacks in a hospital established for this purpose. In 1889 he published a collection of impressions and stories based on his experience that is particularly interesting for the way in which it mingles detailed accounts of what he saw in the lumber camps he visited with romantic views of the loggers' work and the forest itself.[17]

In Fitzmaurice's book one can see the beginnings of the process of mythologizing, with its efforts to frame the lives of the lumberjacks in ways that would appeal to a literate, mainly urban audience. He assembled details about the daily routine of the logger in the woods and the conduct of river drives, facts about the lumber industry, fragments of songs, personal anecdotes enlivened by convincingly realistic dialogue, and tragic stories of "disaster and death," including a version of the death of Jack (or Charlie) Monroe. In Fitzmaurice's version, which he represents as having been told him by Silver Jack Driscoll himself, Monroe's death is wildly mourned by a young, pregnant wife who arrives in camp to find his broken body and promptly delivers a stillborn baby and dies. She is buried with Monroe under a pine tree on the bank of the Au Gres River ("The Lone Pine of the Au Gres"), which no logger will touch. Near the end of his haphazardly organized book, much of it consisting of stories he wrote for newspaper publication, Fitzmaurice includes prescriptions for reform directed to the loggers he claimed he wanted to instruct and amuse. These include condemnations of debauchery in town and approving accounts of temperance campaigns, along with practical advice to all those involved in the lumber industry: stop cutting the stumps so high and find some way to control destructive forest fires. Like other early observers, Fitzmaurice was conscious of the immense waste involved in common lumbering practices.

Fitzmaurice's book offers an odd combination of convincing observations about the character of the shanty boy (hardworking, combative, a spendthrift but generous to those in need) and life in the camps, on the one hand, and self-consciously literary efforts to cast this life as an epic struggle on the other. For him the loggers constitute the "army of the pine," engaged in what he characterizes variously as "the battle of the saw log" and "the war against King Pine." The discontinuity between the loggers' pragmatic view of their work (looking at a pine and seeing only how many saw logs it would make) and his own, more romantic one did not prevent Fitzmaurice from describing the men as acting out "The Romance of the Forest" daily. In an episode that he calls "The Romance of King Pine" Fitzmaurice personifies an ancient pine and shows this "mighty monarch of the forest" peopling the valley with its "children" and towering over them in "sublime majesty," defying storms and floods for centuries. He concludes the story with self-conscious irony by showing a French Canadian shanty boy, a comic figure who boasts of his prowess in broad dialect, bringing the great pine's life to a "ridiculous" conclusion by chopping it down in an afternoon with his ax. Fitzmaurice could undercut his portrait of proud King Pine by describing its ignoble end and then dismiss the story as "nonsense" in comparison with one of the death of a shanty boy from a falling tree that he will go on to tell in his next short chapter. Unresolved tensions between a tendency to idealize the forest and the deeds of those who contended with it and recognition of the practical and economic necessities of logging characterize much early writing about the white pine era in Michigan. Fitzmaurice can rhapsodize over "the gorgeousness of a Michigan forest" and the "silent forces of nature" at work in it, and indulge in a fanciful evocation of the majesty of an ancient pine, and then celebrate victories in the "war" against such pines that he chronicles.

Fitzmaurice concludes his little book with verse that summarizes his defense of the "Shanty Boys" to whom he dedicates it, betraying no sense of concern about the fate of King Pine.

> All hail to the pioneer army grand—
> > The men of the axe and the saw—
> In labor's formost [*sic*] rank they stand,
> > And the car of Progress draw;
> The forests so brown at their march go down,
> > Towns and cities rise where they fell;

> While work well done and wealth well won,
> Speaks the shanty boy's labor well.

In his effort to ennoble the labor of the shanty boy Fitzmaurice links it to the grander ideal of the progress of civilization, as the inscription on the Lumberman's Monument would later, by making the settling of the prairie states the embodiment of this progress. He assumes that towns and cities will spring up in place of the forest, although in fact efforts to establish the agricultural economy necessary to sustain such towns would fail on much of the cutover land. At one point Fitzmaurice defends the "lumber barons" and "pine kings" against the criticisms of the press and politicians, chiefly on the basis of their philanthropy. His reference to "wealth well won" has the effect of including these owners in his vision of the march of the "pioneer army grand." In most of the songs of the lumber camps, as well as in the reminiscences that appeared with increasing frequency in the first half of the twentieth century, there is little if any sense of the cost to the environment or the economic future of the state of the race to log Michigan's old-growth pines. Sending "many a tall and stately tree . . . tumbling to the ground" was part of the adventure and achievement of the shanty boy. The prevailing philosophy of the owners who put them to work in the woods was "cut out and get out." Once they had taken the pine, most of them moved on, leaving others to find uses for the cutover lands and the remaining trees (hardwoods, cedar, hemlock, and jack pine) they left behind.

Belding's *Tales,* published over half a century after Fitzmaurice's book, reflects the radical shift in the public mood in the intervening years. In his prologue Belding denounces the "tide of the lumberman's greed," which he associates with tycoons sitting in city offices who looted the riches of the northern forest after gaining title to millions of acres of timberland cheaply through the connivance of politicians. He laments the ravishing of the "ageless" forest itself in melodramatic verse representing the voice of "The Timberland's Ghost": "Haunting, nostalgic, my wailing floats along / Denuded slopes; drifting, lamenting." Yet, with the apparent contradiction characteristic of writing about the logging era, Belding absolves the loggers themselves of responsibility and proclaims them "a brave, vanished breed." He frankly acknowledges the nostalgia evoked by his memories of "caulk-booted lumberjacks, vigorous, bearded fellows, lopping the limbs from the fallen trees, swamping, skidding, toploading, driving. Memories of old Onaway on a Saturday night, the streets swarming with rugged fighting men swaggering and carousing," celebrating their energy and roughness in almost Whitmanesque fashion.[18]

Local histories of Michigan's logging rivers and lumber towns sometimes reflect another kind of nostalgia, not only for the lumberjacks but also for the pioneering lumbermen who built the mills, spurred the growth of the towns, and often left their names on the landscape.[19] They describe the rise and fall of lumber companies and the role of important mills in local economies, celebrating the individuals whose enterprise was responsible for the emergence of the towns and whose philanthropy sustained their institutions. Some tell stories of transforming rivers to make them fit for driving logs to the mills.[20] Building dams to create holding ponds was a major part of such stories, along with clearing obstructions, including trees that had fallen across the river (sweepers). The results of clearing and widening the Au Sable and logging its heavily forested banks included warming the river, silting its clear waters, and destroying spawning beds, ultimately dooming the grayling, a famous freshwater salmonoid fish native to northern Michigan. A book tracing the history of the river, *The Old Au Sable*, is, among other things, an elegiac tribute to the grayling, "the greatest game fish in Michigan."[21]

A history of the white pine era in the Saginaw River basin graphically re-creates the bustling scene on the Saginaw River as logs were conveyed to the mills from its various tributaries, in an effort to recall a time of astonishing energy and productivity when lumber was the dominant industry of the state and the major source of employment.[22] Its accounts of how logs were sorted into holding pens at the confluence of the Tittabawassee and Saginaw rivers, then rafted to the more than a hundred mills that had grown up along the twenty-mile course of the Saginaw River by the 1870s, illustrate the impressive scale of Michigan's lumber industry in its peak years. The Tittabawassee Boom Company, the largest in the state, sorted and delivered to mills over ten billion board feet of logs between 1864 and 1894. In the most productive years the Saginaw River was crowded with tugs, barges, lake schooners, mackinaw boats, and steamers coming from Lake Huron to deliver supplies and pick up lumber at mills along the riverbanks and transport it to markets.[23] A foldout map identifies the sawmills and related industries along the river in 1884, while accompanying photographs show expanses of wharves with great stacks of lumber. The map's legend describes a scene difficult to imagine today: "Almost overnight new sawmills suddenly appeared. Some mills were giant complexes of mill booms, wharves, drying yards—with company boarding houses, barracks, and stores . . . cooper shops, offices, salt blocks, saw and belt repair shops—shingle and lath mills. One mill. . . . even had its own schoolhouse and library."

William S. Crowe's account of his experiences in the lumber industry in Manistique, first published in 1952 and twice revised, offers a fuller and more detailed view of the white pine era in the Upper Peninsula near the end of the nineteenth century.[24] As the chief bookkeeper for most of the 1890s for the Chicago Lumbering Company, the dominant employer in the Manistique area, Crowe saw all aspects of the lumbering operation, from the logging camps and the management of the river drives to the dealings of the owners with their employees, numbering around fifteen hundred at the time. In addition to describing his experience of camps and drives he re-creates the scene at the Manistique waterfront, with sawmills running nonstop and tall-masted schooners loading lumber at the docks. He shows a visitor greeted by a cacophony of sounds and the mingled smells of fresh pine lumber and smoke from numerous burners and kilns. Crowe insists that no other tree anywhere had so much "romance" or was so closely associated with the way people lived as the white pine. Coming to Manistique after two years on a cattle ranch in Colorado, he was struck by the similarities he found between lumberjacks and cowboys, despite the obvious differences in their environments. For him they had "the same spirit of daring, resourcefulness, initiative, independence and romance bred by close contact with nature at her best and worst in a vast, free country."[25] What Crowe seems to mean by romance is what others, especially in the late nineteenth and early twentieth centuries, called the pioneer spirit, regarded as formed by direct interaction with an untamed natural world and its challenges.

Crowe was writing fifty years and more after his early years in Manistique, with a nostalgia that enabled him to see life in a booming lumber town and the camps that supplied it as "picturesque." His own nostalgia is reinforced by that of a former Manistique lumberjack, one he regarded as his "ideal old-time lumberjack" and visited at the lumberjack's comfortable ranch in California's Santa Clara Valley: "It's nice [here]," he quotes the lumberjack as saying, "but I miss the woods, I miss the wind in the pine tops. I miss the early morning breakfast gong, the cry of 'timber.' The snow, the frosty creaking of the log sleighs, the sprinkler and the ice roads and the big horses straining to start the load. . . . I even miss the straw bunks of the earlier days, and I'd give all this to bring those days back. That was a man's country."[26] It was no doubt easier to relish straw bunks and early winter mornings in the Michigan woods at a considerable re-move in space and time, yet such reminiscences reveal a retrospective at-traction to a simpler and more primitive existence, even to the hardships that lumberjacks liked to complain about when they were experiencing them.

Nostalgia for the challenges and the intensity of such a life is typical of reminiscences of the white pine era by the ordinary lumberjacks who ex-perienced it firsthand. A narrative created from interviews in the 1950s with Louie Blanchard, who grew up along the Chippewa River in Wiscon-sin and worked in the Chippewa pineries from 1888 to 1912, suggests that the attraction to a river driver's life could be irresistible to a boy growing up watching the drives: "Everybody looked up to these men who wore caulked boots and red mackinaws and walked on logs as they shot the rapids. Us boys said that someday we'd ride logs down the Chippeway." For Blanchard and his brothers riding logs became a form of play, and in his later life he still felt the urge: "[T]he life of the lumberjack was a good life. It was a hard life, but if I had to live my life over, I'd be a lumberjack again and ride the logs down the Chippeway."[27] Other old lumberjacks looked back with similar nostalgia on the "good life" of the lumber camps.[28]

Those who were enterprising and capable enough to work their way up to become operators of lumber camps and sometimes buy tracts of timberland themselves expressed their own kinds of nostalgia. John Munro Longyear, who became one of the largest landholders in the Upper Peninsula and the wealthiest man in Michigan, looked back on his five years as a landlooker in the early 1870s as a highly satisfying and formative period of his life, despite the hard work and adventures such as getting lost in the woods, running short of food, and being followed by a wolf on a frozen river at night. After a time in the city, he writes, he was "eager to re-turn to outdoor living, which tended to develop a man's self-reliance, pa-tience, and perseverance; in fact, all his physical and mental resources."[29] Isaac Stephenson, who came to the Upper Peninsula from Bangor, Maine, in 1846 and became one of the most successful lumbermen of his time and subsequently a U.S. senator from Wisconsin, prided himself on the rugged and demanding life he led in his early days in the woods. In a 1915 memoir he describes himself driving ox teams, proving that he could manage men as a camp boss, and learning to do whatever was necessary to meet the needs of lumberjacks in a remote logging camp.[30] This included treating illness and sewing up wounds, even amputating an arm on one occasion, and performing the functions of preacher and lawyer when necessary. A late-nineteenth-century history of the lumber industry largely devoted to celebrating the accomplishments of the early lumbermen of the Northwest presents Stephenson as the archetypal self-made man and someone who delighted in recalling how he "attacked the virgin forests" with a broadax, "shoulder to shoulder with his men."[31]

The 1929 memoir of another self-made lumberman, John Emmett Nelligan, boasts of the rough ways of the early lumbering business and the toughness they called for in anyone trying to manage lumber camps and logging drives, which he did as a camp foreman and river boss before building his own business. Nelligan was the son of Irish immigrants who settled in New Brunswick; he left home at fifteen to work in Maine lumber camps and migrated to Michigan four years later after a brief stay in Pennsylvania. His narrative, constructed from his notes by a young writer to whom he turned for help, emphasizes his ability to keep order with his fists and to outsmart or intimidate rivals, for example, in contending with another company for primacy in the use of a river for a spring drive. The world he describes is one where violence is never far from the surface and success goes to the strong, determined, and quick-witted, all of which he portrays himself as being. Nelligan liked good stories and provides colorful ones about fights, disasters on river drives, and the troubles that lumberjacks' inability to resist whisky could get them into. He tells a story of five men from one of his camps who decided to sleep off a drunk on the way back to camp from town by lying down on the railroad tracks, with fatal results when a train was unable to stop in time. He also shows a tendency to mythologize both the lumberjacks and the early lumbermen who "played great roles in the drama by which the lake state pineries were leveled," a tendency that would become more pronounced in writers as the nineteenth century receded. Nelligan's memoir ends with homages to some of the more prominent of the lumbermen, including Longyear and Stephenson, and with a final, approving observation: "They have passed and are passing, but they will always be remembered as splendid pioneers, as men who unmercifully bent and broke the wilderness to their wishes."[32] Their success at forcing nature to submit to their will, by cutting and turning to lumber great swaths of white pine, becomes the measure of their greatness.

Nelligan celebrates the lumberjacks themselves earlier in the book as unsung pioneers and heroes of a "passing epic drama."

They were strong and wild in both body and spirit, with the careless masculine beauty of men who live free lives in the open air.
They seemed the finest specimens of manhood I had ever seen.
. . . [and] even in their annual periods of dissipation, when they
flung away the wages of a winter's work in a wild orgy lasting only
a week or so, they were magnificent. Drunk or sober, they would
fight at the drop of a hat and fight to a bitter finish. They had
their code and it was a chivalrous code. . . . no man could even
speak lightly of a woman of good reputation without suffering
swift and violent justice at the hands of his fellows.[33]

The ghostwriter's literary aspirations are obvious here, but the basic attitude toward the masculinity of the lumberjack and his honorableness
with regard to respectable women is consistent with the views of Nelligan
that emerge from the memoir as a whole and with those of others who recalled their experiences in the early days of the lumbering era. A few
women visited lumber camps or came to work in the kitchen or the office,
but the camps were unquestionably a man's world. Nelligan's memoir is
more explicit than most in celebrating and justifying the masculinity that
was a major part of the appeal of life in the woods, particularly for those
who looked back with apparent envy at the adventure, freedom, and male
camaraderie of a less "civilized" and constrained time than their own.

National and regional popular histories of lumbering and lumberjacks,
which began to appear toward the middle of the twentieth century, emphasize the more colorful and extravagant aspects of the culture of logging, accentuating its masculinity and contributing to the mythology surrounding the lumberjack. While they document the daily activities of
loggers and river drivers and the evolution of the industry, their authors
often seem more interested in entertaining readers with stories of idiosyncratic characters and wild behavior in the lumber towns. In *Holy Old
Mackinaw* (1938), the first and most influential of these, Stewart Holbrook
presents the lumberjack as a neglected figure who should be regarded as a
type of American pioneer, a member of a "tough race" distinguished from
farmers and townsmen by his "primitive purity" and a man who knew
how to play as hard as he worked.[34] Holbrook, who began as a lumberjack
himself and took up a career as a writer in the 1920s, admired lumberjacks
for being perpetual pioneers who stayed one jump ahead of civilization

and the drudgery of grubbing stumps and laying out towns; his final chapter is a lament for "The Passing of a Race." Holbrook characterizes this "race" primarily through anecdotes about legendary characters. He devotes a chapter to Jigger Jones, a Maine foreman notorious for his swearing and monumental drinking bouts, and most of another to Silver Jack Driscoll, the subject of numerous and sometimes conflicting stories in the camps of the upper Midwest and the prime exemplar of the kind of extreme fighting practiced by the lumberjacks, which could include eye gouging and the trampling of downed opponents with caulked boots. Holbrook does comment on the difficulty of separating fact from legend in the case of Driscoll and notes the less than heroic aspects of his career, including serving two sentences for robbery in Michigan's Jackson prison and finally dying in a rooming house in L'Anse near his favorite haunts in the Upper Peninsula, broken physically by the life he had led.

Part of what Holbrook sees as making the lumberjacks unique is the pattern of carousing in lumber towns at the end of the season, one that he traces back to Bangor, where, as he tells it, men emerged from the woods to seek out "booze, bawds, and battle with roistering loggers."[35] Holbrook characterizes the logging boom in Michigan, and subsequently in Wisconsin and Minnesota, as a "hell-roaring era" dominated by the excesses of lumbermen, who stole timber from property adjacent to their own by urging foremen to cut around their forty-acre parcels (giving rise to the concept of the "round forty"); of timber pirates, who rustled logs during river drives; and especially of the lumberjacks themselves, whom he describes as regularly blowing their season's earnings in a few days in the rough districts of the lumber towns. Such binges were clearly a part of the culture of logging, but it was easy to exaggerate their pervasiveness and importance. Holbrook gives more attention to the saloons and brothels of Saginaw and Bay City (with its notorious Catacombs, an establishment that allowed lumberjacks to pursue all their vices in the same place) than to the broader story of logging in the Saginaw River basin. He shows a similar bias in his treatment of Muskegon in the west, giving most of his attention to a spectacular celebration in its red-light district of Sawdust Flats. Seney, in the Upper Peninsula, provided Holbrook and other chroniclers of the logging era in Michigan with numerous stories of violent and flamboyant behavior by lumberjacks and the women and saloon keepers who worked at separating them from their earnings. Seney earned its notoriety partly because it was close enough to the camps of fifteen logging companies to attract lumberjacks during the winter, as well as in the spring when the season was over. Along with a few other particularly rough towns that flourished briefly in the late nineteenth century (including Hurley, across the river from Ironwood in Wisconsin), Seney gained a special reputation for lawlessness.[36] This was amplified by the national press after a visiting temperance lecturer returned with stories of debauchery fed her by traveling salesmen. Some locals enjoyed spinning tall tales for visiting writers, which contributed to Seney's image as "Hell Town in the Pine."[37]

In his "Natural History of the American Lumberjack," as he subtitled his book, Holbrook shows a raconteur's instinct for lively stories featuring the wild freedoms of a less conventional age than his own and a pronounced nostalgia for a breed of men who knew how to "roar," as well as to handle an ax and a peavey. In his final chapter he laments the loss of virility in the language with the disappearance of loggers' slang, as well as in the life he finds in the more domesticated lumber camps of his own time, marred for him by the presence of wives and "the civilizing drone of the electric washing machine." Celebrating the "hell-roaring" ways of the lumberjacks became a way of criticizing what he saw as the growing tameness and effeminacy of the age in which he wrote. Holbrook felt compelled to defend the "Lumber Barons" that he saw increasingly demonized in the twentieth century for leaving nothing but stumps, pointedly observing that "they left farms and towns and cities as well."[38] For Holbrook, as for many others, opening up land to farming and urban settlement became the justification for the business practices of these lumber barons and for the state in which they left the extensive forests through which they swept with their logging operations. He does not mention the fact that efforts to promote cutover land for agriculture led to widespread failures of small farms established on sandy soils more suitable for pine than food crops.

John Bartlow Martin, a nationally prominent journalist and speechwriter for leading Democratic politicians, perpetuated the image of the lumberjack as "hell-roarer" in a book on the Upper Peninsula from the same period. Martin offers a highly readable account of the working life of the lumberjack in the woods and on the river, but he gives more space to stories of wild behavior when the lumberjacks, "equally starved for liquor and women, overran the sawmill towns like pillaging conquerors."[39] Martin describes the "good people" of Manistique, Escanaba, and Menominee as staying indoors for days until life returned to normal, and he devotes a whole chapter to the excesses of Seney and almost as much attention to those of Hurley. Such stories of the more notorious towns in the northern pineries are a staple of accounts of the white pine era in the Upper Peninsula and reflect patterns of behavior that were typical of lumberjack life but also exaggerations and biases of the sort that characterized some of the lumberjacks' own stories. A lumberjack who wrote a memoir of life on the Tittabawassee boasts that it and the Saginaw River "were lumbered and driven by the strongest, toughest men from all parts of the world" and tells stories of famous fights at the camp known as "Old Sixteen," as well as others involving Silver Jack, who surfaces in some way or another in most such memoirs.[40]

Accounts of memorable fights survive because the lumberjacks themselves passed them from camp to camp, adding variations and embellishments in the process. Yet the image of the hell-roaring "timber beast" could be overplayed, presenting a distorted picture of actual life in the lumber towns, or at least in the more substantial ones. On the basis of his experience in Manistique William Crowe claimed that portrayals of the old lumberjacks as "a red-eyed, hell-roarin' rough and tumble, fighting gang" were "fantastic and unrealistic." He rejects the story that women kept off the streets when lumberjacks came to town and estimates that out of a thousand that he knew only twelve or fifteen sought out fights, usually in saloons, and only forty or fifty would spend their stakes on extended sprees. He recalls many investing in certificates of deposit issued by the Chicago Lumbering Company. In his view, the "lurid stories" represented only a small percentage of the lumberjacks and not a true picture of "the pine lumber days."[41] Crowe was a company man who spent most of his life in Manistique and would have been concerned with defending its reputation. Yet even if one allows for defensiveness on his part, and for the fact that Manistique was known for the efforts of its lumber bosses to preserve order, his responses serve as a useful corrective to the tendency to sensationalize the behavior of lumberjacks as a whole as a way to entertain readers and explicitly or implicitly convey admiration for the wild freedoms of pioneering days in "a man's country."

A more subtle and complex treatment of the activities of lumberjacks and the landlookers who prepared the way for them, as well as of the tension between the demands of the lumber industry and a growing interest in preservation, can be found in the stories of William Davenport Hulbert, which were published in national magazines between 1903 and 1906 and subsequently reprinted in a posthumous collection edited by his brother, *White Pine Days on the Taquamenon*.[42] Hulbert had established a reputation as a writer of animal stories based on his experiences growing up in northern Michigan. These appeared as a series in *McClure's* magazine before being collected in 1903 as *Forest Neighbors,* which was subsequently adapted for use as a reader in the schools. Hulbert wrote at a time when the popular essays of John Burroughs were bringing new attention to "nature writing" and the vogue for realistic wild animal stories was at its height. His own animal stories reflect an interest in natural history he developed during his childhood years on a remote northern Michigan lake he called "the Glimmerglass," after James Fenimore Cooper's fictional lake, with only wild animals as "neighbors." His father had acquired the entire shoreline of the lake, now known as Hulbert's Lake, after discovering it on one of his forays as a landlooker. Hulbert's "life stories" (about a beaver, trout, lynx, porcupine, loon, and buck) show the tendency toward anthropomorphism characteristic of such stories but are firmly grounded in his understanding of natural history. While he humanizes his beaver by giving him a "wife" and "children" and comparing his skills with those of a logger, Hulbert portrays its behavior realistically. The plots of his stories typically involve the disruption of animal life by human intervention, shown from the perspective of the animals. His beaver loses a paw in a trap and sees its "city" of beaver lodges devastated by repeated trapping; his loon is wounded by a hunter after its mate is caught in a gill net and drowns. Hulbert's emphasis on the sentience of animals is characteristic of animal stories of the time, which were linked with the rise of the animal welfare movement, but he avoided sentimentalizing his subjects in the fashion of popular writers such as Ernest Thompson Seton and William J. Long.[43]

Hulbert was prevented from joining his family's lumbering business by a childhood case of polio, which limited him to being an observer of working life in the woods, a role he made use of in his stories of lumbering. These stories typically feature an outsider, in several stories identified as a naturalist, who goes out on scouting trips with landlookers and visits lumber camps, sometimes to witness river drives in progress. Hulbert begins the first story in the collection, "The Naturalist and the Landlooker," by identifying the forested country in which it and the others are set with that of *The Song of Hiawatha,* invoking Shawondasee (the South Wind) and quoting Longfellow.

From his pipe the smoke ascending
Filled the sky with haze and vapor
Filled the air with dreamy softness.
Gave a twinkle to the water,
Touched the rugged hills with smoothness,
Brought the tender Indian Summer
To the melancholy North-land.[44]

Hulbert uses Longfellow here to establish the season and also give his own "North-land" the romantic aura associated with the landscape inhabited by Hiawatha in the poem and in the minds of many of his readers. He identifies the "rushing Taquamenon" of his stories as the river in which Hiawatha launched his birch canoe.

The landlooker and his party regard the forest as a place in which to find marketable pine, and they briskly go about their business of looking for it. For the naturalist, by contrast, the forest assumes something of the mystery given it by Longfellow. Whereas the sound of wind in the pines serves as a welcome signal to the landlooker that the object of his search is nearby, it triggers a memory of Longfellow in the naturalist, who hears the sound as "a murmur / As of waves upon a seashore / As of far-off tumbling waters."[45] When the naturalist comes into the grove itself, he is awed by the beauty of the scene, with rays of sunlight breaking through the canopy to form flecks of gold on the brown pine needles of the forest floor. Hulbert describes him as "[murmuring] something about God's first temples" (10), sanctifying the grove in the fashion of those who described woods dominated by tall, straight tree trunks as cathedrals. For most of the story Hulbert portrays the interests of the naturalist in the forest as compatible with those of the landlooker. We see him admiring the landlooker's skills in the woods, first in setting up camp and then in discovering promising stands of pine from a lookout tree, leading the way to them through challenging terrain (cedar swamps, poplar thickets, windfalls), and finally identifying the section in which they are found by locating the witness trees on which surveyors have marked township and range. In this and several other stories we learn how landlookers embrace their strenuous and "healthy" life in the out-of-doors and hear something of their adventures, for example, in a campfire story about winning a race to the Land Office in Marquette to buy land with promising pine stands. Hulbert's naturalist soaks up such stories and shows a lively curiosity about the work of landlookers, but he is most excited by seeing a great buck. The landlooker, on the other hand, is much more pleased at finding "five-log-pine" that he estimates will run to 10 percent in "uppers" (knot-free wood that commands the highest price). The inherent tension between their very different ways of perceiving the forest surfaces in the narrator's ominous recognition near the end of the story that, although he hears the same old hymn of pines in the wind, "man, the great enemy of all pine trees had been there, and though he had gone away he would surely come again" (16). When the lumberman has finished, he knows, the "glory of the woods" will be gone.

In the second story, "The Naturalist Goes to the Logging Camp," Hulbert presents a sympathetic and realistically detailed view of daily life in a logging camp, including an account of an accident in which a man's arm is crushed under a load of logs that slips and another of a logger's being sent on his way for drunken violence in camp. His naturalist narrator responds with greater emotion, however, to the beauty of the winter woods on a moonlit ride on the sprinkler wagon and to his various encounters with wild animals. He shows much more interest in watching a mink catch fish than in spending time with the lumberjacks. The unexpected sight of bear cubs playing with their mother at the den becomes the climax of his visit. In this story the naturalist takes a harsh view of the visible effects of logging, recoiling at the sight of the "raw" stump and the tangle of branches "where a great pine had stood" (25). He comes to see the loggers as "mining the woods" and driving the animals out of their homes so that pine trees "might be killed and their bodies carried away to be ripped and torn and sawed into boards and planks and beams" (29), imagining lumbering as a violation of the natural life of the woods. This welling up of anguish over the consequences of logging does not cause an overt breach between the naturalist and the loggers, however, or disrupt the flow of the narrative. Hulbert ends the story by showing the naturalist left with mixed feelings of relief and apprehension as camp breaks up after the season and he joins the "skylarking" loggers in tramping out on the tote road. Although the naturalist is a sympathetic figure, and the vehicle for Hulbert's observations about the life of the forest, he appears impotent in comparison with the loggers, distinguished by his sensibility rather than any capacity for action.

In a majority of the stories in the collection Hulbert focuses on some aspect of the lives of loggers or landlookers without questioning their activities. Two of the most effective deal with crises in river drives at Tahquamenon Falls, now the centerpiece of Tahquamenon Falls State

Park and a major tourist attraction. Hulbert presents the action in each as seen through the eyes of an observer fascinated by the skills of the rivermen and by the beauty of the environment in which they work. The slighter of the two, "With the Taquamemon Drive," builds to a scene in which rivermen work at breaking up a side jam at the top of the falls by attaching a rope to a succession of logs, which are then pulled free by a team of horses on the shore. Hulbert's treatment of the scene is remarkable for the way he aestheticizes this highly dangerous activity: "[T]he leaping, roaring water flashed and sparkled and gleamed as it pitched over the ledge and dropped out of sight in its own mist and spray. . . . The man on the brink seemed posing for a sculpture, now standing erect on the outermost log, now stepping back and bracing himself as he hauled in the line" (48). The sun is shining "gloriously," the falls making "splendid" music. This climactic scene serves as a way of celebrating the poise and grace of the rivermen. To the rapt observer they appear less as laborers coping with a difficult challenge on a logging drive than as figures in a landscape, blending harmoniously with their stunning natural setting.

In "On the Brink of the Falls" Hulbert again evokes the aesthetic appeal of the natural setting, here by suggesting the sunny tranquility of river and woods above the falls. The more complex plot of this story turns on the rivalry between two young rivermen, Tommy and Barney, over Polly MacLain, the daughter of the camp boss. Her father engineers a birling competition between the two suitors, which Tommy loses when he distractedly looks back at Polly and lands in the water rather than on the log on which he is trying to jump. The crisis of the story is precipitated when the men are interrupted in their subsequent efforts to break up a center jam just above the falls by the sight of Polly in her canoe with a broken paddle being swept helplessly toward the brink. First Barney jumps on a log to pursue her, "like a circus rider on a bareback horse, the log bucking and rolling and twisting underneath him"(9), and succeeds in getting Polly out of the canoe and onto a rock well out in the river where both are stranded. Then Tommy, the camp favorite who had been displaced by the more aggressive and flamboyant Barney, risks his own life to save both of theirs by getting a rope to them before being swept past on his log to the very lip of the falls. There he must birl for his life, jumping onto a succession of logs headed for the falls to keep from being carried over with one of them. He finally works his way upstream over the swiftly moving logs back to the jam and safety, escaping with a last desperate leap. Fittingly, Tommy wins back Polly's affections through the heroism of his sacrificial act and his subsequent demonstration of nerve and skill. This is scarcely a typical river drive, but the improbable plot enables Hulbert to tell a dramatic love story that showcases the spectacular birling skills of the rivermen while exploiting the fundamental competitiveness of life in a logging camp.

Hulbert's collection ends with "The Story of the Pine," which makes explicit the conflict between preservationist impulses and the economic imperatives of the logging industry that simmers in his first two stories. In basing a story on the life of a pine tree Hulbert was reworking what had become a familiar motif in early writing about lumbering. Fitzmaurice had been attracted by the figure of the solitary, besieged pine, making it a symbol of the majesty and dignity of the ancient forest by personifying it as a "monarch" (King Pine) presiding over the lesser trees of the river valley in which it stands beside a swift northern river. Referring to towering white pines as monarchs became conventional in writing about the white pine era. Monarchs were appropriate to epics, as the struggle of the loggers came to be seen. An anonymous poem titled "The Old White Pine" that was found on the back of a lumber company ledger sheet from 1879 begins:

> Far in the north in the trackless wild
> A grand old pine tree stood
> Towering aloft in its majesty
> The monarch of the woods . . .[46]

The "grand old pine" of the poem suffers the fate that Fitzmaurice's does when loggers find it, although the poet goes on to describe this emblematic tree as serving the "good of man" by becoming lumber. He could indulge a sentimental view of the pine without questioning the human needs that determined its fate. Another anonymous poem contrasts the poet's view of an ancient pine with the woodsman's, clearly favoring the latter. We are told that while the poet "raved of majestic age" and "sang the tale of the tree" the woodsman worried about "shake" and "rot." The final stanza describes the "grand old tree" transformed into "lumber, shingles and lath" and the poet left with nothing but his song ("But the lumber—why, that's in cash.").[47]

The habit of identifying and celebrating "monarch" pines survives at Hartwick Pines State Park, where one of the stops on the Old-Growth Trail marks the location of "The Monarch," formerly the largest white pine in the park at 155 feet in height and 12 feet in circumference. In 1992, when the tree was about 325 years old, a storm broke off its top, killing it, yet the dead tree is still separated by a protective barrier and remains "The Monarch." The pamphlet that serves as a trail guide orients us toward its glorious past, suggesting that we may have heard a story about it from our parents or grandparents or may have known someone who hugged the tree. The broken trunk could just as well be seen as an emblem of the changing nature of the forest, comparable to the fallen and decaying trees on the forest floor and those uprooted by more recent storms. The practice of personifying remarkable trees dies hard, particularly in a place dedicated to preserving Michigan's white pine heritage.

Hulbert does not call the ancient white pine of his story a monarch, avoiding the cliché, but represents it as "the last of his race" and makes it symbolic of the "character and dignity" he saw white pines as giving to the forest. Scattered clusters of tall pines are visible in the distance, like rocky islands against which the surrounding sea of hardwood breaks, in Hulbert's metaphor. When the wind blows, the pine of the story sings a "low, peaceful hymn," rising to "a mighty roar" in a storm. Like those of *The Song of Hiawatha*, Hulbert's pines invariably sing. In telling the story of how this pine grew and survived he displays greater awareness of natural history than Fitzmaurice and interweaves a more detailed account of the impact of the human history that has swirled around it, including the passage of Indians and voyageurs and trappers and, more recently, that of the surveyors who first subdivided the land in 1839. The most decisive event for the purposes of the story is a recent fire that spared the pine but brought in loggers to salvage burned timber. The action involves a confrontation between the foreman of the logging crew and a former landlooker and lumberman who bought the forty acres on which the tree stands, or thought he did. His wife had fallen in love with the solitary pine after they and other city friends camped under it, listening to its "song" and singing their own songs in response.

In the story the "city man," as Hulbert refers to the presumptive owner, has returned with his three sons years later to fish the northern river on whose banks the pine stands, only to find the foreman insisting that the tree is on his company's land and preparing to cut it. After futile attempts to resolve the dispute by pacing off distances from surviving witness trees, the owner realizes that his only hope lies in finding the corner stake left by surveyors a half century before and dispatches two of his sons to paddle overnight to the courthouse to get the surveyors' field notes before the foreman returns with his crew to cut the tree the following day. Hulbert shows the boys racing back in their canoe just as the loggers have finished notching the tree with axes in preparation for sawing it down. Once he has the surveyors' measurements indicating the distance and direction of the corner stake from the pine, the owner digs until he finds fragments of the original cedar stake and its copper cap in a location that vindicates his claim. The story concludes with his triumphant demonstration of the authenticity of the stake, as he splits a fragment to reveal its grain and release the unmistakable fragrance of cedar. After this, the foreman can only retreat.

Hulbert's story anticipates the emergence of preservation as an ideal and a political force in the early decades of the twentieth century and the eventual shift of popular sentiment against logging and especially against the lumbermen who pushed to log all the pine they could find as fast as they could, without regard for the condition of the land they left behind. The story focuses on the damage this particular group of loggers inflict, progressively diminishing the "dignity" of the forest as they decimate the islands of white pine, and on the aggressiveness of the foreman. Hulbert refers to the threatened trees rather than the loggers as "the army of the pine." The bullying foreman embodies the greed of the lumber company, pressing his claim to a prize tree despite uncertainty about its ownership, whereas the true owner displays something closer to the sensibility we see in Hulbert's naturalist, recognizing the role the pine plays in the life of the forest and the pleasures it gives human visitors. Interestingly, Hulbert shows him drawing on his former skills as a landlooker to prove his own claim to the pine, employing them in the service of preservation rather than that of the timber industry. As a "city man," he no longer makes his living in the woods and can now appreciate the inherent value of the pine as opposed to its worth as a commodity. Yet this appreciation, strong enough to have motivated him to buy the forty acres on which the pine stands and to fight to save it, must owe something to the intimate knowledge of the woods gained in his former career. As a landlooker turned preservationist he anticipates the modern environmentalist, more interested in the aesthetic, recreational, and ecological value than the economic worth of old-growth forest, in this case a surviving pine that has come to symbolize that forest. Yet he is less a protoenvironmentalist than a bridging figure, like Hulbert himself, who can understand and sympathize with the late-nineteenth-century world of loggers and lumbermen and also appreciate the inherent worth of the pine forest, to the point of wanting to see at least parts of it preserved.

The heroism in the service of civilization enshrined in the Lumberman's Monument has no place in Hulbert's story, which celebrates the defeat of the foreman and the interests he represents and the resilience of the pine itself, which is described as having survived gales and fire and as blooming more profusely than ever before in the aftermath of the most recent forest fire. Hulbert implies that it will continue to flourish, safe at least from further human harm. The conflict he dramatizes in the story would persist, of course, and for some time so would the romance of the pioneer logger. This would receive its richest and most influential expression in the fiction of Stewart Edward White, whose work is interesting not only because of its role in establishing the figure of the logger in the public imagination and its success in capturing the drama of the logging era in Michigan and the upper Midwest but because White's writing career reflects changes in thinking about conservation and attitudes toward forests in a critical period spanning the late nineteenth and early twentieth centuries. White was influenced by Theodore Roosevelt, becoming a defender of Roosevelt's conservation agenda and the pioneer spirit that Roosevelt embraced, and in turn influenced Aldo Leopold. He was a bridging figure himself, one who combined a strong attraction to the natural world and a strenuous outdoor life with a commitment to the progress of civilization.

4 // Stewart Edward White and the Logger as Frontier Hero

In his 1929 memoir lumberman John Nelligan recalls a winter when a young man named Stewart Edward White spent forty days working for him as a "regular hand" on the tributaries of the Menominee River in the Upper Peninsula. Nelligan remembers White as a hard worker, popular with the men for his storytelling, who surprised him by refusing to take any pay when he left. White claimed he had been working for his health, but, as Nelligan came to realize, he was quietly gathering material for the novel that made his reputation and established the logger in the popular imagination as a new kind of frontier hero, *The Blazed Trail*. In Nelligan's view, the lumberjack was not an easy man to understand, but "young White studied him and understood him and made him live in his books."[1] White had become a famous writer by the time Nelligan published his memoir and contributed a brief foreword in which he included his former woods boss among the "unique and heroic race of men" who worked in "the old pine forests of Michigan and Wisconsin."

Stewart Edward White grew up mainly in western lower Michigan as the son of a prosperous lumberman, T. Stewart White, exposed to the life of lumber camps and to logging drives on the Grand River. Nelligan may have hired him because his father was one of the principals in the highly regarded White-Friant Lumber Company, which had done him a favor by helping sort out logs that had become mingled with his and his partner's on a drive on the Menominee River. White developed an early interest in natural history and published a precocious article on the birds of Mackinac Island in the *Auk*, the premier journal of ornithology of the time. At the University of Michigan, White studied philosophy and led the life of a well-heeled and popular undergraduate. He occupied one summer vacation working in a Black Hills mining camp and others sailing with friends in the North Channel of Lake Huron. After graduating from the university in 1895 he spent three semesters at Columbia Law School, where his most influential teacher was his writing instructor Brander Matthews. White began to publish adventure stories set in the Black Hills and, encouraged by Matthews and his success in getting published, abandoned law school determined to become a writer. After several years of publishing stories and reviews while working in Grand Rapids for his father's firm and then in Chicago, he succeeded in publishing two novels drawing on his western experience, *The Westerners* (1900) and *The Claim Jumpers* (1901).

White managed to write his first logging novel, *The Blazed Trail* (1902), while working in Nelligan's logging camp in the winter of 1901. It was serialized in newspapers and *McClure's* magazine and went through eleven editions in ten months. *The Blazed Trail* was still selling three thousand copies a year thirty years later.[2] White capitalized on the novel's success with a collection that included more stories of lumbering, *Blazed Trail Stories* (1904), and a second logging novel, *The Riverman* (1908). His Michigan writings and Canadian and western novels of outdoor life and the frontier, along with nonfiction accounts of his own outdoor adventures in Ontario and subsequently in the Sierras, made White one of the most popular practitioners of a kind of masculine writing best exemplified by his contemporary, Jack London.[3] White's fiction can be seen as part of the broader romantic revival that flourished in the late nineteenth century as an alternative to the domestic realism typified by the fiction of William Dean Howells. Fiction ranging from historical romance to stories of wilderness adventure challenged the preoccupation of the new realism with moral dilemmas and social agendas. It substituted a world of elemental passions and heroic action for one regarded by some as overly civilized and genteel. Mass circulation magazines, including *McClure's*, responded to the public's taste for entertaining stories of adventure. Those who championed this romantic revival, which has also been characterized as antimodernism, appealed to Sir Walter Scott and contemporary writers such as Rudyard Kipling and Rider Haggard.[4] Some were particularly attracted to medievalism and chivalric romance, revived by Scott and others, valuing it for providing examples of a manliness and martial spirit that could serve as a counterweight to what they saw as the "feminization" of American culture. Action, whether in sports, struggles with the challenges of the wilderness, or military adventure, came to be seen as a means of achieving moral and psychic regeneration.[5] Such fiction tended to celebrate Anglo-Saxon culture and, in some cases, to praise the extension of this culture through imperialistic ventures.

White's logging novels responded to the vogue for entertaining stories of masculine adventure and offered a new version of the distinctively American genre of the frontier romance, of which James Fenimore Cooper's Leatherstocking Tales were the most influential example.[6] His signal contribution was to establish the logger in the popular imagination as a type of frontier hero who displayed something of Natty Bumppo's courage and ingenuity in meeting different kinds of challenges, from unscrupulous competitors rather than treacherous Indians and from the kinds of dangers to which felling large trees and driving logs down streams and rivers regularly exposed him. White's logger is comparable to the backwoodsman and the cowboy in the boldness and self-reliance with which he meets challenges, a "strong man" of primitive instincts who draws his strength from living close to nature.[7] The hero of *The Blazed Trail*, Harry Thorpe, based in part on his father's lumbering experience, progresses from a greenhorn doing the lowest camp jobs to a landlooker who stakes his own claim to pinelands he has discovered in the Upper Peninsula. As his own boss he proves himself capable of doing anything he demands of his men and independent enough as an entrepreneur to withstand assaults from powerful and unscrupulous lumber barons to save his fledgling company. Thorpe appealed to readers as a rugged outdoorsman and also as a self-made businessman at a time when both tales of wilderness adventure and Horatio Alger success stories were becoming increasingly popular.

When White published *The Blazed Trail*, Jack London's stories of the Far North had just begun to appear; London would soon become famous with *The Call of the Wild* (1903). Theodore Roosevelt was proclaiming the virtues of the strenuous life, influenced by Frederick Jackson Turner's argument about the transformative influence of contact with wilderness on the American character, as well as by his own experience ranching in the Badlands of South Dakota and hunting there and elsewhere in the West.[8] Through his writings about his experience in the West and his public pronouncements he exerted a significant influence on the emerging fiction of masculine adventure. By projecting a public image of strenuous virility— as an avid hunter of big game and a founder with George Bird Grinnell of the Boone and Crockett Club, as the leader of the Rough Riders, and subsequently as a president who made extended trips to Yellowstone and Yosemite and vigorously promoted conservation—Roosevelt helped to create an audience for the kind of manly fiction that White and others were publishing.

Roosevelt became an admirer of White's writing, recommended to him by his friend Brander Matthews, and started an extended correspondence with White that lasted almost to the end of his life. After White spent time with Roosevelt in 1903 as part of a delegation welcoming him to California the two developed a friendship that led to invitations to the White House and Sagamore Hill, Roosevelt's Long Island home in Oyster Bay.[9] White won Roosevelt's admiration for his marksmanship in shooting matches at Sagamore Hill as well as for his fiction: "The best man with both pistol and rifle who ever shot there was Stewart Edward White."[10] In an essay titled "Roosevelt and the Pioneer Spirit" that he wrote for the memorial edition of Roosevelt's complete works, White praised him for exemplifying the pioneer spirit in his adventures and for capturing this spirit, as well as a sense of intimacy with wilderness, in reminiscences of western life such as *The Wilderness Hunter,* which his essay introduces. White associated the pioneer spirit primarily with wilderness, asserting that "the strong stark primitive forces of nature are always ready with their tests of [a man's] physical and moral strength."[11]

In his logging novels White exploited the great popularity of what had become a national myth of the frontier by placing the logger in the line of manly adventurers that included Daniel Boone, the fur-trapping mountain men of the West, and the cowboys who had become familiar figures with the rise of cattle ranching in the latter part of the nineteenth century.[12] Dime novels, influenced by Cooper's frontier romances, had made cowboys into heroic figures in the popular imagination.[13] It was a natural leap for White to portray logging as a heroic and inherently dramatic form of frontier experience. Loggers worked in the woods and on the rivers under primitive conditions and risked their lives daily, pushing themselves to their limits and beyond when necessary to overcome natural obstacles or challenges from rival logging operations. White saw loggers, as opposed to workers subordinated to the demands of the factory, as "the last incarnation of the heroic age, when the man is bigger than his work."[14] His hero, Thorpe, characterizes the logger's work as "a struggle, a gasping heave and tug for supremacy between man and the wilderness" (144). In describing Thorpe as grappling "fierce winter by the throat" White sounds very like Jack London, or Robert Service describing the sourdough clinching and closing with the "naked North." Like London and Service, White personified nature as an antagonist that calls forth all the energy and determination the hero can summon. The fact that White was writing at a time when the frontier had been declared closed (in the census of 1890) and the great age of the logger and other frontier types had passed, at least in the East and the upper Midwest, made his heroic portrayal of logging all the more appealing to an audience hungry for stories of times and places where a frontier experience was still possible.

The Blazed Trail and *The Riverman* also have a muckraking dimension, exposing devious business practices with which the heroes must contend while battling natural forces. White's typically melodramatic villains embody the greed and ruthlessness that characterized some of the principals in the rush to exploit Michigan's white pine. In *The Blazed Trail* Thorpe discovers early on that the powerful firm of Morrison and Daly is illegally cutting timber in the watershed in which he succeeds in buying pineland, following the common practice of homesteading (through proxies) forty-acre tracts and cutting pine around as well as on them. He comes to realize that the owner Daly and his agent Dyer will employ any tactics they can to bankrupt him, from financial manipulations to the destruction of dams in order to sabotage a logging drive. In *The Riverman* villainy takes the form of a mill owner who obstructs the logging drive managed by White's hero, Jack Orde, and a treacherous partner who nearly succeeds in ruining him financially. Both protagonists, Thorpe and Orde, prevail in the end through charismatic leadership, daring, and irresistible force of will. They exemplify a kind of business success that depends on the drive and moral probity of a strong individual who can command absolute loyalty from his men and prevail in the end against all challenges.

In both *The Blazed Trail* and *The Riverman* White made a logging drive the climax of the action. Working as a "river pig" was the most dangerous job a lumberjack could undertake and the most important. The success of a whole winter of logging depended on getting the logs safely downriver to a mill at the river's mouth before the high water of early spring receded and then preventing them from being carried out into the big lake and lost. The men involved in a drive, the most skilled in camp, had to be able to clear obstructions, ride unstable logs downstream, retrieve strays with their peaveys, and, when necessary, risk their lives trying to break up a logjam. White presents them as handling the peaveys with which they manage the logs in much the same way a cowboy does a rope. He embraces their roughness and their capacity for violence along with the courage that enables them to ignore the danger of being drowned or crushed by logs and the endurance with which they work backbreaking days, in and out of the cold water. Authorized violence, against a gang of workers from a rival company or a mill owner who blocks the river or anyone else who gets in the way of a drive, serves as proof of their manhood and loyalty to the boss. Rivermen epitomized the heroism of the logger for White.

White's two Michigan novels portray Thorpe and Orde as leaders alternately driving and inspiring their men in a battle with natural forces that they can win only through almost superhuman effort and will. He says of the loggers that Thorpe goads to get out a record cut despite severe winter conditions, "Nothing could stand against such a spirit" (322). The "epic" drive in which the men must work through their exhaustion to get out thirty million board feet of logs in ten days is followed by a struggle to keep them from being swept into Lake Superior by rising waters, which threaten the boom that holds them. A feeling of sustained warfare pervades White's narration of dramatic events in his logging sagas. At the climactic stage of the action of *The Riverman,* when the accumulated logs are about to break through the last restraining boom and escape into Lake Michigan, Jack Orde appears as a "general" commandeering whatever resources he needs and driving men "afire with the flame of combat" night and day until the crisis has passed.[15] At one point White describes the contest as one between seventy-five men and "the weight of twenty million tons of logs and a river of water" (309), presenting a version of the struggle of man against the "stark primitive forces of nature" that he would praise in Roosevelt's writing.

White based the logjam of *The Riverman* on an actual event, the memorable jam of 1883 on the Grand River, which he had described in a magazine article.[16] In the novel White closely followed the struggle to break the actual jam, which extended over several days and developed in stages as bridges and booms that were holding back logs upstream gave way, reproducing incidents and some of the language he had included in the article. The focus of the fictional account, as of the article, is the prolonged effort to drive enough piles in the river to keep the final boom from giving way. Orde's role conflates that of the hero of the article, John Walsh, a one-armed worker who refused to abandon the pile-driving tug he commanded in the face of escalating danger, and that of the owners directing the fight, most of whom abandoned it in the face of odds that seemed hopeless. Orde, like Walsh, insists on chaining the last logs himself, jumping to safety at the latest possible moment. Throughout the struggle Orde exercises the leadership that White attributed to Walsh in his account of the actual event: formulating new strategies as the old ones fail, commandeering boats, and authorizing the men working with him to find the necessary piles by seizing those belonging to the Detroit and Milwaukee Railroad and even by cutting down farmers' trees. They hold off the enraged farmers with their peaveys. The stakes were clearly high—White claims that loss of so many logs would have caused the failure of mills and banks and the loss of thousands of jobs—but one gets the sense that White found the real justification for violence and disregard for the law in the heroism and determination of the men in such a struggle.[17]

Thorpe and Orde constitute White's fictional equivalents of the self-made men who began with the lowest jobs in the lumber camps and worked their way up to positions of ownership, building their own logging companies. They have a stature and appeal that derive from combining the virtues of the foreman and river boss with those of the entrepreneur capable of building a business empire and taking his place in polite society. Thus they bridge the gap between the rough, frontier world of the logging camps and the more civilized one of his educated readers. In part I of *Blazed Trail Stories,* White created fictional versions of classic lumbering types that Thorpe and Orde resemble in some respects but ultimately transcend. Jimmy, the hero of "The River-Boss," excels at his job because of his knowledge of the river and his ability to do better himself what he asks his men to do. He is also willing to attempt anything necessary to fulfill the unspoken imperative of the river boss: "Get the logs out. Get them out peaceably if you can, but *get them out*."[18] When it becomes apparent that a section of the river is too low to get the logs to the mill in time to satisfy the company's contract, he leads a party of men on a nighttime mission to raise the level of a critical dam, accomplishing his aim of releasing the logs but flooding town cellars in the process. When the outraged citizens arrest Jimmy and give him the choice of a jail term or a substantial fine, he pays the fine with a large roll of bills provided by his boss, who insulates himself from responsibility by publicly chiding Jimmy. In *The Riverman* Thorpe leads his men on a comparable raid, in this case illegally raising a sluice gate that a belligerent mill owner refuses to open, flooding the mill but getting his logs down the river. In both cases, White clearly sympathizes with the interests and the tactics of the loggers. The demands of the logging drive trump those of the law.

The hero of another story, Richard Darrell (Roaring Dick) of "The Foreman," responds to the imperative to do whatever is necessary to make the cut agreed on for the season. As the "walking boss" responsible for all the camps in the area, Darrell draws on deep reserves of energy and determination to drive an insufficient number of men to work ever harder in a winter that presents more than the usual challenges. His greatest test comes when two bartenders from the nearby town, one of whom is White's fictionalized version of Silver Jack Driscoll, attempt to enter his headquarters camp to distribute free whiskey in an effort to persuade the men to quit and come into town for a spree. White makes Silver Jack, the legendary fighter of logging camp stories, a blustering bully who handles the undersized Darrell easily when he comes to town to drink but is stymied by Darrell's fierce resistance on the snowy road outside his camp. When after a bloody but inconclusive fight Darrell grabs an ax and smashes not only the whiskey jugs but the horse-drawn cutter in which Silver Jack and his companion were traveling, they have no alternative but to give up and set out on a long, frigid walk back to town. White shows them turning to see a backlit Darrell assuming heroic proportions: "[H]e stood there huge, menacing against the light—the dominant spirit, Roaring Dick of the woods, the incarnation of Necessity, the Man defending his Work, the Foreman!" (38). White's stagy conclusion makes the point that in the Michigan woods, as in London's North, the most desperate and determined is the likeliest to come out on top. It also has the effect of ennobling the work of the loggers. Their labor, in making the cut as in getting the logs to the mill, had to take on extraordinary importance for logging to appear the epic enterprise White sought to portray.

White celebrated the pioneering spirit and the dedication to their work that he found in self-made men such as Thorpe and Orde operating at the edges of civilization, as well as in the logging crews whose respect and loyalty they commanded, proving himself adept at constructing stories of wilderness adventure that effectively exploited the romance logging would come to hold for his wide audience. The novels follow a predictable trajectory, with the hero eventually overcoming all obstacles, positioning himself to achieve business success, and sooner or later achieving wedded bliss with a genteel but spirited wife who after the sparring of courtship devotes herself to supporting him and his career. What is more surprising, and interesting, is the submerged tension the novels reveal between the imperatives of logging and the appeal of the natural world in which the loggers spend so much of their time. White, himself a naturalist and outdoorsman, celebrated the wilderness experience in nonfiction based on his own outdoor adventures such as *The Forest* (1903), a narrative account of canoe trips in the Canadian "North Country" in and around Georgian Bay and in the Algoma country north of Lake Superior in the summer of 1902. He portrays camping and canoeing as a way of testing himself, of "proving his essential pluck and manhood" by fronting the wilderness stripped of the comforts of towns.[19]

White knew how to tell a story of personal adventure that would capture his readers' attention, embellishing it with anecdotes about "woods Indians" and descendants of the fur traders and details about the challenges of travel in the bush. Yet he was also concerned with awakening in these readers a sense of what he called "the wonder of the Forest," understood as a generalized presence combining the "cathedral solemnity" of pine woods, the "gloom" of cedars and tamaracks, and the "transparent shadows" of great hardwood forests. He offers a lyrical description of a particular forest of huge maple, beech, and birch trees, "the most magnificent primeval forest" he has ever seen, dwelling on its cool, shadowy greenness and the springiness of the decaying forest floor (179–81). White represents this forest as a luminous and mysterious place in which his "deep physical joy" makes him forget his fatigue. In the Apologia with which he concludes he becomes lyrical about the variable moods of "the Forest," from fierce to gentle, and confesses his inability to capture it in the pages of a book. A book that presents itself as a travel narrative, with practical tips about canoe camping, becomes something more: an evocation of the romance of the "primeval" forest for an audience increasingly susceptible to the appeal of wilderness.

White also published two early novels based on the fur-trading activities of the Hudson's Bay Company in northern Ontario, *The Conjuror's House* (1903) and the best-selling *The Silent Places* (1904), both of which draw on a more challenging, months-long canoe trip to Hudson Bay that White had made in the summer of 1901. *The Silent Places*, which White regarded as his most coherent work, presents the story of the single-minded pursuit of a renegade trapper through the wilderness and into the Barren Grounds.[20] The novel turns into a harrowing survival story that anticipates and may have influenced London's 1907 short story "Love of Life," with the protagonists fighting starvation and hallucination as they pursue the fugitive to the point of collapse and the North itself becoming an ever more threatening presence. Silence assumes two radically different aspects in the novel. As the pursuers make their way through woods occupied only by widely scattered Ojibwa trappers they become conscious of a "great, brooding silence," a "primal" hush in which the wilderness itself becomes the only measure of time.[21] White invests this silence with a sense of mystery and peace, qualities that writers before and after him have associated with the forest, but he shows it giving way to a more menacing stillness as the hard cold of winter sets in. When the pursuit turns northward, out of the forest and eventually into the barrenness and the "gigantic spaces" of the "true North," the pursuers experience the terror of the sublime. As White puts it, "[T]he woods are quiet with an hundred lesser noises; but here was absolute, terrifying, smothering silence,—the suspension of all sound" (246). Here the romance of the forest gives way to romantic fatalism of a sort that was becoming popular in stories of the Far North as the pursuers refuse to abandon their mission even though they assume that this means they will die of starvation, as in fact the young Ojibwa woman who has joined them does. White undercuts the fatalism in this case with an improbable ending in which he shows his heroes surviving by unexpectedly finding a band of caribou and then returning to the Hudson's Bay post with the renegade trapper they have been pursuing.

Given White's early interest in natural history and his extensive outdoor experience, it is not surprising to find him becoming interested in conservation. After moving to California, he spent his summers in the Sierras beginning in 1904 and became active in the conservation movement championed by Roosevelt. He familiarized himself with current controversies about how the forest reserves, established by Congress in 1891, should be managed and from 1905 to 1909 served as a special inspector for the California forest reserves, appointed at Roosevelt's request. Roosevelt also connected White with Gifford Pinchot, his principal adviser on conservation policy and the force behind the creation of the U.S. Forest Service. Pinchot had become chief of the Division of Forestry (in the Department of Agriculture) in 1898 and was appointed the first chief of the new Forest Service in 1905. White and Pinchot became friends, even vacationing together, and White became an aggressive supporter of Pinchot's vision for managing public lands, which involved defending them against destructive exploitation while recognizing their potential value to local economies. Pinchot expressed his deep gratitude for articles that White wrote for the *American Magazine* defending him and the Forest Service against the assaults of what both men saw as predatory business interests in Pinchot's heated controversy with Richard Ballinger, subsequently secretary of the interior under President William Howard Taft, over Ballinger's alleged favoritism to business acquaintances in approving the sale of public lands in Alaska.[22] Taft supported Ballinger and fired Pinchot in 1910. Years later Robert Sterling Yard, then executive secretary of the National Parks Association, credited White's writing and particularly his forest novels with educating the public, "which in turn stood behind those who defended the Forests in Congress against innumerable bills to divert them to private gain."[23]

How could novels that glamorized logging and made loggers and entrepreneurs such as Thorpe and Orde heroic figures be seen as advancing the cause of conservation? Yard, and the public he invokes, no doubt responded to the strain of appreciation for the natural world that runs through White's novels. One contemporary reviewer of *The Blazed Trail* praised White's descriptions of forest life for capturing "the very breath and spirit of the woods."[24] The novels reflect White's intimate familiarity with the landscapes he describes and his strong attraction to them, yet they also celebrate the pioneering spirit that pits daring men against a nature that seems to stand in the way of the advance of civilization. White sometimes acknowledges this paradox or even exploits it in dramatic confrontations, such as that between Thorpe and his great love and future wife Hilda Farrand over whether to cut the grove of pines in which they met. At other times he ignores or fails to recognize what may seem to modern readers to be contradictory impulses. White came to embrace the view of forest reserves taken by Pinchot and endorsed by Roosevelt, namely, that they were intended for public use ("wise use" in Pinchot's phrase, appropriated in the 1980s by the Wise Use movement in its war against federal regulation of public lands in the West), including managed logging and grazing. Conservation meant not only acquiring public lands (Roosevelt tripled the acreage of the forest reserves when he was president) but ensuring they were used properly and not wasted or exploited by private interests in ways that degraded them. This view allowed for sustainable logging that served the public by providing revenue for the federal government and encouraging the development of the West. White dramatized the conflict between private and public interests in the Sierras in *The Rules of the Game* (1910), a sequel to *The Riverman* and a different kind of forest novel, one that shifts the focus to Jack Orde's son Bob's struggle to discover whether his vocation lies in managing his father's timber interests in California or in pursuing a career in the Forest Service.[25]

White's Michigan forest novels describe an earlier period characterized by the frenetic race to log the pines and then the hardwoods of the upper Midwest. With their celebration of the pioneering spirit, particularly in *The Blazed Trail*, they mask tensions between the demands of logging and the romantic appeal of wilderness that would become more pronounced as the logging frenzy subsided. In his first encounter with logging, as a green hand in a Lower Peninsula logging camp, Thorpe experiences the forest as a place of mystery, where the tracks and sounds of animals and the silent comings and goings of Indians testify to a complex, hidden life. He perceives the pines themselves as "beautiful and solemn and still" (38). White makes the forest seem even more alluring when describing Thorpe's experience as a landlooker camping in the Upper Peninsula, with its "solemn" and "grand" pine groves, hardwood forests "mysterious" and "full of life," dark swamps, and "aromatic" and "enticing" thickets of spruce and balsam. He describes the creatures Thorpe encounters, partridge and lynx and wolf among them, with a detail that suggests his own fascination with the northern forest. When Thorpe eventually finds the great stands of pine with river access for which he has been looking, White describes him as initially awestruck by "the grandeur, the remoteness, the solemnity of the virgin forest" but then feeling "the spirit of the pioneer stirring in him," awakening an instinct to clear the way for civilization (120). Whatever his emotional response to the forest, he has been navigating it with map and compass in pursuit of unclaimed land that meets the conditions for successful logging.

Thorpe appears unaware of any conflict between wonder in the presence of the forest and the reflexive desire to stake his claim to the pines and successfully log them. White's way of dealing with these seemingly contradictory impulses is to invoke the claims of civilization and to treat awareness of its costs as an acceptable form of nostalgia: "We regret . . . the passing of the Indian, the buffalo, the great pine forests, for they are of the picturesque; but we live gladly on the product of the farms that have taken their places" (120). His use of the phrase "of the picturesque" here grants the aesthetic and emotional appeal of what is lost while limiting its significance. White shared a sense of the inevitability of progress with Roosevelt, who recognized ranching, along with "primeval forests," as belonging to a transient, "primitive stage of existence" and scorned any form of sentimentality.[26] What matters most in White's novel is the challenge of the wilderness to the "hardy," not so much to appreciate it or to adapt to its conditions but to win the struggle with nature in the interest of the advance of civilization.

White contrasts Thorpe's practicality and naturalness in the woods with the more studied and self-conscious attitude of Wallace Carpenter, a rich young Chicagoan who with his Indian guide comes on Thorpe by canoe in a campsite that Wallace finds "picturesque." Thorpe is in the process of learning to make a bark canoe with his self-appointed companion, "Injin Charley," during the six weeks he spends cruising for pines in the Upper Peninsula. White describes Wallace as "too young as yet to go behind the picturesque or romantic" (141) yet enthusiastically embracing Thorpe's vision, once he understands his real purpose in the woods, and providing the funds that Thorpe needs to launch his enterprise. Wallace quickly outgrows his initial dreamy fascination with life in the woods through his admiration for the vitality he perceives in Thorpe's pioneering spirit: "You are subduing the wilderness, extending the frontier. After you will come the backwoods farmer, to pull up the stumps; and after him the big farmer and the cities" (144). Thorpe's life impresses him as "real" in a way that his is not. His sudden transformation reinforces the sense that the forest itself, whatever the nature of its appeal, is less important than the achievement of the heroic individual in extending the reach of civilization.

In presenting the developing relationship between Thorpe and Hilda Farrand, another young Chicago socialite, White makes the tension between practical and aesthetic responses the basis for dramatic conflict. He shows the two meeting in a grove of giant pines, which he gives an aura of sanctity by invoking the familiar metaphor of the forest as cathedral, after first revealing Thorpe perceiving Hilda from a distance more as an ethereal vision of beauty than as a woman. The way White presents Hilda, as a delicate figure listening raptly to the song of the white-throated sparrow in a moonlit glade, explains Thorpe's tendency to idealize her. When Thorpe and Hilda subsequently meet in the grove, their inhibitions are dissolved by the haunting violin music of a chore boy who improvises on the song of a hermit thrush. The combination of music and place creates an irresistibly romantic mood, heightened for Hilda because the grove epitomizes to her the mystery of the forest. To her the romance of the wilderness, symbolized by the towering white pines, is much more important than the work of logging that she and her party have come from Chicago to see. In their subsequent meetings Hilda proves herself to be a very real and assured young woman, more than able to hold her own with Thorpe, but by the end of the novel she has embraced her future role as a wife dedicated to advancing her husband's career.[27]

White's presentation of Hilda's counterpart in *The Riverman*, Carroll Bishop, conforms to a similar pattern. The heroines of White's forest novels function as idealized feminine figures who, despite showing a capacity for spirited exchange when they are being courted, metamorphose into submissive wives whose principal role is to support a strong husband. He displaces onto them a capacity for emotional response to the natural world that his heroes possess in varying degrees but rarely reveal, as if aware that yielding to sentiment would undermine their ability to do their work. Women become the primary vehicles for expressing the aesthetic and spiritual appeal of the natural environment in these novels. In each case this appeal is subordinated in the novel as a whole to that of the central story of triumph over all obstacles. This constitutes the real work to which White's heroes dedicate themselves.

The "story of the woods" that Thorpe tells Hilda is one of fighting to finish roads, haul logs, and complete the logging drive under intense pressure in order to defeat the wilderness and secure the future of his company. She admires his manly force, "the strong spirit that wins," but is shocked by the evidence of his work in a scene of recent logging that has the appearance of a battlefield to her, with "stumps of trees, the dead branches, the trunks lying all about, and the glaring hot sun over everything!" (311). We have seen her earlier naming the trees in the grove, which she continues to seek out in solitary walks, personifying pines that Thorpe has to think of as so many board feet if he is going to do the job he has set himself. For Hilda Thorpe is both a heroic figure and someone flawed by not being "poet enough" to see the woods as she does, with little awareness of the nature of his actual work or the imperatives that drive him. White creates a dramatic crisis by having Hilda insist that Thorpe not cut the grove and by making this the definitive test of his love for her. Thorpe agonizes over the choice but refuses to agree because he has factored those pines into the cut he must make that winter in order to keep his company solvent. What White calls Hilda's "sentimental association" of Thorpe with the grove she regards as a shrine conflicts with his "masculine indifference" to sentiment. Their inevitable rupture reflects White's sharp separation of gender roles. She practices a form of the religion of nature, he a religion in which the primary claim is the "duty of success," even when this conflicts with love.

If White makes Hilda appear naive in her romantic view of the woods and her refusal to recognize the economic necessities that motivate Thorpe, he portrays Thorpe as inept in his social awkwardness and his failure to explain the immediate source of financial pressure, a debt his partner Wallace has foolishly incurred through a bad investment. Thorpe appears unable to weigh the claims of love against those of ambition, so fully is his identity defined by the ideal of business success. He is obsessed with the immediate need to inspire his men to accomplish whatever they have to in order to meet the challenge of completing the logging drive. The ultimate reunion of the lovers becomes possible only because Thorpe, having accomplished the heroic feat of getting a record number of logs downstream, releases them into the lake to save the life of one of his men, a widely publicized act that Hilda regards as noble. Thorpe makes a hurried train trip south to find her at her elegant lakefront home in Chicago and declare that she was right about the primacy of love, not stopping to change his woodsman's clothes or his caulked boots.

The scene offers a dramatic, at times comic version of the confrontation between the rough frontier world to which Thorpe is accustomed and the genteel one that Hilda inhabits. Thorpe pushes past the aloof butler, who tries to send this disreputable-looking caller to the back door, leaving the butler looking on in horror as the spikes on his boots cut triangular pieces out of the hardwood floors. To Thorpe's great relief, Hilda embraces him as he is, caulked boots and all, happily agreeing to marry him. Her reversal is plausible because he has shown that he prizes feeling over business success, first in valuing the life of his man over his logs and what they represent and then in making his urgent trek to Chicago to declare his love. Predictably, Hilda's fortune saves the firm. In White's sanguine view, love and the ambition and capacity for heroic action that drive success in the demanding enterprise of logging can be reconciled in the end. Hilda's passionate concern about the devastation left by logging and the loss of the great trees with which she has formed a spiritual bond evaporates as she subordinates herself to Thorpe's sense of purpose. At the end of the novel we see Thorpe, revived emotionally as well as financially by Hilda, prepared to return to the woods and the inevitable success for which his determination and natural leadership destine him.

White created a similar dynamic between hero and heroine in *The Riverman,* set in 1872 in the western Lower Peninsula in the vicinity of the Grand River, where he spent many of his early years, yet the contrast between the sensibilities of the two is less sharply drawn in the later novel. Orde seems more able to relax and enjoy his natural surroundings than Thorpe as he works his way down the river trail with his men in the summer, having "fallen into the wild life as into a habit" (136). He appears as a tanned figure in faded clothes, comfortable with his outdoor life and susceptible to the appeal of the midsummer deciduous woods, which offer a "lazy invitation" with their mysterious shadows, shimmering aspens and poplars, and background noise of birdsong and the drone of insects. The river itself appears invitingly green and cool, with overhanging branches casting shadows. The scene functions as a pastoral interlude, allowing for ease and reflection, in a novel dominated by the urgency of the logging drive and Orde's struggles with a succession of enemies, finally including his devious partner Newmark.

Near the end of the novel, when Orde retreats to the high beech woods in the hills beyond the town where he makes his home after discovering that he has been betrayed by Newmark to think through what he will do, the forest appears as a charmed place, a refuge in which he can recover from the uncharacteristic listlessness and depression into which his disillusionment with Newmark has thrown him. As he sits leaning against a tree, birds and squirrels become accustomed to his presence, and the noon heat pours "down through the forest isles like incense" (351). Orde becomes a part of this seductive scene by giving himself up to its natural rhythms and patterns of light, as if absorbing the sense of order and peacefulness the woods offers. By the time he becomes conscious of the lengthening rays of the late afternoon sun he has been sufficiently restored to return to town and calmly figure out how to deal with Newmark. His choice, anticipated by an earlier scene in which he demonstrates his boxing prowess at his future brother-in-law's club in New York, is to give Newmark the beating of his life and drive him out of town rather than turning him over to the authorities for criminal prosecution. This rough justice, of a sort that would be understood by any lumberjack, is consistent with Orde's straightforward way of dealing with everyone and another manifestation of the manliness at the heart of White's characterization of him. It offers a kind of release and cleansing he could not have found through the tedious workings of the legal system. The resolution is one that White's admirer Roosevelt, an avid boxer himself, would have admired.

A pivotal episode in Orde's relationship with Carroll Bishop, who will subsequently become his wife, begins and ends in the woods outside town when they are carpeted with spring ephemerals and alive with the sounds of migrating birds. White describes Orde as "lost in an enjoyment" so integral a part of his nature that it drew him from town into these woods on a spring morning. When he emerges at the Lake Michigan shore, he discovers Carroll and yields to her invitation to join her in digging in the sand of the beach, then shows her the way through the woods back to town. Orde's natural reserve, with a visitor from New York whom he scarcely knows at this point, contrasts with Carroll's high-spirited playfulness. She delights in calling the birds to her and then, as she walks ahead, in simply throwing her head back and breathing the air, "revelling in the woods sounds and woods odours and woods life with entire self-abandonment" (112). Her spontaneity makes her seem a more natural and credible figure than Hilda Farrand, with her reverential response to the pines. White's tone is lighter in *The Riverman,* and he creates a more convincing chemistry between the prospective lovers. Carroll takes a carefree joy in the beach and woods while showing a canny awareness of her power over the more inhibited Orde.

White makes logging a source of potential friction between Orde and Carroll, as well as between Thorpe and Hilda, yet an incipient breach between them quickly dissolves. When they come out of the woods into rolling country marked by burned, scarred pine stumps as far as they can see, Carroll suddenly turns serious and accusing: "You do this" (113). Orde responds by directing her gaze to a landscape visible in a different direction where they can see farmhouses with cultivated fields, orchards, and tidy woodlots, "all fair and pleasant across the bosom of a fertile nature."

> "And this," said he. "That valley was once nothing but a pine forest—and so was all the southern part of the State, the peach belt and the farms. And for that matter Indiana too, and all the other forest states right out to the prairies. Where would we be now if we *hadn't* done that?"

The visual contrast between the "cultivated countryside" and a landscape of burned pine stumps, of the sort that Hilda imagines as a battlefield in *The Blazed Trail,* makes explicit the logic that justifies the careers of both Orde and Thorpe. By this logic what Carroll and Hilda see as devastation marks a stage on the way to settled and agriculturally productive land.

Orde's dismissive phrase, "nothing but a pine forest," denies southwestern Michigan's stands of white pine any claim to continued existence. What value they have is purely economic, and the logging industry in this view serves society by turning "wilderness" into the kind of pleasing and agriculturally productive middle landscape that Orde points out to Carroll. Unlike Hilda, however, Carroll is quickly satisfied, as if she has simply been testing Orde to see if he can offer an acceptable rationale for his vocation. The romantic story line is less central to the plot in *The Riverman* than in *The Blazed Trail,* and the obstacles to Orde's courtship have more to do with the challenges of getting Carroll out of New York and away from a possessive, semi-invalid mother than with any ideological differences about lumbering. She professes herself content with the rural Michigan landscape in which she takes such pleasure on the spring morning she shares with Orde, describing it as offsetting for her the cultural attractions of New York: "Here are the woods and fields, the river, the lake, the birds, and the breezes" (114). The interplay of woods and fields becomes part of the charm of this settled landscape. Carroll is lively and playful, even mischievous, in her early encounters with Orde, but once she marries him (midway through the novel) she becomes a conventionally devoted wife, entirely supportive of her strong man, whom she calls her "Rock of Gibraltar" and her "whole life" (183, 221). White offers a sentimentalized view of their marriage, typically portraying Carroll as waiting to welcome Orde home from his various adventures to a comfortable domestic scene. The novel concludes with Orde returning from administering Newmark's physical punishment, newly energized and optimistic about his ability to make a success of his logging business, to find Carroll playing a harp in soft light, ready to melt into his protective embrace.

In his second Michigan novel White found ways to reconcile his hero's responsiveness to the aesthetic appeal and the restorative character of the woods with the qualities (manly vigor, decisiveness, ingenuity, daring) that command the allegiance of his men and enable him to meet the escalating challenges involved in getting his logs safely down the river. If Carroll's response to the natural world is more abandoned and playful than Orde's, they nonetheless share an attraction to the woods and an ability to take mutual pleasure in them. And the necessities of logging do not threaten the appeal of the forest as they do in *The Blazed Trail,* at least as seen through the eyes of Hilda, for whom the cutting of the giant pines where she meets Thorpe is a painful violation of the sanctity of the grove. White makes no effort to evoke the romance of grand and solemn pine groves in *The Riverman,* focusing instead on the appeal of the deciduous forest to which we see both Orde and Carroll responding and implying that this forest has a kind of permanence and cultural value that the pines do not. In fact, the lumber industry in southern Michigan moved on to old-growth hardwoods (including beech and maple) once the stands of white pine were depleted. Not all of the cutover land it left behind was suitable for agriculture, and some was reclaimed for nonpayment of taxes from the aspiring farmers who were persuaded to buy it. The pastoral scene that Orde points out to Carroll as a way of justifying his vocation offers a version of the story of logging in southern Michigan that is only partially true.

In *The Riverman* White presents two faces of the natural world. In one aspect, nature is a force that must be controlled, without regard for the consequences to the natural environment, if the logging enterprise is to succeed. Orde uses his ingenuity to modify the river that is the locus of the most important action of the novel by building a dam, blasting boulders, channeling the current with log cribs, and having his men cut seventy-five trees from an adjacent hardwood forest to build a spillway that will carry logs over a waterfall without causing a jam. Such alterations, and others such as clearing obstructions, sacrifice what we would now call ecological concerns to the necessities of the river drive. After preparing the river and getting their logs down it, Orde and his men must summon all their energy and determination to keep dangerously rising water from destroying the boom holding their logs and sweeping them into Lake Michigan. Yet, as we have seen, nature has a more benign face in the novel as well, and Orde has a gentler side than one sees in his efforts to control the river. While the episodes that show Orde enjoying an intimate connection with the woods are clearly subordinate to the underlying story of the conquest of nature that drives the plot of *The Riverman,* as well as that of *The Blazed Trail,* White's second logging novel shows him beginning to give more scope to the pleasures and psychological benefits of contact with the natural world.

Toward the end of *The Riverman* White describes Orde starting to buy timberland in California in anticipation of shifting his operations there when Michigan's forests are depleted. In its sequel, *The Rules of the Game* (1910), Orde has become a congressman and his son Bob is being groomed to take over the new family lumbering business in California. At the beginning of the novel we learn of Bob Orde's college career as a football star, a validation of his manliness comparable to his father's boxing prowess, but he comes to embody a different vision of the role of the lumberman. In *The Rules of the Game* White's focus has shifted from the individual's struggle with wild nature on the frontier to the emerging cause of conservation, although he recognizes the contribution of pioneering western lumbermen: "They opened a new country for a new people" (379). We see Bob Orde struggling to reconcile his attraction to the challenging mission of the young Forest Service with a projected future in lumbering he finds unappealing. He is nostalgic for "the riverman and shanty boys of the vanished North" (200), regretting that "the pioneer work of the industry [is] finished" (284). The kind of logging practiced by his father's old friend and partner in California, Welton, lacks the excitement of the early days in Michigan and perpetuates old-fashioned habits of cutting all the available timber as quickly as possible, without regard to the future health of the forest.

The Forest Service, by contrast, offers the challenge of a young, idealistic enterprise dedicated to protecting the forest reserves from the "private greed" of entrenched logging and grazing interests for the benefit of the people. It represents a future in which Bob Orde can believe. This future offers the appeal of living the life of a forest ranger, joining "rough mountain men" turned rangers riding through the wilderness and sleeping under the stars. White describes these rangers as "knights errant," playing on the revived popularity of chivalric heroism (387). He shows Bob deciding to abandon his apprenticeship to Welton and the role for which his father has been grooming him to become a ranger, in the process educating himself about the value of leaving enough trees standing to protect watersheds and conserve water, one of the stated aims of the legislation establishing the forest reserves, and coming to understand the "real use" of the reserves. Bob throws himself into the work of learning the skills and responsibilities of a ranger, including policing the reserves and settling disputes, fighting fires, and, as it turns out, assessing timber in preparation for the future sales that his supervisor anticipates on public land.

The forest ranger was emerging as yet another kind of frontier hero when White published *The Rules of the Game.* In 1917 a former forest supervisor, John Guthrie, published a collection of verse by forest rangers that had appeared over the previous fifteen years, prefaced by a letter from Gifford Pinchot praising the dedication of the men of the Forest Service. Guthrie presents these poems and songs as "expressions of the spirit of the men who have heard the call of the forest and of distant places." Some present the life of the ranger in highly romantic terms, contrasting it with life in the city. One describes signing up with Uncle Sam "as a ranger bold, to ride the forests free"; another represents the pleasures of solitude in the mountains, spending nights in the open "under the whispering trees." Some offer a version of the romantic sublime, associating this primarily with the appeal of the mountains at sunset when the fading light plays over rocky walls: "And soft across the ramparts' face a magic splendor falls." Not all the poems idealize the ranger's life. Another group, including several written by Aldo Leopold during his early career in the Forest Service, presents a more realistic view of the actual work: building trails, fighting fires, planting trees, chasing thieves. Some offer humorous complaints about the less desirable aspects of life on the trail (mosquitoes, bad food) or the tedium of some of the ranger's chores (counting sheep, dealing with tourists). Yet despite the complaints, comparable to those of lumberjacks' songs about the conditions of life in the camps, the image of the early forest rangers that emerges from this verse is that of a band of rugged men dedicated to their calling and drawn to the challenges of the outdoor life, "clear-eyed, weather-bronzed rangers," as one poem characterizes them.[28] An occasional woman served as a ranger in the early years of the Forest Service, typically as a fire lookout, but female rangers were rare until the second half of the twentieth century and were not given dangerous jobs such as firefighting and law enforcement until the late 1970s.[29]

In the same year in which White's *The Rules of the Game* appeared, Hamlin Garland published *Cavanagh, Forest Ranger,* with a prefatory letter from Gifford Pinchot praising Garland's understanding of the problems faced by the Forest Service in the West and of the accomplishments of western rangers.[30] Garland and White were acquaintances, friends and supporters of Roosevelt, who corresponded on political matters and shared an intense interest in spiritualism.[31] Like White, Garland was attracted to the mountain West and the story of the early struggles of the Forest Service to impose its authority on westerners accustomed to treating public lands as their own. Garland cast his story as a contest between the old and new West, with the old epitomized by cattlemen who use violence (particularly against sheep men) to get their way and the new by his exemplary ranger hero and his supervisor, Redfield, who grew up with the old ways but has come to embrace the vision of the future represented by the Forest Service. Redfield praises Roosevelt and his chief forester, Pinchot, for creating a force that will work to bring law and order to what has become "a lawless no-man's land" of range wars and abuse of the public domain by "free-range monopolists" (54). Garland made his protagonist Cavanagh a well-born Englishman who became a Rough Rider, serving under his hero Roosevelt, and was then drawn to the American West and subsequently to the Forest Service. As a ranger, Cavanagh remains a soldier in temperament but one who has transferred his loyalty to Pinchot and takes pride in seeing himself as "a defender of the forest." His heroism takes the form of courage to stand up to the accusations and threats of cattlemen and other defenders of the status quo and an unshakable determination to enforce "the impersonal, even-handed justice of the Federal law" (46).

In a memoir Garland describes how he patterned Cavanagh on the rangers he encountered in their isolated cabins during his explorations of the mountain West and came to admire for their hardiness, daring, and loyalty to their distant chief. For him the ranger was "the prophet of a new order."[32] He presents Cavanagh as a transitional figure, halfway between the cowboy and the "trained forester" of the future, who combines an idealistic commitment to the mission of the Forest Service with a responsiveness to the aesthetic appeal of the mountains that he found to be characteristic of rangers. Garland shows Cavanagh drawn to the beauty and purity of the mountains, where he lives in a remote cabin, spending as little time as possible in the rough, squalid town of Roaring Fork. He elaborately describes Cavanagh's emotional reaction to a particularly splendid sunset, with radiant peaks breaking through a rolling sea of clouds, building to a climactic moment of "mystery and grace" when Cavanagh sees his shadow projected on the clouds and suddenly understands Goethe's reference to "the Shadows of the Brocken." Cavanagh's epiphany convinces him to remain in the Forest Service and the "high world" where he can experience such wonders and also to marry the woman he loves, Lee Virginia, raised and educated in the East but compromised by her family connections with the crude social world of Roaring Fork. When Lee Virginia finally experiences the mountains, she shows her own sensitivity to their appeal, feeling herself "carried into another world—a world that was at once primeval and peaceful" (262–63). Garland's treatment of the mountains recalls evocations of the romantic sublime more typical of mid-nineteenth-century descriptions of spectacular American scenery and gives them a timelessness that suggests earlier reactions to the "primeval" forest. The novel ends with a reinvigorated Cavanagh assured of promotion in the Forest Service and committed to remaining in the West, with Lee Virginia.[33]

White's descriptions of mountain scenery are less obviously romantic than Garland's, but he makes Bob Orde's attraction to Sierra landscapes in *The Rules of the Game* part of what draws him to the mission of the Forest Service and ultimately transforms his attitude toward lumbering. White shows Orde developing an intimate familiarity with the mountains he patrols on horseback looking for signs of fire, never tiring of the vistas that open up on his rides. He responds to the "spirit" of the woods as he conducts his timber surveys with a partner, finding himself refreshed and calmed by his interaction with the Sierra "wilderness." One stand of giant sugar pines they survey appears as a "magnificent open forest" with a floor of pine needles, "temple-like" in its austerity and silence.[34] White describes his own attraction to sugar pines, the "most spiritual" of trees and a reminder of the white pines he knew in Michigan, in a book of essays about time spent in the Sierras he called *The Cabin* (1912) after a rebuilt sheepherder's cabin that became his summer retreat. In *The Mountains* (1904), a western counterpart of *The Forest* in which he evokes "the lure of the trail," he combines practical advice about taking pack trips in the mountains with narratives of his adventures that reveal his pleasure in discovering new vistas of peaks and canyons and in riding through pine forests and mountain meadows. White gives Bob Orde something of his own delight in being in the mountains, but he also makes Orde conscious of the potential value of the Sierra forests as timber. The remarkable forest of sugar pines functions in the plot as the object of the machinations of the devious Baker, the principal villain of the novel, who is scheming to get timber rights to it under the mineral act.

The grazing conflicts that generate the central drama of Garland's novel play a limited role for White, who was more interested in the implications of the new conservation ethic for the future of logging in the forest reserves. Bob Orde proves himself an exemplary ranger and worthy hero, defeating an array of villains (including a revived Newmark, who surfaces in California as Baker's henchman) through a combination of physical daring and moral integrity. Yet White shows his experience as a ranger leading him, surprisingly, to recognize that he can find the challenge and fulfillment he seeks by transforming his father's lumbering business. The woman he is destined to marry, his forest supervisor's daughter, Amy Thorne, can urge Bob to leave the Forest Service in whose mission she passionately believes because she is convinced he can do the most good running his father's mill in a way that proves that sustainable logging can be profitable, in the reserves as well as on private holdings. He eventually recognizes that he can have more influence as a progressive lumberman serving as a model for others logging on public land by managing his father's Wolverine Company in ways that show how watersheds and the long-term health of the forests can be protected.

This resolution of the novel was consistent with Pinchot's efforts to demonstrate that sound, science-based forestry could be profitable in order to persuade lumbermen to bid on timber sales in the reserves.[35] White shows Bob recovering a sense of the excitement of logging and implies that he will demonstrate how to succeed in the timber business while practicing conservation, for example, by ending the practice of leaving combustible piles of slash in the forest. Thus he will pave the way for an acceptable kind of logging in the forest reserves that makes sense to both the businessman and the conservationist. At the end of the novel White shows Bob seeing the mill with new eyes and a conviction that he has found his true calling: "The yellow sawdust and the sawn lumber; the dark forest beyond; the bulk of the mill with its tall pines; the dazzling plume of steam against the very blue sky, all these appealed to him again with many voices, as they had years before in far-off Michigan" (643–44). This scene would have filled John Muir with gloom, but it expresses a vision of the harmony of industry with the natural world that White joined Gifford Pinchot in embracing. White makes the machine in the garden, in this case a steam-driven sawmill rather than the intrusive locomotive that disrupted the pastoral world of Hawthorne and his neighbor Thoreau, appear a benign part of the scene.[36]

The evolution of White's thinking about logging reflects the emergence of forestry as a science, as well as his experience in California and his engagement with the progressive conservation agenda of Roosevelt, which was significantly influenced by Pinchot's efforts to shape the future of forestry. For White, as for Pinchot, the question was not whether to log in the forest reserves but how. At a time when even conservationists accepted the need to open up unsettled country, and recognized that lumbermen who bought tracts of private land could play an important role in generating economic development, it seemed possible to reconcile a passion for outdoor adventure and natural history with logging. Trained foresters, it seemed, could provide guidelines for managing a forest in a way that would ensure its long-term health and enable them to justify continued economic use of protected natural areas. These areas were increasingly defended, however, by an incipient preservationist movement for which Muir had become the most influential spokesman.

In 1922 White wrote a letter as chairman of a group seeking to form a new association of writers who would commit themselves to publishing something each year, either an article or a work of fiction, that would promote the interests of the association.[37] These interests, as White's letter defines them, blend an attraction to "the memories and traditions of outdoor America—the days of pioneering and conquest of the West" with promotion of conservation, especially as embodied in the movement to establish national parks.[38] The letter credits writers with playing a major role in the conservation movement and seeks to expand this by forming the new association and identifying publishing venues for its members' work. White's list of objectives is interesting for the way it shows how he, and presumably the ten other writers who signed the letter, saw the conservation of natural resources as a way of keeping alive a tradition of adventure on the frontier. The first objective calls for "the preservation of the romantic west and the reminder of its glories" and the second for "the perpetuation of the memory of the pioneers," from Daniel Boone to Theodore Roosevelt. Clearly nostalgia for a glorious past, the "old days" that White and others continued to mine in their writing, was part of the attraction of efforts to conserve "what is left of our forests and our game," in the words of another objective. Through his efforts to shape public attitudes toward conservation and engage other writers in the cause, he was trying to hold onto a vision of a primitive America that is reflected in one way or another in virtually all of his fiction.

In view of White's strong attraction to outdoor adventure and his continuing fascination with the frontier, it is not surprising to find him starting to spend summers sailing in Alaskan waters and turning to Alaska for subjects for fiction, including his last novel and one of his most popular, *Wild Geese Calling* (1940). Muir, in writings based on a series of trips to Alaskan coastal areas beginning in 1879, had helped establish Alaska in the popular imagination as "pure wilderness" and a place of extraordinary natural wonders, including the glaciers that fascinated him. Reports from the Harriman expedition of 1899, which included Muir and the naturalist John Burroughs along with artists and numerous scientists, brought more attention to Alaska, as did the popular fiction of Jack London and Rex Beach. London, whom White entertained at his southern California estate outside Santa Barbara, tended to erase distinctions between the Yukon Territory and Alaska in his fiction. White would have followed his stories of masculine adventure in the Far North with keen interest and been influenced, like many others, by the image of Alaska as the last frontier that London helped create. In the late nineteenth and early twentieth centuries Alaska assumed two distinct and potentially conflicting identities, as the ultimate American wilderness and as the last frontier, a place ripe for settlement and for exploitation of its vast natural resources.[39]

The protagonist of *Wild Geese Calling,* John Murdock, is a composite of the qualities of the frontier hero that appealed to White. As the product of a family that emigrated from Scotland to New England and then moved west across the Alleghenies with Daniel Boone and subsequently to Oregon by wagon train, he inherited the restlessness and desire to seek out new frontiers that White associated with the pioneer spirit. In a foreword written to defend the ideal of the pioneer as a heroic figure against debunkers, who were criticizing pioneers as escapists unable to deal with the complexities of modern civilization, he characterizes the pioneer movement as a matter of "receptivity to a racial urge. The man who is attuned to that impulse must go."[40] The Anglo-Saxon Murdock embodies this irresistible impulse, moving from the ranch country of eastern Oregon, where as a young man he learns to be a cowboy, to eastern Washington, where he becomes a logger, then to a lumber mill in Seattle and finally to coastal Alaska. Along the way he becomes proficient not only at cowboying and logging but also at sailing and tinkering with the machines that drive the lumber mills and canneries (in Alaska) seen as the backbone of emerging western economies. In the fictional boomtown of Klakan in southeastern Alaska, Murdock even proves himself to be a gunfighter, humiliating a bullying outlaw known as Pirate Kelly in a classic showdown in a saloon.

In Murdock, White created a complete frontier hero, blending the skills that Roosevelt and his friend Owen Wister associated with older kinds of western heroes, including Wister's Virginian, with those of early loggers. Murdock combines these skills and a few others with the kind of resourcefulness necessary to survive on the wild Alaskan coast where he finally settles with his wife Sally. He displays the manliness and courage White gave the heroes of his Michigan logging novels, Thorpe and Orde, if not their ability to organize and lead groups of men and their drive for business success. Murdock typically acts as a solitary individual, with the determination and adaptability needed to meet a broader range of challenges than those faced by Thorpe and Orde. White was more interested in the mentality of the frontier hero in *Wild Geese Calling*. He presents Murdock as capable of acting quickly and decisively in moments of crisis because he can focus on immediate problems and not brood over the past or the uncertainties of the future. White explains his behavior at one point by asserting that "the pioneer is driven by an urge, not a plan. If he thought things away out to a conclusion he would never be a pioneer" (391).

In Alaska Murdock is driven by a compelling urge to prove that he can master the technique of solo logging ("hand logging") that would enable him to make a living in the secluded coastal valley to which he and Sally retreat from Klakan. The most formidable challenge Murdock faces in the novel is sailing their ketch to Klakan by himself in a storm to bring help when Sally is about to give birth; he survives wild seas and extreme cold only by willing himself to continue when he has reached what he thinks are the limits of his endurance. This is the ultimate test that proves his heroism, analogous to the climactic logging drives of White's Michigan novels. But an important turning point in the action comes earlier, when Murdock finally demonstrates that he can succeed at hand logging by felling a big spruce in such a way that he can get it to "run" down to the sea, clearing the way for him to fell other trees that will skid along the same course. This is logging in its purest and most demanding form, depending on the skill and ingenuity of one individual. Rather than pit himself against the forces of nature, as Harry Thorpe did, Murdock solves "the problem of using the forces of Nature against herself" (402) by learning to rely on the weight of felled trees to generate momentum that will cause them to slide downhill to the sea where they can be held by a boom. He had learned the rudiments of hand logging earlier from a solitary Canadian they encountered on the coast of British Columbia on their way to Alaska, insisting on delaying their journey until he fully understood the process (186–90). White uses the episode to illustrate the difficulty of this kind of logging, which demands not only extraordinary skill with an ax but also the ability to use a jack and clear away obstacles in order to get a difficult tree (limbed, stripped of its bark, and greased with dogfish oil if necessary) into position to slide unobstructed to the water.[41]

Murdock's wife Sally, whose grandmother gave birth in a covered wagon on the way to Oregon, represents a new kind of heroine for White. She shares her husband's adventurous spirit and is even more eager than he is to go to Alaska. Once there, she displays a more intense kind of the responsiveness to natural beauty that White associated with his earlier heroines, achieving "a rapture of intimacy with her surroundings" on long walks while Murdock is preoccupied with trying to master hand logging, absorbed in what Sally sees as his "man's world" of work. The natural world to which she responds has a dynamism and sense of teeming life unlike anything in White's rendering of Michigan's forests or the California Sierras. White describes Sally as nearly overcome by the spectacle of a salmon run, with the air "electric" with the screaming of birds, and taking a wary delight in observing grizzlies fishing for the spawning salmon. The rush of the salmon themselves suggests "the upswelling, powerful flow of the very stream of life" (429). Her ability to lose herself in the surging life around her makes Sally see an element of tragedy in Murdock's felling of giant trees, part of the fabric of the vibrant natural world that absorbs her, but she accepts his logging as essential to their effort to sustain themselves in this country. She adamantly opposes the use of steel traps because of the suffering they cause, however, and forces Murdock and their friend Len to follow the traditional Indian practice of using snares and deadfalls for trapping. Her realism about the need to accumulate furs to earn needed funds in the spring allows White to insist that she is "no sentimentalist." We are told she can accept the "sudden clean death" of animals (489), if not the use of steel traps.

While White continues to delineate gender roles clearly in *Wild Geese Calling*—Murdock is practical and Sally empathetic, he most stirred by crises and physical challenges and she by her engagement with her natural surroundings—he shows Sally embracing the role of pioneer wife and the hardships that go with it. She even learns to smoke salmon for the winter from a solicitous old Indian couple who live in the valley seasonally, and she prides herself on giving birth "in a log cabin in a remote wilderness, during a winter snowstorm, without benefit of medicine" (560). Sally finds this as romantic a "pioneer show" as her grandmother had put on in delivering the baby's namesake while crossing the plains, at the same time recognizing she risks being sentimental by entertaining the comparison. White's efforts to insulate her from the charge of sentimentalism are another indication of his concern with distinguishing her from more conventional heroines. Where he had made Hilda Farrand (in *The Blazed Trail*) seem naive and sentimental in her attitude toward the forest, he represents Sally as combining a sturdy resilience with the sensitivity that allows her to experience and express wonder at what Muir called the "grand wild country" of Alaska. Murdock shares this wonder to some degree but lacks her capacity to articulate it. Sally became White's principal vehicle for evoking for his readers the kind of appeal he found in the natural abundance of Alaska.

If Sally shows traces of the stereotyping we see in White's earlier female heroines, marveling at the physical skills Murdock reveals and looking to him in times of crisis ("Her man would take care of that," 464), in other respects she represents a new kind of heroine, more vital and tougher than her predecessors. She shares fully in the decision to leave a promising life in Seattle to pursue the vague hope of Alaska and then embraces Murdock's suggestion that they abandon their plan to go to the Klondike in the spring and instead homestead in the valley they have found, having come to the conclusion that they should do this well before he does. She and Murdock share a vision of the life they can make in this unspoiled place and accept the challenges that life there will involve. White shows Murdock's imagination leaping ahead to the possibilities the valley and the adjacent coast offer, not only in logging but in fishing for salmon in deeper water than usual with a new kind of floating fish trap he has already devised, both ways of producing income by serving the needs of Klakan.

Murdock envisions serving their own needs by establishing a truck garden and orchard, even a small dairy herd, taking advantage of the five hundred acres of meadowland the valley offers. We see him embracing the role of the pioneer who opens up new country to settlement, ready to exercise his varied skills to make his way in a wild country that offers both greater challenges and greater opportunities than the Oregon in which his parents settled. White includes friends Len and Annabelle, a good-hearted prostitute who comes to act as midwife to Sally, in the group colonizing the valley and implies that others will join them in the future. He suggests as well that the town of Klakan will flourish as settlers pour into Alaska, implicitly endorsing the kind of American expansionism this represents. Klakan would not be out of place in one of London's stories of the Far North, nor would its cast of typically Alaskan characters; there is even a heroic dog, Chilkat, who saves Sally from being raped at a critical point in the action. But in *Wild Geese Calling* White moved beyond the fortune seeking and the Darwinian struggle for survival that characterize early fiction about the Far North to articulate a new and more domesticated vision of frontier life.

White's happy ending projects an idealized future of homesteading in the Alaskan wilderness untroubled by the kinds of tensions we see in his earlier logging novels. There are no villains in sight once Murdock has disposed of the thuggish Pirate Kelly early in their Alaskan experience, and, apart from Sally's regret over the need to cut down trees, there is no sense of loss or destructiveness in the exploitation of natural resources. The late-nineteenth-century Alaska that we see through their eyes is a place of such natural abundance that scenes of destruction such as fields of stumps are unimaginable in the context of the novel. The vision of the Murdocks promises a future in which their narrow, isolated valley will become an agrarian utopia, White's version of an earlier American ideal but one with a distinctly Alaskan flavor. He evokes a pastoral landscape embedded in wilderness, hemmed in by mountains with dense forests on their lower slopes and guarded by a rugged coast that allows access to the interior only through a scarcely visible "hole" that leads to the river flowing by the Murdocks' cabin. The towering peak that Sally thinks of as her "Protector of the Wilderness" will still preside over the valley, the forests will remain, and their lives will continue to be governed by tidal and other natural rhythms. In presenting this remote valley as a kind of paradise for settlers White found a way of celebrating both the Alaskan wilderness and the resilience, array of skills, and pioneer spirit necessary to live with it.

When White wrote *Wild Geese Calling* in 1940, the early-twentieth-century struggles to establish the conservation ethic championed by Pinchot and to legitimize the role of the Forest Service had receded into the past, and the political battles of our own time over large-scale commercial logging in roadless areas of Alaska's Tongass National Forest were well in the future. White could appeal to readers captivated by the image of Alaska as the last frontier while indulging a fantasy of a time and place in which the pioneer could continue to be tested by "strong stark primitive forces of nature" and wilderness would not inevitably give way to civilization. While he recognized that Alaska had changed because pioneering settlers had opened up parts of the backcountry, it was still a wild enough place when he wrote to nurture his ideal of the pioneer hero and stimulate him to develop this ideal in ways that he had not before. Logging, of a kind that requires understanding and using natural forces rather than simply combating them, remains an essential part of this heroism but no longer the dominant part. Writing *Wild Geese Calling* allowed White to move beyond the kind of contest between man and nature that dominates the action of *The Blazed Trail* and *The Riverman,* and in even starker ways that of *The Silent Places,* to imagine how the pioneering spirit could coexist with a life spent in the presence of wilderness.

5 // Loss and Renewal

Stewart Edward White's Michigan novels and stories appealed to the public taste for adventure on a vanishing frontier, offering a dramatic version of what John W. Fitzmaurice called "the romance of the forest" and emphasizing the theme of heroic struggle with "wilderness" in the name of progress. Much of the subsequent fiction dealing with logging in Michigan and the Lake States explores its social, economic, and environmental costs. The novel published in the immediate aftermath of the logging era that is most interesting for my purposes, Harold Titus's *Timber* (1922), enjoyed an influence out of proportion to its literary merit. It addressed an issue that provoked contentious debate at the time, what to do with Michigan's extensive cutover lands, and, through the vision and determination of its protagonist, Helen Foraker, presented a compelling case for how the pine forests could be regenerated. Titus effectively challenged the heroic view of lumbering popularized by White and dramatized the case for restoring the state's pine forests by making his protagonist a young woman who triumphantly applies the principles of the relatively new science of forestry, overcoming natural and human challenges to her plan. His popular and timely novel influenced foresters and state legislators who were trying to deal with forestry issues, including the problem of forest fires, when it had become apparent that most efforts to convert cutover lands to agriculture had failed or were in the process of failing.

Two novels that appeared a little more than a decade after *Timber* illuminate the changing climate in which Titus wrote and are interesting in their own right as successful fictional explorations of the social and environmental costs of the logging era. Both reflect shifts in the public perception of logging toward a much more critical view of prosperous lumbermen and their companies, if not of the lumberjacks themselves, and a recognition of the waste and destructiveness of the logging boom. Mildred Walker's *Fireweed* (1934) describes the social and economic consequences of the decline of logging in the Upper Peninsula in a dying mill town modeled on Big Bay, where she spent her early married years before moving to Great Falls, Montana, with her physician husband. Edna Ferber's *Come and Get It*, published in the same year, traces the rise and fall of a self-made Wisconsin lumber baron and the education of a grandson, who comes to see him as no better than a cattle thief but is nonetheless fascinated by the culture of logging. These novels offer complementary views of the evolution of the lumber industry, Walker's from the perspective of mill workers and the company towns on which they depended and Ferber's from that of the new aristocracy of lumber barons.

In *Fireweed*, her first of thirteen published novels, Mildred Walker tells the story of a young wife and mother, Celie Linsen, coming to terms with the hardships and frustrations of life in a failing mill town on the shore of Lake Superior from which she dreams of escaping. The action of the novel takes place in the late 1920s and early 1930s, during the hardwood era that followed what Walker characterizes as the "great massacre" of the white pine in the Upper Peninsula. An early scene in which Celie impulsively yields to her boyfriend Joe in the ghost town of Mead, with its tumbledown buildings and streets in the process of being reclaimed by grasses and sweet fern and "magenta masses of fireweed" (64), both determines her future and foreshadows that of her own town of Flat Point. After their lovemaking Celie shivers at the thought that Flat Point could be similarly deserted someday and insists on making a quick retreat from the deserted town.

Walker shows Celie finding pleasure in the communal rituals of Flat Point and in the big lake and the nearby woods and meadows when the weather softens in spring and summer, and, at least at times, in her new experience of marriage and motherhood. Yet for most of the novel she remains determined to escape to the more expansive life she imagines outside. We see the limitations of the town through her eyes. Its inhabitants are trapped in jobs that depend on the will of the impersonal "city bosses" of the Lake Superior Lumber Company, who visit periodically from Detroit but do not "belong" to the place as the workers do and have no real commitment to their well-being. The company provides a store, a doctor, and modest houses to which the workers and their families are assigned, and it dictates the conditions of employment. Celie reads her future in the worn face of her mother and ultimately blames the mill town for the deaths of both her parents, her father's from an accident in which he is crushed by logs and her mother's from typhoid fever contracted while nursing the sick children of a poor family that brought the disease to the town. Uncertainty about the future of the mill, at a time when readily available timber is running out and mills in comparable towns are closing, only makes her situation seem more hopeless. The eventual closing of the mill, precipitated by the crash of 1929 and the onset of the Great Depression, has come to seem inevitable by the time it happens.

Walker found no romance in logging and the lumber business. She describes an industry in decline, with the fates of the mill workers determined by financial forces beyond their control or understanding. We see the impact of the mill's closing in the hollowing out of the town of Flat Point as the store disposes of its stock and virtually all the inhabitants leave to seek work elsewhere. Walker finds hope for the future not in the possibility that the mill will reopen but in Celie's growing recognition of her attraction to the place she has sought to escape. She becomes confident that she and Joe can find a way to live off the land (fishing, trapping, cutting firewood, and making wreaths to sell in the nearby town of Clarion). Celie realizes that such a life will have its hardships and constraints but nevertheless embraces it, finding satisfaction in the prospect that she and Joe will be independent. If Walker romanticizes anything, it is the natural environment. She describes the shrill sound of the mill whistle marking the end of the final workday as fading quickly, "louder only for a second than the deeper, everlasting sounds of the wind and the trees and waters of Lake Superior."[1] Celie had always enjoyed canoeing on Superior with Joe when the ice broke up in the spring. When the big house on the bluffs is abandoned, and the company's representative Arthur Farley and his glamorous wife have separately decamped for Detroit, she realizes that the life it symbolized for her was an illusion. She takes more pleasure in being outside the house in the sun with her children than in looking through the window at the now "dark and ghostly" room where she had once been a dinner guest dazzled by the splendor of her surroundings. The landscape itself, the environment of lake and woods, emerges as the primary locus of value in the novel and becomes the bedrock of Celie's life.

Walker concludes her novel by showing Celie and Joe enjoying a picnic at Mead after a trip to Clarion in which Joe succeeds in selling a load of firewood and Celie realizes that she would not want to live in a cramped apartment like that in which they find their friends who have moved to the city, a fictionalized version of Marquette. As they lie in the grass enjoying the sunshine, the abandoned town no longer troubles Celie. The winter wind has blown away "the ghosts of the old town," and spring rain and summer sun have "cleansed and sweetened" the tumbledown houses, as if banishing thoughts of the economic ruin and suffering that the houses recall (312). The fact that nature is steadily reclaiming the deteriorating town has come to seem a form of purification. Celie now finds the masses of fireweed appealing, "pretty enough for a garden, almost, and sturdy to grow in that burned out ground" (312). They have become a symbol of renewal, and of a simpler existence in which natural rhythms displace the relentless commercial logic of the lumber industry that formerly dictated the pace of life in Flat Point. Walker asks the reader to believe that Celie and Joe can survive without depending on the industrial economy, relying on their knowledge of the resources provided by the land. Walker avoids sentimentalizing this existence by showing Celie recognizing that her life will be marked by more childbearing and winters that cut them off from the rest of the world and that her children will go away and make their lives elsewhere. Yet she also shows Celie finding a new kind of peace as she meditates in the "stillness" of the scene beside the lake, with Joe napping in the sun, and embraces the future she can imagine unfolding for her in an environment free of the influence of lumber companies.

Edna Ferber offered a more ambitious and complex reassessment of the lumber industry and its effects in *Come and Get It*. Ferber grew up in Kalamazoo, Michigan, and became one of the most popular novelists of her time, winning a Pulitzer Prize for *So Big* (1924); her novels were frequently adapted for the screen (including *Cimarron, Giant,* and *So Big*) or the stage (including the musical based on her novel *Show Boat*). She wrote *Come and Get It* in midcareer, returning to Michigan and Wisconsin to research the lumber industry. The dynastic saga she presents in the novel owes most of its force to the dominant personality of Barney Glasgow, her version of the lumberjack become wealthy and respectable businessman. Barney, given the nickname Gusto in his early days in the lumber camps, displays not only the skill and determination to rise from chore boy to foreman but also the shrewdness to convince the most successful lumberman in eastern Wisconsin to take him on as a partner. His ambition drives him to assure his future by marrying the lumberman's spinster daughter. When the novel opens, in 1907, we see Barney at the height of his success, enjoying the luxuries of life in the family mansion in Butte Des Morts while presiding over the Glasgow Pulp and Paper Mill and the vast timberlands that supply it. He is a robust, dynamic figure who radiates confidence but chafes at the social regimen imposed by a wife for whom he has no affection. Barney relishes his opportunities to escape to the woods at the northern lumber town of Iron Ridge, where he can reconnect with his friend Swan Bostrum and the lumber camps in which he began his career.

Ferber patterned Barney Glasgow in part on Big Bill Bonifas, one of the pioneering Michigan lumbermen and someone she visited at his lodge on Lake Gogebic near Ironwood in the western Upper Peninsula in the course of her research for the novel.[2] Her account of this research in her autobiography makes it obvious that she regarded the "paper-mill millionaires" she interviewed as midwestern versions of the robber barons of the East: "Cutting and slashing, grabbing and tricking, they had seized and destroyed millions of acres of forest land with never a sprig replanted; they had diverted and polluted streams and rivers; had falsely obtained right-of-way on either side of trumped-up railroads and thereby got control of untold mineral wealth as well as woodland, water, and farm lands."[3] Ferber deplored the state of the cutover land she saw, with its "miles and miles of rotting stumps where once a glorious forest had stood," rendering this landscape more luridly in *Come and Get It* as "a wasteland of bleeding pine stumps left there to rot and dry like corpses on a battlefield."[4] In the novel she makes Barney an unapologetic defender of the breed of pioneering lumbermen that he represents, railing against Theodore Roosevelt's ideas about forestry and conservation and dismissing replanting as too expensive. Instead he simply allows his cutover land to revert to the government for nonpayment of taxes, a common practice among the lumbermen of his time. Ferber describes Barney and his fellow millionaires as "pirates in fine linen and diamond shirt studs" who "saw what they wanted and grabbed it, as all their lives they had" (39). He appears supremely self-assured and resistant to suggestions that he change his way of doing business, including sensible ones about potential innovations made by his forward-looking son Bernie.

Ferber prevented Barney Glasgow from becoming simply a caricature of a plundering lumber baron by giving him a complicated and flawed personal life. His unhappiness with his marriage and the social pieties of Butte des Morts makes him susceptible to an infatuation with the granddaughter of his lumbering buddy Swan and the woman he rejected to pursue his ambition, an infatuation that ultimately causes his downfall. Barney imagines the granddaughter, named Lotta after her grandmother and possessing her grandmother's magnetism, as offering the prospect of enjoying the happiness in love that he had rejected before. His indulgence of his obsession and his eventual devastating recognition of its folly, in a scene in which nineteen-year-old Lotta reveals her love for his son Bernie and dismisses Barney as "old," constitute the major drama of the novel. Barney violently breaks off relations with his son and dies shortly afterward, in an explosion on the family boat caused by his carelessness that claims his wife and daughter as well.

Ferber subsequently recognized that killing off Barney with more than a third of the novel to go was a mistake, in that it removed the most vital character in her story.[5] The remainder of the action traces the dramatic growth of son Bernie's business empire and the escape of Lotta, who has become his wife, from the snobbery of the matrons of Butte des Morts into the high society of New York and Europe on the strength of her charm and Bernie's wealth. The decline of Bernie's fortunes and health in the Depression and the preference of Brad and Dina, the teenage twins of Lotta and Bernie, for America over Europe bring the action back to Butte des Morts, where Bard concludes that his future lies in running the family business. The novel ends in Iron Ridge with the celebration of Swan's eighty-fifth birthday and the simple virtues of the old-time lumberjack that he embodies. The final scene shows Bard joining Swan in ceremonially felling a hundred-year-old white pine, one of a stand that must go to make way for a new airplane beacon.

Samuel Goldwyn's 1936 film adaptation of the novel, directed by William Wyler, avoided the problem that Ferber acknowledged by focusing on the story of Barney's relationships with the two Lottas and ending with Barney's disillusionment.[6] The film opens with a robust evocation of life in a north woods lumber camp, with Barney asserting his dominance by physically subduing two rebellious lumberjacks and Swan Bostrum playing the comic Swede, in a role for which Walter Brennan won an Oscar for best supporting actor. The opening scenes show white pines toppling in rapid sequence as if choreographed and logs stacked on rollways spectacularly catapulted into the river for the spring drive with the liberal use of dynamite. The vividness of these early scenes, based on Ferber's sketches of camp life, hints at something the film loses by foreshortening the action of the novel, the sense of the importance of the heritage of logging and the role of the lumberjack that Ferber managed to communicate in the course of bringing the story of the family dynasty into the 1930s. She differentiates the rapacity of the timber owner from the achievements and ethic of the lumberjack, who had become a fixture of American folklore, by elevating the stature of Swan Bostrum and showing Barney's grand-children finding a way to embrace the legacy of the pioneering loggers.

Tom Melendy, the grandson of one of Swan Bostrum's fellow lumber-jacks, plays a pivotal role in the novel as the mentor who weans the twins Brad and Dina from the effete European life for which Lotta has prepared them by arousing their interest in America and their American origins. Ferber portrays Melendy as a radicalized college teacher who publishes a book entitled *The Rape of the American Forest* yet paradoxically retains a fascination with the lives of the old woodsmen. If he sees Barney and his fellow timber owners as thieves who stripped the land, he nevertheless finds them "splendid" ones and larger-than-life figures. Barney's ghost hovers over the latter part of the novel, eclipsing the presence of his son Bernie, who proves himself the model of the efficient modern business-man but lacks his father's passion and collapses physically and mentally under the pressures that follow the 1929 crash of the financial markets. Swan Bostrum emerges as the survivor, who prefers the old ways of the lumberjack and the simple life of Iron Ridge, earning the admiration of Tom Melendy and the twins.

Ferber shows the appeal of America for the twins partly through their early memories of Iron Ridge and their attraction to the room of their grandmother Karie, Lotta's mother, in their grand London house. There two pictures establish the presence of Iron Ridge, one of Karie and Lotta as waitresses in the dining room of Ridge House before Barney removed them to Butte des Morts and the other of Swan in winter lumberjack's gear seen against a snowy forest of pine and hemlock, "enlarged to stu-pendous proportions so that he actually looked like the giant he was" (467). The twins recognize in Swan and Iron Ridge a kind of authenticity they fail to find in their experience of Europe, mediated by the exclusive schools in which their mother places them. Their mentor, Tom, for all his criticisms of the rapacity of the lumber barons, sees the hardiness and vi-tality of the early lumberjacks as manifesting an American spirit he ad-mires: "The best of them lived on the land and the forests and the water and fought it out with their bare hands" (498).

Another picture, a painting based on a tintype that Barney commis-sioned and then displayed in his office, symbolizes life in the early lumber camps for Ferber. It shows Barney's gaunt mother bent over the stove in the cooking shack, with "bearded giant shanty boys" on benches waiting for their meal and young Gusto the chore boy looking on. The picture, titled "Come and Get It," serves as a reminder to Barney of his origins and also as an ironic commentary on the extent to which he has physically and psychologically distanced himself from these origins. When he returns to Iron Ridge to visit his camps with Swan, Barney assumes his old manner but feels the physical strain of cutting down a pine, which he does to prove that he has not lost his touch, and finds the camp food that he once relished unpalatable. He cannot help thinking of himself as a "great man" who achieved a success that the others could not, and he cuts off Swan's stream of reminiscences about their early adventures in the woods, unwilling to acknowledge his age or imagine himself in a life so at odds with his present one. By showing Swan embracing the simplicity of this life and continuing to work as a lumberjack, Ferber gives him a dignity and moral stature that Barney lacks. Swan's observation that Barney and his father-in-law should have replanted the pine they cut only irritates Barney, while it marks Swan as the one who feels a sense of responsibility for the future use of the land.

The final scene of the novel reaffirms the values that Swan embodies, as the oldest working lumberjack in the woods at eighty-five, and a way of life that the community of Iron Ridge preserves. Bard excitedly tells his sister: "this is the real thing. . . . Look at old Swan. This is America, all right" (514). Wearing a lumberjack's mackinaw and boots, he proves he can handle ax and saw as he joins his great-grandfather in ceremonially cutting down the designated white pine. Swan reflexively calls him Gusto, as if re-creating his bond with his old friend and acknowledging Bard as a worthy successor. In an earlier scene Ferber had shown the young Barney satisfying "a savage sense of destruction and his sense of power at the same time" (97) by cutting down a giant white pine two or three centuries old. She describes the great tree as having seen the passage of Indians and Jesuits and voyageurs, incorporating Barney into the familiar story of the pine. In her conclusion she justifies the felling of a hundred-year-old pine by Swan and young Bard, in only fifteen minutes, by having Melendy point out that it is dying anyway. The act of expertly felling this symbolic pine becomes a way of acknowledging what is valuable about a distinctively American tradition and of implying a future in which Bard embraces his American heritage. The mood of the final scene is entirely celebratory, with townspeople turning out by the hundreds to observe the spectacle and honor Swan and with Karie, dominating her daughter Lotta for once, summoning people to dinner by calling "Come and get it!" Ferber gave her title a double meaning, alluding to the plundering of the pine forests and the colloquial expression,[7] but in choosing to end her novel with a festive, modern version of the old camp dinner scene she suggested the possibility of separating the spirit of the pioneering lumberjacks from the recklessness and greed she saw in the lumber barons that Barney came to represent. Unlike Walker, she imagines a future for the lumber industry, one free of the vices she associated with the old-style lumber barons, ending on an optimistic and patriotic note likely to appeal to her Depression-era audience.

Walker and Ferber explored the human drama of the aftermath of the great era of logging in the Lake States while acknowledging, from different perspectives, the environmental degradation and waste of resources that it involved. By the time they wrote, the need for reforestation had been broadly accepted, along with the related need to find effective means of controlling wildfires. Government policies regarding taxation and rural zoning encouraged reforestation and timber production. With the increase in tax reversion of cutover lands, state and federal holdings of forestland were growing rapidly, and these lands were beginning to be managed for recreation as well as timber production.[8] The future direction of forest policy, although it would continue to be debated vigorously, had become clearer than it was when Titus wrote *Timber* in the early 1920s, in part because of the influence of Titus's novel on public opinion.

By the end of the nineteenth century the "cut out and get out" philosophy of the pioneering lumbermen had left deep scars on the landscape, including "cleaned" rivers and streams with altered flows and eroded banks. Efforts to make streams usable for logging drives, including dynamiting obstructions and building multiple dams, inevitably affected aquatic life and the health of the watershed, particularly when coupled with logging along the shore. The drives themselves compounded the damage. Jeff Alexander has written about the ways in which logging degraded the Muskegon River, sending great amounts of sand into the stream and making it wider, shallower, and warmer. Fish habitat was buried and spawning beds scoured by logs. David Cassuto has described comparable damage to the Pere Marquette: "The river ... lay in utter ruin, its banks and ecosystem destroyed by the removal of tree cover and the widespread aquatic destruction wrought by the logs, the log jams, and the dynamite used to clear them."[9] The most obvious effects of logging could be seen in the expanses of cutover lands, amounting to more than forty million acres in northern Michigan, Wisconsin, and Minnesota combined.[10] These cutover lands presented scenes of devastation characterized by numerous stumps and snags, slash left by logging operations, and emergent brushy growth, often showing the marks of fire. Comparisons of cutover land with the desolation of World War I battlefields began to appear when images of formerly forested European landscapes laid waste by artillery bombardment became familiar to the public and took hold in the popular imagination.

Boosters of various kinds, including state officials and large landholders such as railroads and lumber companies, had begun to tout the agricultural potential of the cutover lands as early as the late nineteenth century. Their promotional literature appealed to those drawn by visions of developing their own small farms, many of them city dwellers or immigrants. Promoters in the Upper Peninsula, led by the enterprising editor of the Menominee newspaper, began referring to it as Cloverland. A magazine with that title began publishing in 1916, and the Upper Peninsula Development Bureau published a map and history of Cloverland and even a song celebrating northern Michigan as a "land of clover" as well as woods and hills.[11] Cloverland was described as a place where landscapes of stumps could be converted to truck gardens, fields of grain, grazing land for sheep or cattle, or flourishing dairy farms with milk cows thriving where pines once had.[12] Those who were persuaded by this mythologized version of the Upper Peninsula as an agricultural paradise discovered that, although farms might flourish in some places, the sandy soils that grew pines did not so readily grow crops. After a few years of trying, many aspiring farmers found themselves unable to survive financially, eventually losing their land for nonpayment of taxes. Such tax-delinquent land reverted to the state, which in many cases resold it at discounted prices to homesteaders or to speculators who found new buyers so gripped by their dreams of self-sufficiency that they ignored the emerging pattern of failure and repeated the cycle. By 1920 a series of reports and articles had exposed what has been called "the myth that farms follow forests" and had begun to argue for distinguishing between lands fit for agriculture and those more suitable for reforestation.[13] One of the most aggressive of those who challenged the myth, and the related belief that towns would follow the farms, was Titus's friend P. S. Lovejoy, who attacked schemes for developing the cutover lands in articles written for popular magazines beginning in 1919.[14]

In a letter to his publisher suggesting ways to promote *Timber,* Titus argued the need to grow timber as a crop on cutover lands, following long-standing European practice. He cited Gifford Pinchot and the cur-

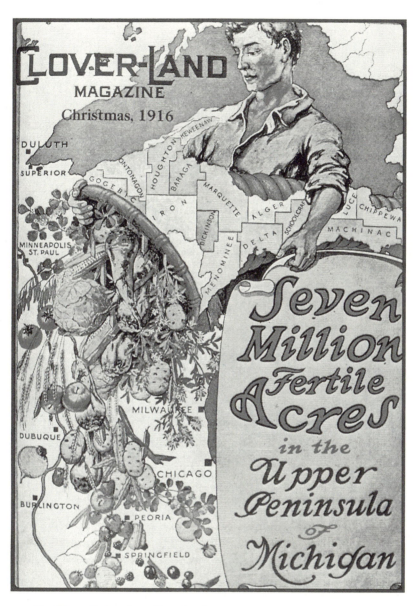

The Upper Peninsula as Cloverland.

rent chief forester William Greeley on the unsustainable rate of consumption of timber in support of the argument that present practices would result in a timber famine. Interestingly, Titus claimed that it was his personal concerns as a sportsman that weighed most heavily on him: "The influences that touched me off were not economic, however. I saw my trout streams going to pot because ransacking lumbermen and neglected forest fires were changing their character: I saw our bird cover in Michigan melting away like snow; I saw lonely pine trees on neglected barrens drop seeds and start a brood which, given a chance would have developed and reproduced again, and then I saw these islands of volunteer pine damaged or licked up by forest fires. . . . That's why I wrote 'Timber!': to show what can be done with land we efficient people call waste land."[15]

Concerns about the prospect of a timber famine had emerged as early as the mid–nineteenth century and were articulated most thoroughly and forcefully by George Perkins Marsh in his influential *Man and Nature* (1864); they were given new impetus when Theodore Roosevelt used the need to avoid a timber famine (as well as to protect watersheds) as a rationale for conserving the nation's forests. By demonstrating in detail how human activity had degraded the natural environment in Europe and was causing similar damage in New England, Marsh encouraged a kind of thinking that questioned the uncritical embrace of progress. He provided the beginnings of a scientific foundation for explaining environmental degradation for those who were troubled by the waste and destructiveness they saw in lumbering operations and the rapid depletion of the forests. One can see the persistence of the agrarian ideal promoted by Thomas Jefferson, who envisioned a nation of yeoman farmers, in continuing justifications of lumbering as preparing the way for agriculture and the society that it would support. White offered a fictionalized version of this kind of justification in *The Riverman* by showing Jack Orde defusing Carroll's objection to his clear-cutting of pines by pointing out the "cultivated countryside" that his lumbering made possible. When White published his Michigan novels in the first decade of the twentieth century, the problem of cutover lands that were not being put to productive use was becoming increasingly apparent in Michigan and the other Lake States. White would come to embrace Gifford Pinchot's vision of a sustainable kind of logging based on scientific forestry, itself part of the broader conservation movement, which responded to the perceived need to protect natural resources on a national scale. Deforestation was one aspect of a larger problem that led to a rethinking of the reflexive embrace of progress, although for Pinchot and other Progressive era advocates of conservation continued development was compatible with responsible stewardship of natural resources. A more radical challenge to assaults on forestlands in the name of progress would come from those who embraced the romantic tradition of emphasizing the aesthetic and spiritual values associated with forests, including advocates of creating more national parks to preserve scenic and monumental landscapes.

By 1920 the need to reforest cutover lands had come to seem inescapable to Titus and others concerned with the future of forests in Michigan and the other Lake States. The related issue of how to control destructive forest fires had assumed a comparable sense of urgency by the time Titus wrote *Timber*. Fire was an ancient way of clearing land, used as late as the 1920s by settlers who were reluctant to give it up. Immigrants had brought with them from Europe the practice of swidden (slash and burn) agriculture and continued to fire their fields in the spring and fall to burn stubble and reduce disease. They could find a local precedent in the habitual use of fire by native tribes (Indian burning) to clear fields and reduce brush as a way of improving conditions for hunting. With the spread of railroads in the late nineteenth century, wood-burning locomotives became an additional cause of fires, in this case accidental ones started by stray sparks. Lightning had always triggered forest fires in dry conditions, and the influx of settlers and the proliferation of railroad lines multiplied the risk of fire. By the latter part of the nineteenth century, settlers had become accustomed to haze and smoke from numerous small fires, particularly in the dry conditions of late summer and early fall. For the most part these fires burned themselves out or were brought under control by rudimentary fire brigades when they threatened towns. But in 1871, and at intervals thereafter, a combination of exceptionally dry conditions, strong winds, and the accumulation of highly combustible slash resulting from logging created circumstances that led to wildfires on a scale that no one had previously seen or imagined, firestorms or "holocaust" fires that destroyed whole towns and took hundreds of lives. The most destructive of the huge fires of 1871 was one that swept through eastern Wisconsin in early October and came to be known as the Peshtigo fire, for the town near the Michigan border that suffered the most devastating losses.

In the case of Peshtigo, two separate fires converged south of the town, spawning a "mass fire" that generated its own weather, with high winds, vortices that created fire whorls, and floating bubbles of hot gas that exploded and started new fires ahead of the advancing wall of flames.[16] A Catholic missionary, Abbe Pernin, who survived along with others who managed to immerse themselves in the Peshtigo River, described witnessing a surreal scene: "Turning my looks from the river, I saw on the right hand and on the left that the firmament showed nothing but fire. Everything was on fire—the houses, the trees, and the atmosphere itself. Above my head, as far as my vision could penetrate space, alas! Too clearly, I could see nothing but flames, immense billows of flame that covered the whole sky, and rolled one upon another, as if violently agitated, as we see clouds driven in a storm—a sea of waves and a horrible tempest of fire."[17] Some who could not get to the river survived by pressing their faces to the earth in plowed fields. Others suffocated in dry wells or cellars where they thought they would be safe or were incinerated, either in their houses or on roads trying to outrun the flames. Some fifteen hundred people are estimated to have died in the Peshtigo fire, which spread across Green Bay to the Door Peninsula and reached north into Michigan, leaping the Menominee River; floating balls of fire ignited an island half a mile offshore in Lake Michigan.[18] The town of Peshtigo and its surrounding forests and farmsteads were completely destroyed in what remains the most deadly fire in U.S. history.

The great Chicago fire had broken out two days before the Peshtigo fire and claimed the nation's attention. Although Wisconsin authorities quickly mobilized relief efforts, it took longer for the scale and destructiveness of the Peshtigo fire to become widely known. The same weather conditions that triggered the Wisconsin fires produced firestorms in Michigan, on both coasts of the Lower Peninsula, that consumed three times as much forested land as the Peshtigo fire, some 2.5 million acres, but claimed fewer lives and drew less attention outside the state.[19] The 1871 fires in Michigan's Thumb area destroyed a string of villages along the Lake Huron shore and were described by eyewitnesses in terms similar to those used of the Peshtigo fire. The *Detroit Tribune* for October 11, 1871, reported an eyewitness account that describes hurricane winds and a sound from the approaching fire like the roar of the sea: "The flame, as it arose, drew in the surrounding atmosphere, already parched and heated in extreme degree, until it became a tornado of fire, sweeping everything before it."[20] Those who could took refuge in Lake Huron. Another firestorm erupted in the same area in September of 1881 during similar weather conditions and was even more devastating, burning over two thousand square miles and claiming 280 lives, with winds so strong that they uprooted trees and flames moving fast enough to overtake fleeing horses.[21]

The Great Fire at Peshtigo. (Reprinted from *Harper's Weekly,* November 4, 1871.)

Fires continued to plague Michigan and the other Lake States, with recurrent forest fires in the Upper Peninsula burning many thousands of acres. In late August of 1896 a firestorm destroyed the town of Ontonagon on the Lake Superior shore along with the surrounding forests and the mill and large stores of stacked lumber of the Diamond Match Company. One of the most notable fires in Michigan devastated the village of Metz along with two hundred thousand acres in Presque Isle County in the northeastern Lower Peninsula in October of 1908. There people crowded into a train, sent to rescue as many as possible, which took them away through burning woods until the wooden cars caught fire and the train itself went off warped rails. Some were able to get out and save themselves in plowed fields, but fourteen died in a burning gondola car. Other train rescues were more successful, most famously one that saved close to three hundred people from the Hinckley, Minnesota, fire of 1895 when a locomotive backed up for four miles with cars catching fire and windows shattering until it reached a shallow pond where the passengers were able to survive as the fire roared over them. The escape, and the engineer who kept the train going in a burning cab with the help of a fireman who repeatedly doused him with water, became the subject of ballads.

Numerous stories of miraculous survivals and horrific deaths survive from the period of the holocaust fires, some recorded in verse, such as a ballad recounting the deaths of all five members of the McDonald family in the Thumb fire of 1871.[22] A lurid poem by George Angus Belding, "Holocaust," describes men in the fields buffeted by a hot gale, then hearing "a sound as of surf on stone," and shortly after seeing a red wall of flame swiftly coming from the south, like a ravenous "dragon of fire." Animals flee the forest in panic and pines writhe in flames that reach the treetops as others explode and crash to the earth. In Belding's superheated verse, "Torture and death were abroad in the land." He describes the flames as leaving nothing but "blackened sand," his way of rendering the phenomenon of fires so intense that they burned through the topsoil.[23]

Belding's poem may have been prompted by the Metz fire in his home county of Presque Isle, but he could have been writing about virtually any of the holocaust fires. Others personified such fires as demonic and strained for figurative language that would convey their astonishing effects. The roar of approaching fire reminded some of the sea, others of locomotives or artillery. Whirlwinds caused by convection, which caught up burning debris, seemed to one observer of the Peshtigo fire like waterspouts of fire.[24] The conditions produced by these fires were so unexpected and terrifying—including darkness caused by thick smoke, roaring and whirlwinds, and fire streaming through the air—that they caused many to believe that the Day of Judgment had come and left them helpless before what seemed to them an act of God.[25] Holocaust fires that devastated populated areas continued into the early twentieth century in the Lake States, ending with the Cloquet fire, which largely destroyed a center of lumbering activity twenty miles west of Duluth in 1918. Cloquet suffered the fate of other towns with sawmills when the winds generated by firestorms picked up stacked lumber and hurled burning planks through the air. If Titus and others concerned with the problem of getting forest fires under control needed a reminder of the devastation such fires could cause, the Cloquet fire would have provided it.

In *Timber*, Titus made fire the great natural adversary rather than the floods that threatened the logging drives of White's Michigan novels and addressed the problem of how to create a basis for sustainable logging in a time when the pine was largely depleted and logging no longer seemed a heroic enterprise. One journalist who read the version of *Timber* serialized in *Everybody's Magazine* as "Foraker's Folly" wrote Titus to ask whether he could use it for an article comparing the novel with White's *The Blazed Trail*, which he saw as portraying "the height of the timbering industry in Michigan": "'Foraker's Folly' chants the requiem for that romantic period and lights the way for a new era."[26] The outdoor writer Ben East credited *Timber* with doing "more than any other single factor between 1920 and 1925 . . . to create a popular demand for better ways of dealing with the problems of cutover lands and forest fires."[27] The novel's emphasis on the promise of reforestation, and on the deceptions of land speculators and civic boosters who promoted the use of cutover land for agriculture, reflects arguments made by the emerging forestry establishment at the time, including those of Titus's friend Lovejoy. Titus dramatized the devastating effects of fire by having a raging forest fire precipitate the resolution of his narrative, in that way addressing the other primary concern of foresters. A feature film based on *Timber* produced by Louis B. Mayer, *Hearts Aflame*, helped to convince the Michigan legislature to begin appropriating money to fight forest fires. The fact that the film invented a scene in which hero and heroine drive a locomotive through the flames to rescue trapped villagers, recalling well-publicized escapes and attempted escapes from horrendous firestorms by train, could not have hurt.[28]

Titus went on to become a leader in conservation politics, appointed by two different governors to the Michigan Conservation Commission, where he pursued his campaign for fire suppression as chairman of the fire committee. He continued to write about conservation issues, most notably in a series of articles in *Field and Stream* in the early 1930s, for which he invented the persona of the "Old Warden."[29] By presenting these issues in the form of discussions around the woodstove in a hardware store or in local gun club meetings, with the Old Warden listening patiently and then intervening to tell a decisive story or invoke "this man Leopold" on strategies for nurturing game, Titus found an effective way to convey the latest theories of game management to ordinary readers. The

Old Warden debunks common complaints and misunderstandings and shares information in an engagingly colloquial style. The series displays Titus's own sportsman's instincts and, in a piece on the Civilian Conservation Corps (CCC), a concern with reconciling the interests of sportsmen and foresters not apparent in *Timber* and his other fiction dealing with forestry issues. The Old Warden, while defending the tree-planting and thinning activities of the CCC, chides foresters who "think of a forest only as so many cubic feet of wood" and wants to see states planning their forests "so they'll grow more fish and game along with their trees."[30] By the 1930s, with forest fires more effectively controlled and the need for reforestation established, Titus could indulge his long-standing interest in the state of hunting and fishing.

Early in *Timber* Titus presents a version of the familiar stump scene that underscores the extent of the destruction caused by the early wave of logging and magnified by subsequent fires. It registers a moral judgment that anticipates the attitude Jim Harrison associates with his narrator David Burkett in *True North*. The scene, which reflects Titus's travels in the area of the Manistee River in the western Lower Peninsula, as well as in the country around his Traverse City home, reveals pine plains (also called pine barrens) stretching for miles, with clumps of jack pine and deciduous trees punctuating a landscape dominated by large pine stumps: "All about stood stumps, big stumps, close together, rotted by time and blackened by fire, ugly and desolate, but marking the places where within the generation mighty pine had reared their ragged plumes in dignified congregation. The same black that was on the stumps was on living trees, too; whole halves had been eaten from the butts of oak by creeping flames; smaller oaks, fire-killed, stood black and dead, while a clump of fresh brush rose from the living roots."[31] For Titus the scene epitomizes "the ruin that was where a forest had been" (28), not just any forest but one of "mighty" pine in "dignified congregation," idealized in recollection.

The devastated landscape exemplifies the kind of land that unscrupulous real estate speculators were luring would-be farmers into buying. Titus dramatizes this process through a melodramatic story of the financial ruin and near starvation of a young couple, the Parkers, who leave office jobs in Chicago to pursue their dream of living on the land but discover that they cannot make the pine barrens produce agricultural crops. Their disillusionment, combined with the loss of their malnourished baby, destroys Jenny Parker's will to live and leads to her decline and death. Her deathbed denunciation of the "shark" who sold them their land, the power company lawyer and developer Jim Harris, establishes Harris as the principal villain of the novel. Helen Foraker, summoned to her bedside by Jenny to hear her story and receive her blessing of Helen's efforts to redeem the land by replanting pines, emerges early in the novel as his moral opposite and the antagonist he must defeat to realize his ambitions.

Titus portrays Helen Foraker as the heroine who hopes to reclaim the cutover land by reconstituting a forest of white pine, over time, and ultimately establishing a self-sustaining forest business. Foraker's Folly, as it is known by skeptical locals, consists of ten thousand acres bought by Helen's father in the mid-1870s, almost fifty years prior to the time of the action of the novel, and developed by him according to principles of the new European forestry. Titus describes his library as containing forestry journals and shelves of books on silviculture, including many in French and German, and presents his experiment as a model for reformers that draws visiting forestry scientists from Europe and the University of Michigan. Helen's fierce dedication to realizing her father's vision, and her skill and decisiveness in managing and defending the forest, make her a strikingly different kind of heroine from the women of White's Michigan novels. She plays a role more nearly comparable to those of White's heroes Thorpe and Orde, though in a very different kind of drama. This turns on challenges to her long-term program of restoration from local antagonists who try to force her to sell by attempting to raise her taxes and otherwise harassing her and, ultimately, from a formidable natural force, in this case a potentially devastating forest fire rather than a river in flood. White shows his frontier heroes relying on manly virtues to defeat natural forces and an array of human antagonists. Titus's Helen, who rivals Thorpe and Orde in her tenacity and capacity for leadership, is sustained by her knowledge of forestry and her vision of a different kind of forest. She knows her success will be measured by her ability to nurture her "baby pines" to the point where they become part of a continuously productive forest, with new pines maturing to replace those that are cut.

Titus represents the pioneering days of logging primarily through the figure of Luke Taylor, retired to Florida in his old age but driven by the need to relive the exploits of his early days of logging "cork" pine and driving the Saginaw River by discovering more Michigan white pine to cut. Titus makes Luke a caricature of the self-made lumber baron, obsessed with the past and arrogantly dismissive of changing attitudes toward logging. He angrily rejects the label of destroyer, as a slander of his sort by "old women," along with any concern for the next generation: "Didn't Michi-

gan Pine build the corn belt? . . . Didn't Michigan Pine build cities that
make the country wealthy?" (5). Helen, explaining her commitment to
restoration to Luke's son John, supplies what amounts to Titus's answer to
the kind of justification of the logging boom offered by Luke, itself a
cruder version of the appeal to progress made by Orde: "Oh, we were
Prussians, we Americans! We were ruthless, heedless. All we saw was
forests and a market for their products, so we butchered" (123). Luke's
ruthlessness and greed manifest themselves in the novel when he learns of
Helen's ten thousand acres of white pine, not yet mature but large enough
to cut, and resolves to gain control of them however he can. His resolve
leads indirectly to various acts of sabotage perpetrated by Harris and others acting on his behalf, culminating in the setting of a fire that threatens
Helen's whole forest.

Luke's son John Taylor has come to the area in which the novel is set,
in the vicinity of the Au Sable River, in response to his father's challenge to
prove his business ability by salvaging timber on one of his properties.
The challenge reflects Luke's cynicism about his well-educated but
untested son's business ability, since he knows, as John does not, that it
will be difficult if not impossible to get the abandoned timber to market
because the rail line connecting the area with the mill has been disman-
tled. Titus shows John gradually won to Helen's cause by her personal
force, impressive business sense, and knowledge of forestry combined
with his growing attraction to her as a woman. The love story can develop
because Helen reveals a need for John's emotional support at times of
great stress, finding refuge in the "sanctuary" of his arms when he offers
promises of protection from her enemies. After a misunderstanding about
his plans for the forest, which estranges her, John proves his loyalty and
love by acting manfully in her defense, giving his father's conniving secretary Rowe a beating when he threatens Helen and working behind the
scenes to thwart schemes to force her to sell. If Titus falls back at critical
moments on the formula of strong man and dependent woman, he more
often shows Helen breaking with conventional expectations regarding a
woman's role by demonstrating her superior abilities. John succeeds in
transporting his father's logs to the mill by river only through Helen's
guidance and active help, after realizing how much he has to learn from
her about the timber business. She also displays self-confidence and a capacity for heroic action under stress, most remarkably through the leadership she exercises in rallying her men to defeat the fire that threatens her
forest.

Titus shows this fire overwhelming the efforts of Helen and the men she marshals to try to contain it with homemade fire extinguishers, fire lines, and backfires. He portrays it as an irresistible force once it reaches the crowns of the trees and begins to rain embers on the men, who drop their tools and run: "Fire, man's first friend, had turned into his raging enemy, mighty in its wrath, terrible in its manifestation of power" (348). Once the fire reaches the swale where Helen has determined to make a final stand it races through a balsam thicket and down one side with "triumphant" ripping and tearing sounds "against the background of savage roar" (352). By personifying the fire as demonic, a "fiend" exulting in its power, Titus magnifies its challenge and evokes the firestorms that had periodically terrorized the pineries. He characterizes Helen as a general rallying her troops for one last effort and refusing to let them give up when the battle appears to be lost. Her saving inspiration to dynamite the sandy ridge on the other side of the swale as a last-ditch measure proves decisive, as she persuades the men to risk their lives stringing the dynamite along a two-hundred-yard stretch and then watches as the explosion buries the center of the fire in tons of sand, reducing it to disorganized remnants that can be controlled. Her effort recalls that of Orde in White's *The Riverman*, rallying his men to contain the force of the river, which threatens to scatter his logs into Lake Michigan. Titus transformed the kind of frontier hero that White had popularized into a fearless heroine acting in the service of conservation. He suggests that Helen is able to summon extraordinary energy and exercise cool and unwavering leadership throughout the ordeal of the fire because of the strength of her vision of a restored forest that perpetually renews itself.

Helen faces a series of challenges prior to the climactic one of the forest fire and needs the help of a paternal, small-town newspaper editor and state senator, Hump Bryant, as well as that of John Taylor, to meet them. The most important of these challenges involves a plan engineered by Harris and the township supervisor, Sim Burns, a rejected suitor turned vindictive, to finance a new county courthouse and additional roads that will serve Harris's development by raising the assessed valuation of Helen Foraker's property. The scheme reflects actual ones employed by townships to take advantage of absentee timberland owners, another practice that concerned Titus and one that would subsequently be addressed by the Michigan legislature. Hump Bryant is able to defeat this scheme at the last minute by addressing the meeting of county supervisors ready to vote for the necessary bond issue and producing evidence that they have all been bribed by the power company to ignore the fact that its own properties are drastically underassessed. Bryant gets his chance only because a plan devised by John and executed by Black Joe, a longtime employee of Helen and her father (who is actually swarthy rather than black), delays Harris's return to the supervisors' meeting after lunch by tricking him into listening to a fantastic Paul Bunyan story about a giant cornstalk.

Titus made Joe an idealized version of the classic lumberjack and a loyal worker who also happens to be a skilled storyteller. He delights those who hear him hold forth from the "deacon's bench" in the men's "shanty" on Helen's property, pointedly excluding Harris and anyone else of whom he disapproves. Harris is unable to resist the opportunity to hear a story when Joe finally offers it, despite his need to get back to the meeting. Joe establishes the slow, deliberate pace that had become traditional for such stories, allowing for listeners' questions and spinning out digressions and plot complications that put off the conclusion. In his story an emissary arrives from Congress with a warrant for Paul's arrest because the roots of his cornstalk are draining Lake Huron and Lake Michigan, stranding boats; fifty broadax men fail to bring down the stalk because it grows faster than they can cut. By the time Joe finally reaches the climax of the story, in which Paul pinches off the stalk with quarter-mile-long rails that he strips from his logging railroad, Harris has lingered so long that the supervisors have adjourned the meeting without acting, having been scared off by Bryant. Titus's plot device, improbable though it may seem, has the effect of showing the slick-talking speculator ironically undone by his fascination with the tale telling of the old-time lumberjack, who cannily exploits Harris's curiosity about a tradition that has more vitality than anything in his own world of moneymaking schemes. Joe functions in the novel as something of a hero himself, an authentic "woodsman" who can call on his old skills as a river driver in the push to get John's logs to the mill and yet embrace Helen's conservationist agenda, devoting himself to tending the young forest and the nursery in which pine seedlings are raised to be transplanted. Like Ferber and others who reassessed the logging era, Titus could find virtue in the individual lumberjack while condemning the greed and short-sightedness of his bosses.

When a bullying Luke Taylor finally confronts Helen directly, in a scene near the end of the novel interrupted by an urgent summons that takes her away to fight the fire, he is aware that she is unable to make a pending mortgage payment and confident that he can force her to sell. She refuses to buckle, responding with a vigorous and ultimately successful appeal to him to invest in her property, thereby enabling her to wait to begin to log it until the timber is "ripe." She would then log only two hundred acres a year, an amount that would enable her to carry the investment, by this practice ensuring the "continuous output" that had become the goal of foresters and extending the life of the forest indefinitely. Titus makes her a proxy for the kind of progressive, scientifically informed forestry that he opposes to the old practice of cutting whole stands of pine at once, thus creating more ravaged landscapes of stumps. He asks his readers to believe that Luke can be convinced to "take a chance with [her]" because he admires her nerve and her command of the economics of logging, as well as the mettle that she demonstrates in successfully fighting the fire, and, surprisingly, because Helen persuades him to see the renewed forest as something in which he can take pleasure. The last reason is the most interesting, in that it suggests a way of reconciling seemingly opposed uses of the forest for emotional satisfaction and economic benefit.

Titus establishes Luke's susceptibility to the emotional appeal of the forest in a scene that shows him finally opening himself to it. When he enters Helen's pine woods, he reflexively steps off a quarter acre and estimates the yield, then walks on to the riverbank where he gradually relaxes and allows himself to respond to the aesthetic appeal and the sensuous stimulation of the place: from the bark of a pine he touches, the wind in the tops of the trees, the song of a white-throated sparrow, the murmuring of the river gleaming in the sunlight. Titus, with an explicitness with which he typically renders emotion, describes Luke as unconsciously allowing "sentiment" to break through the walls he has built against it as he indulges the play of his senses, then wrenching himself abruptly back to the present and his preoccupation with "board feet." Helen has observed the scene without Luke's knowledge and relies on her awareness of his susceptibility to the sensuous appeal of the woods in making her final argument to him one based on emotion. In it she suggests he can find a "contentment" he has missed since his early logging days by participating in the new, sustainable kind of logging that she envisions, linking this contentment with the emotional response to the forest she has seen in him. She shrewdly evokes scenes and sensations associated with logging that she knows that Luke would have experienced in the past, conjuring up his future pleasure in seeing cork pine floating in the water and smelling the "resin blisters" raised on the logs by the sun (340).

Titus implies that such contentment, from participating in a different kind of logging in a pine forest that can always be enjoyed because the forest will last "forever," can displace the greed that formerly drove Luke and others like him to cut as much as they could with no regard for the future. He shows Luke redeemed by a surprising willingness to trust Helen and her vision, conditioning his support on her agreement that he can come up when he wants and "listen to 'em talk" (363), his way of reconnecting with his early experience of logging pine. By conflating the pleasures of sensuous enjoyment of the forest with those inherent in the work of lumbering, as Helen describes it, Titus makes the aesthetic and psychological appeal of the forest seem inseparable from progressive management of it as an economic resource. What he does not acknowledge is the difference between the complex old-growth forest found by the early loggers and the new one that Helen is nurturing, which amounts to a pine plantation.

Titus describes the young forest as consisting of ranks of small, nearly uniform pines about a foot in diameter with cleared strips (fire lanes) at regular intervals (35, 71). The pine forest is thickly planted with pines that appear even aged, although we learn that Joe regularly sets out seedlings. While Luke recognizes that these are not the massive pines he knew but "baby pine" that will yield only two sawlogs instead of four or five, he is nonetheless delighted at seeing such a dense forest of white pine: "It was solid, without a Norway, without a hardwood tree in sight" (317). What he celebrates is a monoculture, without even red (Norway) pines or the hardwoods among which stands of white pine normally would have been found. The fact that these young trees whisper in the breeze, allowing him to imagine the white pines he used to know, is enough to revive the old feelings. Titus championed the ideal of scientific management represented by European forestry (Helen cites the example of Sihlwald in Zurich to make her point that a forest can be sustained for centuries) and saw this as the key to a revived lumber industry and the productive use of Michigan's cutover lands. Helen's orderly forest is a model of efficiency, dedicated solely to the production of timber. Recognition of the value of a more diverse forest, functioning as a healthy ecosystem, would have to wait until later, as would recognition of the potential ecological value of fire. For Titus and his contemporaries, as for the Forest Service of the time, forest fire was simply a destructive natural force that threatened the recovery of forests and had to be brought under control.[32]

In *Timber* Titus foreshadows the triumph of Helen's vision by showing John Taylor experiencing his own epiphany after hearing her long explanation of the origins and purpose of Foraker's Folly. As he subsequently walks through her pine forest at night it comes alive for him, assuming a dynamism that he associates with its future productivity. His new sense of the life of the forest grows out of a recognition of the idealism of Helen's struggle to reclaim waste land without regard to material gain for herself, and of the pettiness of his own ambition to prove himself to his father and secure his financial future. This recognition precipitates a decision to ally himself with Helen and attempt to undo some of the devastation by which his father made his fortune. He embraces the new standard of heroism that she represents, which is more credible to the reader because Titus makes her struggle emblematic of the larger battle over the future of former forestlands in Michigan and elsewhere.

In Helen's view stripping the forests from millions of acres of land produced a devastation like that of World War I, a particularly apt analogy for an audience in the early 1920s. Titus presents her as engaged in a prototypical act of re-creation, making ruined land productive again, not by attempting to convert it to agriculture but by restoring the white pines that were Michigan's natural heritage. Helen explicitly rejects "sentiment" as a motivation for restoring forests, displaying practical business sense about the profit necessary to sustain the investment involved in reforestation. She also communicates a sense of urgency owing to the "timber famine" that she perceives: "Logs, lumber, forest products are the foundation of national life" (124). Her extended justifications of her vision, to John and subsequently to his father Luke, serve as vehicles for Titus's progressive agenda. They reassert the importance of the lumber industry to the development of the country, with the difference that they assume timber resources must be managed in a way that will ensure they last. In using Helen's story to suggest the power of a forward-looking and determined individual to reclaim the land and bring about a new kind of forest management Titus offered a utopian vision of the future of Michigan's forests. In fact, their management would become increasingly centralized, for public lands the job of professionals working for the state government (and the Forest Service in the case of Michigan's national forests).[33]

Making the case for restoration through Helen's story enabled Titus to give her forest the kind of presence that it assumes for Luke, when he walks into it and finds himself coming alive emotionally for the first time since his early experiences in the woods, as well as for John, when he senses its promise after falling under the influence of Helen's vision. Titus sets the stage for her persuasive elaboration of this vision as she and John sit on the riverbank by describing the vitality of the reviving June landscape with its greening sedges and ferns, tremulous young leaves, birdsong, and new needles seeking the light in the pine forest (115). The sense of joyousness and benevolence with which Titus invests the landscape helps to explain Helen's faith in the promise of the forest and John's susceptibility to her persuasion. Titus suggests this benevolence again in an idyllic scene that brings John and Helen together on the river. She holds their canoe steady while he fly-fishes in the cool, sweet air of late afternoon: "The water above them was old rose, like the sky, and a faintly violet mist hung over the stream, blending with the bottle-green of pine trees" (182). Such scenes imply that Helen's vision is inseparable from her aesthetic response to the landscape, despite her rejection of "sentiment" and her businesslike embrace of efficiency in managing her forest. For the Titus who responded to the degradation of favorite trout streams, restoring Michigan's pines was a way of recovering an important part of its natural heritage whatever other purposes it served, and appreciating this heritage depended on an ability to respond to its aesthetic and emotional appeal.

The sense of a harmonious and easy relationship with the landscape apparent in these river scenes contrasts with the exploitation of the land demonstrated in different ways by Jim Harris and by Luke Taylor, before he softens under Helen's influence and that of the forest itself. The novel's conclusion offers another manifestation of this harmony in which the benediction of the pines seems to affirm Helen's vision. The conclusion follows a final demonstration of Helen's heroism when she rescues John from an attack by her dangerous pet wolf dog, released by her foreman and jealous suitor Milt, and seals the reconciliation of the two: "Behind them the Blueberry [River] hurled itself at the high bank and above, between them and the clouds that sped across the brilliant sky, the canopy of pine trees that would never be of the past spread their peaceful shadow over the two, like a blessing" (379). The denouement is framed by a romantic vision of the personified pine forest, its future assured by the fact that Helen now has the financial security to practice the kind of forestry she has been advocating. The earlier, mistaken view that Michigan's forests were inexhaustible has been replaced by her vision of a forest that can be managed in such a way that it will indeed last forever. The closing scene of *Timber* represents the culmination of Titus's efforts in the novel to fuse the emotional appeal of the forest, expressed here in the peacefulness with which it seems to envelop the lovers, with a scientifically informed design for restoring and logging it. By evoking the romance of the pines, here and elsewhere in the novel, Titus implies that we can have a thriving timber industry without sacrificing the beauty of the forest. Helen's vision neatly reconciles economic and aesthetic values.

Titus saw the potential of fiction to popularize the case for restoring pine forests on cutover lands in ways that neither his journalism, as a reporter for the *Detroit News,* nor academic papers and popular articles by foresters could have. He was able to engage the public and influence legislators and state officials by juxtaposing Helen Foraker's struggles with speculators, outmoded attitudes toward logging, and a potentially disastrous forest fire with her vision of restoring Michigan's white pine on waste land. Three years after *Timber* appeared James B. Hendryx published *Connie Morgan with the Forest Rangers* (1925), one in a series of eight novels for boys featuring the triumphs of an invincible young hero in Alaska and subsequently in the timber country of Minnesota and Michigan.[34] Hendryx was a popular and prolific writer of novels and stories set mainly in the Yukon Territory and the American West who became a friend and fishing buddy of Titus after settling in the Traverse City area. The fact that he would make the plot of a novel in his well-known Connie Morgan series turn on efforts to restore pine on cutover land suggests the reach of the theme of reforestation in the 1920s.

Hendryx set *Connie Morgan with the Forest Rangers* in the fictional former logging town of Pine Tree, Michigan, located in the western Lower Peninsula, telling his readers that there are a hundred more like it where the timber has been "skinned off."[35] The locals illegally burn the pine plains around the town every year to stimulate the growth of blueberries, in the process preventing the natural regeneration of the forest by suppressing brush that normally would shade emerging pine and other seedlings and keep out grass. Connie's adviser in his plan to regenerate the forest and establish a sustainable lumber business is a seasoned forester, McLaren, who makes a case for the scientific logging of township lands and argues that this is a way of conserving game for sportsmen while still allowing timber production (89). An older resident, Whitlock, deplores the gray stumps that mark the landscape as "the graveyard of the forest" (59), allowing trees to grow back on his own land and arguing that restored forests and natural features such as a lake and river will draw tourists to the area. Hendryx uses McLaren and Whitlock to offer complementary arguments for renewing the forest, one based on forestry science and the other rooted in memory of the land's past and an aversion to its continuing degradation. Both function as spokesmen for the recreational potential of restored forestlands.

With characteristic ingenuity and daring Connie defeats both the hostile locals and a predictably villainous lumber baron, Crump, who denounces conservation and proclaims his indifference to future generations. Crump's plan is to strip the land, after gaining control of it and its timber one way or another. After various schemes fail, he tells his men to "burn him [Connie] out" by setting a fire in the swamp that will spread to threaten the remaining timber. As in Titus's *Timber*, a raging forest fire precipitates the resolution of the novel by calling forth an act of heroism. In this case, Connie boldly dynamites a dam, releasing a flood that drowns the fire before it can do major damage. After rounding up the villains, he succeeds in buying the contested land himself (twenty-three thousand acres) and employs McLaren to develop a plan for regenerating the forest and sustainably logging it. We are left with the assurance that the burned-over pine plains, with their vistas of blackened stumps, will be used for something besides agriculture and blueberry picking and that the locals of Pine Tree will prosper in the revived economy.

Hendryx went so far as to present reforestation as the key to the moral, as well as economic, recovery of the area. The sheriff attributes the moral deterioration of the most influential and also the most corrupt of the locals, Clayt Mimms, to the decline of the lumber industry in which he and others worked: "I know that the reforestation of the cut-over would save more souls than all the missionaries could." Hendryx shows Mimms transformed by the hard labor of cleaning up the slash from cedar he has stolen from the swamp, a form of penance insisted on by Connie. Through this enforced labor Mimms regains his physical fitness, as well as his former sense of moral purpose, and subsequently begins a new life in the woods as the foreman of a timber crew working for Connie. If Hendryx offers a simplistic and overly optimistic view of the promise of reforestation, his fiction nonetheless points, with that of Titus, to the direction that Michigan would take in recovering and charting the future of its forestlands. By turning a boys' adventure story into a moral tale about the benefits of restoring Michigan's forests, he contributed to popularizing the redemption of cutover lands for a broader audience.

Hendryx introduced issues that do not come into play in any significant way for Titus in *Timber*, notably the use of reforested lands to provide habitat for game and to promote tourism generally. Titus subsequently addressed the potential for tourism in a novel and in a story about the emergence of a river town as a destination for sportsmen, but he clearly felt the need to focus on reforestation and the problems surrounding it in *Timber*. He found an effective way of doing this by dramatizing the struggles of Helen Foraker and her vision of making the cutover land pay by growing pine as a crop.[36] Her strict adherence to contemporary aims and methods of forestry in nurturing a uniform and highly regulated kind of forest, however, would seem less obviously exemplary when questions about the use of regenerated forests became more complicated. Commercial logging—whether of pine, hardwoods, or aspen and other species used for pulpwood—would become one of a number of competing uses that would shift in relative importance as different constituencies for them emerged. Given the economic arguments for timber production from public lands, and the fact that the budgets of agencies responsible for managing them would become linked to the amount of timber they produced, this use would continue to dominate. But the conviction that the highest use of public forestland was to guarantee a sustainable supply of timber grew out of a particular historical moment when concerns about a looming timber famine were high and the rise of scientific forestry appeared to offer the answer to questions about how to reclaim degraded land. The Forest Service and state agencies charged with managing public lands, most of whose employees were trained in silviculture, would continue to view guaranteeing the continuous production of timber as their primary concern, but they would find themselves forced to recognize rapidly growing public interest in a wide range of recreational uses of forests. Those primarily interested in hunting and fishing or automobile touring or hiking and camping were more concerned with maintaining aesthetically appealing forests that offer habitat for wildlife than with keeping lumber mills busy.

6 // The Forest as Playground

Harold Titus and James B. Hendryx anticipated the commitment to sustainable forestry that would be institutionalized in government agencies, and Hendryx's references to the suitability of forestlands for game and tourism mirrored the policy of multiple use that informed national forestry planning and would come to guide planning for the recovery and management of Michigan's public forestlands. A network of state forests and game areas, parks, and protected natural areas would evolve gradually as the state took possession of tax-reverted lands and purchased others, with an escalation of acquisitions in the 1930s.[1] National forests would become part of the mix of public lands, with large holdings in the northern Lower Peninsula (now the Huron-Manistee National Forests) and the Upper Peninsula (the Hiawatha and Ottawa National Forests). Foresters charged with managing Michigan's regenerating state forests grew and planted seedlings, thinned young stands to produce larger trees, and improved fire control, beginning these efforts in the first decade of the twentieth century and accelerating them as funding permitted. They practiced a kind of active management designed to produce timber and other forest products, following the principles of European forestry that Titus used the example of Helen Foraker to illustrate.

From 1933 to 1942 the Civilian Conservation Corps gave these and other management activities a powerful boost, with CCC workers in camps throughout Michigan building roads and fire towers, establishing public campgrounds in state forests, thinning hardwoods, and planting almost five hundred million trees. The most visible result of their planting was the proliferation of red pine plantations, which presented a striking departure from the mixed forests that predominated before the timber boom. In the 1940s Michigan's timber production would jump sharply in response to wartime needs, drawing on maturing second-growth forests. As Michigan's public forests regenerated, and could be relied on for regulated and sustainable timber production, expectations about a high level of production became established and were codified by the legislature. At the same time the demand for recreational uses of these forestlands continued to grow. Theodore Roosevelt and his Forest Service chief, Gifford Pinchot, had recognized the potential of the national forests for recreation, Pinchot in the 1907 *Use Book* for forest rangers, where he acknowledged that the forests "serve a good purpose as great playgrounds for the people . . . campers, hunters, fishermen, and thousands of pleasure seekers from the near-by towns."[2] Recreational use of the forests had risen sharply by the 1920s and became an increasingly important priority, recognized in Michigan by a major expansion of state campgrounds. The needs of recreational users have always had to compete, however, with those of timber and mining interests, supported by politicians who have often been slower to see the economic potential of recreational tourism than that of traditional extractive industries. The story of the growth of recreational use of public forests is marked by continuing tension between those concerned with protecting habitat for wildlife and gaining increased access through trails and facilities and foresters primarily concerned with managing forestland for the production of timber and wood products. As recreational use has escalated and new kinds of uses have emerged, tensions among different kinds of recreational users have become part of the story as well.

A debate between foresters and sportsmen that took place in the 1940s illustrates the kind of struggle between recreational users and managers that has increasingly shaped the development of Michigan's forests. State game areas had been designated in the 1920s and a Game Division created under the new Department of Conservation, precursor of the present Department of Natural Resources (DNR), in recognition of public interest in hunting.[3] In the 1940s sportsmen expressed concern about the loss of forest openings, prime habitat for sharp-tailed grouse and prairie chickens, as forests grew back. Foresters resisted setting aside potential forestland to be managed for prairie birds, species that for the most part had moved in from the west after massive logging and the fires that followed it, but in the end the sportsmen's interests prevailed. Maps were developed to guide the management of openings, and the state began controlled burns and applications of herbicide to preserve habitat for prairie birds, along with a program of stocking sharp-tailed grouse in the Upper Peninsula to build a sustainable population.[4] The DNR currently maintains sharp-tailed grouse habitat (grassland and mixed grassland and shrubland) on the eastern end of the Upper Peninsula through rotational clear-cuts.[5]

The dominant recreational uses that emerged as priorities for public forestlands were hunting and fishing, tourism (particularly as this surged with the widespread availability of automobiles and the expanding network of roads created to serve them), and exploration of the forest, the latter initially on foot or horseback and later on skis or mountain bikes or by machine (snowmobiles and off-road vehicles). The economic impact of such uses of public forests, on surrounding communities and state economies more generally, magnifies the influence of recreational users on forest policy, as does their ability to generate political pressure. I am primarily concerned, however, with their influence on ways of perceiving the forest (as a place for sport or adventure, a refuge from the pressures of contemporary life, a source of aesthetic pleasure, or a means of achieving physical or spiritual regeneration) and thus on ways of valuing it other than the utilitarian ones (supplying timber, protecting watersheds) that served as the rationale for setting aside the forest reserves that established the concept of public forestland.

Hunting and fishing, in streams whose health depends on forested banks, were not new uses of the forest, of course. Woodland Indians were subsistence hunters intimately familiar with the forest and expert in tracking and killing the game to be found there. They used whatever methods worked, including shining deer at night with torches and capturing larger animals with deadfall traps and smaller ones with snares. Daniel Boone, for Theodore Roosevelt "the archetype of the American hunter," was so skilled in the ways of the forest that he was said to be half redskin, half paleface.[6] His fictional counterpart, James Fenimore Cooper's Natty Bumppo, possesses similar skills, which enable him to thrive in the forest and more than hold his own with his Iroquois antagonists. Cooper's Leatherstocking Tales and biographies of Boone played a major role in making the hunter a respectable and even heroic figure. In the early years of the republic the dominance of the agrarian ideal promoted by Thomas Jefferson had contributed to the view of the hunter as someone who was too lazy to pursue the honorable occupation of farming and preferred the relative lawlessness of the frontier. In J. Hector St. John de Crèvecoeur's memorable characterization, hunters were made savage by living in the woods or near them: "[O]nce hunters, farewell the plow. The chase renders them ferocious, gloomy, and unsociable."[7] Early European settlers in Michigan and the upper Midwest came to farm, however, with the aim of extending the kind of agrarian civilization with which they were familiar. They hunted primarily to supplement their diet and protect their property from marauding bears, wolves, and foxes. These pioneering settlers bore little resemblance to the legendary Daniel Boone or Natty Bumppo and were scarcely as comfortable in the forest as members of the Algonquian tribes they found there, but they learned to hunt their new terrain out of necessity and developed the skills they needed to get the deer, turkeys, and other game they relied on for food. They also developed a knack for telling stories calculated to reveal their prowess as hunters while entertaining their audiences.

In *The Bark Covered House* William Nowlin draws out a convoluted tale of pursuing a group of four bears for two days that involves scaring off an Indian competitor and bringing in dogs that lose a furious battle with the bears.[8] The fact that the bears ultimately got away mattered less to Nowlin than the story's entertainment value and its usefulness in convincing his readers in the 1870s that bears indeed roamed the woods of Southeast Michigan in 1842. Nowlin establishes his skill as a hunter earlier in his memoir by describing how he shot wild turkeys in their roosts at dawn, locating them by the sound of their gobbling and making his way through prickly brush in the dark woods quietly enough to get a shot at first light. He boasts of his skill in calling turkeys, imitating them so well with a turkey call made from a hollow wing bone that they would run to him. Nowlin's accounts of successful deer hunts demonstrate his ability to bring down deer with his muzzleloading rifle and entertain his readers with stories of bizarre incidents, such as two in which he rescues companions from irate bucks trying to trample them. Hunting white-tailed deer was a common activity for early settlers in southern Michigan, given the abundance of deer at the time and their desirability as a food source. Nowlin hunted deer for the market as well as for the pot, taking advantage of a newly established rail connection with Detroit to ship skins and meat to markets there. He describes hunting through one winter with a friend in order to pay off the mortgage on his family's property, making a rule of staying out long enough to kill a sled load of at least six deer. With no hunting season or bag limits to restrain them they simply killed as many as they could.

The hunting journals of Oliver Hazard Perry, a namesake of the naval hero of the War of 1812 but no relation, represent a relatively early stage in the development of sport hunting in the Midwest. They offer a different kind of narrative, one that illustrates the process of evolution by which hunting became a recreational activity for those with the leisure to pursue it. Perry grew up in Cleveland and went on extended hunting expeditions in Michigan, as well as in Ohio, mainly in the 1840s and 1850s. He would take the train to Port Huron or Saginaw and then strike out by ox-drawn wagon for wild country known to have abundant game. Setting up camp was a matter of felling trees and constructing a primitive shelter from available materials, sometimes using remnants of abandoned wigwams from old Indian camps. Perry and his companions would stay for as long as two months in the fall, hunting along the Black River or the Cass for deer and elk and the occasional duck or partridge to vary their diet. His day-by-day accounts of his expeditions include stories of coming on individual bucks or groups of elk, tracking wounded animals, and listening to wolves at night, as well as glimpses of routines of camp life such as eating elk meat on improvised wooden plates and stretching skins on poles Indian fashion. They also offer a graphic portrayal of the hardships of primitive camping and of hunting in what Perry describes as a "wild wilderness," including bouts of ague (malaria) and times of "extreme exhaustion caused by so long an exposure to wet and cold, poor diet, and the labor of walking through cedar swamps, windfalls, and thickets" carrying a heavy rifle and pack.[9] Perry complains frequently about the deer mice that would overrun their camp, eating gloves and shoes as well as food supplies. He kept a running tally of the number he trapped (sixty-eight on one trip).

Some deer camps had become considerably more comfortable by the 1870s, when William Laffan described for the readers of *Scribner's Monthly* his adventures with "a party of gentlemen" he traveled from the East to join for their annual deer hunt on the Au Sable River. Their camp offered quarters in a deserted logging camp with a cook and her handyman husband to serve the hunters' needs, and the hunt had become more ritualized. Dogs were used to drive deer toward runways leading to the river where they could be shot either as they reached the river or when they were swimming in it.[10] The Nichols Deer Hunting Camps in the northern Lower Peninsula set an even higher standard, offering parties as large as twenty such amenities as a floored cooking and dining tent with china and silverware and comfortable chairs.[11] Guests at the Nichols camps would have been well-heeled sportsmen accustomed to regarding hunting as a leisure activity and concerned with maintaining the conditions that made it possible, including abundant deer.

The ideal of the gentleman sportsman, adapted from English models, had become well established in America by the middle of the nineteenth century, in part through the writings of an expatriate Englishman, William Henry Herbert, who used the pseudonym Frank Forester. Hunting came to be seen, by Herbert and others, as a way of ensuring health, moral vigor, and manliness, particularly for wealthy city dwellers but increasingly for the middle class as well. Hunting also came to be associated with the pursuit of natural history and with a conservation ethic grounded in scientific knowledge.[12] The most influential proponent of sport hunting, Theodore Roosevelt, was a lifelong student of natural history who wrote highly regarded accounts of the behavior of the animals he hunted. He maintained a long relationship with the American Museum of Natural History, which his father had helped to found.[13] By the late nineteenth century numerous sportsmen's clubs had formed in the Midwest on the model of those established earlier in the East and South, some with their own game preserves. The most influential of several national magazines dealing with hunting and fishing, *Forest and Stream,* began publishing in 1873. After he assumed the editorship in 1880 George Bird Grinnell used *Forest and Stream* to champion the values and the conservation agenda of the Boone and Crockett Club, launched in late 1887 at a New York dinner of upper-class sportsmen hosted by his friend Theodore Roosevelt. Encouraging preservation and advancing natural history were among the club's stated purposes.

The first article of the Boone and Crockett Club's constitution was "To promote manly sport with the rifle," and one of the initial requirements of membership was to have killed one each of three different species of large animals by "fair chase."[14] The chase, as Roosevelt understood it, involved one in the "free, self-reliant adventurous life" of a wilderness hunter and encouraged a "vigorous manliness" important to the nation as well as to the individual.[15] For Roosevelt hunting became an expression of patriotism. His ideal of the wilderness hunter was strongly colored by his own western hunting adventures and his fascination with frontier types, but he could adapt it to other settings such as the Adirondacks, where he had gained his early experience of hunting and primitive camping. The antithesis of the ideal, for sportsmen generally as well as for the members of the Boone and Crockett Club, was the market hunter. Pot hunters were objectionable as well, since they were assumed to have no regard for principles of conservation or "fair chase" (such as shooting birds only on the wing), but market hunters threatened the very existence of game species. The rapid depletion of buffalo herds and the immense flocks of passenger pigeons by the end of the nineteenth century presented alarming examples of the consequences of unregulated hunting, driven in large part by the demands of urban markets such as New York and Chicago.

The role of sportsmen in lobbying for game laws, particularly that of the influential members of the Boone and Crockett Club, has been well documented.[16] For the Boone and Crockett Club conservation meant preserving habitat, particularly large blocks of forested land, and stopping such practices as jacklighting (shining) deer and using dogs to drive them into the water where they could be shot more easily, practices in common use in the Adirondacks. More broadly, the club campaigned to establish bag limits, restricted hunting seasons that avoided breeding periods, and effective systems of enforcement, with game wardens responsible to state game commissions. By the early twentieth century most states had put in place game laws enforced by game commissions, funded at least in part by fees from hunting and fishing licenses. In 1900 the Lacey Act undermined market hunting by making the interstate shipment of illegally taken wild birds and mammals and products derived from them a federal offense, and in 1918 the Migratory Bird Treaty between the United States and Canada outlawed spring shooting of migratory birds and set daily bag limits in season for those classified as game.[17]

William B. Mershon, the Saginaw lumberman who became active in conservation causes in the early twentieth century and subsequently led the campaign to fund the Lumberman's Monument on the Au Sable River, presents an unusually interesting example of the sportsman. Mershon belonged to the generation of hunter conservationists who believed strongly enough in the value of outdoor sport to become actively involved in political battles to regulate hunting and fishing and conserve the natural resources on which they depend. In his case this meant playing a significant role in the Michigan Sportsmen's Association (founded in 1875 and the precursor of the Michigan United Conservation Clubs), working to strengthen and enforce game laws, and campaigning for the creation of state forest reserves as a member of the Forestry Commission.[18] In a memoir based on his experience as a sportsman over a period of fifty years Mershon offers an elegiac view of a time when grouse, wild turkeys, and waterfowl were abundant, before forests were cleared for farms and marshes were drained and before the automobile made remote hunting and fishing areas easily accessible. He argues for the creation of state game reserves so people can continue to enjoy "the grand, health-giving, mind-purifying sport with rod and gun."[19] For Mershon and others like him such sport was a therapeutic and character-forming kind of recreation, to be sharply distinguished from the reckless commercial exploitation of game by market hunters.

Mershon learned to hunt from his father, beginning by shooting squirrels in the hardwood forests near Saginaw and passenger pigeons on their spring flights through the area. Stewart Edward White's novel about the boyhood of Bobby Orde shows him learning the principles of sportsmanship and acquiring the skills he needs to hunt squirrels, then waterfowl, and finally more elusive grouse and partridge. His mentor is an older friend, Mr. Kincaid, who takes an interest in him while his father is away tending to his lumbering enterprises.[20] White, a notable sportsman himself, shows Kincaid communicating the ideal of the "true sportsman," who hunts for pleasure rather than money or fame, presenting Bobby's extended tutorial in how to handle a gun and find and shoot game as a form of moral education. White and Mershon, both sons of prosperous lumbermen, would have enjoyed similar educations in the ways of sportsmanlike hunting.

Mershon's lively stories of his hunting and fishing experiences, intended like all such stories for readers who can appreciate the thrills and nuances of the chase, offer a window on the evolution of this form of recreation in Michigan in the late nineteenth and early twentieth centuries. His chapter on the wild turkey, for him "the grandest of all game birds," traces his experience from an early hunt with his father, on which they encountered a flock of as many as forty turkeys, to one in 1886 on which he made a difficult shot to kill a large gobbler flying from a treetop. Mershon speculates that this may have been "the last wild turkey in Michigan" and describes having it mounted. Whether or not it was the "last of its race," as Mershon wanted to think, wild turkeys were hunted out in Michigan in the late nineteenth century. They have since been reintroduced and are once again flourishing. Unlike William Nowlin, Mershon declined to shoot turkeys coming off their roosts and thought it unsportsmanlike to shoot the birds after calling them, choosing instead to track them with bird dogs, at times following one elusive bird all day. How one hunted, and the experience itself, had become more important than how many birds one could put in the game bag. Mershon, of course, was not hunting to feed a family as Nowlin and other early settlers were when they stalked wild turkeys.

Like virtually every other male at the time, Mershon took advantage of the immense spring flights of wild pigeons. In an earlier book on the passenger pigeon, most of which consists of reprinted articles and letters, Mershon describes his boyhood excitement at rising before dawn to shoot pigeons on the wing as they emerged over a point of woods in their rapid flight.[21] The main purpose of his book was to describe the mass destruction of the great nestings of pigeons that had become common in Michigan by the 1870s, the last and largest of which spread north from Petoskey for forty miles in the spring of 1878, and the eventual disappearance of the pigeons. Mershon reprinted an article by his friend H. B. Roney of East Saginaw from *American Field* documenting violations of existing state laws meant to protect such nestings: by hunters firing shotguns into the nesting area, including homesteaders collecting wagon loads of pigeons to be shipped by steamer to Chicago; by boys and Ottawa Indians coming from the Petoskey area to knock squabs out of nests with poles; and, especially, by the "pigeoners" who converged from all over the country and set up their netting operations impermissibly close to the nesting, capturing as many as ninety dozen birds a day by luring them with improvised salt licks.

For Mershon, as for Roney, the chaotic scenes that accompanied such a nesting represented the worst excesses of market hunting. Yet he also reprinted a retort to Roney by a Chicago game dealer who challenged some of his allegations and insisted on the economic benefits to homesteaders of the bounty of pigeons, arguing as well that pigeons would destroy crops if not taken. Whatever the economic self-interest of the dealer, his criticisms expose the class differences between the sportsmen who were appalled by the massive assault on the passenger pigeon and those who regarded pigeons as legitimate and lucrative prey and took whatever advantage of the roostings they could. The breach between sportsmen and farmers (and other rural hunters) had become apparent in less extreme cases than that of the passenger pigeon. The imposition of strict game laws, along with the rise of private hunting preserves, aroused resentment among those used to hunting when, how, and where they wanted. For them hunting, whether for the pot or the market, was not so much an occasional sport as a way of life, sometimes a means of subsistence, which they saw as threatened by the aggressive efforts of affluent sportsmen to restrict their liberties.

Mershon and his well-to-do Saginaw friends shot ducks and geese on trips to North Dakota, as well as on outings in Michigan, taking numbers well in excess of today's bag limits. Mershon, reluctant to be seen as a "game hog," defended the "old-time sportsman" on the grounds that game was more abundant and hunting pressure much less than it had become by the time he wrote in the early 1920s. Yet he acknowledged, in retrospect, that he and his companions had not realized at the time "that the game was disappearing."[22] He and his friends traveled to western hunting grounds in the Dakotas in a private railroad car built in 1894 for the Saginaw Hunting Club and used for hunting trips in Michigan as well. The expansion of railroad lines (with the Flint and Pere Marquette linking Saginaw and Ludington, the Grand Rapids and Indiana reaching northern Michigan on the west side of the state, and the Michigan Central doing the same on the east side) made for a dramatic increase in comfort, as well as in ease of access to prime hunting and fishing places. Railroad lines published brochures advertising cars equipped with berths, stoves, and utensils that could be rented for ten dollars a day and dropped off on a siding. Sportsmen could go out for a day's hunting or fishing and return to their railroad car where they could reminisce about the old days of going into the woods by wagon to hunt deer and sleep in a heavy canvas tent. Those with private railroad cars could enjoy more luxuries, such as the bathroom and tub with which the Saginaw Hunting Club's car was outfitted.[23] In an account of annual hunting trips from 1898 to 1904 in the Tahquamenon area of the eastern Upper Peninsula, which he took pains to link with landmarks in Longfellow's *The Song of Hiawatha*, A. D. Shaffmaster deplored a decline of game, which he attributed to insufficient game laws and the expansion of "the great net of railroads which have penetrated nearly every portion of our once impenetrable fastness."[24]

If railroads extended the reach of hunters, the ready availability of automobiles by the 1920s made it possible for them to go anywhere that a rapidly expanding road system would let them and also freed them from dependence on railway schedules. The automobile also had the effect of democratizing sports hunting. Anyone with a Model T could light out for the woods of northern Michigan in deer season, and increasing numbers did, many from cities in southern Michigan and neighboring states. Deer licenses jumped from 28,000 in 1920 to 75,000 in 1930.[25] By the end of the 1970s as many as 500,000 hunters could be found in the woods on opening day of deer season (out of about 700,000 with licenses), and a distinctive hunting culture had developed, with buck poles, bars ready to welcome the November invasion, and camp followers. Anyone not wearing blaze orange in firearm season (bow-hunting and muzzleloading seasons had been added by then) risked being shot, along with some who would be shot regardless of what they were wearing. Mortality reports became a regular feature of deer season. As their numbers increased so did the variety of the hunters, including not only those taught how to hunt by families that perpetuated a tradition of responsible hunting but also such new types as "slob hunters," "sandwich hunters" (up for the day), and "road hunters" (unwilling to venture far from the security of the road).[26] Arguments flared over the ethics and consequences of the relatively new practice of bait hunting, luring deer with piles of vegetables, leading to efforts to regulate baiting by the DNR. While the tradition of the gentleman sportsman persists, particularly in hunting clubs, deer hunting has become more of a blue-collar sport. It has also become a more commercialized one, with an infrastructure serving hunters' needs. For those who want to be guaranteed success there are deer ranches specializing in trophy bucks that offer hunting in enclosed spaces. In recent years, hunting has been losing ground as social patterns have shifted and other forms of recreation have become more popular. The number of deer licenses issued in Michigan has declined from a peak of 870,000 in 1997 to 725,000 in 2009, prompting the DNR to establish programs designed to recruit more hunters.

One wonders what a Perry or a Mershon would make of the contemporary deer-hunting scene in northern Michigan or how they would react to a visit to a giant Cabela's outfitting store such as the one in Dundee, Michigan. There they would discover all that the well-equipped hunter could possibly need, including every imaginable kind of rifle and shotgun (along with laser scopes and range finders to improve the odds), portable tree stands, camping gear, camouflage outfits, motivational DVDs, and video games that make it possible to hone one's skills while enjoying a virtual experience of the chase. They would also find increasingly sophisticated camouflage clothing, with patterns based on computer-enhanced images of bark, leaves, and tree limbs created by such manufacturers as Mossy Oak and Realtree, with the option of scent control (by Scentlok) to give the hunter a further advantage. The latest 3-D clothing features hooded jackets, pants, and even face masks, with attached polyester leaves designed to break the hunter's silhouette and make him or her indistinguishable from tree or bush, enhancing the illusion of having become a part of the forest. As one satisfied user quoted on Cabela's website reports, "The turkeys never seen me." The ideal of fair chase has clearly undergone a metamorphosis.[27] To walk into a Cabela's megastore is to enter a hunter's (and fisherman's) fantasy world, with its mounted game animals in simulated habitats, including a towering "Conservation Mountain" displaying North American big game in quasi-realistic settings. Many of the simulated scenes (wolves pursuing caribou or fighting with polar bears over a carcass, moose locking horns, a mountain lion leaping on a deer's back) are calculated to raise the adrenaline level. The proximity of life-sized animals and the blizzard of accessories could almost cause the modern sportsman to forget the actual conditions that make hunting an arduous and chancy enterprise. In Cabela's anything seems possible.

Tourism was well established as a leisure activity by the mid–nineteenth century, encouraged by railroad companies promoting travel to resort areas reached by their lines. Those affluent enough to afford it had become accustomed to leaving town for extended summer vacations, seeking woods, mountains, lakes, or seashore. In the East the Catskills became a popular destination in the 1840s, the Adirondacks in the 1850s. The White Mountains of New Hampshire became a favorite retreat of landscape painters, among them Thomas Cole, Asher Durand, and John Kensett. Popular resorts and spas sprang up at such places as Saratoga in New York and White Sulphur Springs in West Virginia.[28] In Michigan the Grand Hotel opened on Mackinac Island in 1887, funded by railroad and steamship companies, one of many resorts accessible by rail that appeared in the upper Midwest in the late nineteenth and early twentieth centuries. The most famous of the popular pageants based on *The Song of Hiawatha* was sponsored by the Grand Rapids and Indiana Railroad and staged at Round Lake, between Petoskey and Harbor Springs in the northern Lower Peninsula, an area heavily promoted as a destination for vacationers from the Midwest. Seventy-five Indian actors were imported from Ontario, where the pageant had originated, and pantomimed actions as *The Song of Hiawatha* was recited and sung offstage, with forest and lake providing a natural setting for the outdoor performance.[29]

Railroads regularly published promotional literature encouraging tourism, as well as hunting and fishing expeditions. Charles Hallock, the first editor of *Forest and Stream,* offered reflections on a trip to Michigan that combined hunting with tourism in an 1878 publication of the Grand Rapids and Indiana Railroad. Hallock describes northern Michigan lakes ringed by "beautiful forests of oak, hemlock, pine, beech, maple, radiant mountain ash" and is pleased to find "Nature everywhere . . . in its wild

My Rambles in the Enchanted Summer Land of the Great Northwest, 1882.
(Courtesy of the Bentley Historical Library, University of Michigan.)

state."[30] A small illustrated book, *My Rambles in the Enchanted Summer Land of the Great Northwest,* consisting mainly of letters purporting to be from an anonymous lady to a southern friend that describe the delights of resorts in Wisconsin and Michigan in gushing prose, went through three editions; it was offered free on request by the Chicago and Northwestern Railway. Unlike Hallock, an easterner impressed by the wildness of the country available to sportsmen in Michigan, the writer of the letters was attracted to "cultivated wilderness" of the kind she found in lakeside resorts that offered "elegant and first-class accommodations in the very midst of the wild wood!"[31] The "enchanted summer land" she describes is more picturesque than wild and offers comforts for the vacationer along with the assurance that she is following a path favored, or soon to be favored, by the fashionable crowd.

A series of illustrated brochures on summer resorts created by the Passenger Department of the Pere Marquette Railroad in the early twentieth century is more typical of the efforts of the railroads to promote travel to forested and other scenic areas. These include descriptions of resorts served by the railroad along with pictures of the area, accounts of game laws, train schedules, and in some cases foldout maps. They are addressed to a potential audience from the Midwest and beyond, consisting of anyone who might respond to the appeal of northern Michigan. This was described as "the paradise of votaries of recreation," offering happiness to be found "upon the placid surface of its inland lakes, within its balsam-scented forests, near its gurgling brooks and murmuring streams."[32] A parallel series put out by the same railroad, *Fishing and Hunting in Michigan,* includes brief essays on such subjects as canoeing on the Manistee River and current conservation efforts in addition to accounts of accessible hunting and fishing areas.

One theme that surfaces repeatedly in such literature is the benefit to health and emotional well-being of escaping the city for what one brochure describes as "a refreshing summer of contentment in land of the pines" where one could find a natural forest "untouched by the axe of the lumberman or the scythe of the forest fire." A resort owned by the Detroit and Mackinac Railway Company in the Tawas area, on the shore of Lake Huron, was touted as a "natural sanitarium" where one could experience the tonic effect of inhaling the "health-giving and delicious odors" of the "noble pines" while enjoying the purity of the waters. The railroad's publicists promised relief from all the maladies of city living.

> Men, women and children who are rundown, exhausted, and tired out, whose lungs are filled with miasma . . . their nerves unstrung and entire systems an easy prey to malevolent microbes, come to Michigan woods, and after enjoying a few weeks of the restful conditions and energizing air which prevail, return home invigorated, strengthened, nearly all cured and others greatly relieved—the certain result of communing with nature.[33]

This brochure, like others, appealed to hunters and fishermen as well as those fleeing "malevolent microbes," with pictures documenting successful hunting and fishing trips. The railroads cast a wide net in their efforts to capture business for the resorts they served, combining practical information with the kind of florid prose that would become a staple of later tourist literature. A subsequent publication from the West Michigan Tourist and Resort Association credits the passenger agent of the Pere Marquette Railroad with inventing "color week" and raves about the "lanes of scarlet and gold" to be found on the Leelanau Peninsula and the beauty of the forests surrounding its inland lakes.[34] Such travel writing, whether published by railroad companies or the tourist offices that succeeded them as boosters, appealed to the leisure traveler primarily through descriptions of scenic wonders. The "beautiful forests" of northern Michigan, even more dazzling in their fall colors, offered visual spectacles that could be enjoyed from train or car windows or relished at leisure if one lingered at a resort.

The rapid growth of automobile use by the 1920s (from fewer than 500,000 in 1910 to 17.5 million registered in 1925) launched an era of auto tourism, as well as opening up new territory to hunters and fishermen.[35] Mass production of automobiles and the development of an infrastructure to support the new vogue for auto camping had a profoundly democratizing effect on leisure travel, with major implications for the use of public forestland. The automobile revolutionized tourism, altering patterns established by the proliferation of railroads and their promotion of travel to areas and resorts served by the expanding network of railroad lines. Visits to national forests and parks, as well as to newly established state parks, jumped sharply as more people took advantage of the freedom the automobile allowed and responded to the appeal of escaping cities for a temporary nomadic life on the road. For most this included camping, which offered the opportunity to sample a more basic kind of existence in contact with the natural world. As urban society became increasingly industrialized, the appeal of experiencing a simpler life grew. Auto tourism was one manifestation of the broader "back to nature" movement that took hold in the early decades of the twentieth century. This movement was characterized by the idealization of country life, the rise of the scouting movement and summer camps, a vogue for nature study and nature writing, an outpouring of fiction dealing with wilderness adventure, and heightened awareness of scenic beauty.[36] The availability of a family car invited weekend escapes to the country and longer road trips, on which one could find at least temporary respite from the pace and growing complexity of urban life.

Taking to the road in the early years of auto touring could be an adventure, complicated by bad roads and breakdowns and the uncertainties of finding a place to camp, often in a farmer's field or an inviting grove of trees. With the expansion and improvement of roads and the proliferation of auto camps in municipalities eager to attract visitors, as well as in state and national parks and forests, such tourism became easier and more orderly. Organized auto camps reduced the litter, pollution, and fire hazards associated with more random camping. Articles promoting auto tourism and offering tips about camping appeared in national magazines, along with advertisements for improved tents, camp stoves, and sporting as well as camping gear. A 1923 book on auto camping championed it as "romantic, healthful, educative, and at the same time economical" and offered listings of campgrounds and evaluations of equipment in addition to comprehensive advice on what to take and how to camp.[37] A similar book that appeared in the same year featured comparable advice and product analysis and emphasized the class dimension of auto camping, presenting it as a way of escaping a mode of travel dominated by the rich ("Haughty Pullman cars and stifling coaches, gouging hotels and insolent waiters") for the freedom of the highway.[38]

In a 1924 article in *American Forests and Forest Life* James E. Scott argued that in the previous decade national forests had become "truly national playgrounds" and stressed their potential for meeting recreational needs, including those of city children. Beginning around 1916, when the National Park Service was established, the Forest Service had begun to promote the recreational use of national forests, broadening its definition of multiple use in response to both public demand and a perceived threat to its mission from a rival agency.[39] The Forest Service had resisted the creation of the Park Service, fearing, with reason, that this would make it more likely that new national parks would be carved out of national forests. The relationship between the two agencies was competitive from the beginning and became increasingly complicated, reflecting differing philosophies of land management. The Park Service sought out visitors and embraced outdoor recreation as a central part of its mission. The Forest Service, dominated by professional foresters, was more concerned with preserving the capacity of public forests to provide a reliable supply of timber. At least initially, Forest Service efforts to accommodate recreational users were defensive, a way of controlling visitors while remaining relevant to a public becoming more interested in national forests as places for recreation and aesthetic pleasure.[40] The difficulty foresters had in accepting aesthetic values became apparent in agency controversies over whether to preserve forested "beauty strips" along roads to shield tourists from having to look at logged areas; protecting "viewsheds" subsequently became common practice.[41]

Scott wrote after the Forest Service had accepted recreation as a legitimate use of the national forests and in the immediate aftermath of the 1924 conference on outdoor recreation convened by President Calvin Coolidge, the first of two such national conferences.[42] The "See America First" campaign, vigorously pursued by railroad companies as a way of boosting transcontinental travel, promoted the western national parks as "the people's playgrounds."[43] National parks and forests and many state parks expanded their road networks and offered campsites for auto campers, usually without charge. A publication of the Michigan Conservation Department from the 1920s proclaims the virtues of outdoor recreation and offers promotional descriptions of twenty-three existing state parks, including such features as a "semi-circular grove of white pine, said to have been planted by early Indian tribes for tribal pow-wows" at Onaway State Park. The underlying message is that state parks are "the pleasure grounds of every one. There is no class distinction."[44] Use of Michigan's expanding network of state parks grew rapidly, from 220,000 visitors in 1922 to 7 million (in fifty-two parks) in 1929.[45]

Auto camping offered a more direct form of interaction with wild nature than that enjoyed by those who patronized the resorts, although such camping had more to do with enjoying the new freedom of the road and mastering camping rituals than with making extended excursions into the woods. The literature of auto camping describes increasingly sophisticated gear designed to make camping easier, including air mattresses, a foldaway bed designed for Ford sedans, and trailers ("motor bungalows") to be pulled behind one's car. Municipal campgrounds, established by

Advertisement from *American Forests and Forest Life,* 1928 (Courtesy of American Forests.)

towns alert to the potential of travel to benefit local economies, offered amenities that included water, electricity, showers, and laundry rooms.[46] Auto campers learned that they could rough it without leaving all the conveniences of civilization behind. In fact, they could reconstitute a version of domesticity on the road.

As they expanded their road systems and improved their camping facilities national forests and parks became increasingly popular destinations for auto campers. Assistant Forester Leon Kneipp argued for the recreational use of the national forests in a 1930 article in which he describes the public as becoming less concerned with the forests as sources of materials or food and more interested in them as sources of "beauty, inspiration, and recreation."[47] In promoting the increased use of national forests (almost twenty-five million visiting motorists in 1929), which he correlated with improved forest roads and the increase in private ownership of automobiles, Kneipp was indirectly addressing the concerns of foresters who wanted to restrain such recreational use. He insists that improved campgrounds reduce fire danger and risks to public health and justifies providing facilities for outdoor recreation as a way of countering "the intensity of modern existence" and recognizing "the widespread impulse to get back to nature." One way in which the Forest Service recognized this impulse was by granting permits for summer homes in the national forests, over ten thousand by the end of 1929. Kneipp was sensitive to the concerns of some about extending forest roads and conscious of the need to protect "the best remaining examples of the primitive in nature within the national forests." He had been given the responsibility of writing the Forest Service's Regulation L-20 (1929), which required that district foresters identify potential areas for preservation as wilderness and submit reports with plans for administering them to the chief of the Forest Service.[48] His 1930 article assumes that preservation can coexist with significantly increased recreational use of the national forests, although there inevitably was tension between these contrasting goals.[49]

Kneipp was writing after the wave of auto campers had caused a backlash among defenders of the national forests, reflected in editorials in *American Forests and Forest Life* commenting on the strains caused by the influx and the "roadside" problem of advertising signs, hotdog stands, and other development associated with the increase of automobile traffic. One writer complained about the tourist invasion of the national forests over primitive roads established for fire prevention and the problems of enforcement, sanitation, and fire prevention this generated. Another, deploring the loss of much of the Maine wilderness to lumbering, lamented the fact that roads into the forest now brought "the jar of radio jazz" and "the stench of gasoline."[50] Such complaints were manifestations of the strong reaction against the rapid expansion of roads and the motorized recreation that they made possible by those who valued a more primitive kind of camping and a different experience of the national forests, unmarred by the intrusive sounds and smells that accompanied the automobile. Paul Sutter has argued that the real impetus for founding the Wilderness Society and campaigning to set aside federally designated wilderness areas came from resistance to opening up formerly wild areas to roads and automobile traffic. One of the Wilderness Society's founders, Aldo Leopold, denounced what he called the "universal motorization of the forests" and argued for primitive forms of wilderness recreation, without the support of roads, hotels, and the new industry that had grown up to supply the needs of auto campers.[51]

Leopold saw mass tourism, encouraged first by the railroads and then by the proliferation of automobiles and roads, as destroying wilderness and threatening the kind of primitive recreation he advocated by extending the reach of automobile camping ("woodcraft becomes the art of using gadgets").[52] Bob Marshall, who played a pivotal role in founding the Wilderness Society and privately funded it in its early years, imagined the westward expansion of the country as a story of highways invading secluded valleys, with neat gardens and orchards replacing "the tangled confusion of the primeval forest," factories belching smoke, and the wildflowers of the forest floor "transformed to asphalt spotted with chewing gum, coal dust and gasoline."[53] Marshall's charged language suggests revulsion at the contamination of natural environments that he regarded as not only wild but pure. The automobile with its gasoline fumes and the asphalt roads that accompanied it violated what seemed to him a pristine natural order and symbolized the threat that an industrialized and mechanized society posed to wilderness and the values he associated with it. Marshall preferred what he called "the freedom of the wilderness" to the "freedom of the road" embraced by the multitudes who escaped to the countryside and national and state forests and parks in their automobiles. His attraction to this freedom depended on a vision of wilderness that excluded roads and settlements. Enjoying the kind of recreation that he promoted required getting out of the car and truly experiencing the woods: "A large fraction of the vacation motorists enjoy what features of the forest they can observe at a velocity of over 40 miles an hour, but never really transfer their lives from the highway to the forest."[54]

Like Aldo Leopold, whose arguments for wilderness influenced him, Marshall advocated more primitive forms of outdoor recreation.[55] He grew up climbing the high peaks of the Adirondacks and later spent several summers exploring Alaska's remote Brooks Range, the basis for his posthumously published *Alaska Wilderness* (1956). Although Marshall recognized the practical need to accommodate auto tourism in the national forests by setting aside campgrounds and preserving scenic areas along roads, he was more interested in designated "wilderness" and "primeval" areas and in the kinds of experience they made possible. He justified wilderness recreation as promoting health and satisfying an urge for adventure, in the spirit of the American frontiersmen, resembling Leopold (and Theodore Roosevelt) in valuing a kind of strenuous outdoor life he saw as threatened. Primitive recreation offered possibilities for contemplation and a communion with nature resulting from "cutting all bonds of habit and drifting into the timeless continuity of the primeval." Such "drifting" into a sense of timelessness gave him at least temporary release from the discontinuities of modern life. It also offered the assurance of an ongoing natural order. Marshall saw the kind of hiking and camping he advocated as making possible an experience of beauty divorced from evidence of human activity, a beauty more than merely scenic that depended on appreciating the immensity and dynamism of the wilderness.[56] In linking what he called the "dynamic beauty" of the forest with natural cycles of decay and rebirth and insisting on the complexity of the processes by which forests evolve, Marshall sounded themes that Leopold would subsequently develop. His own career was unexpectedly cut short by a fatal heart attack, at the age of thirty-eight, in 1939.[57]

The embrace of the primitive by Marshall, Leopold, and others became a way of resisting the modernizing tendencies they deplored, particularly as these affected natural forests and other wild places, which they feared would be seriously compromised by the expansion of roads and auto tourism. In advocating primitive ways of experiencing wilderness areas, whether on foot or on horseback or in a canoe, they were reaffirming a tradition they associated with pioneer America. Hunters and fishermen who ventured into remote areas were part of this tradition, but relatively few of them wrote about their experience or tried to articulate its benefits. In the mid–nineteenth century William Murray, the minister of Boston's Park Street Church and one of the most popular preachers of his day, had launched an invasion of the Adirondacks with a popular account of his summer adventures there that appeared in 1869.[58] Murray opposed the pristine character of the "North Woods" of the Adirondacks to the Maine woods, which he described as having been devastated by logging, and began his book by offering detailed advice for the traveler. The primary appeal of the book, in addition to the liveliness and humor of Murray's stories, had to do with his vision of the Adirondacks as a paradise not only for sportsmen but for those seeking to find God in nature or to restore their health. To illustrate the curative properties of the mountain air, he describes his own restorative sleep ("Many a night have I laid down upon my

bed of balsam-boughs and been lulled to sleep by the murmur of the waters and the low sighing melody of the pines, while the air was laden with
the mingled perfume of cedar, of balsam and the water-lily") as a prelude
to a story of a consumptive who was miraculously cured by several
months of wilderness living.[59] In the Adirondacks, Murray promised, one
could apprehend God instinctively in the silence of the woods, the pure
waters, and the mountains and also enjoy the healing powers of the fragrance of spruce, hemlock, balsam, and pine.

Murray presents himself as an adventurer paddling his "cedar shell"
all over the Adirondacks, carrying it around waterfalls and over ridges
separating lakes, but he describes camping in terms that emphasize its
comforts and sociability. He established his own camp at Raquette Lake,
first on Constable Point and then, for greater privacy after his book
brought unwanted visitors, on Osprey Island. In both places he and his
wife entertained numerous guests who came to escape the city and enjoy
the sport and pleasure of outdoor life in the Adirondacks, as well as their
reputed health benefits. Not surprisingly, the influx of tourists prompted
by the appearance of his book encouraged a rapid expansion of the tourist
infrastructure and also left many of these tourists, unprepared to venture
beyond the periphery into what Murray regarded as the true Adirondack
wilderness, disgruntled at not finding the paradise he had promised. Jour-
nalists and cartoonists satirized "Murray's fools" and questioned his
claims, but his book and the lectures he gave around New England promoting the Adirondacks had a lasting impact on tourism and helped establish the "refining and spiritualizing influences of nature," an aspect of
what he called "the religion of the forest," in the public consciousness.[60]

John Muir offered a more idiosyncratic and provocative example of
wilderness exploration in accounts of his rambles in the Sierra Nevada,
beginning with *The Mountains of California* (1894), in which he portrayed
himself as taking no more provisions than tea and bread and finding shelter wherever he could. In "A Near View of the High Sierra" he describes
making his bed in a pine thicket, which he finds as snug and well-venti-
lated as a squirrel's nest, "full of spicy odors, and with plenty of wind-
played needles to sing one asleep."[61] Muir delighted in his ability to make
himself at home in his natural setting, imagining himself less as a human
intruder than as one more wild creature. Not being a squirrel, however,
and having failed to bring a blanket, he found himself having to creep out
to the fire frequently during the night to keep warm. In his solitary adven-
turing and indifference to the kinds of gear and provisions others would

have found necessary, Muir practiced a particularly austere form of camping, one strikingly at odds with the domesticated kind that would develop with the auto-camping movement. He was if anything more evangelical than Murray in celebrating his own version of paradise, but unlike Murray he was wary of the threat to it posed by tourism. Muir was more intent on sharing his vision of the wildness and purity, and the divine lessons, of forests, peaks, rushing streams, and "sky meadows" with those he thought might share his sense of exultation, enthusiasts of the sort he would subsequently lead into the mountains on the earliest Sierra Club excursions.

In the stories of his hunting and camping adventures in the West collected in a series of three books that culminated with *The Wilderness Hunter* (1893), Theodore Roosevelt projected another kind of image, as a rancher and latter-day frontiersman, describing how he adapted himself to the rigors of camping and stalking game in the Badlands and on the northern plains in his hunting expeditions. By all accounts, he thrived on harsh weather and rough conditions. His own stories of camping experiences serve as demonstrations of his hardiness and as briefs for the kind of primitive experience of nature he advocated. Roosevelt describes being forced to take shelter from a snowstorm in a lean-to when riding alone to his Elkhorn Ranch, getting through the night with only tea to sustain him while wolves howled outside. The next day, we learn, he was able to shoot some sharp-tailed grouse and roast them.[62] He tells his eastern readers about camping on another occasion in a grove of cottonwoods on a horse blanket with an oilskin spread over it.[63]

Roosevelt embraced the privations as well as the pleasures of the trail, wrapping himself in his buffalo robe in subzero cold as if trying to recapture the pioneering spirit he admired in the mountain men of the early nineteenth century who survived by trapping in the Rockies. He delighted in wearing a custom-made buckskin suit on his hunting trips and cultivating the appearance of a mountain man or frontiersman, to the point of using a picture of himself in his buckskin suit as the frontispiece to *Hunting Trips of a Ranchman* (1885). As a privileged easterner, and one who had endured a sickly childhood, Roosevelt needed to prove his toughness to his acquaintances and employees in the Dakota Territories to earn their respect. He also had to recover from the double shock of losing both his mother and his young wife on the same day, February 14, 1884. Adventure and vigorous exertion, including working alongside his ranch hands, proved to be the tonic he needed. Roosevelt was reinvigorated physically and mentally by his western experience and reinforced in his belief in the benefits of a strenuous life in the out-of-doors. Ranching and hunting big game in the West, more challenging than any hunting he had done before, gave him the confidence and authority to argue that a more primitive mode of life encouraged manly frontier virtues that could counteract the debilitating effects of civilization.[64]

Stewart Edward White's popular narratives based on his outdoor adventures were less well known than those of Muir or Roosevelt, to whom he was much closer in spirit than to Muir, but *The Forest* (1903) and two other nonfiction books dealing with his subsequent experience in California, *The Mountains* (1904) and *The Cabin* (1911), constitute a fuller introduction to traveling and camping in primitive conditions. They offer more practical advice, on pack trips (*The Mountains*) as well as surviving in the wilderness, while making a case for the benefits of what Leopold would call "facing nature alone." In the account of his extended canoeing and fishing expedition in the Algoma country of Ontario in *The Forest*, White describes a primitive kind of camping, which he regarded as a contest to see how much he could rely on his wit and what the forest offered rather than on "the ready-made of civilization." This minimalism persisted in *Camp and Trail* (1907), a manual for those taking pack trips into the Sierra in which White defines skill in woodcraft as a matter of being comfortable in the woods with as little equipment as possible.[65] Unlike the guides to auto camping that would appear in the 1920s touting the advantages of the newest camping equipment designed to make outdoor experience more palatable, *The Forest* urges readers to "go light" and use an ax to make what they need (tent pegs, camp chairs, a bed of layered balsam boughs). White prides himself on his success in stripping away everything but necessities: one shirt, one pair of pants, a good blanket, a few essential tools and utensils. For him this was a matter of playing the "game" of matching himself against the forces of nature fairly, "a test, a measuring of strength, a proving of his essential pluck and resourcefulness and manhood."[66] For someone who plays the game well, as White would have us believe he did, one of the rewards is enjoying one's ease after a strenuous day of "woods-walking" and the brisk effort of setting up camp. He ends one chapter by showing himself smoking his pipe in the protective circle of the campfire, feeling "at home": "Nothing can disturb you now. The wilderness is yours, for you have taken from it the essentials of primitive civilization,—shelter, warmth, and food" (49).

For White the journey he describes in *The Forest* was a version of the "Long Trail," a term popularized by Kipling that became synonymous with the call to adventure in remote places.[67] Like the fur traders and explorers before him, White saw himself as leaving civilization to respond to the summons of "the North Country," where he expected to experience the mystery and sublimity of "the Silent Places" that he described more fully in his novel of that name. Encounters with the native Ojibwa, the "Woods Indians," were part of the romance for White. While he admired the pioneering spirit and would praise Roosevelt for embodying it, he found a compelling ideal in these Woods Indians, including one who sometimes served him and his companion as a guide, Tawabinisay. They functioned as exemplars of woodcraft, displaying an easy expertise that he found "almost beyond belief." White marveled at the ability of the Woods Indians to fashion what they needed from the materials of the forest with knife and light ax: a bark container, snowshoes, and "a thoroughly waterproof, commodious, and comfortable bark shelter made in about the time it would take one to pitch a tent" (215). As a sportsman himself, White was particularly impressed by their superior hunting skills, which he associated with their acute senses and knowledge of the woods: "The forest is to [the Woods Indian] so familiar in . . . its subtle aspects that the slightest departure from normal strikes his attention at once" (209). White's admiration for the Indians he describes in *The Forest* recalls the fascination with his Indian guides and Indian ways that Thoreau reveals in the essays of *The Maine Woods,* his account of three wilderness expeditions on which he learned methods of primitive camping. The conviction that Indian ways provided the best examples of woodcraft had become established by the early nineteenth century and had grown as wilderness exploration became more popular. Practices based at least loosely on Indian woodcraft would play a critical role in the early success of the Boy Scouts and subsequently that of its female counterpart, the Campfire Girls.[68]

Ernest Thompson Seton was largely responsible for the vogue of playing Indian as a way of initiating youth into camping and woodcraft. Seton, who was born in England and spent his early years in Canada, was a prolific writer and illustrator who developed much of the framework that would be adopted by the Boy Scouts of America (he was responsible for the first edition of the *Boy Scout Handbook,* published in 1910) and exerted a strong influence on early summer camps for children. In 1901 Seton founded the Woodcraft Indians and provided the organization with ceremonies, games, and a program of nature study that he tried out on local boys whom he organized into a fictional tribe on his estate in Connecticut. He then publicized his experiment, winning admirers who spread the program nationally.[69] In the preface to *The Book of Woodcraft and Indian Lore* (1912), a compendium of material he had been refining and expanding in annual versions of his *Birch-Bark Roll of Woodcraft* since 1902, Seton offered a rationale for his program. He began from the assumption that the nation was turning to "the Outdoor Life" for physical regeneration and that this shift reflected a recognition that "those live longest . . . who live the simple life of primitive times."[70]

For Seton sport was the primary incentive to outdoor life and nature study "the intellectual side of sport." His youth program worked by combining sport, chiefly in the form of mock hunts and other competitions inspired by Indian practices, with nature study that might involve competitively learning the names and characteristics of trees or butterflies (with the incentive of earning "coups" or "honors," precursors of the modern scouting movement's merit badges). Making Indian costumes and learning Indian songs and ceremonies was a way of appealing to the attraction of the young to imaginative play. The nine principles that Seton made the foundation of his program indicate that he saw such play as having the serious function of shaping character by developing manhood, outdoor skills, and a capacity for self-governance. For him it was a form of moral education that promoted both heroic ideals and an attraction to beauty. Seton envisioned his program, and the scouting movement initiated by Sir William Baden-Powell in England with which he merged it, as a way of preparing boys for adult life by remedying a degeneracy he blamed on the decline of farm life with the rise of cities and industry. Playing Indian became the means of preserving the virility and the moral and spiritual values that Seton and others regarded as having been undermined by industrial civilization.

In the first edition of the *Boy Scout Handbook* Seton explained that he called his movement the Woodcraft Indians "because the idealized Indian of Hiawatha has always stood as the model for outdoor life, woodcraft, and scouting."[71] He saw Indians as embodying an instinctual life lived in harmony with their environment that could be imitated by the young.[72] For Seton's purposes the idea of "the primitive Indian," as a master of woodcraft and the model for virtues that he wanted his program to inculcate (manliness, bravery, self-control, reverence, truthfulness), was more important than the actuality. He nonetheless made a vigorous effort to refute stereotyped views of Indian vices and cruelties, citing George Catlin and George Bird Grinnell, among other visitors to the western tribes, as authorities.[73] What mattered most to Seton was that Indian lore and ideals that could be associated with Indians provided the basis for a program that engaged young people in learning about woodcraft and natural history. They responded to the romance of Indian costumes and Indian names, council fires, teepees, competitions in such activities as scouting and spear throwing, crafts, and woodland remedies.

Seton's rival, Daniel Beard, creator of the Sons of Daniel Boone, based an alternate vision of camping and woodcraft on pioneer heroes such as Daniel Boone and Davy Crockett and cast Indians as the villains in the drama of frontier warfare. Beard, who also merged his movement with the Boy Scouts, would play a major role in driving Seton to resign from the Scouts in 1915, as the organization turned more militant and patriotic and became less oriented toward woodcraft with the advent of World War I. Yet associations with Indians would persist in scouting and camping. A scouting leadership society known as the Order of the Arrow, influenced by Longfellow's *The Song of Hiawatha* and Cooper's *The Last of the Mohicans,* would be established in the late 1920s and continue into the present.[74] Camp Hayo-Went-Ha for boys, established in 1904 on Torch Lake in the northern Lower Peninsula by the Michigan Young Men's Christian Association (YMCA), offers one example of the effort to embrace Indian culture. An early brochure describes an annual trip to an Ojibwa village to see an enactment of the Hiawatha story and explains that the name of the camp was derived from the hero of Michigan poet Benjamin Hathaway's "The League of the Iroquois," the "mighty chieftain who united the five nations of the Iroquois in a common brotherhood and stood for all that was noble and unselfish."[75] A brochure from the late 1930s describes such camp activities as a council ring ceremony, a procession with drumming, and a tribal prayer. A program of wilderness adventure, continued and expanded in the present-day camp, ranges from beginners' canoe trips on northern Michigan rivers to extended backpacking trips on Isle Royale and in the Porcupine Mountains.

Seton's Woodcraft Indians and the scouting movement, along with the summer camp movement, which had its beginnings in New England boys' camps in the 1880s, emerged at a time when the need to reclaim values associated with immersion in the natural world seemed particularly acute. As they evolved, scouting and the traditional summer camp experience would continue to encourage woodcraft and outdoor adventure in various forms and, along with more recent programs such as Outward Bound and the National Outdoor Leadership School (NOLS), to shape attitudes that would contribute to the popularity of backpacking and wilderness trips by canoe or kayak. The modern ideal of low-impact camping, however, reflects a dramatically different understanding of how to function in the woods and other outdoor environments. Whereas White and others who prided themselves on their woodcraft and masculine self-reliance went into the woods with little more than an ax, backpackers today, increasingly female as well as male, trust high-tech gear to make outdoor adventure more manageable and less damaging to the natural environment. They can rely upon global positioning system (GPS) receivers to find their way and lightweight tents, portable stoves, and freeze-dried foods to make the way easier. Gore-Tex and polypropylene have obvious advantages over the kinds of clothing Thoreau specifies in the "Outfit for an Excursion" that appears in the appendix to *The Maine Woods,* including thick pants and waistcoat and an India-rubber coat to serve as rain gear. The modern camping industry thrives on backpackers' appetite for the latest in gear and gadgets, fostering a consumerism that White and other devotees of woodcraft and the primitive wilderness experience rejected. With their high-tech equipment and an ethic that encourages them to "leave no trace," modern backpackers are likely to be kinder to the environment than their predecessors, but they may not know it as well as those who had to depend on their wits and their axes as well as their knowledge of the woods.[76]

Backpackers and day hikers benefit from well-developed trail systems in many state and national parks and forests. The more dedicated hikers are lured by the Appalachian Trail, Vermont's Long Trail, and other cross-country trails such as Michigan's Shore-to-Shore Trail between Empire on Lake Michigan and Oscoda on Lake Huron and the North Country National Scenic Trail, which runs through Michigan's Upper Peninsula and will eventually link the Missouri River (in North Dakota) and the Adirondacks. Those who pursue this kind of outdoor adventure today can be seen as part of a tradition that includes such advocates of primitive encounters with woods, mountains, and rivers as Leopold, Marshall, White, Murray, and the Thoreau of *The Maine Woods,* among others. Hunting and fishing are less likely to be part of the experience than they once were, although a fishing rod would be seen by some as essential camping gear. Hunting, as measured by the number of hunting licenses issued, has been declining as backpacking, hiking, and other forms of outdoor recreation have been increasing.[77] One of these, wildlife photography, offers a version of the chase that appeals to some in ways that hunting no longer does. At the beginning of the twentieth century Theodore Roosevelt saw the potential of "hunting with the camera" to offer physical challenges and opportunities to experience primitive nature comparable to those of hunting with a rifle, with the advantage of preserving scarce game.[78]

When the first book-length guide to auto camping appeared in 1923, the appeal of the primitive was still strong enough for the authors to devote one chapter to "Primitive Camping." They envision "two husky young fellows," representative of the "wild" motor camper, gathering most of what they need from the woods, including utensils, which they fashion from available materials, and making fire without matches. They would learn to recognize and eat wild foods such as cattail roots and wild rice, supplementing their gathering with what they could procure with rod and gun.[79] In a book preoccupied with the liberating effects of automobile travel and the equipment offered to auto campers by companies rushing to supply their needs, such a chapter seems little more than a gesture, an effort by the authors to imagine what an alternate kind of camping might be. In fact, the automobile would become a dominant and accepted presence in national and state forests and parks, served by scenic roads with turnouts and by campgrounds laid out in interconnected loops that offer conveniences such as bathhouses and hookups for recreational vehicles (RVs). Campers in Winnebagos would come to outnumber those who strike out for the backcountry.

The spiritual heirs of Leopold and Marshall can be found today resisting the further expansion of roads and newer forms of motorized travel, mainly by off-road vehicles (ORVs) and snowmobiles, into roadless areas of public forestlands. On a national scale the argument has focused on the Roadless Area Conservation Rule, or "roadless rule," issued by the Forest Service in January of 2001 in the closing days of the Clinton administration to protect the approximately 58 million acres of the national forests still without roads. This was modified by the Bush administration to allow states to decide their own approaches, and subsequently reinstated by court decision and supported by the Obama administration. With challenges to the original rule and subsequent modifications and exemptions still before the courts, the future of the roadless rule remains uncertain. Critics, including timber and mining interests and ORV and snowmobile users, see the rule as restricting their access to public resources. Supporters, including many scientists and a majority of the general public, praise it for preventing fragmentation of forests that would damage wildlife habitats, threaten watersheds, and deprive people of the quiet and sense of refuge they can find in areas free of motorized traffic.

Similar interests and issues come into play in ongoing arguments about extending, or closing, roads on state forest land.

Public support for maintaining intact forests, relatively undisturbed by roads and the kinds of activity they bring, has been influenced by a tradition of nature writing that has helped to define and communicate values associated with such forests, particularly the aesthetic, spiritual, and ecological values that have displaced utilitarian ones for much of the public. In North America this tradition includes such major figures as Thoreau and Muir, both heralded now as pioneering advocates of wildness and wilderness. John Burroughs, little read today but a celebrity in the late nineteenth and early twentieth centuries for popular natural history essays based mainly on his rambles in the Catskills, represents a vein of nature writing that calls attention to the aesthetic and spiritual appeal of the natural world and the pleasures of close observation. Burroughs's essays, published in leading periodicals such as the *Scribner's Monthly* and *The Century Magazine* and then collected in numerous books beginning with *Wake-Robin* (1871) and ending with *The Last Harvest* (1922), often deal with gentler landscapes where fields mingle with forests and the human presence is visible.[80] Burroughs was drawn to the "picturesque" and pastoral rather than the sublime, although he could respond to the appeal of the primitive. A trip to England prompted him to articulate a distinctively American aesthetic, one based on the kind of wildness he found in his native ground of upstate New York. However much he was drawn to the "rural and pastoral beauty" of the English countryside, Burroughs missed the "beauty of the wild—the beauty of primitive forests,—the beauty of lichen-colored rocks and ledges."[81] He admired Wordsworth but felt that his poetry lacked "the subtle aroma of deep woods" and the "Indian's love of forests and forest-solitudes" that he found in the poetry of Bryant and Emerson (43).

Burroughs himself loved the "solitudes" of the dark hemlock forest in which he found more than forty species of birds in the summer, relishing their varied songs, and the rocky forested slopes of the Catskills, which he explored with friends searching for hidden lakes and new trout streams. He camped in the "primitive woods" and occasionally got lost in them, as on the excursion he describes in his early essay "Birch Browsings," marked by his account of several failed attempts to find a lake before he and his friends stumble on it. Burroughs observes that he would make a poor Indian.[82] Yet even on an outing plagued by misadventures, including a night made miserable by a rocky bed and clouds of midges, he can delight in the dawn chorus of thrushes and in the varied birds he encounters (woodpeckers, grouse, a rare waterthrush). If he was not the adventurer and celebrant of spectacular mountain landscapes that Muir was, he could show readers how to discover and appreciate natural wonders on a more intimate scale. From his rustic cabin, Slabsides, only a mile and a half from his stone farmhouse on the Hudson River but at the edge of the mountains, he explored field and forest and demonstrated the pleasures of the close observation of nature that he advocated. Burroughs seems most comfortable with the kind of life at the intersection of the wild and the domesticated that he describes in "Wild Life About My Cabin," an essay that shows him observing the birds that nest around Slabsides or linger on the edge of the clearing in which the cabin sits. When he wanted a wilder scene, he would hike a mile through the woods to put his canoe on a familiar creek. Burroughs was an avid fisherman and an occasional hunter but found his calling as a naturalist writing for a public looking, as he was, for relief from "the petty cares and turmoils of this noisy and blustering world."[83] He found this relief in becoming "a man who looks closely and steadily at nature" and in redefining the chase to place the focus on discovery and appreciation rather than success in the hunt: "The ideal observer turns the enthusiasm of the sportsman into the channels of natural history, and brings home a finer game than ever fell to shot or bullet."[84]

Burroughs was an early advocate of a kind of outdoor recreation that has grown to include armies of bird-watchers and increasing numbers of day hikers, backpackers, nature photographers, and others who go to the woods for the pleasure and awareness they experience by learning to "pay attention," as poet Mary Oliver would put it. Thoreau offered a model that Burroughs could imitate, with his daily practice of taking long walks through the countryside within range of Concord, journal writing grounded in observations of the natural world, and natural history essays (including "Walking" and "Wild Apples"), as well as his other writing. Burroughs's genial prose, with its reliance on emotive language, has little in common with Thoreau's.[85] Burroughs's influence has waned as Thoreau's has increased, yet his essays reached a broad public receptive to the appeal of a natural world that he made emotionally engaging to them, and he popularized a genre that would find many practitioners. The list of winners of the John Burroughs Medal for a "distinguished book of natural history," beginning in 1926, reveals how elastic the boundaries of the genre have become and how many talented writers have adapted it to their purposes.[86] Burroughs's actual legacy is more apparent in the continuing flow of essays and journal writing in local and regional publications describing observations or excursions, often organizing them around the changes of the seasons: a collection of newspaper columns by O. B. Eustis recording impressions over the course of the year, for example, Lon Emerick's essays on his encounters with favorite landscapes in the Upper Peninsula, or the more recent phenomenon of blogging about daily observations of natural happenings (with photographs).[87] Whether we call this natural history or nature writing or something else matters less than the fact that it reflects a continuing exploration of human interactions with the natural world. Such writing, which can range from sentimental and nostalgic to lyric to meditative, encourages regarding the woods or other inviting natural settings as places of discovery, physical and spiritual renewal, or simply aesthetic pleasure. It appeals to readers looking for reinforcement of their own appetites for exploring the natural world.

Sigurd Olson, who published nine books of essays based on his experience of the north woods from the mid-1950s to the early 1980s and was awarded the Burroughs Medal in 1974, is particularly relevant for my purposes. Olson's essays belong to the tradition of natural history writing exemplified by Burroughs and Thoreau, both of whom he read extensively. He regarded Burroughs as his favorite American nature writer, admiring him partly for his independence in rejecting organized religion and choosing an unconventional career as a writer, a path that he himself took in preference to the academic career in wildlife ecology that Leopold and others urged him to pursue.[88] Yet Olson was more strongly drawn to primitive experience of nature than were either Burroughs or Thoreau, whatever they professed about the value of wilderness and wildness.[89] Whereas they were most comfortable with pastoral landscapes (Thoreau with those around Concord and Burroughs with those in the vicinity of his rustic cabin in the Hudson Valley), Olson was attracted by the wilder country of the Quetico-Superior area of northern Minnesota and southern Ontario and the more remote reaches of Canada where he spent years taking wilderness canoe trips, initially as a guide. He imagined himself as following in the steps of the Chippewa who inhabited the region and the voyageurs who traversed it, trying to recapture a sense of their experience of the "old wilderness" of forests and lakes and streams. Olson's essays illustrate a fascination with the natural world and a disposition to see it as a source of spiritual truths that recall Thoreau and Burroughs, yet he also preached the value of primitive experience of nature as a way of counter-

Canoe country. (Drawing by Francis Lee Jaques; courtesy of the University of Minnesota Press.)

balancing the demands of what he saw as an increasingly mechanistic and busy modern world. His method was to engage the reader with stories of wilderness canoeing adventures and revelatory personal experiences, using them as vehicles for meditations on the meaning of these encounters with the wild northern landscapes that so powerfully attracted him.

Olson was enough of a naturalist to want to understand the geology as well as the flora and fauna of the terrain he explored. He could read its human history in ancient portage trails first used by the Chippewa and then the voyageurs and in blackened pine stumps that served as reminders of the loggers who had come through more recently and the fires that followed them. He saw the forests of the Canadian Shield country with the eye of someone attuned to the slow working of natural processes, for example, those by which the transformation of an uprooted pine can be observed in the pit and elongated mound ("cradle-knoll," in the idiom of the early settlers) formed on the forest floor by its gradual decay and the new growth that springs from such a nurse log. Or those slower processes by which granite surfaces are broken down over thousands of years by caribou moss and stunted pines, junipers, and cedars whose roots find pathways into the rock.[90] Olson wrote before the movement for an ecologically oriented forestry arose, but his fascination with cycles of growth and decay and the interrelationships of the components of natural systems suggests that he would have embraced it. Emergent ecological thinking, which he absorbed through Leopold's writings and his personal exposure to ecologists during his early studies and later travels with them, reinforced his own instincts and observations.

At the end of *Listening Point,* sitting by his campfire on a greenstone ledge whose age he estimates at over three billion years, Olson reflects on the way modern man still listens to "the ancient rhythms," despite or perhaps because of the noise and the "whirring complexities" of what he liked to call the machine age: "He has come a long way from the primitive, but not far enough to forget."[91] Like Marshall and Leopold decades earlier, Olson embraced the dichotomy he found between primitive experience of nature and modern urban life, but he went beyond either in proclaiming its "spiritual necessity."[92] One of the primary aims of his writing was to revive in his readers an awareness of the primitive that he believed was still alive in most people, at least subconsciously, and to convey the sense of wonder with which he associated it. He attempted to do this by showing the resonance particular scenes had for him: a cliff with pictographs that reminded him that this was once "the spirit land of the Chippewas" or a place where huge boulders, left by a glacier ten thousand years ago, stand among pines, awakening "a powerful sense of the primeval."[93] He encouraged his readers to imagine how the Chippewa would have understood the landscapes through which they preceded him, what the voyageurs and later the early lumberjacks would have seen, and how the forests have evolved over the millennia since the last retreat of the glaciers.

Nature writing has proliferated since Olson wrote, and it continues to shape public opinion about the importance of experiencing and preserving particular natural environments. As environmental battles arose in the latter part of the twentieth century, much of this writing took on a political edge, using descriptions and stories of personal experience to rally support for protecting places under siege. The availability of nature films and television programs and high-quality nature photography (in coffee table books, magazines, and calendars) contributed to growing public support for protecting places remarkable for their scenic or recreational values or, more recently, their biological diversity. As executive director of the Sierra Club from 1952 to 1969, David Brower was the driving force behind a series of books that combined nature photography with texts (essays in some cases, quotations in others) to send strong environmental messages. The first of these, *This Is Dinosaur* (1955), a collection of essays and photographs edited by Wallace Stegner, was sent to members of Congress and helped to defeat plans to build the Echo Park Dam in Dinosaur National Monument. The second, *This Is the American Earth* (1960), featuring photography by Ansel Adams and others and text by Nancy Newhall, drew wide public attention to the cause of conservation. Newhall's text traces a history of increasing human degradation of the environment while the photography mingles images of natural scenes ranging from the intimate to the grand (iconic western landscapes as rendered by Adams) with others suggesting the worst consequences of urban development and the exploitation of natural resources. Successive volumes in the Sierra Club's Exhibit Format Series also sold well and served the purpose of raising public awareness of the appeal of unaltered natural landscapes, sometimes in the service of particular environmental campaigns, for example, the successful one to defeat a proposal to build dams in Grand Canyon. The first of several books in the series showcasing the color photography of Eliot Porter, *In Wildness Is the Preservation of the World* (1962), combined quotations from Thoreau with images of New England and other eastern landscapes portraying seasonal change on an intimate scale. It was widely acclaimed and immensely influential, demonstrating the power of words and images to advance the Sierra Club's goal of building support for the wilderness movement.[94]

Critics have faulted Adams and Porter for presenting selective versions of a sublime nature, in part by omitting signs of human presence, and the Sierra Club series generally for emphasizing aesthetic and spiritual responses to the natural world to the exclusion of other kinds. By ignoring history and the importance of work in human interactions with the natural world, the argument goes, they magnify the opposition between a pristine or Edenic nature and human society.[95] The criticism is important and reflects movement beyond the kind of critique of modern, industrial society that characterized the early wilderness movement, beginning with attacks on the invasion of once remote places by roads and automobiles. A book based on the seventh biennial wilderness conference sponsored by the Sierra Club, edited by David Brower, illustrates the attitudes that were prevalent at the time. In it Ansel Adams describes art as concerned with "the revelation of beauty and the identification of man with his environment" and with generating "spiritual and emotional insight." Justice William O. Douglas sees the machine, in the form of bulldozers plowing roads through forests and jeeps penetrating mountain meadows, as threatening the last remaining wilderness; he argues the need for rallying around spiritual values that he finds undermined by technology. Joseph Wood Krutch urges the importance of contact with "living nature," where one can find "a sense of the mystery, the independence, the unpredictableness of living as opposed to the mechanical."[96] Such arguments lack the nuanced sense of the difficulties of separating nature from culture, and of possibilities for relying on collaboration rather than confrontation, that characterizes much contemporary environmental discourse. Those who made them and the artists who supplied their images, however, grasped the importance of an emotional appeal based on values other than economic ones to winning public support. They responded to what they perceived as an urgent need to change attitudes, and they were effective both in winning particular legislative battles and in stimulating broad public interest in preserving exceptional natural environments.

The influence of the Sierra Club books can be seen in subsequent collaborations between writers and artists or among communities of writers drawn together by a shared purpose. A book of essays by Wendell Berry with photographs by his friend Gene Meatyard helped to defeat the effort by the Army Corps of Engineers to dam Kentucky's Red River and turn the Red River Gorge into a reservoir.[97] Writers have put together collaborative volumes, intended for members of Congress as well as the general public, with the aim of influencing public opinion and legislative debates about the future of such areas as Utah wildlands and the coastal plain of the Arctic National Wildlife Refuge.[98] While some of the contributors to such volumes make direct appeals on political or scientific grounds, more rely on stories and descriptive writing that evoke the beauty, biological richness, or cultural importance of the place in question. Recent books featuring Michigan's natural heritage, some involving collaborations between writers and photographers, are typical of publications focusing on particular states or regions that continue to shape public opinion.[99]

The political activism of writers and artists concerned with protecting natural areas is most obviously directed at major external threats to the integrity of a place from those who would build dams, drill for oil or gas, develop mines, strip timber, or otherwise exploit natural resources. Their evocations of the qualities that make areas worth saving also convey the implicit or explicit message that visitors should use such places lightly, in ways that will not compromise their distinctive qualities. Some kinds of recreational users are obviously preferable to others for those chiefly interested in preservation. Bird-watchers are more welcome than dirt bikers. Nature writing, visual art, and for that matter poetry and fiction, that communicate a sense of aesthetic, spiritual, or ecological values are likeliest to reach and influence those who prefer to experience the woods or other natural landscapes on foot (or, in the case of rivers and lakes, in a canoe or kayak) at a pace that encourages observation and invites reflection. Such visitors, whether or not they come in contact with writing of the sort I have been discussing, may well include hunters and fishermen, many of whom derive as much pleasure from being outside and becoming alert to what is going on around them as from bagging the game or catching the fish that are the ostensible reason for the trip. They are less likely to include those who rely on mechanized transportation for their experience of natural areas: snowmobiles or ORVs, motorboats or jet skis. Such machines may have their uses as efficient means of getting to a desirable place, such as a hunting camp or stand, but they imply a different relationship with the landscape by allowing one to speed through it rather than experience it at a slower pace. For some they invite risk taking and the sense of dominance that this kind of power encourages.

Tensions among recreational users of public forestlands have escalated as the number of users has grown and the incompatibility of different kinds of use, and the values they reflect, has become more obvious. Legal hunting and fishing are generally welcomed in national and state forests and constitute one of the major forms of outdoor recreation. They need not cause tension with other users, although pressure from hunting groups for more intensive management of forests for deer or grouse and other game birds by maintaining existing openings or creating new ones can provoke resistance from environmental and other groups committed to nurturing old-growth forests. Lobbying for more roads and trails allowing motorized access invites similar resistance on the grounds that greater fragmentation of a forested area reduces the amount of deep woods and can threaten the viability of a host of animal and plant species. Conversely, those primarily concerned with increasing and maintaining habitat for game species or expanding opportunities for motorized recreation resist arguments for maximizing old growth.

The creation of campgrounds for automobiles, expanded to include trailers and RVs, has swollen the influx of tourists into state and national parks and forests, but these vehicles are typically confined to the fringes of such areas and in any case are restricted in their mobility. Although plans for expansion of access or facilities for such vehicles can generate controversy, greater concern has arisen over the increasing presence of snowmobiles and especially that of various kinds of ORVs in sensitive natural areas. Michigan now has more than 9,300 miles of trails for snowmobiles and ORVs on public lands. A major concern of critics of such recreation is noise, which disturbs wildlife and can disturb hikers even in areas that are off-limits to motorized vehicles (noise from an ORV can carry for a mile). The contemporary ORV, larger and more powerful, as well as more agile, than its predecessors, would have given Marshall and Leopold fits. Imagine their reaction to the brawny, two-seater Kawasaki Brute Force 750i, capable of churning its way through wetlands and powering over logs and up steep slopes. Ads for ORVs and the more popular all-terrain vehicles (ATVs) and articles in trade publications sometimes present them as workhorses (Honda markets a utility model called the Big Red to farmers), but most are aimed at the large audience of recreational users, the "mud runners" and "rock crawlers" looking primarily for adventure. Manufacturers compete to produce models that accelerate faster, have a higher top speed, and can handle tougher challenges. Many of the model names (Rhino, Grizzly, Trail Blazer, Outlaw, and Renegade, to mention a few) suggest a culture of aggressiveness and defiance of rules. If you are out for thrills and a sense of power, and have read that after a few rock crawls your Yamaha Rhino "makes you feel like a superhero," you will be less likely to worry about staying on the trail or considering the impact your machine has on the terrain.[100] In the world of contemporary ATVs the older rhetoric of masculine adventure and frontier values has been replaced by the language and imagery of action movies, with nature in the role of the adversary to be dominated.

The metaphor of parks and forests as playgrounds becomes problematic when the play involves the potential for significant environmental degradation and conflict with other recreational users. The Forest Service has classified damage from "unmanaged outdoor recreation," especially off-highway-vehicle (OHV) use, as one of the four greatest threats to the national forests (along with fire, invasive species, and the loss of open space).[101] The reaction of state and federal agencies responsible for public forestlands to such abuse, as well as wear and tear from other kinds of recreational use, reflects both an awareness of the need to do more to educate users and restrain irresponsible ones and a significant shift in the perception of forests. This shift, toward greater recognition of the importance of preserving and restoring healthy ecosystems and the biological diversity they foster, has changed the environment in which forest policy is made, if not always how it is implemented.

Tensions among recreational users represent one aspect of the larger controversy over how public forests should be used, a controversy that most often has taken the form of conflicts about how much timber should be cut from these forests. The reluctance of many in government agencies, including their leadership, to abandon the traditional priority given to managing forests to produce timber as recreational use was rapidly growing intensified this conflict. The vision that Harold Titus attributed to Helen Foraker, so promising to those concerned with the problem of the cutover lands, leads ultimately to the ideal of forests as tree farms engineered for maximum productivity. The Forest Service and managers of state lands vastly increased the production of timber from public forestlands after World War II as pent-up demand for housing expanded (in the case of the national forests, from about three billion board feet in 1945 to over eleven billion in 1970). They relied on more intensive management and revised estimates of sustainable yield upward, often using flawed assumptions about future growth, as they responded to pressures from industry and legislators intent on exploiting forest resources as fully as possible. Multiple use for government foresters and their allies in the timber industry came to mean use compatible with a high level of timber production. To achieve this yield, road building had to accelerate, along with clear-cutting. The Multiple-Use Sustained-Yield Act of 1960, although it gave statutory protection to the variety of uses specified by the Organic Act of 1897, which it superseded, did little to change prevailing management practices.[102] By 1989 timber production was still receiving a percentage of the Forest Service budget ten times that devoted to recreation and wildlife.[103] It took effective protests by groups lobbying for greater support of recreation and protection of wildlife on public lands, as well as challenges from ecologists developing new ways of understanding and managing forests, to begin to change the priorities of those ultimately responsible for forest policy on federal and state lands.

7 // The Forest as Ecosystem

Those who managed public forestlands had to learn how to accommodate competing interests, adjusting management practices to respond to pressure from recreational users, as well as from their traditional clientele in the timber and forest product industries and the legislators who supported them. They were slow to acknowledge that postwar levels of timber production, which depended on ever more intensive management, were unsustainable and to recognize that they were alienating a public more interested in forests as places for recreation and aesthetic enjoyment than as sources of wood products. As road networks were extended and patchworks of large clear-cuts became more visible this public grew alarmed. By the 1970s the managers of public forestlands found themselves in a new policy environment as a confluence of forces triggered a revolution in ways of thinking about forests. These forces included passage of a series of federal environmental laws, advances in the understanding of forest ecology (and the parallel emergence of the new discipline of conservation biology), and dramatically heightened public interest in preserving and restoring natural forests, forcefully represented by environmental advocacy groups (including the Sierra Club, Audubon Society, Wilderness Society, Environmental Defense Fund, and Natural Resources Defense Council), which had grown rapidly and developed national constituencies.

The growth of national environmental organizations reflected rising public concern about a broad range of environmental issues. The publication of Rachel Carson's *Silent Spring* in 1962 had dramatized the dangers of pesticide use. A major oil spill from a blown-out well off the coast of Santa Barbara in 1969 alerted the public to another kind of environmental damage, one of many receiving more notice, including polluted rivers, contaminated urban neighborhoods, and lakes made sterile by acid rain. The massive turnout for the first Earth Day (April 22, 1970) reflected a new sense of urgency about the degradation of the environment. Debates about the consequences of the population explosion, runaway development, and excessive consumption became part of public discourse. One manifestation of the sense of environmental crisis was a concern with protecting threatened natural areas, for ecological as well as aesthetic and other reasons. The public recognition of ecology as a scientific discipline in the 1960s and 1970s raised awareness of the importance of healthy ecosystems to sustaining biological diversity and helped to create a climate that made it possible for Congress to pass major environmental acts with broad implications for the management of forests and other natural areas.[1]

The new federal legislation—especially the National Environmental Policy Act (NEPA) of 1969, the Endangered Species Act (ESA) of 1973, and the National Forest Management Act (NFMA) of 1976—had the effect of opening forest policy regarding public lands to greater scrutiny and forcing attention to ecological science. The ESA effectively gave the U.S. Fish and Wildlife Service veto power over forest policy by requiring that habitat for endangered and threatened species be protected. The NEPA had previously introduced the requirement that an Environmental Impact Statement (EIS) be prepared for "major federal actions significantly affecting the quality of the human environment," mandating disclosure of potential environmental impacts of proposed actions and allowing for public response. The NFMA required the Forest Service to develop long-range management plans for each national forest that would conserve biological diversity and maintain "minimum viable species" of forest populations, a clause that would have far-reaching implications. These forest plans were to be developed by means of a process involving a high level of public participation.[2] The cumulative effect of these and other acts from the same period that added new environmental regulations (including the Clean Water and Clean Air Acts and the Wild and Scenic Rivers Act) was to shift the focus of public discourse about forestry policy from guaranteeing a sustainable timber supply, while ostensibly protecting watersheds and considering recreational interests as required by prior legislation (the Organic Act of 1897 and the Multiple-Use Sustained-Yield Act of 1960), by giving a new prominence to maintaining and restoring biological diversity on federal forestlands.

The major scientific development affecting forest policy since the 1970s has been the emergence of ecological forestry, which emphasizes such objectives as sustaining biological diversity, focusing on habitats rather than stands of trees, and encouraging native forests and old growth.[3] This "New Forestry," as it was known when it appeared in the Pacific Northwest, was grounded in pathbreaking studies of forest ecology that looked beyond traditional silviculture to new ways of logging and managing forests that would be less disruptive of the dynamics of forest ecosystems.[4] For proponents of ecological forestry the "health" of forests depended on sustaining the rich mix of flora and fauna on which forest ecosystems depended rather than on simply protecting trees from threats such as insects and fire in order to preserve their potential value as timber and wood products.[5] The forestry establishment advocated intensive management of forests designed to simplify and regulate them; the simplest, most fully regulated kind of forest was a monoculture, for example, a clear-cut area replanted with Douglas fir seedlings after the area was effectively cleaned with fire and herbicides. Ecological forestry, by contrast, stressed the complexity of the forest ecosystem and the adverse effects of management practices such as removing logs and branches from the forest floor, suppressing natural fires, pushing roads into roadless areas to open them to timber cuts, and creating a mosaic of clear-cuts.

Clear-cutting proved to be the issue that brought together scientists concerned with biological diversity and the future of natural forests and a public increasingly concerned with the visible effects on public lands of high levels of timber cutting. Local and national environmental advocacy groups encouraged and channeled this public resistance, increasingly resorting to lawsuits to achieve their aims. A case in federal court challenging the practice of clear-cutting in West Virginia's Monongahela National Forest, brought by a group of turkey hunters who were joined by the Izaak Walton League, led to a decision that clear-cutting was contrary to the Organic Act of 1897 and a precedent-setting injunction banning clear-cutting on federal land in West Virginia. The prospect of a general ban on clear-cutting in national forests became a matter of urgent concern for the Forest Service and the timber industry. Congress responded to this concern by passing the NFMA, which allowed for clear-cutting under some circumstances while also requiring a planning process that would guarantee attention to biological diversity. The act did not significantly slow the pace of timber cutting in the national forests, but by requiring environmental impact statements it had the effect of forcing the Forest Service to hire new staff with expertise in wildlife biology and forest ecology, and it allowed environmental groups unhappy with the forest plans mandated by the act and the assumptions on which they were based to contest them, in court if appeals within the Forest Service proved unproductive. The Forest Service found its management authority eroded by the courts, and its leaders deplored what they came to regard as "judicialized decision making."[6]

The question of whether to protect existing old-growth forests, and the related question of whether to allow more old growth to develop, became the fundamental issue in the controversies between environmentalists and scientists advocating ecological forestry, on the one hand, and agencies responsible for federal and state forestlands (along with the timber industry and those who depended on it) on the other. Foresters trained in traditional silviculture and committed to using forest resources primarily to guarantee a sustained yield of timber over time, the philosophy that had dominated the Forest Service since Gifford Pinchot articulated it in the early years of the agency, viewed old growth as overmature and decadent. An old-growth forest, in this view, was decaying faster than it was producing new growth and should be replaced with younger, rapidly growing trees that could be harvested when they reached the requisite size, before their rate of growth significantly slowed. The ideal was an orderly, efficient, "regulated" forest that could be nurtured by intensive management, with thinning to promote more vigorous growth and the application of herbicides and pesticides as necessary. T. C. Boyle satirizes this kind of forest in his futuristic novel *A Friend of the Earth*, showing it through the eyes of his volatile protagonist, Ty Tierwater, at the height of his environmental activism: "They weren't the yellow pines, the Jeffreys, the ponderosas, cedars and sequoias that should have been here, but artificial trees, hybrids engineered for rapid and unbending growth. . . . Neat rows of them fanned out along both sides of the road, as rectilinear as rows of corn in the Midwest. . . . Tree farming, that's what it was, tree farming in the national forest, monoculture, and to hell with diversity."[7] Early settlers had seen the tangled forest they discovered as disorderly and threatening, an ominous wilderness that had to be mastered if they were to establish their farms and towns. Foresters for much of the twentieth century regarded an old-growth forest, with its dead and dying trees and a floor littered with fallen limbs and other forest debris, as an emblem of waste and a challenge to their management skills.

Although argument about the definition of an old-growth forest continues, most would agree that it includes uneven aged trees, with some 150 to 200 years old (more in the case of long-lived species such as white pine and hemlock), a multilayered canopy with gaps created by natural disturbances, broken-off trunks of dead trees (snags), organic litter, and a variety of habitat niches.[8] Proponents of ecological forestry value the messiness of old-growth forests, including snags and decaying matter on the forest floor, for its role in sustaining biological diversity and forest health. They describe the interdependence of species and its importance to the functioning of healthy ecosystems, using examples such as voles, which eat the truffles that develop from the mycorrhizal fungi that help tree roots to extract nutrients from the soil and then spread mycorrhizal spores through their excrement.[9] One of the chief lessons of research on forest ecosystems in Oregon's Andrews Experimental Forest and elsewhere is how little their complexity is understood. Nancy Langston has described the unintended consequences of Forest Service efforts to manage the forests of the Blue Mountains of eastern Oregon, where previously "complexity allowed the forest to ride the waves of fires and epidemics and droughts."[10] The sustainability of the open forests of giant ponderosa pines of the Blue Mountains depended on periodic light fires, and suppressing these fires affected the capacity of the pines to regenerate. The combination of suppressing fires and harvesting the older pines resulted in a forest dominated by firs, which were devastated by insect pests when stressed by drought. Langston's argument that less management is better when those in charge do not sufficiently understand the dynamics of forest growth is one that has been made repeatedly by proponents of ecological forestry. For Langston, the pursuit of "maximum efficiency" should be replaced by ideals that allow for "complexity, diversity, and uncertainty."[11]

The principal battleground on which the controversy about old-growth forests has played out is the Pacific Northwest, particularly the temperate rain forests of western Washington and Oregon, where the economic stakes are highest and the biological diversity is richest. This controversy reached its peak in the period between the late 1980s and 1994, when the Northwest Forest Plan for federal lands in Washington, Oregon, and California brokered by the Clinton administration was announced. The plan, developed in ninety days of intensive deliberations by a committee of scientists, was widely publicized at the time and has been extensively analyzed and debated in the years since.[12] It represented an effort to resolve a controversy that had developed against a background of rising concern on the part of scientists and a large segment of the public about the extent and methods of timber cutting on federal lands, mainly in old-growth forests, and threatened to halt most timber cutting in the region. The controversy was brought to a head by a series of lawsuits by environmental groups, most notably one led by the Seattle Audubon Society charging the Forest Service with failing to develop a conservation plan for the "threatened" northern spotted owl that would comply with relevant federal acts (NEPA, ESA, NFMA). When Judge William Dwyer in 1991 ruled in favor of the Audubon Society and issued a restraining order prohibiting timber cutting in "owl habitat," the threat to the timber industry in the Northwest and the communities dependent on it became alarmingly real. The owl had already earned the hostility of loggers, who displayed their feelings with slogans such as a pair worn on suspenders, "Save a Logger," "Shoot an Owl."[13] Scientific experts argued that the northern spotted owl was an indicator species whose decline mirrored that of the old-growth forests on which it depended for nesting sites and prey; environmental groups seized the opportunity to make the owl a surrogate for what they preferred to call "ancient forests," a more emotionally charged term than "old growth."

The scientists who developed the Northwest Forest Plan gave priority to maintaining the more than five hundred species of flora and fauna found in old-growth forests in the region rather than to timber production. At the same time they called for a sustainable level of timber sales. The chief means of protecting biological diversity they recommended was to include 80 percent of existing mature and old-growth forests on federal land in large reserves (of over a hundred thousand acres) where logging would be banned. Implementation of the plan and subsequent litigation had the effect of ending the heavy reliance of the timber industry on old growth, with public resistance making it more difficult to log old growth even on private lands outside the reserves, and of causing a dramatic reduction in the timber harvest generally. Communities economically dependent on logging and already suffering from declining timber cuts and automation in the industry, which had eliminated many jobs, were hit particularly hard, with some mills closing and others retooling to handle smaller logs. When the effects of the Northwest Forest Plan were assessed ten years after its implementation, it was clear that the plan had succeeded in protecting biological diversity and increasing the amount of old growth (by allowing younger trees to mature) but not in maintaining the level of timber production that was anticipated or in ending the debate about old growth. Nor, for that matter, did it assure the survival of the spotted owl. Populations of spotted owls have declined in some areas, suffering from a continuing loss of habitat and also from an influx of larger and more aggressive barred owls, which can adapt to forests fragmented by clear cuts.

Recent discussion of forest policy in the Pacific Northwest has questioned the iconic status that old growth has achieved, calling attention to the variety and distribution of what is considered old growth and arguing for paying more attention to the forest landscape as a whole, including early successional stages. Some critics of the Northwest Forest Plan have challenged the sharp division of federal forestland between unmanaged old-growth reserves and areas in which forests can still be actively managed and logged, observing that the reserves were established at a particular moment in the life of forests that will continue to change. They contend that the present old-growth forests of the reserves would be likelier to persist with the benefit of active management such as thinning, prescribed burning, removal of invasive species, and reintroduction of species that have disappeared.[14] Such arguments reflect a fundamental belief in the necessity of actively managing forests to ensure their health and productivity. They represent an effort to redefine and justify the role of forestry science after decisive losses for federal forest policy in the courts and the shift of public opinion toward regarding forests as ecosystems that must be protected. This effort has been complicated by pressures on agency budgets that had come to be linked to timber production, making it difficult to afford sufficient staff to pursue such activities as extensive thinning in a period of declining timber sales. Disagreements about the nature and scale of the management of public lands underlie many of the continuing debates about forest policy, in other areas of the country as well as in the Pacific Northwest. These debates raise fundamental questions about the relations between humans and forests. To what extent, and to what ends, should we attempt to shape our forests rather than allowing them to regenerate naturally? What kinds of management are likeliest to foster the ecological health of forests? What are likely to be the long-term effects of our interventions? Of our efforts to accommodate the multiple uses of forests mandated by federal law and established by tradition?

The Healthy Forests Restoration Act of 2003, an outgrowth of the Bush administration's Healthy Forests Initiative, represented a victory for more intensive management that was welcomed by advocates of traditional silviculture and by the timber industry. The act, passed in the aftermath of severe western forest fires in 2002, including Oregon's massive Biscuit Fire, affirmed the importance of protecting and restoring stands of old growth but expedited salvage logging by streamlining environmental regulations, chiefly by waiving the requirement of an environmental impact statement for timber sales of a thousand acres or less (successfully challenged in court by the Sierra Club). The stated goals of the act include reducing the hazard of future fires by thinning forests and protecting communities vulnerable to forest fires. Environmentalists immediately attacked it as an indirect way of justifying logging and road building in the national forests, thus letting timber companies back into areas from which they had been excluded and allowing them to log healthy as well as dead trees.[15] Arguments by industry and forestry scientists for extensive cuts (including logging of the large-diameter, old-growth trees necessary to make the operation profitable) only heightened their skepticism. The continuing controversy has been fueled by litigation challenging portions of the Healthy Forests Restoration Act and efforts in Congress to amend the act, as well as by the absence of scientific evidence that salvage logging will reduce the intensity of future fires. What research has been done points to the negative environmental effects of salvage logging due to soil disturbance by heavy equipment, erosion, river siltation, and removal of the woody debris needed for forests to regenerate.[16]

Other actions taken by the Bush administration, and subsequent actions taken by the Obama administration to reconsider or undo them, illustrate the difficulty of definitively resolving a controversy as deep seated and contentious as the one over old-growth forests in the Pacific Northwest. By settling lawsuits brought by the timber industry aimed at opening up more federal land to logging the Bush administration undercut the Northwest Forest Plan and set a course that would result in the weakening of environmental regulations protecting salmon, as well as spotted owls, and in a substantial reduction of protected "critical habitat." A new plan for protecting the spotted owl, mandated by the settlements entered into by the federal government, that significantly reduced protected habitat was finalized despite the objections of the scientists who reviewed it, prompting a lawsuit by a consortium of environmental groups. In 2005 and again in 2008 the Bush administration issued revised NFMA planning regulations for all national forests that would have weakened environmental protections and reduced public participation in forest planning. Both revisions were rejected by federal courts.[17] In July of 2009 the Obama administration declined to appeal the second of these court decisions and announced its own effort to rewrite the regulations. The proposed new regulations (officially the new "Forest Planning Rule") were announced in February 2011, with the final regulations to follow after a period of public comment.

Collaborations involving representatives of groups ranging from loggers to environmentalists on plans for the Gifford Pinchot and Siuslaw National Forests designed to thin younger trees and get them to mills pointed to another, more promising way of settling disputes.[18] Negotiated agreements, including a recent one between the timber industry and environmental groups to support federal legislation that would settle long-standing disputes about harvest levels and watershed and old-growth protection in central and eastern Oregon, reflect a mutual recognition of the changed scientific and political context. About a decade after the appearance of the Northwest Forest Plan, William Dietrich, a journalist who had attempted to represent all sides of the controversy in his book *The Final Forest* (1992), published an article in which he concluded that the old-growth wars would never end, but the plan proved that the democratic process worked and also "codified a paradigm shift in the way people saw national forests: no longer simply as a resource base, but as an ecosystem with biological, aesthetic, and spiritual qualities as valuable as timber."[19]

The revolution in scientific understanding of forest ecology and related arguments for protecting biological diversity, particularly as represented by old-growth forests, would not have had the impact on the public they did without an emotional appeal based partly on what Dietrich describes as aesthetic and spiritual qualities. A book commissioned by the Wilderness Society explaining the scientific case for conserving the "ancient forests" of the Pacific Northwest for a lay audience argues that the temperate rain forests on the west side of the Cascade Mountains are "extraordinary for their cathedralesque beauty," as well as for providing fine timber, rich biological diversity, and pure water.[20] The appeal to "cathedralesque beauty" by a biologist engaged in demonstrating the complexity of old-growth forests reflects the persistence of aesthetic and spiritual values associated with the romantic view of forests that arose in nineteenth-century America. Such appeals play on public attraction to, and nostalgia for, qualities associated with North America's presettlement forests, taken as representing a kind of wholeness and naturalness that our forests have largely lost. One commentator has characterized forestry scientists eager to eliminate the "messiness" of old growth as being most troubled by "the re-enchantment of the natural world."[21] Using the term *ancient forests,* an alternative to the *primeval* favored by nineteenth-century writers, was one way of contributing to the process of reenchantment. To call forests ancient is to give them an aura of mystery and permanence and to contrast them implicitly with the ideal of simplified, highly regulated forests embraced by foresters and the timber industry for much of the twentieth century.

The growth of a public sense of aesthetic and spiritual values associated with forests, as well as ecological ones, was stimulated by the effort to establish federally protected wilderness areas, commonly known as the wilderness movement. This effort began in earnest in the 1920s with calls for dedicated wilderness areas by Aldo Leopold and Arthur Carhart, subsequently joined by others including Bob Marshall, Robert Sterling Yard, and Benton MacKaye who came together to found the Wilderness Society in 1935. The movement gathered momentum in the 1940s and 1950s, eventually resulting in passage of the federal Wilderness Act of 1964. The Wilderness Act established criteria for including designated areas, many in national forests, in a National Wilderness Preservation System and affirmed the value of wilderness, defined by the act as a natural area that retains "its primeval character and influence, without permanent improvements or human habitation" and as a place "where the earth and its community of life are untrammeled by man, where man himself is a visitor who does not remain." The act reflects the strong biases of its proponents in favor of primitive experience of nature and against mechanized recreation. It specifies that wilderness should offer "outstanding opportunities for solitude or a primitive and unconfined type of recreation" and that there should be no permanent roads and no use of motor vehicles or any other form of "mechanical transport" except to satisfy minimal administrative requirements such as protecting safety.[22]

In recent years the idea of wilderness embodied in the act has drawn vigorous criticism and just as vigorous defense. Among other things, critics have challenged the exclusion of a lasting human presence from areas defined as "wilderness" and have deplored the presumed effects on thinking about land use policy of the strict separation of nature and culture envisioned in the act.[23] They have also traced the origins of the prevailing concept of wilderness to the attraction of the American frontier and of the romantic sublime and have faulted its advocates for ignoring history, particularly that of indigenous tribes.[24] Whatever the merits of arguments about the cultural assumptions embodied in the concept of "wilderness" and about the validity of the term itself, the Wilderness Act has led to the creation of an expanding network of federal wilderness areas, now amounting to over 109 million acres, and has validated the concept of wilderness for the broader public. It has had a powerful political effect, in other words, and the wilderness ideal remains a potent force. My concern here is with the role played by some of the values associated with this ideal, as it developed in the twentieth century and continued to take on different meanings, in shaping the public perception of forests.

Two figures are particularly important to the developments I am tracing, John Muir and Aldo Leopold. Both articulated views of the value of public forestlands that challenged the "wise use" philosophy of Gifford Pinchot, based on his utilitarian conviction that conservation should produce "the greatest good, for the greatest number, for the longest run," and the federal and state forest policy that followed from it.[25] Muir was initially friendly with Pinchot and supportive of his efforts to establish forest reserves as a way of protecting forested land from private exploitation. In "The American Forests," one of a series of essays championing national parks that Muir published in the *Atlantic Monthly*, he embraced the need to establish public forests to protect watersheds and "produce as much timber as is possible without spoiling [the forests]" for public use.[26] Yet these essays contain the seeds of Muir's future breach with Pinchot, which was to lead to their intense, nationally publicized controversy over the future of the Hetch Hetchy Valley, included in the expanded Yosemite National Park for which Muir had successfully campaigned. Muir's failure to stop the conversion of Hetch Hetchy to a reservoir to supply San Francisco with water left him bitterly disappointed at his defeat by the "temple destroyers," as he called those he regarded as profaning a landscape that rivaled that of Yosemite Valley, but the prolonged controversy had the effect of raising public awareness of arguments for wilderness preservation to a new level.[27]

The *Atlantic Monthly* essays that Muir collected in *Our National Parks* alternate between celebrations of the magnificence of American forests, especially those of the western national parks he knew well (Yosemite, Sequoia, Yellowstone), and condemnations of those he saw as threatening them and the surrounding forestland: loggers, miners, shepherds and the "hoofed locusts" they tended, and the shake makers who cut large slabs out of sugar pines and left them to die. Someone who could characterize loggers and shepherds as "mere destroyers . . . tree-killers, wool and mutton men, spreading death and confusion in the fairest groves and gardens ever planted" (363) was bound to fall out with Pinchot, who believed that providing grazing land as well as a sustainable timber supply was among the highest uses of the forest reserves. Muir begins his essay "The American Forests" with a panoramic and lovingly detailed view of presettlement forests spreading "in glorious exuberance" from the East to the West Coast and on to Alaska as a prelude to an exhortation to "Save what is left of the forests!" (336–37). Settlers who cleared forests were "pious destroyers" who waged "interminable forest wars" (346). Loggers had reduced the "magnificent coniferous forests around the Great Lakes" to "lumber and smoke" (346). Muir could acknowledge the inevitability of the changes brought by settlement and grant the necessity of reserving public forestlands to guard against a timber famine, but his passion was communicating his enthusiasm for "God's woods" to a national audience, which he sought to enlighten about the forces he saw as threatening the forests he loved, including a growing influx of tourists.

Early in the first essay in his collection, "The Wild Parks and Forest Reservations of the West," Muir asserts that "Thousands of tired, nerve-shaken, over-civilized people are beginning to find out . . . that wildness is a necessity; and that mountain parks and reservations are useful not only as fountains of timber and irrigating rivers, but as fountains of life" (1). The phrase "fountains of life" echoes Thoreau's injunction in his seminal essay "Walking" to "go in search of the springs of life."[28] Muir was deeply influenced by the idea that transcendental truths are to be found in the natural world, which he discovered in his reading of Thoreau and Emerson. He saw encounters with mountains and their forests and streams as having spiritual as well as aesthetic value and often relied on biblical or more general religious language to convey this, substituting his own religion of nature for his father's severe Calvinism. Thus he wrote about the "divine lessons" to be found in Sierra landscapes and described forests as temples and windblown pines as "a bright, waving, worshipful multitude," transferring his own religious enthusiasm to the trees.[29] He called his initial public defense of forests "God's First Temples," echoing William Cullen Bryant's "Forest Hymn."[30]

Muir could find in forests places of refuge and of meditation, as others have, describing the "deep peace of the solemn woods" and the "deep, brooding calm of the wilderness."[31] It was more characteristic of him, however, to emphasize their animation and to describe how he was energized and delighted by this.[32] When Muir wrote of the need to seek out the "fountains of life," he was trying to persuade his readers that they could be spiritually rejuvenated by the vitality they could find in the natural world, as he was. One of the best-known essays from *The Mountains of California*, "A Wind-Storm in the Forests," exemplifies Muir's response to nature's kinetic energies, in this case appreciated from a swaying perch at the top of a Douglas spruce he climbed in order to experience the storm more intensely. He associates the exhilaration he feels with the thrashing trees themselves, imagining them as "holding high festival." Muir renders the beauty he finds in the scene by registering its effect on his heightened senses, with the varied sounds and fragrances that he distinguishes mingling with visual impressions he describes himself as *feeling:* "Now my eye roved over the piny hills and dales . . . and felt the light running in ripples and broad swelling undulations across the valleys from ridge to ridge, as the shining foliage was stirred by corresponding waves of air" (176–77). Muir frequently refers to the beauty of Sierra landscapes and occasionally describes them as picturesque or sublime but rarely places himself in the position of a detached observer. He typically associates aesthetic perceptions with the spirit and dynamism he finds in the natural world and registers through his own heightened sensations.

Through his writings and his public stance as the most prominent advocate of his time for national parks and the protection of wilderness, as well as his role as cofounder and president of the Sierra Club (for twenty-two years), Muir exercised a major influence on public perception of the spiritual and aesthetic values of natural forests.[33] Aldo Leopold played a different kind of role, that of a figure who could bridge the gap between scientific and popular understandings and articulate an ecological vision that later would prove important for those promoting the cause of ecological forestry. Leopold brought ethical and aesthetic dimensions related to ecological awareness of the dynamics of natural systems to the discussion of the value of forests, primarily through the vision he articulated most forcefully and comprehensively in his influential essay "The Land Ethic," included in *A Sand County Almanac* (1949). His ideas were frequently cited by those advocating ecological forestry and influenced a land ethic canon adopted by the Society of American Foresters in 1992, though not to the degree that proponents of his vision would have wished.[34]

In "The Land Ethic" Leopold brought together ideas he had been developing since the 1930s through a series of essays, including the radical view that all species deserved continued existence as a matter of "biotic right." He had come to believe that we should regard ourselves as members of the "biotic community" rather than as its masters and that we should act out of an "ecological conscience," concerning ourselves primarily with "land health" (which he defined as "the capacity of the land for self-renewal") rather than with the economic value of what could be produced from the land.[35] The oft-quoted maxim that he offers near the end of the essay constitutes his most succinct statement of the values he opposed to economic ones: "A thing is right when it tends to preserve the integrity, stability, and beauty of the biotic community. It is wrong when it tends otherwise" (224–25). The "integrity" of a biotic community depended for Leopold on preserving the original complement of species whose interactions ensured the healthy functioning of the community. To remove parts of the biotic community, by exterminating wolves or allowing cattle to destroy vegetation by overgrazing their range, for example, was to destabilize it. Ecologists today, more conscious of the dynamism of ecosystems and their susceptibility to change, would not promote stability as an ideal. For Leopold "stability" was a way of referring to land with a healthy circulatory system, able to cycle nutrients and sustain itself over time, hence resilient. As its association with "integrity" and "stability" implies, "beauty" was for him inseparable from ecological function; beautiful land was healthy and productive land.[36] By linking beauty with ecological science and beginning to develop what he called a "land esthetic," Leopold provided additional justification for making an appeal to beauty a part of the new way of thinking about old-growth forests.[37]

Leopold had a practical sensibility shaped by his early years in the Forest Service (after training at the Yale Forest School) and by his subsequent career in game and wildlife management, a field he was instrumental in establishing. He recognized the need to use natural resources to a much greater degree than Muir had and encouraged sustainable ways of logging public and private lands. Throughout his career Leopold worked to educate farmers in methods for producing game, as well as crops, while conserving the health of their land. Yet whatever his utilitarian concerns, he was also convinced by his early experience as a Forest Service employee in the Southwest of the need to designate some national forest land as "wilderness areas," a concept he pioneered. Leopold had the satisfaction of seeing his idea realized when portions of the Gila National Forest were designated a wilderness area in 1924, as he had urged they be. He initially argued for wilderness areas as the "highest recreational use" of some parts of national forest land, working within the framework established by Pinchot as Forest Service policy. His early definition of a wilderness area reflected his own view of a satisfying outdoor experience, "a continuous stretch of country preserved in its natural state, open to lawful hunting and fishing, big enough to absorb a two weeks' pack trip, and kept devoid of roads, artificial trails, cottages, or other works of man."[38]

The kind of manly recreation Leopold associated with wilderness areas aligned him with Theodore Roosevelt and Stewart Edward White, both of whom he had read on outdoor adventure in his youth.[39] They embodied what he saw as "a distinctively American tradition of self-reliance, hardihood, woodcraft, and marksmanship."[40] After moving to Madison, Wisconsin, in 1924 and beginning to take canoeing trips in the Quetico-Superior area of northern Minnesota and Ontario, Leopold added explorations by canoe as well as by pack train to his justifications of wilderness areas. Both were "primitive" modes of travel that he associated with the pioneering spirit that appealed to Roosevelt and White and with what he called "the wilderness of Covered Wagon Days" and contrasted with both organized campgrounds ("Wood and Water Furnished") and the domesticated nature of city life.[41] The chief threat to wilderness that Leopold saw at this time was the rapid spread of tourism, especially the motorized tourism encouraged by the Good Roads Movement, which he regularly denounced: "[W]e are crushing the last remnants of something that ought to be preserved for the spiritual and physical welfare of future Americans."[42] Leopold's appeal to spiritual as well as physical welfare here, like his argument for the "cultural value of wilderness" (as embodied by canoe and pack trips in unpopulated areas), was a way of broadening the sense of the value of wilderness that he was trying to communicate beyond a narrow focus on recreation. He would broaden it further in the 1930s and 1940s as he developed and articulated the ecological understanding that would inform "The Land Ethic" and *A Sand County Almanac* generally.

Spending the fall of 1935 in Germany and Austria on a fellowship to study game management in relation to forestry helped focus Leopold's views of forest management and the value of wildness. In a two-part article that resulted from his travels Leopold emphasized the negative effects of the German practice of silviculture, in particular the intensive cultivation of spruce plantations for timber, including excessive acidity of the topsoil ("soil-sickness"), failure of forest litter to decay, and insect epidemics.[43] Leopold found some hope of counteracting the sterility and declining yield produced by this kind of management in efforts to restore mixed forests and encourage more wildlife but concluded that it was difficult for the Germans to escape their passion for geometry in planting forests and their attachment to artificial methods of managing wildlife (including feeding deer and eliminating hawks and owls to protect pheasants). His dominant impression was of the lack of "wildness" in the German landscape.[44] Leopold's German experience sharpened his sense of the importance of preserving wilderness areas in America and gave him vivid examples, from the very cradle of forestry science, of the hazards of excessive regulation of forests. This experience would continue to resonate in his subsequent elaborations of an ideal of conservation based on land health rather than economic return in essays that included examples of the ecological damage caused by "artificialized" management of wildlife and overly regulated forests.

Leopold's involvement with two large forested areas in Michigan's Upper Peninsula, in 1938 and 1942, reveals both how he responded to practical problems of forestry and wildlife management and how he continued to refine his thinking about the value of wilderness areas. In the summer of 1938 Leopold made two visits to the private Huron Mountain Club to develop and then present a management plan for the property, at that time amounting to fifteen thousand acres of relatively undisturbed maple-hemlock forest to the west of Marquette, with shoreline on Lake Superior. The members eventually acted on virtually all of the recommendations Leopold made in his report, including the most consequential one: that they create a five-thousand-acre protected reserve in the center of the property surrounded by a buffer of selectively logged land.[45] Leopold recommended selective logging less as a source of revenue than as a way of creating habitat for wildlife (including ruffed grouse and snowshoe rabbits) through the introduction of gaps in the forested areas. He urged that wolves not be exterminated or driven away but accepted as a way of controlling the deer population, arguing that their presence made the property more valuable and unique than deer ever could. He made a point of including otters, which were competing for fish with the club's fishermen, among the predators that should be left alone. The more conservation-minded members of the club, who ultimately carried the day, responded readily to these suggestions and the further one that they encourage scientific studies, in cooperation with universities in the region, and register the property as a state natural area.

Leopold's reputation as the leading expert on wildlife management at the time, along with his pragmatism, gave him the authority to be persuasive. He was able to show his clients how they could enjoy their remarkable property, since grown to almost twenty-two thousand acres, and manage it according to enlightened forestry practices, at the same time persuading them of the value of preserving its wildness. His design for the property, establishing a biological reserve at its core and designating other areas for different uses, was consistent with the system of differentiating areas (zones) by intended use that was introduced in national parks in the 1930s and adopted by the Forest Service and state agencies for managing public lands.[46] Current members of the Huron Mountain Club have continued to follow Leopold's recommendations closely and have recently undertaken a process that will lead to updating them, after more than seventy years, based on an inventory of species on the property conducted by the Huron Mountain Wildlife Foundation and a survey of members' attitudes.

In 1942 Leopold responded to an appeal from Robert Sterling Yard, then president of the Wilderness Society, by writing an article for *Outdoor America* urging protection of a large stand of old-growth hardwood forest in the Porcupine Mountains of the western Upper Peninsula. This was being whittled away by logging operations accelerated by the wartime demand for timber. Leopold had remained actively involved in the Wilderness Society since helping to found it, periodically contributing articles to its publication *Living Wilderness,* including one to the inaugural issue offering a rationale for the society. His article on the Porcupine Mountains combines rhetoric calculated for popular appeal with a scientific explanation of the consequences of what he characterized as the "violence" of slashing (clear-cutting). The article begins with a dramatic evocation of the crashing fall of a giant maple, "the last merchantable tree of the last merchantable forty of the last virgin hardwood forest of any size in the Lake States," and modulates into elegiac prophecy: "There will be an end of cathedral aisles to echo the hermit thrush, or to awe the intruder. There will be an end of hardwood wilderness large enough for a few days' skiing or hiking without crossing a road. The forest primeval, in this region, will henceforward be a figure of speech."[47]

Leopold's rhetorical strategy was to spur his readers to action by shocking them with an image of destruction and then evoking the sense of wonder that could be experienced in a north woods old-growth forest, relying on such charged phrases as "cathedral aisles" and "forest primeval," the latter echoing the familiar beginning of Longfellow's poem *Evangeline.* He devoted most of the article, however, to arguments for conservation of the sort that had become natural for him, drawing on his convictions about the proper uses of forestry. Leopold observes that logging such a mature hardwood forest would destroy "the best schoolroom for foresters to learn what remains to be learned about hardwood forestry" and argues for the symbolic importance of the sugar maple ("as American as the rail fence or the Kentucky rifle"). He uses the example of the Spessart forest in Bavaria to demonstrate the long-term damage done by clear-cutting. The slope of the Spessart that was only selectively logged produced the finest cabinet oak in the world, Leopold observed, while the slope that was clear-cut yielded only inferior pine, having failed to recover over a period of three centuries from the depletion of the microflora in the soil on which the biotic community that sustained it depended.[48] Leopold's overall argument has as much to do with the advantages of selective cutting as with the case for wilderness protection, yet he recognized the need to appeal to values that would resonate with a public less attuned to debates about forestry practices than he was. He concluded his essay by returning to the rhetorical mode of the beginning, describing the Porcupine forests as not just timber but a symbol of "a chapter of national history which we should not be allowed to forget. When we abolish the last sample of the Great Uncut, we are, in a sense, burning books."

Leopold knew that the forests of the Porcupines were not the only example of the "Great Uncut" in Michigan, and in a letter responding to Jack Van Coevering of the *Detroit Free Press* he agreed that most of the uncut remnant was "scrubby," as a friend of Van Coevering's had claimed. He might have agreed with another correspondent of Van Coevering's, W. F. Ramsdell of the University of Michigan, that the Huron Mountains had more and better "virgin northern hardwoods" than the Porcupines.[49] Yet Leopold and others whose opinion Van Coevering sought could agree readily that the Porcupines held enough pockets of outstanding old growth to be worth fighting to preserve. Those who led the public campaign for preservation revealed no doubts about the value of the Porcupines, appealing to history and to aesthetic and spiritual values. In an article published in *National Parks* magazine, Raymond Dick, an Ironwood merchant who helped to found and then led the Save the Porcupines Association, quoted *The Song of Hiawatha* on the forest beside the shores of Gitche Gumee and invoked the Chippewa and the visit of the explorer Pierre Esprit Radisson in 1659. He colorfully described the forests of the Porcupines as about to disappear, "leaving desolation and ruin in the place of beauty and grandeur." Dick imagined the Porcupines as a remnant of the frontier where Americans could regain their spiritual values. Responding to the wartime mood, he associated peace and independence of thought with experience of the forests. In Dick's view such qualities were particularly needed when the American people were facing the materialistic and dictatorial regime of Nazi Germany.[50] In a long article for the *Grand Rapids Press* published in the same year, outdoor editor Ben East, a friend and ally of Dick, argued that the Porcupines constituted a little-known treasure rivaling the Ozarks and speculated that Robert Service would have been as inspired by the view of the Carp River from the high escarpment overlooking it as he was by Alaskan valleys.[51] When the Michigan legislature authorized a million dollars to be spent purchasing forty-six thousand acres in the Porcupines in February of 1944, after efforts in Congress to create a national park or monument had failed, East celebrated the victory as the preservation of a sacred place: "Here is a forest shrine that Michigan has decided to keep. Here is a vast cathedral of trees that is to remain a cathedral. Here is a region of forest-cloistered lakes and foaming brawling mountain rivers that are to be left in their wild setting."[52]

In an article published earlier in *Living Wilderness,* "Wilderness as a Land Laboratory" (1941), Leopold had introduced an important argument for wilderness that would become part of his thinking about conservation, writing that "a science of land-health needs . . . a base-datum of normality, a picture of how healthy land maintains itself as an organism."[53] Signs of land sickness were evident enough to Leopold, including declining fertility, erosion, loss of species, and irruptions of pests. As ecological science developed a fuller understanding of what contributed to forest health, including the microflora in the soil, the benefits of having old-growth forest such as that of the Porcupine Mountains function as a norm became more apparent. Recreation grew less important to Leopold as a justification for wilderness areas, "not their only or even their principal utility."[54] He argued the need to develop an awareness of what he called "the complexity of the land organism," as well as a land ethic. Leopold also insisted on the importance of an aesthetic appreciation of land. One of Muir's recurrent themes was the beauty he found everywhere in the Sierras, in evidence of the violence of natural forces as well as in mountain meadows, and he recognized that an ability to see such beauty fed the passion to preserve a place. Theodore Roosevelt echoed Muir on the beauty of the Yosemite Valley and the importance of preserving it after spending three nights camping in Yosemite with him and listening to his arguments for national parks during his 1903 visit to California. Leopold's contribution was to associate beauty with the health of the biotic community, making appreciation of it a dimension of ecological understanding.

When a 1935 editorial in the *Journal of Forestry* criticized the newly established Wilderness Society and declared that aesthetic judgments were not the business of foresters, Leopold responded with a letter to the editor arguing that each person must judge what is beautiful, as well as what is right. He insisted on the importance of beauty as a criterion for determining the value of wilderness: "The question of the 'highest use' of remaining wilderness is basically one of evaluating beauty, in the broadest ecological sense of that word."[55] Leopold's position makes clear his divergence from the utilitarian views of the forestry establishment and his determination to link a sense of beauty with ecological awareness, if not exactly what he meant by "the broadest ecological sense of the word." He would have been conscious of the long-standing opposition of foresters, and the Forest Service, to aesthetic standards of value. Gifford Pinchot had resisted them vigorously, recognizing the threat that an emphasis on beauty posed to scientific forestry and the "wise use" of natural resources that he championed.[56]

While he never developed his land aesthetic as fully as he did his land ethic, Leopold attempted to distinguish the kind of aesthetic appreciation he valued.[57] He begins his "Marshland Elegy" with a dazzling scene of clangorous sandhill cranes descending on a marsh through the dawn mists, then establishes the ancient relationship between cranes and marsh by describing the slow evolution of the landscape. The peats that the cranes stand on, he tells his readers, are "the compressed remains of the mosses that clogged the pools, of the tamaracks that spread over the moss, of the cranes that bugled over the tamaracks since the retreat of the ice sheet."[58] For Leopold it was impossible to appreciate the quality of the cranes, or that of the marsh, without understanding this ecological and evolutionary context. Elsewhere he describes Daniel Boone as seeing "only the surface of things" because he lacked the kind of "mental eye" made possible by ecological science.[59] In "Marshland Elegy" he goes on to claim that "our ability to perceive quality in nature begins with the 'pretty,'" his equivalent of the picturesque, and proceeds through stages of the beautiful to "values as yet uncaptured by words," where the quality of cranes lies. If these ultimate aesthetic values remain elusive, Leopold nonetheless shows throughout *A Sand County Almanac* that they differ from conventional notions of scenic beauty and derive from natural processes rather than the fact or illusion of a landscape shaped by human actions. The thrust of "Marshland Elegy" is to link beauty with ecological quality and to make wildness the measure of this quality: "The ultimate value in these marshes is wildness, and the crane is wildness incarnate."[60] For crane marshes, as well as forests, the threat to quality lay in human interventions that disrupted natural processes, in this case efforts to create agricultural land by draining the marshes, with the unintended consequence of creating the conditions for unmanageable peat fires.

By challenging traditional assumptions about the advantages of intensive management of forests and articulating a holistic view of forest health based on ecological science Leopold prepared the way for the emphasis of the New Forestry on forests as ecological communities whose biological diversity should be protected. His efforts to link ethical and aesthetic considerations with ecological ones helped to justify introducing these into arguments for reforming forest policy.[61] If Leopold provided support for proponents of ecological forestry, he also influenced attitudes about the relationship of humans to wilderness, and the natural world more generally, that played an important role in public controversies about old-growth forests, especially in the Pacific Northwest. Muir was a more charismatic and more public figure in his day, inspiring support for preservation with rhapsodic accounts of his experience in the Sierra and prophetic denunciations of "temple destroyers." Leopold, as *A Sand County Almanac* won a growing following in the years after his premature death in 1948, helped to create a constituency educated in the functioning of healthy biotic communities and receptive to arguments for thinking about the value of forests in new ways.

While Sigurd Olson's influence does not compare with that of Muir or Leopold, he played a prominent role in the wilderness movement. Moreover, he made a determined effort to articulate spiritual values that he associated with the "north woods" of the upper Midwest, which he did as much as anyone to establish in the popular imagination as a distinct region.[62] Olson described spiritual and other values he associated with wilderness in ways that gave him a wide audience and made him a pivotal figure in the effort to protect the Quetico-Superior country (including what is now the Boundary Waters Canoe Area Wilderness) and in the broader struggle to pass a federal Wilderness Act. His commitment to these values led him to embrace a public role as president of the National Parks Association, and subsequently the Wilderness Society, and to serve as a consultant to Secretary of the Interior Stewart Udall, who called on him to help identify lands for federal protection in Alaska and elsewhere. Olson became a popular speaker at meetings of national park supervisors and training sessions for Park Service employees and gave addresses on the meaning and value of wilderness at meetings of national environmental groups, including the biennial conferences on wilderness sponsored by the Sierra Club.[63]

Whereas Leopold tried to articulate aesthetic values and link them to ecological ones, Olson concentrated on what he called "spiritual" values or sometimes "intangibles." He associated these values with a kind of outdoor experience that he saw as primitive, simple, and physically and emotionally challenging. In an essay on why we need wilderness Olson invokes Thoreau ("We need the tonic of wildness") and asserts that the purpose of preserving wilderness is to give Americans "the opportunity to find themselves and their real qualities, to rejuvenate their spirits through simple living in the out-of-doors."[64] Engagement with wilderness, of the vigorous sort he advocated, was for Olson a way of recovering a serenity and equilibrium missing from modern life and also a sense of wholeness and oneness with the natural world. This was a matter of returning to our roots in what he regarded as "the ancient rhythms, silences, and mysteries of the once unknown."[65]

Olson tends to conflate the spiritual values that he invokes and often associates them with silence. He begins an essay simply called "Silence" with a description of the quiet just before dawn and goes on to argue the importance of preserving "the great silences of the wilderness," which he associates with heightened awareness and receptivity and also with a sense of timelessness, all made possible by the absence of familiar human sounds. The silence that he sees as belonging to "the primitive scene," and returns to repeatedly in his writing, becomes for Olson a measure of the sanctity of the remote places he explores and the spiritual dimension of his experience of them.[66] This silence held none of the "religious terror" of the silence that Tocqueville experienced in the deep woods on his journey to Saginaw. Rather, it was vital to the appeal of the "wilderness" that he found in the Canadian Shield country.

Olson's preoccupation with the value of silence, and the solitude with which he associates it, reflects his sense of continuing threats to the Quetico-Superior area from the incursion of roads and motorboats and the more general effects of the "grind of motors" and the "roar of jets" that represented for him the mechanized character as well as the noisiness of modern life. To invest silence with the importance he did was to sharpen the dichotomy between wilderness and civilization, seen as increasingly clamorous, and to make noise a symbol of an intrusiveness incompatible with the spiritual values he associated with wilderness. Olson would have found it harder to make silence a touchstone of spirituality today, when it has become increasingly rare. As acoustic ecologist Gordon Hempton has shown, the places in the continental United States in which it is possible to experience something like Olson's "great silences" are rapidly diminishing, as are the intervals between interruptions by noises such as those of motors or jet engines. Even the "one square inch of silence" in Olympic National Park that he takes as symbolizing the possibility of natural quiet must be defended from the intrusion of man-made noise, chiefly from overflights.[67]

One could fault Olson for projecting onto others his own sense of the allure of the primitive and for embracing an extreme form of antimodernism. One could also criticize the outmoded ecology that led him to describe wilderness areas as "museum pieces of primitive America," using a metaphor popular with conservationists at the time that implies a stability at odds with contemporary understanding of forest ecosystems.[68] Olson was more flexible than some of his assertions about wilderness would suggest, however. He knew he had to be able to function in the modern world and showed that he could do this effectively in his role as an environmental activist. And he accepted technological advances despite his instinctual attraction to the primitive. Olson also showed that he could find wild nature in a secluded nook of a city park and in the surroundings of his cabin on Burntside Lake a few miles outside of Ely, Minnesota. His writings, which still find an audience, are significant partly because of the way they broadened the discussion of humanistic values involved in our interaction with wild places.

Efforts to articulate humanistic values associated with wilderness, and particularly with old-growth forests, have continued and have become more closely linked with ecological ones, as in a recent essay in which the philosopher and nature writer Kathleen Dean Moore tackles the challenge of defining spiritual values.[69] Moore acknowledges the ecosystem services provided by forests along with cultural values, including recreation and aesthetic appeal, but she concerns herself primarily with ways in which an old-growth forest, in her case Andrews Forest in the Oregon Cascades, can enhance spiritual well-being. She invokes Leopold several times and Muir once, careful to differentiate her sense of "secular spiritual practice" from Muir's religion of nature. Her enumeration of sources of spiritual value integrates older ways of talking about the forest with others dependent on modern, ecological understanding. The scale of the old growth through which she walks, with its giant trees, invites humility and wonder. The silence of the forest, and implicitly the solitude that one can experience there, fosters tranquility and prompts her to appeal to the familiar metaphor of "cathedral forests," which she gives a new twist by invoking the medieval understanding of cathedrals as places of sanctuary for fugitives.

Moore finds beauty not in scenic values but in the harmonious working of the forest's parts, what she calls its "organic wholeness," associating this with Leopold's "integrity." Her other sources of spiritual value show the influence of ecological awareness even more clearly: the sense of the continuity of life given by the presence of trees of all ages; evidence of the "stream of living things" in which death mingles with rebirth; a complexity that derives from structural diversity and the interrelationships of the forest's parts; and the wildness that results from natural succession, unaltered by human attempts to manage it, and provides an ecological baseline showing what a forest can be. Moore's description of the rawness of an adjacent clear-cut slope gives her delineation of spiritual values added force. Like many efforts to define the noneconomic values associated with forests, her essay grows out of a sense of ecological wounds inflicted by human actions.

Moore's success in blending scientific and humanistic perspectives suggests ways in which they can complement each other, deepening our understanding of an old-growth forest and changing the way we perceive it. Her essay illustrates how a tradition of finding aesthetic and spiritual value in forests that reaches back into the nineteenth century can be given new vigor and intellectual force by ecological understanding of the sort taught by Leopold. It complements writing by scientists who have argued for the importance of values other than strictly scientific ones, for example, biologist Donald Waller in an essay written as a response to William Cronon's "The Trouble with Wilderness." Waller insists that "many biologists and environmentalists find ecocentric approaches to conservation fully compatible with the more traditional attitudes based on reverence, aesthetics and recreation" that Cronon faults for creating a dichotomy between wilderness and human culture, arguing that those most directly involved in protecting wildlands "have converged on biotic values for both ethical and scientific reasons."[70] Leopold, among others, exemplifies for him the ability of scientists to combine scientific and humanistic values.

Moore's essay, like many others that grow out of observation of a particular place and reflection on it, demonstrates the importance of emotional attachment to natural landscapes. We are more inclined to work to protect places that strongly attract us, whatever their scientific value. Yet, as ecologists and the writers and artists who have been active in conservation efforts know well, the struggle to protect and nurture such places can be a prolonged and contentious one. For public forestlands this involves a complex process that frequently results in conflicting interpretations of federal environmental laws, among them the National Forest Management Act, which mandates multiple uses of forests (including economic and recreational ones) and at the same time requires the protection and restoration of biological diversity. This process has evolved into a continuing and sometimes loud debate over the development, revision, and implementation of forest plans and related documents for managing public forestlands. The agencies responsible for planning decisions, including those involving particular actions such as timber sales and mining leases, have had to develop procedures allowing for interaction with the public and to deal with vigorous criticism from elements of a diverse constituency. An elaborate, sometimes ritualized dialogue plays out in public hearings, written comments and responses, administrative appeals, and not infrequently the courts. The ongoing drama determines how, and to what degree, we design our forests.

8 // Designing the Forest

As the traditional emphasis on managing public forestlands for maximum timber yield was increasingly challenged, nationally as well as in the Pacific Northwest, the Forest Service began to incorporate the orientation and vocabulary of ecological forestry in its public discourse, although continuing resistance to change from many of those trained in silviculture meant that debates over the actual management of public forests were far from settled. Ecosystem management emerged as the preferred term for an approach that appeared to absorb the ecological orientation of the New Forestry, and protecting biological diversity became a stated priority and an essential element of forest plans. Mike Dombeck, who became chief forester in 1996, adopted an approach to natural resources policy that echoed Leopold's emphasis on "land health" and a "land ethic" as part of an effort to reorient the Forest Service.[1] The fact that federal legislation mandated protection of threatened and endangered species, environmental impact statements, and a planning process that required weighing possible uses of public forestland against the need to protect biological diversity made it difficult to avoid giving ecological concerns this new prominence. Whether they translated into significant changes in the actual management of individual forests was another matter.

The contrast between the Nicolet National Forest in northeastern Wisconsin and the adjacent Menominee Forest, approximately 220,000 acres managed by the Menominee tribe since the mid–nineteenth century, is revealing. The tribal forest has been described as recalling what the Great Lakes forest looked like before the massive logging of the late nineteenth century, with "dense stands of tall white pines, stands of large northern hardwoods, and mixed stands of hemlock, sugar maple, and yellow birch."[2] It has a richer mix of species and more large trees than the Nicolet National Forest, despite continuing to produce more timber for harvest per acre. One factor explaining the difference is the continuing reliance of the Forest Service on the doctrine of multiple use, both to serve the needs of a broader public and to justify a persistent bias in favor of authorizing ever larger timber sales. The resistance to change of those responsible for the initial forest plans for the Chequamegon and Nicolet National Forests in the 1980s prompted controversy with reformers over the extent of the Forest Service's commitment to biological diversity and eventually a lawsuit that challenged the methods by means of which the agency developed the required environmental impact statements. Federal court rulings upheld the Forest Service on the grounds that the application of conservation biology was still too uncertain to require the degree of analysis and disclosure in the environmental impact statements that was sought.[3] Subsequent lawsuits challenging proposals by the Forest Service for timber sales have continued to question the ways in which environmental impact statements have been framed and the adequacy of the research they incorporate.

Attitudes of the Menominee toward their forest reflect a fundamentally different orientation from that of the Forest Service, apparent in a belief that maintaining the health of the forest, in perpetuity, is critical to preserving tribal identity. Their practice of sustainable logging, under the supervision of a trained forester who employs loggers drawn from the tribe, is informed by the principles of modern silviculture but also reflects a traditional culture that leads the Menominee to place the long-term welfare of the forest above short-term economic gain and results in forestry practices such as culling diseased and slow-growing trees rather than focusing solely on those with the highest commercial value. Logging is limited to about 1 percent of the forest a year.[4] A recent tribal forest plan asserts that "the Menominee people do not view themselves as separate from the forest, or the forest and its creatures [as] independent from them. The Menominee culture exists in harmony with Mother Earth, understanding the circle of life."[5] Belief in "the circle of life" means, in the words of an account of Ojibwa life in Minnesota, "that both good and bad return to the place where they began. We believe that if we start a deed, after the fullness of time it will return to us, the source of the journey. If care is not used when the circle is begun, then the hurts along the way will be received in the end."[6] Commercial logging has been a part of Menominee culture since the mid–nineteenth century, with current practice represented by a large, modern sawmill at Neopit and past practice by a Logging Camp Museum in the Menominee forest outside Keshena on the Wolf River. The Logging Camp, with seven reconstructed log buildings and a vast collection of logging artifacts, functions as a tribal cultural center as well as a tourist attraction, hosting powwows, an annual lumberjack breakfast in the camp dining hall with its giant woodstove, and meetings and repatriation ceremonies (marking the burial of remains that have been returned) in the large open space of the bunkhouse.

Recent management of Michigan's three national forests and its extensive state forest system, with 3.9 million acres the largest in the country, incorporates an ecological approach (ecosystem-based management) in policy statements that mirrors what has by now become a well-established national trend. The old-growth controversy in Michigan and the upper Midwest always had less to do with preservation than restoration, since very little old-growth forest remained in comparison with that of the Pacific Northwest, but the question of how much public forestland should be dedicated to actual or potential old growth became a focus of debate when the controversy heated up in the early 1990s.[7] A 1994 report written by Anne Woiwode for the Sierra Club argued for a policy of managing forests to protect biodiversity and against state Department of Natural Resources (DNR) practices that favored early successional forests. The report presents the old-growth, presettlement forests of northern lower Michigan as a model of forest health against which present-day forests transformed by logging and other unnatural disturbances should be measured.[8] Ecologists in the Forestry Department of Michigan State University in collaboration with associates elsewhere had been developing a landscape ecosystem approach to northern Michigan forests, which they codified in a field guide to ecological classification and inventory of the Huron-Manistee National Forests that was published and used as a model by the Forest Service. For the first time, foresters had a practical aid to management grounded in ecological science. Applying the approach embodied in the guide, the Huron-Manistee National Forests allocated 177,000 acres for future old growth as part of a new emphasis on old growth and biodiversity.[9] The 2006 Forest Plan allows for further increases in old growth and further decline of aspen, while also providing for maintaining and expanding openings, though not sufficiently to satisfy hunters concerned about the loss of prime deer and grouse habitat.

By the end of the 1990s the focus of attention in planning for state forests had shifted from arguments about the definition and importance of old growth to recognition of the complexity of functioning native ecosystems of all kinds and the need to develop ways of assessing and preserving them.[10] The Michigan Natural Resources and Environmental Protection Act (NREPA) of 1994 consolidated existing laws and established a framework for developing policies that would protect biological diversity and provide for the continuing viability of ecosystems and ecosystem processes. Michigan is now using a biodiversity conservation planning process to create a network of biodiversity stewardship areas to be managed with the primary goal of conserving and enhancing the native biodiversity of "high quality natural communities." The process includes an assessment of candidates for inclusion by core design teams for each of the state's four major regions made up of DNR members and diverse groups of stakeholders. The ongoing effort to establish such reserves represents a significant change from the former emphasis on maximizing timber production, although it remains to be seen to what degree the DNR will accept the results of the process. Policies have been put in place to protect wildlife (species designated as endangered, threatened, or of special concern) and guide timber harvests, with the object of mimicking natural disturbance to the greatest degree possible. A Wildlife Action Plan implemented in 2005 calls for identifying and monitoring vulnerable populations and focusing on maintaining ecological processes. Guidelines for timber cutting established the following year stress attention to increasing the structural complexity of stands, retaining underrepresented tree species, and protecting endangered or threatened species (for example, the red-shouldered hawk).[11]

The current DNR plan for managing Michigan's state forests describes the management emphasis as having shifted "from a narrow focus upon conserving or restoring native old growth forests to a more holistic view of conserving and restoring some portion of the native biological diversity of Michigan" and offers detailed guidelines for assessing ecosystem health and measuring progress in conserving biodiversity.[12] Present practices reflect a requirement imposed by the Michigan legislature in 2004 that the DNR manage state forests according to the principles of sustainable forestry, as certified by a third party, and develop a long-term management plan. While the motivation for requiring certification was primarily economic, to enable the industry to satisfy the demand for certified forest products, the certification process has influenced forest policy broadly. Maintaining certification requires annual audits by an independent certifying organization (in practice this has meant audits by both the

Forestry Stewardship Council [FSC] and the Sustainable Forestry Initiative [SFI]) to assure that Michigan's forests are being managed in environmentally responsible and sustainable ways. Despite questions about how closely both certifying organizations monitor the forests and how rigorously they apply their standards, the fact that they conduct regular audits and can require changes in management practices (through "corrective action requests") has reinforced the emphasis on ecosystem health among state forest planners.[13]

While the plans and procedures developed in recent years by Michigan's DNR, as well as those developed by the Forest Service, reflect a public shift toward management based on the principles of ecological forestry, the ability to act on these principles is limited by multiple constraints. Since the late 1990s the state legislature has established annual targets for state timber sales, averaging fifty-three thousand acres a year, an action that obviously restricts the flexibility of the DNR. The fact that the legislature has progressively withdrawn general fund support from the timber management program for state forests has made its budget highly dependent on revenues from timber sales.[14] A statutory requirement that no more than 10 percent of the land managed by the DNR may be designated as natural areas (a category including special conservation areas, high conservation value areas, ecological reference areas, and now biodiversity stewardship areas) limits the department's capacity to conserve native biological diversity by establishing such areas, a slow process in any case. Conflicting interests among different divisions of the DNR may inhibit the development and implementation of plans. Foresters may push for policies that would result in substantial reduction of the deer herd in order to lessen environmental damage caused by excessive browsing while their counterparts in Fish and Wildlife work to improve deer habitat and resist changes that might anger the deer hunters who make up a large part of their constituency and provide the bulk of their financial support through license fees. The DNR as a whole must concern itself with social and economic as well as ecological goals and must respond to political pressures from groups as diverse as the Sierra Club, the Ruffed Grouse Society, and the Michigan Association of Timbermen. Forest planning may appear to be a deliberate and rational process, but it cannot be understood apart from its social and political contexts.

The Michigan DNR's current forest management plan addresses the challenge of protecting biological diversity, while accommodating a variety of human uses of the forest, by asserting that the principles of ecosystem management require balancing "the concepts of biological, social, and economic uses and values" without regard to priority.[15] Pursuing the ideal of "balancing competing uses" of forest resources, however sensible a response to the problem of managing finite resources in the face of increasing claims on them this may seem, can result in emphasizing following proper procedures over making judgments about the relative value and desirability of different uses. As long as the competing claims are considered, including those having to do with ecosystem values, one can justify a particular management decision on the grounds that it represents a judicious balancing of these claims. The plan ensures that there will be openings to appeal to hunters concerned with particular game species and expanses of intact forest to appeal to those more interested in the recovery of natural forests, but it gives relatively little guidance about how to determine the proportions of each.

Given the concentration of public forestland in northern lower Michigan and the Upper Peninsula, the economic and cultural interests of residents of these areas inevitably influence the management of state (and national) forests. Timber production and recreational activities involving public forests provide significant economic benefits and, in the language of the management plan, are "essential to the social and cultural fabric of the region." Many of the activities that embody the social and cultural values of area residents pose relatively little threat to the ecological health of the forests: regulated hunting and fishing, traditional gathering of forest products by native peoples and others (berries and wild fruits, mushrooms, sap for maple syrup), forms of recreation that cause little or no environmental degradation or inconvenience to other users. Yet some kinds of recreation can pose a threat to ecological values and become a source of controversy, for example, the increasing use of off-road vehicles (ORVs), including unauthorized but difficult to control use of these off the established trails and forest roads on which they are permitted. The growing popularity of ORVs is proof that they are part of the social and cultural fabric of the region, and this popularity makes it harder to resist political pressures for additional dedicated trails and "scramble areas."

The continuing expansion of ORV trails, even if only by providing connectors linking existing ones, results in further fragmentation of the forest with consequent pressures on wildlife species dependent on large areas of continuous forest. Fragmentation that results from extending roads and trails, whether for recreation or timber or mining operations, creates corridors and edge effects that make it easier for invasive species to penetrate the forest (e.g., brown cowbirds, which lay eggs in woods warblers' nests, and invasive plants that colonize the borders of forest roads). Planners embrace the optimistic view that providing more opportunities for authorized use of ORVs will inhibit unauthorized, off-trail use, but it has proved difficult to control the tendency of some ORV users to create their own trails regardless of whatever trail system is provided. The DNR's management plan avoids discriminating among uses, mingling different kinds of trail and water use (e.g., Jet Skis and canoes) without regard to their environmental and human impact. It is easier to focus on measuring user days and gauging the significance of an activity by its economic impact and importance to "traditional social well-being" than to make the hard calls about what kinds of disturbance and environmental damage conflict with legal mandates.[16]

Statewide criteria and indicators (with appropriate metrics) are provided to guide the development of four ecoregional plans covering the Upper and Lower Peninsulas. The first two criteria ("conservation of biodiversity" and "ecosystem condition and productivity") are followed by a criterion that lumps spiritual values with social and cultural ones ("social/cultural/spiritual") and defines them similarly, by reference to what people seem to like: "Spiritual values or existence values are personal feelings and sentiments that natural resources stir within the human spirit. This criterion is concerned with the continued ability of the resources to provide these values. Because spiritual values are personal in nature and to a large degree intangible, the indicators pertain primarily to ecosystem features . . . that appeal to the senses or address the ability of people to use those resources."[17] This definition is so inclusive and vague as to make identifying specific spiritual values virtually impossible. It exposes the limitations of the kind of cautious, generalized language invited by a management plan, especially in comparison with the efforts of Aldo Leopold or Sigurd Olson or more recently Kathleen Dean Moore to articulate spiritual values associated with natural landscapes. The plan's specified indicators for spiritual values are the same as those for social and cultural ones: the extent of archaeological or historic sites, undeveloped natural resources, aesthetically appealing landscapes, and traditional gathering activities and celebrations. Outdoor recreation obviously embodies social and cultural values but is presented as a separate criterion, with its own indicators and metrics, for the purposes of the plan.

An earlier pilot project that anticipated planning for sustainable forest management, by trying to develop appropriate guidelines for the Lake

Superior State Forest in the eastern Upper Peninsula, offers more insight into how spiritual values might be interpreted, through the record of two workshops in which members of the public were asked to assess the usefulness of possible values and indicators. The project summary, describing the effort to adapt to the new requirements of certification, recognizes the need to develop a process for tracking nontimber values holistically and looking at landscape concerns (as opposed to traditional compartment-level ones limited to individual compartments of fifteen hundred to three thousand acres, 10 percent of which were reviewed annually).[18] The challenge was to develop good indicators by which to measure progress in realizing nontimber values, including spiritual as well as social and cultural ones. The indicators for spiritual values assessed by workshop participants included the relative absence of development, "natural sounds/quiet," remoteness, aesthetics, stability of land use, and experience of "spiritually important" wildlife and plant species.[19] Despite the vagueness of the term *spiritually important,* these indicators suggest a particular kind of landscape, relatively free of human traces (structures, roads) and human sounds and home to species other than the most abundant ones, such as those whose favored habitat is the interior forest. Silence, a quality associated with old-growth forests by Sigurd Olson and Kathleen Dean Moore and with "primeval" forests by nineteenth-century observers, was seen as the least feasible indicator by participants, perhaps because they thought it too difficult to find or measure.

The 2008 state Forest Plan recognizes the importance of "large undeveloped forests" to spiritual as well as social and cultural values, specifying the size and distribution of natural areas and their use as a proper metric, but it makes less effort than the pilot project does to indicate the sources of spiritual values. It was simpler to be more specific about aesthetic values. These could be defined, narrowly, by association with scenic vistas, natural beauty roads, and lakeshore areas whose aesthetic qualities could be protected through the creation of "visual management areas." The DNR, like the Forest Service, manages the difficult job of integrating competing uses chiefly by segregating them. Campgrounds, trailheads and trails, and public access sites are classified as "concentrated recreation areas." Timber cuts are restricted to areas regarded as suitable for them, as visual management areas clearly would not be. Dedicated management areas, for example, the Sand Lakes Quiet Area near Traverse City, allow only "non-intrusive forms of recreation," defined as including hunting and trapping, hiking, wildlife viewing, and cross-country skiing. In this context ORVs and snowmobiles are regarded as "intrusive." Such "dominant-use zoning" has become a pragmatic way of accommodating different uses regarded as legitimate, yet the practical expedient of separating activities regarded as incompatible masks continuing tensions among users with different visions of the forest. These tensions emerge in public commentary about proposed policy decisions and complaints about uses of particular areas or adjoining areas that are perceived as incompatible.

The complexities involved in the effort to balance competing uses while sustaining the health of forest ecosystems can be seen in the record of the most recent long-range planning process conducted by the U.S. Forest Service for Michigan's three national forests. This process culminated in 2006 in the adoption of revised plans intended to guide the management of the Hiawatha, Ottawa, and Huron-Manistee National Forests for the next fifteen years, replacing prior ones adopted in 1986 in the first round of long-range planning required by the National Forest Management Act (NFMA). The revised plan of 2006 for the Hiawatha National Forest recognizes comments from Chippewa tribal leaders; timber interests; groups representing the interests of snowmobilers, mountain bikers, and users of off-highway vehicles (OHVs); hunting groups, including the Sharp-tailed Grouse and Ruffed Grouse associations; environmental groups, including the Sierra Club, Defenders of Wildlife, and The Nature Conservancy; Friends of the Hiawatha; state and federal agencies; and local school boards. Because school boards benefit from the requirement that the Forest Service return 25 percent of the revenue from timber cuts to the counties in which they occur, these boards have a vested interest in the level of the timber harvest. Local communities benefit from jobs generated by the need to log and mill the timber from authorized timber cuts. They also benefit, increasingly, from jobs related to recreation in the forests.

In a preface to the Hiawatha plan the regional forester for the Eastern Region of the United States describes the final version as reflecting the desires of the public for the present and future of the forest, as the 1986 plan had reflected the desires of the public twenty years before, while establishing "a strong foundation for ecological, social, and economic sustainability over the long-term."[20] Like the DNR's plan for the state forests, the Forest Service plan for Hiawatha relates the values it promotes to those of the public it serves and attempts to reconcile competing interests. It conflates cultural and spiritual values with "social" ones and makes no effort to define these, although they are implicit in the alternatives by means of which the required environmental impact statement frames the choices available to the decision maker, the regional forester. The approved plan rejects alternatives that would strongly emphasize ecological considerations, on the one hand, and those that would emphasize economic and certain social considerations (favoring timber and forest products interests, sportsmen, and advocates of motorized recreation) on the other, opting for one that represents a compromise between these extremes. The NFMA requires the regional forester to justify not choosing the "environmentally preferable alternative" if another alternative is the one selected. In the case of the Hiawatha National Forest Plan he does this on the grounds that this alternative gives too little attention to social and economic considerations and would harm the timber and tourism industries, the latter by restricting snowmobile and OHV use. He also argues that it would limit the use of timber harvesting as a management tool to promote early successional species that provide habitat for some species of wildlife, including the federally endangered Kirtland's warbler. Linking an argument to restoration of the Kirtland's warbler tends to disarm critics. One of the Forest Service's successes in Michigan has been helping the DNR to bring back a healthy population of the warblers by maintaining the young jack pine plantations in which they nest, a process that involves clear-cutting followed by replanting or a controlled burn to simulate the effects of the fires by means of which stands of jack pines were periodically renewed in the past.

Changes from the 1986 Hiawatha plan reveal a shift toward greater encouragement of biological diversity, particularly in its objectives. The 2006 plan allows for a larger proportion of long-lived pine and hemlock and places more emphasis on managing forests for uneven age classes rather than the even-aged classes preferred by the timber industry. Under the new plan the amount of old-growth forest is to remain about the same, but it is to be withdrawn from timber production, along with other "unsuited" lands, and maintained in ways that will increase connective corridors for wildlife. Other changes, recognizing the wishes and actual practices of advocates of motorized recreation, work against the goal of promoting biological diversity. The new plan opens several lakes in semi-primitive areas to motorboat access and promises increases in snowmobile and OHV routes. The approved alternative initially banned cross-country snowmobile travel, but the final version removed this restriction in response to protests by snowmobilers, while maintaining the prohibition of cross-country OHV travel. Although the revised plan recognizes the risks of environmental damage and reduced species viability from allowing greater motorized access to the national forest, it justifies this action by predicting that increased access will not make things worse, on the questionable assumption that present levels of use will continue.

In 2005 the Forest Service issued new regulations for OHVs in national forests, acknowledging that previous ones had not proved sufficient to control the proliferation of routes and consequent environmental damage, including soil erosion and effects on water quality and wildlife habitat.[21] The new regulations recognize the need of other kinds of users to enjoy a quiet recreational experience. They address the perceived problems by calling for designating systems of authorized roads, trails, and areas at the local level "in a manner that is environmentally sustainable over the long term." Forest Service responses to comments on the draft regulations rejected arguments for excluding OHVs from national forests altogether, on the customary grounds that federal law authorizes multiple use of the forests, and affirmed the policy of finding an "appropriate balance" of uses and minimizing conflicts. In developing the "travel management" plans called for by the regulations, national forests are required to determine which roads and trails are suitable for motorized travel and to make atlases indicating those available to the public. The 2005 regulations recognize the possibility of designating new roads or trails based on ones created by unauthorized off-road use, implicitly creating an incentive for the kind of illegal behavior that the regulations were intended to address.

At times the language of the Hiawatha Forest Plan reflects the strain of trying to blend conflicting visions of what the forest should become, for example, in the assertion that not increasing OHV trails "could lead to unauthorized OHV cross country travel and user created trails," which would cause environmental degradation and decrease the "opportunities for solitude and feelings of remoteness" that some visitors value. Increasing trail mileage in response to public pressure thus becomes a way of preventing greater harm, at least in theory. In fact, unauthorized cross-country travel by OHVs continues to be a serious problem for managers of Michigan's national forests and also for the DNR, which currently spends approximately four hundred thousand dollars a year remedying environmental damage caused by such travel. A similar justification for allowing motorboats on more inland lakes cites an "increased risk of user created access resulting in greater potential to reduce water quality and non-motorized recreation experience," claiming to be avoiding harm while paradoxically legitimizing it.[22] Visitors seeking clean water and quiet might not be so conscious of the difference between authorized and unauthorized motorboat traffic.

Forest Service policy regarding motorized recreation, as reflected in forest plans and in travel management plans for individual national forests, assumes that this can be successfully managed and that all uses authorized under the multiple-use mandate are commensurate. Yet, as critics of expanded ORV access to public lands have argued, use that causes significant and lasting environmental damage or disturbs other users to the point of driving them away is fundamentally different from other recreational uses.[23] A few national forests have banned ORV use altogether (Monongahela in West Virginia, Hoosier in Indiana), and others have responded to campaigns by regional environmental groups to restrict use in particular areas.[24] Conflicts over ORV access and lawsuits arising from them are likely to increase, with regional environmental groups (including Colorado's Quiet Use Coalition, Montana's Bitterroot Quiet Use Coalition, and Minnesotans for Responsible Recreation) campaigning to restrict ORV access and user groups, supported by the national BlueRibbon Coalition, fighting to expand access and prevent the decommissioning of forest roads. The fact that much of the BlueRibbon Coalition's funding comes from industry (timber, oil, and mining companies, as well as manufacturers of recreational vehicles) reflects the reality that struggles over motorized access are often part of the larger struggle over the future of roadless areas, particularly in the West. Once ORV (and snowmobile) use is established in an area it is less likely to be a candidate for wilderness designation.

In addition to allowing for more motorized recreational use of the forest in the final plan for Hiawatha, the regional forester raised the minimum goal for the amount of aspen to be maintained, responding in this instance to protests from the timber industry and sportsmen eager to maintain more habitat for grouse and woodcock. The controversy over how much effort should be made to retain aspen and other early successional species such as paper birch has become one of the most significant that both the Forest Service and DNR have to resolve and one that epitomizes the persistent conflict over management philosophies. After the logging boom and the catastrophic fires that followed it, aspen growth exploded, to the extent that aspen became the dominant tree species in northern Michigan forests. The abundance of aspen became the basis for a pulpwood industry and also served the interests of sportsmen, since young aspen stands constitute prime habitat for ruffed grouse, woodcock, and white-tailed deer.

The current overabundance of deer, encouraged by the policy of maintaining openings and a specified amount of early successional forest, has prevented some kinds of trees from regenerating (hemlock, for example) and led to a decline in native wildflowers in areas where the deer population is high. Management activity designed to increase the population, pursued aggressively in the 1980s by the DNR until the deer herd swelled to 2 million in 1989, and still practiced to a lesser degree, has the effect of changing the character of the forest. The deer herd has declined somewhat in recent years, from a peak of 2.2 million to approximately 1.8 million in 2008, but it remains high.[25] Research on northern forests in Wisconsin has shown that an elevated deer population alters the structure of forests, with hemlock yielding to sugar maple and mixed hardwoods to black cherry. It also reduces the diversity of plant species in the understory, with native wildflowers such as trillium virtually disappearing from some areas.[26] Despite the fact that hunters kill 400,000 to 500,000 deer a year in Michigan, their numbers remain well above the target levels established by the DNR.

In the absence of disturbance such as fire or logging, aspen will be replaced by later successional species, including white pine and shade-tolerant northern hardwoods.[27] One can see this natural process happening in mature aspen stands such as one near the University of Michigan's Biological Station on Douglas Lake in the northern Lower Peninsula, where impressively large aspen one hundred years old or more can reach 130 feet in height. Younger hardwoods, including sugar maple and beech, are beginning to compete with the aspen in this stand and will eventually displace it. The amount of aspen in Michigan's forests has been declining since the mid–twentieth century, despite extensive clear-cutting intended to promote its regeneration, prompting sportsmen and representatives of the timber industry to continue to lobby for more active management. One can assume that fire and windstorms will create new gaps in the forest cover that will be colonized by aspen and birch, but relying on such natural processes does not satisfy those who want to maximize their opportunities for hunting or pulpwood production.

Recent summaries of public comments on draft planning documents reveal conflicting views on such issues as how large a timber cut should be allowed annually in state and national forests (projected by the DNR to continue at about fifty-three thousand acres for state forests), how actively

forests should be managed to maintain early successional species and promote even-aged classes of other species, whether biomass such as fallen
trees and other forest debris should be used commercially or allowed to
decay on the forest floor, to what extent roads should be maintained and
extended, and what conditions are necessary to sustain viable populations
of different species of wildlife. Some of those in favor of managing for
early successional species accuse the DNR of seeking to restore forest conditions approximating those of 1800, a charge that the DNR rejects. Some
object to what they perceive as a bias toward old growth. Those lobbying
for active management to maintain more early successional forest are primarily interested in sustaining game species, while those who lobby for increasing the percentage of old growth advocate more passive management
that would allow for natural succession. In the Upper Peninsula passive
management is likely to provide more habitat for nongame species such as
pine martens, eastern timber wolves, and red-shouldered hawks, all
species that depend on extensive tracts of undisturbed forest.

The language of the DNR's responses, as well as that of comments by
industry groups, often reflects traditional silvicultural perspectives, as in
references to trees being "unused" or "lost" through natural mortality or
to the need to harvest "overmature" trees. Such language is not surprising
given the traditional training of many foresters and the commitment to
economic uses of the forest. It embodies assumptions about what constitutes a healthy forest and how the forest should be used, however, that are
challenged by those who define forest health primarily in terms of functioning ecosystems and habitats that sustain a wide variety of species.
These critics, more likely to be trained in ecology or to have been
influenced by ecological perspectives, question the priority that continues
to be given to maintaining a high level of timber cutting. For example, the
Sierra Club objects to giving age-class data for tree species in increments
of 10 years culminating in 100+, a form of classification that reveals a
mind-set attuned to rotations for commercial harvesting, when the natural life span of many species is well over 100 years (350 or more years for
white pine). The objection reflects a fundamental disagreement with a
policy of maintaining early successional species at present levels rather
than allowing natural succession, which the Sierra Club argues would be
consistent with the state forest management plan's announced goal of
"sustain[ing] fundamental ecological processes."[28] The Mackinaw Forest
Council, a citizens' group associated with the Mackinaw State Forest in the
eastern Upper Peninsula, offers similar but more pointed criticism:

"[H]ow can sustainability be assured in a forest system largely maintained in an unnaturally disturbed state? . . . What is the cost? What pieces of the web of life will we lose?"[29]

Criticisms such as these represent a minority of the comments on the draft management plan summarized by the DNR and do not mention the fact that old-growth forests typically had gaps caused by natural disturbances, but they illustrate a basic difficulty faced by both the DNR and the Forest Service. These agencies incorporate the principles of ecological forestry in planning documents yet face the political need to develop policies reflecting economic and social values that often conflict with ecological ones. Thus we find the DNR, in response to Sierra Club criticisms, justifying a policy that maintains aspen by defining ecosystem management as "not exclusively a matter of ecological processes" but of fiber and habitat needs as well (in this case habitat for desirable game species).[30] In such a formulation ecosystem management sounds more like traditional forest management under the familiar doctrine of multiple use, here employed as a defense against arguments that focus primarily on ecological values. The DNR could resist arguments of the Michigan Association of Timbermen as well as those of environmentalists, for example, by insisting on the need to limit the number of roads and trails to avoid more fragmentation of the forest. Yet one is frequently reminded when reading forest management plans that they are ultimately political documents subject to public scrutiny. Such plans typically reflect compromises intended to reconcile conflicting demands and pressures while at the same time asserting that they meet the requirements of relevant state and federal laws, including procedural ones. They are influenced by a public audience that includes a heterogeneous collection of users who have learned how to make their desires and expectations known, directly or through interest groups, and who can be counted on to protest any policy contrary to these expectations.

The concluding comments of the regional forester on the revised plan for the Hiawatha National Forest reflect both political sensitivity and the bureaucratic nature of the document. They attempt to protect the autonomy of Forest Service managers while at the same time reassuring a diverse constituency. The regional forester is careful to explain that "adaptive management" will allow for modifications of the plan in the future to reflect changes in the Forest Service's evolving understanding of "ecological, social and economic environments," invoking a principle that preserves flexibility for managers to take into account the results of management practices and also shifts of public opinion. In a summary comment the regional forester argues that the revised plan, along with the expected cycle of "learning and adjustment," will allow the national forest "to provide the most appropriate package of benefits to the American people."[31] Speaking of a forest as offering an appropriate package of benefits makes it sound more like a health insurance plan than a dynamic ecosystem. The unfortunate choice of words reduces the forest to a bureaucratic abstraction drained of all life, a delivery system rather than a community of trees, myriad animal and plant species, soil types, and microclimates bound together by complex biological interactions.

In 1986 the Wilderness Society, as part of the public comment process, issued a detailed critique of the first draft forest plan developed by the managers of the Ottawa National Forest, which it regarded as representative of the seven north woods national forests in the Lake States. The critique is a harsh one, faulting the managers for projecting substantial increases in timber production, despite the fact that previous timber sales had lost money and the likelihood that the projection of future demand was unrealistically high, and also for failing to enhance the possibilities for recreation and tourism. It criticizes the planners for not recognizing sensitive species and protecting the kind of habitat they need (by creating more semiprimitive areas) and for not reducing the already extensive road system (four thousand miles) rather than expanding it. It also challenges the methodology and assumptions of the draft plan and many of the assertions made in it.[32] If the Wilderness Society had given comparable attention to the 2006 Ottawa Forest Plan, it might have found some grounds for approval. Three wilderness areas have been established in the Ottawa since 1986 (Sylvania, McCormick, and Sturgeon River Gorge), and the present plan gives considerably more attention to ecological processes than does the first one. It specifies, for example, that "to the extent practical, timber management will seek to restore ecological structure, function, and processes (e.g., northern hardwood forest types), and will emulate naturally occurring disturbances (e.g., fire and windstorms)."[33] The plan also recognizes the need to match openings to ecosystem capabilities and allows for more regrowth of northern hardwoods, as well as for restoration and regrowth of conifers.

Yet no forest plan is likely to satisfy all of its potential critics or to settle the continuing debates about forest policy. Those who offered public comments on the 2006 Ottawa draft plan challenged its evaluations of species viability and alleged a lack of thorough analysis of the effects of timber harvesting and a failure to give sufficient attention to the impact of fragmentation on the forest, among other things. Responses by the Forest Service to comments on drafts of the latest forest plans for all three of Michigan's national forests offer specific answers or objections in some cases but more general and guarded, or nonresponsive, answers in many others. These official responses may appeal to a law such as the Multiple-Use Sustained-Yield Act without acknowledging that how it is applied is subject to interpretation and that some uses may be incompatible. Or they may say, as they must in many cases, that determinations will be made on a site-specific basis and avoid taking a position on the underlying issue that prompted the comment. They may simply reiterate a boilerplate response intended to demonstrate a commitment to balancing conflicting demands and to imply that this is possible. One formulation repeatedly invoked in responses to comments on the draft 2006 Huron-Manistee forest plan asserts that "the Selected Alternative strives to achieve a balance between, and integration of, ecological, economic, and social factors into a comprehensive strategy aimed at protecting and enhancing sustainability, diversity, and productivity."[34] Such ritual assertions project confidence in the ability to balance and integrate disparate goals without addressing questions about how, for example, increasing the timber cut can be reconciled with the obligation to maintain the viability of species by preserving their habitats.

Another kind of assertion that frequently appears in the 2006 forest plans and Forest Service responses to public comments on them attempts to harmonize economic and ecological goals by linking the health of the forest with active management to counter threats to it (disease, pests, fire, damage from blowdowns). A Forest Service response to a public comment questioning the practice of salvage logging claims that "the Ottawa cannot rely upon natural processes to take care of forest health issues caused by destructive weather events" and defends salvage logging as a more efficient way "to assure recovery of damaged lands to a healthy and productive condition." Besides, the respondent notes, selling dead and damaged trees can help offset the cost of restoration.[35] Salvage logging can be a useful management tool in some circumstances, but it is easily abused, as experience in the Pacific Northwest under the Healthy Forests Act has shown. And readiness to authorize salvage logging may be motivated by a desire to generate revenue or assert control lest the natural process of recovery proves too unpredictable or slow. Ecologists and advocates of ecological forestry have argued that leaving dead and damaged trees along with forest litter (what they call "biological legacies") is a better way of promoting forest health than removing them, challenging the traditional view that a forest that suffers major disturbance needs to be cleaned up to aid recovery.[36] The answer to the question of whether, and to what extent, we need to "take care of forest health issues" caused by natural disturbances depends on what kind of forest we imagine in relation to what purposes and to what time scales. And, implicitly, on how we define forest health. John Muir, contemplating the effects of the Sierra's wild storms on its forests (from "plucking off a leaf or limb as required" to "removing an entire tree or grove"), reaffirmed his faith in what he called "Nature's forestry."[37] It would be hard to imagine Muir as a supervisor of a national forest, but it is worth recalling his radically different perspective. Even after a violent storm, he could see only beauty and perfection in the Sierra forests. It would not have occurred to him that they needed human intervention to recover.

Annual monitoring and evaluation reports by the Hiawatha National Forest (required by NFMA) reflect a kind of management primarily intended to restore and maintain forest ecosystems, in accordance with goals set forth in the 2006 Forest Plan. The reports for fiscal years 2008 and 2009 document efforts to identify and limit damage to wetlands and soils from timber cuts, to combat nonnative invasive species, to maintain habitat for sensitive (and endangered or threatened) species, and to assess compliance with federal and state best management practices and the 2006 Forest Plan, among other things.[38] They offer evidence of the impact of insect pests and diseases (damage from the jack pine and spruce budworms and beech bark disease, the progress of the emerald ash borer) and of an influx of invasive plant species. They also reveal the extensiveness and sophistication of the monitoring efforts conducted by Forest Service staff and the scope of their management activities, which include maintaining grasslands for sharp-tailed grouse and young jack pine forests for the Kirtland's warbler (by ensuring that diseased jack pines are harvested and the forests regenerated), rerouting a snowmobile trail away from a wetland, opening a new motorcycle trail, and working to repair the damage from illegal OHV use. The magnitude of the challenges faced by the staff is apparent from such reports, as is the extent to which they spend their time in various forms of environmental damage control. Much of the disturbance that they monitor and attempt to mitigate is caused by humans, chiefly through timber cutting and OHV use, both activities authorized by the forest plan in keeping with the multiple-use mandate of the national forests.

It is apparent from monitoring patterns that much of the invasion of nonnative species in the Hiawatha follows routes opened up directly or indirectly by timber cuts, along forest roads and into areas cleared or substantially cleared by harvesting. The Forest Service extensively monitors the soil disturbance and compaction that result from timber cutting, measuring the degree of disturbance (reported to be below the 15 percent level judged acceptable in the Forest Plan) but not its impact on native plant species. Conclusions about how to mitigate the damage caused by heavy equipment testify to the importance of informed planning in determining where, when, and how to cut and also reveal how disruptive such operations can be. Descriptions of illegal OHV use in the reports, with illustrations, suggest the environmental costs of this kind of activity, including destabilization of sand dune slopes, erosion, degradation of wetlands and lakeshores, and damage to snowmobile trails and the North Country Scenic Trail. The reports document a dramatic rise in reported incidents of illegal use, from 167 in 2008 to 365 in 2009, although they attribute this primarily to increased enforcement. The Forest Service uses funds supplied by the DNR to rehabilitate degraded areas and collaborates with OHV users' groups on educational efforts but clearly must struggle to control the abuse. The fact that all eight of the gates used to close snowmobile trails to OHV use in the summer months of 2009 that were monitored were found to be either damaged or circumvented suggests how difficult it will be to change established patterns of behavior.

The requirements of the planning process for national forests, with mandated environmental impact statements and opportunities for comment on draft plans or proposed actions by anyone from ecologists to area residents concerned with preserving activities they enjoy, have led to new modes of thinking and to regular monitoring of progress toward goals. Planning now involves interdisciplinary teams with expertise in areas not previously represented in the Forest Service. Whatever the requirements of the process, however, those who manage the planning process for the agency determine the issues to be addressed by the plans and frame the alternatives from which the regional forester must choose. And they determine the language of the final plans. They may choose to keep this language relatively opaque on matters that require clear statements of position or detailed analysis to be useful. They subsequently decide when to authorize a specific action such as a timber sale or mining project, subject to their reading of the language of the plan and the requirements of the relevant legislation and agency regulations, after soliciting public reaction. Unless a lawsuit results in a different outcome.

In July 2008, a decision by a federal district court blocked a plan by the Forest Service and the Bureau of Land Management, approved by the Michigan DNR, that would allow slant drilling from a site in the Huron-Manistee National Forests intended to tap reserves of natural gas thought to lie under an adjacent state wilderness area (the Mason Tract, consisting of 4,700 acres along the South Branch of the Au Sable River). The federal government subsequently decided not to appeal. The court, finding that the Forest Service had not satisfied various requirements of the National Environmental Policy Act (NEPA), cited inadequate environmental assessments and a failure to consider potential degradation of recreational aspects of the Mason Tract. The case is interesting for the issues it raised, the considerable political and popular support it galvanized, and the fact that the lawsuit was pursued by an unusual alliance of the Anglers of the Au Sable and the Sierra Club (along with the grandson of the donor of the land that became the core of the Mason Tract).

The proposed project calls for a well site a third of a mile from the Mason Tract in a portion of the Huron-Manistee National Forests designated as a semiprimitive nonmotorized area. It would involve clearing 3.5 acres of old-growth forest, widening and upgrading two forest roads, and adding a production facility 1.5 miles from the well with a pipeline connecting the two locations. On the basis of environmental and biological assessments, the latter dealing with potential implications for the endangered Kirtland's warbler, the forest supervisor issued a "finding of no significant impact," which meant that a more thorough environmental impact statement was unnecessary. The district court's decision reports that the magistrate judge who heard the case "viewed with skepticism the conclusion that a gas well drilling project that admittedly would alter scenic and primitive areas for up to 30 years, double noise levels in areas isolated from human contact, involve clearing old growth forest, and emit petroleum and engine exhaust odors would have no significant environmental impact."[39] The Forest Service has since been preparing an environmental impact statement, with the usual provision for public comments, in an attempt to remedy the deficiencies identified by the court.

Comments by the late Rusty Gates, founder and president of the Anglers of the Au Sable, give a human dimension to the case and suggest why it aroused the widespread and passionate support that it did. Gates described the Mason Tract as a "very, very revered recreational spot" that offers "solitude for those seeking quiet places." One concern of those who opposed the plan was the impact of removing three acres of old-growth forest and widening roads to establish the well site, but a more fundamental one was noise. Gates was convinced that the qualities that made the Mason Tract revered would be compromised by the "drone of diesel generators" and the sound of trucks coming and going every day within earshot of the Au Sable.[40] A sign welcoming visitors to the Mason Tract describes it as offering solitude and standing ready "to renew your soul." Solitude and silence are not the only values that came into play in the case—the potential impacts of drilling from the proposed location on recreational tourism and the Kirtland's warbler were significant factors—but they are critical to the appeal of wild areas such as this one, and they seem to be difficult ones for those who write forest plans and proposals and implement them to take seriously.

Pursuing litigation against the federal government over actions proposed by the Forest Service is not a course that many can afford to take, and lawsuits challenging agency plans and proposed actions must overcome the "deference" given them by the courts on the grounds of the expertise of the agency.[41] In 2009 a district court judge dismissed a lawsuit by Kurt Meister challenging the 2006 Huron-Manistee Forest Plan for allowing gun hunting and snowmobiling in the immediate vicinity of primitive and semiprimitive nonmotorized areas.[42] The suit symbolizes the frustration of those seeking quiet and solitude in such areas, values recognized in the forest plan as goals but described in Forest Service responses to comments on the draft plan as only "desired" or "aspirational." Its initial outcome illustrates the tendency of judges to defer to the Forest Service unless it can be shown that its position is inconsistent with the language of a forest plan or that the process by which it was reached did not follow legally mandated procedures. In this instance, however, a panel of the Sixth Circuit Court of Appeals overturned the decision of the district court, finding that the Forest Service had failed to provide "quality" recreation and was not entitled to deference unless it was earned. The Forest Service was instructed to come up with a management plan that complied with the law. The court faulted the agency for its methodology and a failure to follow its own regulations and pointedly asked it to consider whether bird-watchers and snowshoers should be able to enjoy primitive and semiprimitive nonmotorized areas without ducking gunshots or "hearing the whine of snowmobile engines."[43] An earlier lawsuit by Northwoods Wilderness Recovery against the Ottawa National Forest seeking to stop a proposed timber sale (provocatively called Rolling Thunder after a Vietnam War bombing campaign) was also successful on appeal. In this case the Sixth Circuit Court of Appeals ruled that the proposed sale was inconsistent with the language of the forest plan about estimates of acreage to be devoted to timber production and that the circumstances demanded an environmental impact statement. The language of a forest plan and the qualifications and exceptions it incorporates can become critical factors in such cases. Plaintiffs have been successful more often, however, by demonstrating that a proposed action fails to satisfy the requirements of federal legislation (typically NEPA, NFMA, or ESA) because of inadequate assessment of its potential environmental impacts.

Challenges to proposed Forest Service actions are often rejected by judges on the grounds that procedural requirements of the relevant federal legislation have been met, but in some cases litigation has led to settlements, typically entailing a modification of plans for a timber cut. Other cases have resulted in an injunction preventing a proposed action until the Forest Service develops a satisfactory environmental impact statement. The Environmental Law and Policy Center has had considerable success in winning injunctions against proposed timber sales and forcing negotiated settlements through litigation on behalf of the nonprofit Habitat Education Center against the Forest Service, prompted by the agency's management of Wisconsin's Chequamegon-Nicolet National Forest over the course of two decades. It has succeeded in part by demonstrating the inadequacy of general assurances of compliance with federal requirements. In three successive 2005 decisions the court granted injunctions blocking timber sales until the Forest Service could produce an environmental impact statement complying with federal law. The fundamental issue in all of these cases involved the cumulative impacts of past and proposed timber sales on the habitat of the northern goshawk and the red-shouldered hawk (in one case on that of the pine marten as well) and the question of whether the Forest Service had taken a "hard look" at these impacts. In one opinion the judge faulted the Forest Service for asserting that its actions would have "minimum impact" on red-shouldered hawks without being specific about what that meant or providing data about the impact of past projects on the species.[44] Litigation can be costly and time consuming for all concerned, but it has proven an effective way of holding the Forest Service accountable for boilerplate language that masks a failure to conduct rigorous scientific assessments of the environmental impacts of its actions. In the case of the Chequamegon-Nicolet Forest litigation has sometimes forced settlements that resulted in modifications of timber cuts (e.g., to protect a sensitive area from clear-cutting or to leave a buffer zone around nests of red-shouldered hawks) and has led to recognition by the Forest Service that more scientifically credible environmental impact statements will be required.[45]

In the early nineteenth century the Ojibwa and other tribal groups still regarded the forest as their spiritual and physical home and a major source of their livelihood. Even after they had begun to be displaced from their homelands, they attempted to maintain their identity as a "forest people" by practicing traditional woodland ways and teaching these to their children.[46] A recent report on the northern white cedar commissioned by the Great Lakes Indian Fish and Wildlife Center reveals the persistence of concerns based on these ways. The report supports arguments about threats to the sustainability of white cedar, including overharvesting, by drawing on interviews with elders to illustrate the sacred qualities, as well as the many practical uses, that give it a significant role in "the Anishnaabe spiritual and material world."[47] As we have seen, early European settlers brought a radically different attitude toward forests, regarding those they found as adversaries that they had to push back in order to colonize a wild frontier. Two centuries later our understanding of the forest and our relationship to it have become vastly more complicated. Whereas the early settlers pitted themselves against a largely unknown and intimidating "wilderness," we attempt to produce the forests that we want by engaging in a collaborative process. What we want, collectively, has come to be determined by a complex interaction of biological and forestry science, cultural attitudes, and political forces. And what we get depends on the resources available for the work of managing forest growth at any given time, as well as on the compromises reflected in management plans, as managers weigh the claims of different potential uses of the forest.

The struggles of forest planners to find the elusive "balance" of uses that will please the greatest number of people while satisfying legal requirements to protect biological diversity can produce contradictory signals and language so qualified or general as to have little meaning. They may interpret federal law and Forest Service guidelines narrowly to preserve management flexibility. Goals and indicators of progress set out in forest plans may not predict what actually happens, given budgetary limitations and changing social and economic conditions, as well as ecological ones. A commitment to meeting timber production goals, and increasing them over time, may undermine other goals. Nonetheless, current planning processes, whatever their flaws, reflect a significant advance over the unexamined commodity orientation of earlier forest planning, and they have prompted efforts to incorporate the goals of ecological forestry in long-range, landscape-level plans that are open to public scrutiny and comment. The current chief of the Forest Service has established expectations for future national forest plans by emphasizing landscape-level planning, the restoration of healthy forest ecosystems, the array of ecosystem services that forests provide, and also the increasing importance of climate change.[48] If planning processes can generate tensions among users and lead to dissatisfaction with outcomes, interested parties nonetheless are given opportunities to influence the thinking of planners or at least to challenge this publicly. And they can sue if other means of influencing the process fail.

Forest planning was a much simpler exercise when the primary goal was assuring a sustainable timber supply, or pretending to while maximizing timber production, and when the process was much less exposed to public scrutiny, but it has always generated controversy. Disputes over how much management is necessary or desirable are likely to continue, with such groups as the Sierra Club, the Wilderness Society, and local and regional environmental organizations that would prefer to see more reliance on natural processes arguing for limiting management to what can be justified on scientific grounds and spokespersons for forest products industries, sportsmen's groups, and some kinds of recreational users pushing for whatever degree of management is necessary to maintain the kind of forest they prefer. Advocates of more opportunities for motorized recreation, and sometimes those for mountain biking as well, will continue to meet resistance from backpackers and day hikers interested in enjoying natural sounds and opportunities for viewing wildlife and, where possible, the experience of solitude. Controversies about such issues as restoration activities, management of habitats for particular species, and conflicts among users will persist, and on public forestlands these will be mediated by the appropriate agencies.

The elaborateness of current planning and management procedures may give the impression that we have thoroughly domesticated our forests, yet efforts to shape and control them are necessarily limited, especially when budgets are shrinking, and they can produce unintended effects. Whatever else recent research on forest ecosystems has demonstrated, this research has made it clear that much remains to be understood about how these ecosystems function. Ecologists tend to argue that recognition of the limits of our knowledge should lead foresters to adopt a more passive, and modest, approach toward management. In the view of some of these, the Forest Service needs to realize "that nature, not the Agency, builds forests" and that localized management efforts often fail to address natural ecological processes.[49] Some forestry professionals interested in reforming their discipline have begun to invoke the science of complexity to argue that forests should be understood as "complex adaptive systems" in which the various parts react to each other, in the process "continually modifying the system and allowing it to adapt to altered conditions." This approach assumes that foresters should abandon the agricultural model that has dominated the profession and think of forests not as stands of trees to be managed by a "command-and-control" method, with interventions to encourage uniform conditions, but as more heterogeneous and dynamic natural systems. According to this way of thinking, influenced by advances in forest ecology, they should worry less about uniformity and predictability and stop "fighting against the inherent behavior of forest systems."[50] In other words, they should learn to live with complexity and some measure of uncertainty.

With their natural resilience forests will continue to expand into cleared or open areas and to evolve toward maturity, where not prevented by development or repeated harvesting. Forests in Michigan have rebounded to the point that the amount of forested land today is comparable to what existed at the beginning of the nineteenth century, although the composition of today's forests is quite different. White pine and northern hardwoods have been making up lost ground at the expense of species that flourished in the aftermath of destructive logging (aspen and birch, oaks) as Michigan's northern forests continue to recover.[51] Yet some species, including hemlock, were reduced so drastically that they will not return on anything like their former scale, and we are unlikely to see the abundant, massive old growth of the "forest primeval" in the imaginable future. Nor are we likely to see in many places the diversity of wildflower species characteristic of the forest floor in a natural forest with undisturbed soils.[52] While certain kinds of change may be irreversible, restoration efforts can go some distance toward recovery, of fauna as well as flora. In the 1980s pine martens and fishers, inhabitants of mature forests, were reintroduced in the Upper Peninsula and are now well established, particularly fishers; moose were reintroduced on several occasions from Isle Royale or Canada and have taken hold in the western Upper Peninsula.[53]

Gray wolves returned on their own and, with their number estimated at close to 600 in the Upper Peninsula and the northern Lower Peninsula, have recovered to the point that they were removed from the federal endangered species list in March 2007 and reclassified as "threatened." They were subsequently reinstated as the result of a successful legal challenge by the Humane Society, then delisted and reinstated again. Their status is likely to remain contested.

In 2004 the DNR approved guidelines for expanding mesic conifers (eastern hemlock, white pine, red pine, balsam fir, and white spruce) by fifty-seven thousand acres on state forest lands in areas of the western Upper Peninsula by 2020. Implementation involves attempting to determine their historic range from early (ca. 1800) vegetation maps and remaining large stumps and downed logs, then deciding what species are likely to thrive in particular areas and whether replanting and other forms of management will be needed to restore them.[54] This project represents an effort to restore a forest closer to its presettlement state, subject to what existing forest conditions will allow. The hope is that restored areas will attract more of the bird species that prefer mesic conifers and provide winter habitat for deer, in order to disperse the herd over a larger wintering area. The 2006 Forest Plan for the Huron-Manistee National Forests envisions restoring barrens, prairies, and grasslands where possible, to an extent (sixty-eight thousand acres) more nearly corresponding to their historic range. Planners defend this initiative, which will involve extensive removal of red pine stands, chiefly on the grounds that it will maintain the viability of over twenty at risk species that depend on the habitats to be restored. On a smaller scale, the kinds of interventions authorized to maintain designated conservation areas (e.g., removing invasive species and conducting prescribed burns) represent an analogous effort to restore and maintain functioning ecosystems. Management efforts such as these are more likely to be embraced by those concerned with ecological values, though not necessarily by those preoccupied with the economic health of the forest products industry.

Through a combination of natural and assisted recovery Michigan's northern forests are moving toward a state closer to what Schoolcraft would have found in the early nineteenth century, if not the same kinds of old-growth forests that he saw. While forests are recovering, however, they face threats that are bringing new kinds of change. Those concerned with the health of our forests now, on private as well as public lands, understand that they must reckon with developments that will affect their evolution, including the accelerating spread of invasive species, outbreaks of disease, and irruptions of exotic insect pests. The effect of the emerald ash borer on forests in southern lower Michigan and neighboring states since it was discovered near Detroit in 2002 (tens of millions of trees killed in Michigan and comparable numbers in several other states) illustrates how rapidly and drastically one of these pests can affect the structure of forests. Developing trends have the potential to transform forests in other ways: rising demand for biofuels, which leads to more cutting of trees (especially fast-growing, early successional species) and more use of forest debris; increasing fragmentation of large landholdings as these are sold by timber companies to investment groups looking to subdivide them; and the effects of climate change on the range of plant and animal species. Those working to recover and maintain high-quality forested lands, including nonprofit groups such as The Nature Conservancy and local land trusts, attempt to mitigate the effects of these factors as they can, not to reconstitute some idealized version of the forests found by the first European settlers but to protect functioning ecosystems with high biological diversity. The work of educating the public in the processes by means of which more diverse and natural forests can be maintained and of enlisting volunteers in stewardship and restoration is increasingly part of this effort, as are collaborations that may involve nonprofits, state and local governments, businesses, and groups of sportsmen or conservationists.

The Nature Conservancy's Northern Great Lakes Forest Project offers an example of large-scale conservation that depends on collaboration with the state and an investment company, The Forestland Group, to protect a network of parcels amounting to over 270,000 acres in the Upper Peninsula under conservation easements that allow sustainable forestry while restricting development. The Conservancy manages 23,338 acres of this network in the watershed of the Two Hearted River that it purchased outright as "working forest" under the Michigan Commercial Forest Reserve Act, with the intent of using sustainable timber harvesting to enhance biological diversity. Foresters with experience in the area act as timber cruisers who identify overabundant sugar maple to be cut in order to open up the canopy. Their aim is to stimulate the regrowth of such species as yellow birch, white and black spruce, hemlock, and American and paper birch. Where the landlookers who were their nineteenth-century predecessors sought out bonanzas in undiscovered stands of white pine, these timber cruisers work in the service of restoration.

A key object of the management plan developed by The Nature Conservancy, with the help of the foresters, is to enhance biological diversity by restoring the ecosystem that existed about 1800, before the proliferation of sugar maple began to crowd out other species and the wildlife that depended on them.[55] Designing a forest in this context means trying to bring back a level of diversity that formerly existed. The plan being implemented by the Conservancy, recently certified by the Forestry Stewardship Council, supports local economies by employing loggers from the area and allows for continuing recreational use of the forest, including hunting and snowmobiling on designated trails. Managing a large forested area long used by local inhabitants has its challenges, for example, removing hunting blinds and bait piles and closing two-track roads formerly used for logging to ORV users accustomed to ignoring barriers. Like the DNR and the Forest Service, The Nature Conservancy must struggle with the problem of controlling unauthorized and potentially damaging ORV use. It benefits from the efforts of an organization based in nearby Newberry, funded by sportsmen's and recreational groups, along with local businessmen, which educates the public about legal and illegal ORV use and discourages the latter by posting photographs of environmental damage caused by irresponsible ORV users on its website.[56]

In the future forests are likely to be differentiated by their functions even more than they are now: urban parks, private woodlots and tree farms, industrial-scale plantations, forested areas protected and in some cases actively managed by land conservancies, and large public forestlands managed by the DNR and the Forest Service that allow a wide range of uses and set aside some areas as wilderness or biological reserves and some as places for motorized recreation. We will perceive these differently according to what we want or have been conditioned to expect. Old growth, where it survives or has regenerated since being logged a hundred years or more ago and has been allowed to reach maturity, will embody the promise of what the natural forest could become to those for whom this is the desired ideal. Forest ecologists will see in it a welcome complexity in the structure of the canopy, the diversity of plant and animal species, the cluttered forest floor, and the organisms found in the soil. For those mainly interested in the potential for commercial timber harvests it is more likely to represent a waste of overly over-mature and fallen trees, for sportsmen a failure to maintain the openings and early successional species needed by the game they hunt, and for some ORV users a denial of the freedom to ride wherever they choose.

Two wilderness areas, both in the western Upper Peninsula, offer models of what can be achieved through a commitment to nurture and protect healthy forests by minimizing management interventions and trusting to natural processes of regeneration. They also suggest how designated wilderness areas can be enjoyed by many kinds of recreational users, including those who come to hunt or fish as well as those who are seeking solitude or a primitive camping experience, without compromising the ecological health of the forest. The Sylvania Wilderness Area of the Ottawa National Forest, near Watersmeet, includes thirty-six lakes set in sixteen thousand forested acres dominated by hemlocks, sugar maples, and yellow birches with a scattering of white pines.[57] Walking into it one is soon surrounded by old-growth forest with mature hemlocks, hardwoods, and pines. Saplings spring from the mossy, ferny floor where light penetrates the canopy. The fact that the trail follows a fading two-track is a reminder that parts of the area were logged in the late nineteenth century. It owes its preservation, and the present state of its forest, to the fact that a group of U.S. Steel executives acquired eleven thousand acres in the early twentieth century and formed a hunting and fishing retreat they called the Sylvania Club. The Forest Service was able to purchase the land in 1966 and maintained it as the Sylvania Recreation Area until it was designated by Congress as a wilderness area in 1987. As part of the federal wilderness system it offers protected old-growth forest with some trees as old as three to four hundred years and a network of clear, quiet lakes and ponds, with wildlife that includes packs of wolves that move through the area, fishers, martens, black bears, loons, ospreys, bald eagles, and pileated woodpeckers. Canoeists and backpackers can reserve primitive campsites scattered around the lakes. On Clark Lake, in the adjacent Sylvania Recreation Area, visitors can find a well-equipped camping area accessible by automobile. Boats with small electric motors may be used on Crooked Lake, where one cabin owner and her guests retain the right to operate motorboats as a result of a lawsuit against the Forest Service when the wilderness area was established. Otherwise Sylvania is wilderness, with no form of mechanized transportation allowed, including bicycles and portaging wheels. Even sailboats are banned.

The Porcupine Mountains Wilderness State Park, enlarged to sixty thousand acres and designated a "wilderness" park since its founding as a state park in 1946, offers perhaps the best example in the Lake States of what an old-growth, north woods hardwood and hemlock forest can become. Like the Sylvania Wilderness Area, it owes its existence largely to the power of the wilderness ideal, although it has remained under state control rather than becoming part of the federal wilderness system. Displays and literature in both places (and in the nearby Ottawa National Forest Visitor Center in Watersmeet in the case of Sylvania) quote the Wilderness Act of 1964 and figures such as John Muir and Aldo Leopold on wilderness. The film shown continuously at the Porcupines Wilderness Visitor Center presents wilderness as an American ideal and describes it as a sanctuary of biological diversity, as well as a refuge from civilization. Near the entrance to Sylvania a plaque commemorating the acquisition of the Sylvania Tract by the Forest Service quotes Thoreau's *Walden:* "We can never have enough of nature. We need to witness our limits transgressed, and some life pasturing freely where we never wander."[58] Those who administer both areas, recognizing that what makes them unique is their wildness, embrace the concept of wilderness and seek to educate visitors about its importance.[59]

The signage at the Summit Park Scenic Area of the Porcupines records the intent of the Michigan Conservation Commission, as it began to acquire lands for the park in 1945, "to preserve forever, as a forest museum, the largest stand of mixed hardwoods and of hemlock still existing in Michigan." While the metaphor of the forest as museum embodies dated assumptions about the forest as an unchanging image of presettlement times, its popularity at the time suggests the high value placed on natural, uncut forest by those drawn to the emerging wilderness ideal.[60] The Michigan Conservation Commission remained committed to preserving the wilderness character of the Porcupines in the face of repeated efforts in the early years of the park to allow logging and mining (both part of the history of the area), to establish a new shoreline road, and even to build fish ladders, which would have required blasting away parts of the waterfalls near the mouth of the Presque Isle River. A subsequent bill funding a shoreline road linking the east and west entrances to the park was passed by the Michigan legislature but vetoed by then governor George Romney after a visit to the Porcupines.[61] South Boundary Road on the outskirts of the park, opened in 1965, connects the two entrances in a more circuitous but less intrusive way.

In 1958 a proposal to grant a lease to mine copper in the park to the local Bear Creek Mining Company, a subsidiary of Kennecott Copper, appeared close to being approved by the Michigan Conservation Commission. The heated debate over the proposed mining lease, which would have involved over nine hundred acres of the park near the mouth of the

Presque Isle River and another fifty-two hundred submerged acres off-shore, pitted local residents who anticipated immediate jobs against those more concerned with wilderness values and the longer term potential for increased recreational tourism. The campaign against mining in the park was led by the Michigan United Conservation Clubs (MUCC) and the Porcupine Mountains Association and enlisted widespread support from national and state organizations. Howard Zahniser, the executive secretary of the Wilderness Society, who would draft the Wilderness Act, testified before the Conservation Commission on behalf of his own organization and several others, and articles opposing the mining project appeared in *Outdoor America, Nature,* and the *New York Times.* One by Samuel Dana, a past president of the Society of American Foresters and former dean of the University of Michigan's School of Natural Resources, argued that the philosophy of multiple use, however sound, did not eliminate the need for choice and that uses such as wilderness and mining were incompatible.[62] The overwhelming public opposition to the proposed lease, which generated a flood of letters to the governor's office embellished with a special stamp issued by the MUCC picturing Lake of the Clouds, persuaded the mining company to withdraw its application several days before the Conservation Commission was to meet to act on it. The commission then unanimously reaffirmed a policy established in 1954 under which the resources of the park were not to be exploited at the expense of recreational values.

In 1972 the Natural Resources Commission approved a master plan for the Porcupines embodying management principles and strategies that had evolved over the course of the early years of the park. Under the plan, which is still in effect, approximately 35,000 acres at the core of the park would be designated as wilderness, with no improvements other than hiking trails allowed and no motorized vehicles. The wilderness area of the park was given statutory protection by the Michigan Wilderness and Natural Areas Act, after previously having been designated a Natural Area Preserve by the Michigan Natural Areas Commission in the 1950s. With the implementation of the master plan the park was renamed the Porcupine Mountains Wilderness Park and divided into four management zones: wilderness (35,605 acres), wilderness study (5,295 acres), scenic sites (2,048 acres), and intensive use (19,000 acres).

The master plan reflected a decision to preserve the "primeval character" of the park's core, where the old growth is concentrated, while making other parts more accessible to a wide range of recreational users. The designated scenic areas (the escarpment overlooking Lake of the Clouds, the waterfalls near the mouth of the Presque Isle River, Summit Peak with its observation tower, and Union Spring) can be reached by car and short trails and, in the case of the Presque Isle waterfalls, by a series of boardwalks and stairways. The intensive use zone includes the Wilderness Visitor Center, a modern campground at Union Bay, and a ski area, all located near the east entrance to the park. The Visitor Center documents the human history of the area, with its waves of mining and logging, as well as its natural history, the latter through exhibits and a self-guided nature trail. Farther along the South Boundary Road a short interpretive trail takes one past ruins of the Union Mine, a reminder of the copper-mining activity in the area, which began in the 1850s and lasted into the early twentieth century. The park manages to exploit the recreational potential of its remarkable setting (including its traditional use as a place for hunting and fishing by local residents), to provide easily accessible scenic views, and to pursue its educational mission without compromising the wilderness character of its vast interior. Hikers and campers can explore the interior through a network of simple trails, from one to sixteen miles in length. Sixteen primitive cabins predating the park's wilderness designation, accessible only by hiking trails, can be rented for as long as a week.

The present state of the park reflects the triumph of the wilderness ideal over efforts to exploit the natural resources of the Porcupine Mountains and to open them up to more commercialized forms of development by building roads and resorts and stocking streams. State senator Joe Mack, who combatively advocated both exploitation and extensive commercial development, complained that those who favored setting aside large areas as wilderness were a minority who felt "that rotting timber, windfalls, [and] inaccessible areas are what a park should consist of."[63] A firm commitment to preserving the wilderness values of the park was an essential bulwark against the kinds of pressure exerted by Mack and others. The present management and educational mission of the park reflect the evolution of the wilderness ideal nationally, from its early emphasis on providing primitive forms of recreation to the current focus on ecosystem health. Recreation remains a priority, but more effort is being made to educate the public about the nature and value of the park's natural diversity, in part by invoking the history of local efforts to preserve the Porcupines and those of the national movement to set aside wilderness areas.

One can get a sense of the wildness and of the unique features that characterize the Porcupines from the major scenic vantage points: the view from the observation tower on Summit Peak of unbroken forested landscapes reaching to Lake Superior; the overlook from the escarpment, which reveals the Big Carp River winding from Lake of the Clouds through marshes three hundred feet below; and the series of three water-falls (Manabezho, Manido, Nawadaha) on the lower Presque Isle River with their distinctive potholes carved by the action of the water.[64] The boardwalks along the Presque Isle border old-growth forest with hem-locks three to four hundred years old and downed trees in various stages of decay, some engulfed by thimbleberry bushes where sunlight reaches the forest floor. For a fuller immersion in the old-growth forests of the Porcupines, and a sense of the solitude possible there, one can explore any of a number of hiking trails. A relatively short trail along the Little Carp River takes one across a cedar swamp and past gentle waterfalls through a forest of old-growth hardwoods with a characteristic pit and mound structure. Longer trails take day hikers and backpackers to Mirror Lake in the heart of the park, along the Big Carp River through meadows and old-growth hemlock, and along the Lake Superior shoreline through second-growth aspen and birch in an area where white pine (along with bass-wood, hemlock, and cedar) was logged in the early twentieth century.

Both Sylvania and the Porcupines offer extensive old growth mixed with cutover areas well advanced in the process of recovery. They illustrate the value of letting the forest heal itself, with minimal efforts to manage it. In Sylvania these efforts are governed by the Wilderness Act and manage-ment plans developed by the Forest Service for the area. Before Sylvania was designated as a federal wilderness area the Forest Service responded to the desires of local residents by paving an entrance road, which gives au-tomobile access to Clark and Crooked Lakes, and developing over sixty campsites with picnic tables and outhouses. After wilderness designation in 1987 the number of campsites was reduced, and the picnic tables and outhouses were removed. Early experiments with selective logging were abandoned.[65] Current management rules mandate the use of handsaws rather than chainsaws for trail work, prohibit cans and bottles in the wilderness area, restrict the size of groups, and bar the use of live bait and barbed hooks in some of the lakes. The greatest threats to the ecological health of Sylvania come from natural forces rather than human use of the area: invasive plant and animal species, including Eurasian earthworms, which consume organic matter on the forest floor, drying out the soil and creating conditions more favorable to invasive plants; climate change, which threatens to alter the structure of the forest and to create a drier environment; and excessive deer browsing, which inhibits the regeneration of hemlock, sugar maple, and yellow birch.

The 1972 master plan for the Porcupines incorporates the definitions of wilderness in the Wilderness Act but is more restrictive, limiting insect and disease control to "disaster conditions which threaten whole ecosystems" and setting out stringent rules for use of the wilderness zone, including prohibitions of horseback riding and of bringing in disposable metal or glass containers.[66] The plan did not envision the looming problem of invasive species, dealt with at present by efforts to eradicate patches of garlic mustard discovered in the park since 2002 and to educate visitors about how to avoid spreading it.[67] Salvage logging was allowed in the Porcupines after large blowdowns in 1948 and 1953 but was subsequently prohibited by the Conservation Commission after a windstorm in 1958, arousing the ire of Upper Peninsula legislators and those concerned with the potential value of the timber. Now, with the commitment to preserving biological diversity firmly extablished, blowdowns are regarded as natural events; salvage logging would not be authorized except when unusually dry conditions create a fire hazard.[68]

Wilderness areas such as Sylvania and the Porcupines represent special cases, where nature is largely left to realize its own designs for the forest. Artists in residence in the Porcupines, who spend two weeks in a primitive cabin built for this purpose, offer their interpretations of these designs through painting, poetry, landscape photography, and in one instance an alphabet based on intimate photographic images of plant and animal forms. The value of such places can be measured in multiple ways. They serve as magnets for recreational tourism, which benefits nearby communities, as what Aldo Leopold called "a base-datum of normality" for scientists, and as habitats for a diverse array of plant and animal species. They offer opportunities for primitive experience of the natural world of a kind that would have been welcomed by Aldo Leopold, Bob Marshall, and others whose sense of the rapid loss of such opportunities motivated them to campaign to preserve wilderness. The appeal that Sylvania and the Porcupine Mountains have for many has to do with the north woods heritage they represent. They give visitors a chance to experience something resembling a kind of northern "primeval" forest that for the most part we can only imagine now.

Even as we develop a better understanding of the complexity of such forests, and of the ways in which they change in response to natural and human disturbances, we continue to value the silences and the opportunities for solitude as well as the biological richness and the aesthetic pleasures they offer. Some prize them more as the noise and the distractions of everyday life intensify. The fact that the chief of the U.S. Forest Service lists "aesthetic beauty and spiritual renewal" among the "ecosystem services" that forests offer, and that forest planners continue to talk about "spiritual values" whether they can define them or not, suggests that they recognize the persistence of a public need to see in our forests more than resources to exploit or venues for sport.[69] If we project onto them desires and expectations that reflect different cultural moments and varying individual needs, we also learn in our different ways to pay attention to the kaleidoscopic displays of changing natural phenomena that they present. Those who have grown up living with forests, hunting and foraging and possibly working there, may see more and be less self-conscious about it than those who come from cities in search of recreation or renewal. They may differ with occasional visitors in their opinions about how forests should be used and enjoyed but are likely to share an appreciation for what makes particular forests remarkable.

Yet all those who value the northern forests, and argue about how they should be managed, may find themselves confronted by changes so great they call into question both the capacity of managers to shape the forests and that of forests to renew themselves. Global warming promises to bring warmer summers and milder winters, which are likely to change the composition of tree species in northern forests and also to trigger intense windstorms that can cause massive blowdowns such as one that involved more than four hundred thousand acres in the Boundary Waters Canoe Area of Minnesota in 1999.[70] Invasive species, including the garlic mustard that has spread quickly through disturbed forests in southern Michigan and the nonnative earthworms that already are consuming the duff on the forest floor in northern as well as southern forests, are likely to accelerate the transformation. If deer herds increase with milder winters, or even remain at their present high levels, some tree species in areas they favor will have difficulty regenerating. The possibility of change on such a scale introduces a new kind of uncertainty about the future of the forests. It may prompt a rethinking of assumptions about how well they can recover from disturbances and how actively they should be managed. Calls for more aggressive efforts to combat invasive species and excessive deer browsing, for more extensive use of controlled burns to aid regeneration, and for more ambitious and widespread efforts to slow global warming are likely to increase. Whether or not present trends can be reversed or significantly slowed remains to be seen. The north woods popularized by Sigurd Olson, and enjoyed by visitors to state and national forests in the upper Midwest, may look very different a hundred years from now. As uncertainty about the future of forests grows the primeval forest of presettlement times, however we imagine it, may come to represent an ever more elusive ideal.

Coda

I live in the woods so I know a few things.

—JIM HARRISON, *Returning to Earth*

Two contemporary novels set in Michigan's Upper Peninsula, Jim Harrison's *Returning to Earth* (2007) and his friend Philip Caputo's earlier *Indian Country* (1987), bring my story of changing cultural attitudes toward the forest back around to the Ojibwa and introduce different perspectives on some of the themes that I trace. They also offer glimpses of ways in which the presence of a heavily forested landscape influences life in the Upper Peninsula in the present. The chief interest of these novels for me lies in the way in which Harrison and Caputo link the redemption of their protagonists to a vision of a spirit-haunted natural world, mediated by traditional Ojibwa beliefs as the writers understand these. Both assume the persistence of these beliefs in their fictions and suggest the possibility of an alternate way of viewing our relationship with the natural world that depends on a sense of the interconnection of human and other than human nature.

Harrison's *Returning to Earth,* a sequel to *True North,* picks up where the previous novel left off but shifts the focus from David Burkett to his sister Cynthia and her husband Donald, who is dying of Lou Gehrig's disease and preparing for his death by embracing the Ojibwa side of his mixed Ojibwa and Finnish heritage. In the family history that Donald recounts in the opening section of the book Harrison brings together two important Upper Peninsula stories, that of the Finnish immigrants who learn to make a hard living in the big woods and that of the Ojibwa who find means of keeping traditional beliefs alive while adapting to the ways of the dominant white society. The struggle of Donald's family to accept his choice of assisted suicide reflects not only grief but discomfort with the spirit world with which he is increasingly preoccupied, to the point that he repeatedly seeks and finally achieves a dream vision on the Ontario hillside where he will subsequently insist on dying and being buried.

Caputo focuses on his protagonist Chris Starkmann's struggles with his memories of the Vietnam War, tormented by a recurrent nightmare related to his guilt over having caused the death of his boyhood friend Bonny George in Vietnam by mistakenly calling in the wrong coordinates for air support. He shows Chris finally recovering his mental health and the capacity to embrace his present life, after a self-destructive descent into violence that leads to his hospitalization, through the efforts of Bonny George's Ojibwa grandfather to heal him. Caputo portrays the grandfather as the last of the shamans on his reservation who follow the way of the Midewiwin, the Grand Medicine Society that played a dominant role in Ojibwa culture until well into the twentieth century and has more recently resurfaced in robust form with a broadened cultural focus, a development not reflected in Caputo's novel.[1]

The forest assumes major importance in both novels, as the environment that shapes everyday life in the Upper Peninsula and as a source of spiritual meaning for Donald and Chris. Both writers tell stories of living, working, and hunting in the woods, and both allude to a past in which the natural resources of the area were exploited relentlessly, Harrison through references to thousands of mining accidents and to landscapes still marked by pine stumps. In these novels experience in the woods typically serves as an index of awareness and a clue to the psychological state of a character. Harrison's David and Cynthia both lose their way in the woods through inattention, David numerous times.[2] Donald, on the other hand, appears assured and highly alert in the woods, with powers of observation that we are told he has learned from his "tribal friends." Harrison has written frequently about his own habit of walking ("To return myself to earth I walk daily with my dog") and makes Donald someone who walks off his anxieties and becomes familiar with wild animals through his frequent rambles in the woods.[3] Donald returns to the earth literally, buried as he wishes without a coffin on the Ontario hillside that he regards as sacred ground, and he embraces his identity and his connection with the natural world more completely than any other character in the novel: "I never saw anyone who so thoroughly was what he was."[4]

Caputo traces the progression of Chris's psychological disintegration by showing him losing his customary assurance in the woods when he imagines a cougar stalking him and flees in panic, tripped up by roots and slapped in the face by branches, until he recovers sufficiently to figure out how to find his way back to the logging road where he has left his truck. Chris's disorientation is remarkable for someone who not only works in the woods (as a surveyor and timber cruiser) but lives there, having persuaded his reluctant wife June to abandon her home in Marquette for a remote cabin on forty wooded acres bordering the Vieux Desert reservation.[5] June illustrates a more common kind of fear that the engulfing woods of the Upper Peninsula can arouse. She hates the isolation of their remote setting and is made deeply uneasy by trips on her rounds as a social worker into the back country of jeep and logging trails, anxious about losing her way in the maze of intersecting, unmarked two-tracks ("The woods gave her the creeps").[6] Chris shows none of this kind of fear, and we know that he has begun to recover when after his hospitalization he succeeds in tracking down Bonny George's grandfather, Louis, at the camp in the Huron Mountains that he had visited in his boyhood with Bonny George but now must find without the help of directions.

The forest assumes even greater spiritual significance in *Indian Country* than it does in *Returning to Earth* and also plays a larger role in the action. Caputo's novel begins and ends in the forested landscapes of the Huron Mountains, and we see Chris mainly in the woods, where he can find the solitude that he seeks and can also experience periods of calm pursuing his work or roaming his own property, hunting grouse and deer and fishing the stream that runs through it. He seems miscast in a work role that calls for him to translate a forest into its market value, and to exaggerate the potential yield of company land to justify a new mill, when his own sympathies are closer to those of the Indians who "saw mystery in some ancient pine or maple, not just so many board feet of saw log or cords of pulp" (93–94). As his anxiety increases and he drinks more and more in an effort to control it, he perceives a logging operation he inspects as a nightmarish scene of slashings and churned mud that recalls his Vietnam experience. To Chris the logging site takes on the "ruined look of a battlefield the day after the battle" (85), and a giant loader-slasher resembles a "monster from outer space." He hears chainsaws "[ripping] the silence of the forest" and imagines them biting into the skin and flesh of trees.

When Chris challenges the bullying woods boss over the sloppy practices that he allows, the confrontation quickly escalates to a violent fistfight. Caputo uses the scene both to critique the destructiveness of contemporary logging practices and to mark the point at which Chris loses control and ensures that he will be fired. The swaggering culture of the woods boss and his men, with their chainsaws and heavy machinery, makes them seem to Chris "phony lumberjacks," the antithesis of old-style loggers laboring with axes in the woods. Yet his nostalgia for a simpler, more challenging kind of work makes him seem even more unfit for life in a world in which Great Superior Iron and Timber is a dominant force. In his preoccupation with his own demons Chris seems oblivious to the manifestations of poverty that June deals with daily and to an economic climate that breeds constant worry about "layoffs, mine shutdowns, declining demands for timber, and foreclosure sales" (221). The emotional pull that he feels is to the Huron Mountains visible in the distance, which Caputo portrays as the epitome of wildness: "wolf and coyote country, uninhabited, never touched by the plow, Indian country" (281). The question posed by the novel is whether Chris is too damaged by his experience with the hostile "Indian country" of Vietnam to recover a sense of the possibilities of this original Indian country.

Caputo develops a sharp dichotomy between wilderness and civilization, establishing wilderness as the primary locus of value in the novel with his opening account of the fishing trip that Chris and Bonny George take to the ominously named Windigo River on the verge of Bonny George's departure for the army and Vietnam.[7] The wilderness character of the Huron Mountains is epitomized by a stand of old-growth white pines on a ridge above the Windigo River too steep to have been logged that Chris encounters on his trip with Bonny George. He is awestruck by the "cathedral columns" of the tall pines as though he has come on a "forbidden temple." Caputo invokes the familiar view of the forest as sacred space, showing Chris imagining these woods with their damp shade broken by shafts of light as "haunted" and "primeval," seeming to belong to "an older America, untouched and unowned" (38). As he and Bonny George sit on an outcrop of the ridge, he envisions the remnant pines as part of one vast forest, "broken only by its lakes and rivers," which reaches south "across the Upper Peninsula into northern Wisconsin, west into Minnesota, east into Ontario, and north five hundred miles to Hudson's Bay" (39). Caputo uses a metaphor that Harrison would recast in *True North* to characterize the logging boom in the Upper Peninsula, describing it as "a slaughter that had been to the north woods what the annihilation of the buffalo had been to the plains" (37). Chris's encounter with the surprising stand of towering white pines combined with his view from the ridge prompts a vision of a recovering north woods "ravaged but never completely conquered" by the white man, a wild "Indian country" at the heart of the continent.

The fishing trip suddenly turns nightmarish when Chris loses his footing in the swift current of the Windigo River and is very nearly swept to his death under a deadfall before Bonny George can pull him out. The experience abruptly ends the trip but does not diminish the appeal of the Huron Mountains for Chris. Bonny George's deep attachment to the place heightens this appeal and helps to explain Chris's decision to settle in the Upper Peninsula after he returns from Vietnam. For Bonny George life in the woods—hunting and fishing, checking traps with his grandfather, even working as a pulp cutter—"make[s] everything all right" (40). Seeking refuge in Canada to escape the draft would mean giving up any chance to continue this life and his close relationship with the grandfather who introduced him to it. The character most completely identified with the forests of the Huron Mountains is this grandfather, Louis or Wawiekumig, the Ojibwa name he assumes after a successful vision quest as a boy in which he discovers his personal *manito,* or guardian spirit, the eagle. He interprets his dream of flying with the eagle as meaning that he should study to join the society of the Midewiwin (or Mide).[8] Caputo uses Mide rituals to represent Ojibwa spiritual beliefs, describing through flashbacks how the youthful Louis/Wawiekumig gained powers in this world and the invisible world of the *manitos,* including the ability to heal. We see him acquiring the "spiritual sight" that commits him to a life as a shaman or medicine man through a series of four initiations into the secrets of the Mide, each confirming his ascent to a higher degree of knowledge.

In the present of the novel Louis is eighty-two, conscious of the waning of his spiritual sight, and of the Mide itself, and still struggling to understand and accept his grandson's death in Vietnam fourteen years earlier. When we first see him, he is getting ready for the Ghost Supper that he conducts each year at his camp deep in the Huron Mountains by fasting for three days and then taking the sweat bath that represents the last stage of his preparation. Caputo emphasizes his vulnerability by representing him as practicing the way of the Mide in a world in which its presence has faded. He is forced to do everything for himself, building the sweat lodge and performing the rituals of purification without the company of fellow initiates that he had in the past, "an old man, Wawiekumig, follower of an archaic creed, fasting alone and naked in the forest" (153). As he struggles to break through the boundary between this world and the invisible one and communicate with the spirit of his grandson he has the additional burden of not knowing whether anyone will perform the rites that will put his own soul on the Path of the Dead. In praying to the power represented by an eagle that appears in his camp, a favorable omen, he confesses that he has fallen out of harmony and declares his intent to restore "balance" by finding answers to his questions through dreams.

Louis's secular counterpart, the Veterans Administration (VA) clinical psychologist Eckhardt, can offer Chris group therapy, hospitalization, and intelligent analysis of his condition but is unable to reach him on the level on which Louis can. To Louis, Chris's unexpected arrival in his camp on the anniversary of Bonny George's death is a mystery that he must patiently wait to see reveal itself. Caputo presents the encounter as a struggle of Chris and Louis to cross boundaries of thought and culture. When an increasingly agitated Chris confesses his responsibility for Bonny George's death and asks for forgiveness, he is frustrated by Louis's impassiveness. Yet Louis cannot simply "forgive" Chris because the word and the concept have no meaning in his view of the world, as he tries to explain. What he can recognize is that Chris is "out of harmony with himself." He reaches him by assuming the manner of a teacher and reducing his complicated sense of his own guilt for Bonny George's death to an explanation that Chris can understand, namely, that he and not Chris was responsible for the decision to go to Vietnam that led to his grandson's death (by advising him to follow the way of his warrior forebears). His advice to Chris, that he needs to learn to live with himself and that the only reason he is ashamed of himself is that he wants to be, resembles what Chris has heard from Eckhardt but carries greater authority because of Louis's experience and the fact that he gives it in the natural setting of the camp rather than the sterile one of Eckhardt's office.

Caputo takes the encounter into another register by describing a "medicine dream" that Louis has while Chris is lost in a deep, restorative sleep on the floor of his wigwam. In this dream an eagle carries him and Chris to "a beautiful forest of towering cedars" where he brushes Chris's head with an eagle feather four times while singing a song of healing and then reenacts the Mide ritual of symbolically killing and then reviving the person needing help that he had undergone himself in the process of his initiation. By this means Caputo suggests the continued vitality of the Ojibwa spiritual tradition for Louis without needing to show Chris consciously participating in it. Louis believes that the events of the dream actually happened in the world of the *manitos* and that once again he has practiced his art of healing, a conclusion that makes him happy and enables him to recover the inner harmony he was seeking. Chris, meanwhile, awakens refreshed to the sight of lake and woods transformed by fog, with the pines on a nearby island showing through the mist like "a ghost sailing-ship," and feels himself convinced by Louis's explanation of the night before that trickster spirits had entered him and infected his reason. In this setting, with firs and birches "looming eerily in the smoky woods," Louis's view of a world infused with spirit gives Chris a new way of understanding the woods, one not shaped by the Christian heritage that colored his view of the grove of white pines above the Windigo River as a hidden temple. He absorbs the peacefulness of the camp, "separate from the woods, yet as much a part of it as the trees" (413), and is excited as he recalls Louis's pronouncement of the night before: "I know that life is a gift. I know that life should be a song and a prayer" (411). The sentiment may sound to a modern ear more like a greeting card cliché than the wisdom of a shaman, but it reflects Ojibwa understanding of nature's offerings as gifts and of the importance of sacred song and prayer. Caputo represents it as Louis's effort to find English words that will reach Chris and enable him to imagine a hopeful future.

However we understand his transformation, Caputo makes the new bond that Chris feels with Louis seem wholly natural. He becomes a willing helper, cutting birch sticks for a snare at Louis's direction and listening attentively as Louis explains the medicine bundle from which he takes basswood twine to complete the snare and a pipe mixture of tobacco and aster to attract game. When Louis returns shortly with two grouse for breakfast, Chris is astonished. Louis's invitation to join him on fishing trips and his suggestion that there are things he could teach Chris point to a future in which he will mentor him in the ways of the woods and perhaps more: "There's a lot of things I know you don't" (416). If Chris cannot embody Bonny George's spirit, he can become a surrogate for him to whom Louis can pass on at least some of his knowledge. Caputo suggests that they have formed a new kinship, "each finding in the other what each had lost" (417).

Caputo completes the story of Chris's psychic healing by showing him returning to the Windigo River to perform personal rites of absolution. His sense of harmony within himself and with his environment gives him the confidence to strip and reenter the river in which he almost drowned, surrendering himself to the current. When he emerges, he is able to speak aloud his forgiveness of his authoritarian and militantly pacifist father, as well as of himself. Chris has come to realize that hatred of his father, a Lutheran minister who expected his son to follow in his path, was a large part of his motivation for enlisting in the army. Sinking his army uniform in the river in an improvised ceremony serves as the final act by which he signals his freedom from his obsession with his Vietnam experience. He experiences what amounts to a symbolic rebirth, delighting in the freshness of the air and imagining the surrounding trees as holding out their arms to welcome him to a world that appears newly created and full of life and promise. By ending the novel with the woods echoing Chris's jubilant shout of "I forgive you," Caputo makes it seem as though they are celebrating the "repatriation" that will enable him to return home and begin a normal life. The forest is a necessary setting for the denouement of the novel, as Louis is a necessary agent in Chris's redemption. The role played by Louis/Wawiekumig's "medicine" remains ambiguous, but his spiritual understanding of the forest and his regained harmony with it are unmistakable, and critical to Caputo's vision.

Harrison presents Ojibwa beliefs more obliquely and economically in *Returning to Earth,* offering glimpses of them through the narratives that constitute the four parts of the novel, each given to one of the central characters. In rehearsing the history of his family in the first part Donald introduces several figures who believe in the interconnection of natural and spiritual worlds (a Cree shaman who appears at the wedding of his great-grandfather, his father's cousin Flower, and the teacher who guides him in the vision quest that he pursues on the hillside in Ontario north of Sault Ste. Marie). Unlike Caputo, who dramatizes Louis's isolation by characterizing the creed he follows as "archaic," Harrison presents characters who find ways of perpetuating Ojibwa beliefs and practices while discovering how to live with contemporary white society. Donald himself seems to occupy two worlds, one dominated by his family and his construction business and another defined by Ojibwa religious beliefs, which he is reluctant to share, treating them as private. When he finally describes his revelatory experience on the Ontario hillside to his wife Cynthia, as his narrative draws to a close, we learn how in the course of three days of fasting he began to have visions: of his future sickness and death (two years before his diagnosis); of his parents sitting by a creek, with a sleeping bear beside them, telling him not to be afraid to "come home"; of his body flying over the earth and walking on the ocean floor. Donald's visions, which he attains after several prior attempts have failed, enable him to cross the boundary between the physical and spiritual worlds in his imagination and convince him that "the spirit is everywhere rather than a separate thing" (71).

Harrison associates Donald's ability to believe in and connect with the spirit world with the fact that, as Donald puts it, he was "lucky to spend a life pretty close to the earth up here in the north" (71). He understands the earth more deeply as a result of his fast on the hillside, receiving the "gift" of being able "to see all sides of everything at once," including how creatures see him. Donald owes what Cynthia calls his "tribal feelings" primarily to his association with his "pure-blood and traditional" cousin Flower, the best exemplar in the novel of a life lived close to the earth and a character who comes across as a less scary and more mischievous version of Louise Erdrich's Fleur Pillager. Flower lives in the woods and supports herself, with some help from Cynthia, by cleaning cottages, gathering herbs and berries, hunting, and trapping. Her unimposing shack reflects her wanderings in the woods in which she spends most of her time. It is a place of "eerie serenity" where she makes pies from the berries she gathers, weaves baskets out of porcupine quills, and spreads out found objects that include feathers, stones, animal skulls, and a soapstone peace pipe shaped like a loon. For David, who describes the calming effect on Donald's grieving daughter Clare of time spent with Flower, "It is hard to imagine a house so totally *on the ground*" (147). Harrison portrays Flower as Donald's principal helper and guide to the spirit world of the Ojibwa, someone who understands animals and tells Donald stories that embody Ojibwa beliefs. Donald's bond with Flower begins when he spends two months with her at age ten and is deepened by continuing contact in his adult life. Cynthia credits Flower's belief "that people must be careful to live in complete harmony with their natural surroundings" (50) with being a formative influence on his character.

The strongest connection between Donald and Flower has to do with their sympathetic understanding of animals, particularly bears, which function in the novel as in Ojibwa belief as a link with the spirit world. Caputo presents bears as mediators between the human world and that of the *manitos* in Ojibwa myth and also as actors in daily life in the Upper Peninsula. He includes a grisly scene in which June kills a bear that breaks the kitchen window of the rural family she is visiting to get at cooling berry pies, shooting it repeatedly and compulsively out of fear and rage. When she sees the bear spread out in the process of being skinned and gutted by the boys of the family, she is shocked by its resemblance to a human form and even more disturbed when she learns that it was a pregnant sow. The bear might well have been shot anyway by hunters that the boys were preparing to guide, but June's reaction to the surprising violence of her act makes us see her killing of the bear as unnatural and disruptive, as if she had violated a taboo. Bears are more elusive and ambiguous figures in Harrison's novel, except in a story told by Donald's great-grandfather of guiding a brewery executive who wanted to use a picture of himself with a bear he had killed in a beer advertisement. The great-grandfather's remorse, after baiting a large female bear and helping the executive to kill it, triggers "bear nightmares" and a decision to swear off hunting as an act of penance (39).

Harrison alludes to stories of men becoming bears and bears mating with young women and shows bears making mysterious appearances in dreams and actuality. Donald's "animal dreams" date from his experience of hearing Flower's stories and those of a friend of hers as a ten year old, some of them scary ones about the Windigo and bad Indians transformed into bears with huge wings that fly down to eat Indian children. As an adult, he has come to know bears from his experiences in the woods and to feel a sense of kinship with them. David claims that he "loves" them. During Donald's three-day fast in Ontario a female bear comes to investigate him one evening and then returns at dawn, giving him the feeling that she is courting him. He talks to three ravens who linger to look at him, telling them about the visions he is having. Donald would have regarded both bears and the ravens that follow them as potential emissaries from the spirit world, to be welcomed rather than feared.

David, by contrast, is uneasy about tribal attitudes toward bears and about bears themselves. He reports a teasing comment of Donald's: "You think a bear is just a bear" (157). Clearly a bear is not just a bear for Donald, or for Flower, who refuses to eat bear meat "for religious reasons" and talks to a bear, who rubs against her, when she is picking berries. In presenting her grandfather's bear-claw necklace to Donald on his last visit to her she gives him something that both would have regarded as having its own medicine. Her prediction that they would "take many walks in the far corners of the earth when they entered the spirit world" (136) is a way of consoling him and reminding him of their shared beliefs. Flower's view that the spirits of the departed enter the bodies of their favorite animals subsequently reinforces Clare's conviction that her father's spirit has assumed the form of a bear and her determination to find a way to communicate with him.

Harrison makes David a foil for Donald in his relationship to the woods as well as in his attitude toward bears. The David of *Returning to Earth* has discovered a new sense of purpose in providing survival kits to Mexicans seeking to cross illegally into the United States, pursuing his own vision of social justice as if trying to compensate for the wrongs of his father and grandfather, and he returns from Mexico to his cabin in the Upper Peninsula only in the summer. He finds some respite from the tensions of his work in Mexico by "retreating to [his] log hideout in the woods where the sound of the river baffles the world's noise" (204). The woods function for David primarily as a refuge and an antidote to what he calls the "illness of history" (149), something that he can never completely shake despite having got beyond the effort to write the history of his own family with which he was obsessed in *True North*. The woods provide him with the stimulus of the insistently real: "History always withers in the face of a raven squawking at me from the bare tamarack tree beside the pump house" (151). The hollow pine stump that served David as a sanctuary in *True North*, another favorite motif of Harrison's and one that reflects his own practice of resting in hollow stumps when hiking from his Upper Peninsula cabin near Grand Marais, reappears in the sequel as an "easy chair" in which he can meditate.[9] Yet David is never truly comfortable or sure of himself in the woods, despite his years of experience there. He locates his favorite stump again only with difficulty and makes a habit of getting lost, neglecting to take such routine precautions as carrying a compass. When a bear appears sitting in a glade fifty feet from his hideaway in the stump, he nervously retreats to his car and drives quickly out of the woods, wondering whether it could be Donald.

David's uneasiness with bears that come too close, including one that he recalls following him on a long hike in the sand dunes years before, has more to do with his sense of what they may represent than with possible physical threats. He has dreams about bears, including one of an old male with patchy fur at his bird feeder from which he abruptly awakes when the bear starts to talk: "I didn't want to hear what it had to say" (184). What David seems to fear is the possibility of boundary crossings between animal and human worlds. He prefers scientific explanations of bear behavior to mythic ones that suggest a kinship between bears and humans, and he does not want to think about the time Donald spent on the hillside in Ontario because the idea of seeking visions of a spirit world unnerves him. For David too much solitude is a dangerous thing, potentially loosening his grip on the sense of "ordinary reality" that he depends on and regularly renews by seeking human company, particularly that of women. Clare, on the other hand, wants to cross the boundary that separates her from the spirit world in the hope of making contact with the spirit of her dead father, believing that it actually could have entered the body of a bear. Thus she devours books about bears and Ojibwa customs, listens to Flower's bear stories, and with Flower's guidance builds a hut in which she isolates herself in the woods. She haunts places such as the one on the Yellow Dog River where she last fished with her father, at times sensing his presence. Cynthia finds such behavior deeply troubling, but her psychologist friend Coughlin, Harrison's more sophisticated version of Caputo's VA psychologist Eckhardt, regards it as a natural attraction to what Clare imagines as her father's way of perceiving the world.

Harrison's novel becomes a study of ways of dealing with grief, which he illuminates by showing the reactions of the principal characters to the Ojibwa belief in the interrelationship of the natural world with the invisible one of *manitos*. Cynthia sees Clare's desperate embrace of this belief in her efforts to contact Donald's spirit as an unhealthy obsession. She had planned to take her daughter to a Ghost Supper, "where you throw tobacco onto a bonfire and release the spirits of the dead you've been clinging to" (186), but instead Clare seeks out her father's teacher in Ontario. Harrison makes this Ojibwa teacher a land surveyor and part-time medicine man, a shadowy figure who carries into the present at least some of the traditional beliefs represented by Caputo's evocation of the Mide in Louis/ Wawiekumig. He shows up at the digging of Donald's grave just before his suicide to line it with cedar boughs. Subsequently, he displays an insight in dealing with Clare in her grief that recalls Louis's more complicated response to Chris. After taking her to a hibernating bear's blowhole near the grave site, he advises her that the fair thing to do is to let her father's spirit go, warning that it could drive her crazy to fool around with such matters without knowing "where she already was in the world" (259). As one who presents himself as a mediator with the spiritual world in which her father believed, he has an authority for Clare that family members lack. She allows him to steer her away from Ojibwa beliefs, which can never have the authenticity for her that they had for Donald, and put her on a path that leads to recovery and a new focus and sense of identity. When we see her last, she is pursuing graduate work in botany and horticulture.

Flower tells Cynthia the story of Clare's experience with the medicine man in Ontario, with the aside that she is just an old lady and stays away from "most of this stuff." Harrison makes her the canniest and most enigmatic character in the novel and someone who is unconventional and strong willed enough to walk out of a hospital and all the way home on an old Indian trail in the middle of the night. Flower has her own kind of wisdom, which has little to do with that of white society. As she puts it, "I live in the woods so I know a few things" (259). When she finally allows Cynthia to see Clare's hut, Flower enjoys making her jump by growling like a bear. Then she takes her through a swamp to a bear's blowhole and, after Cynthia has listened to the bear breathing, tells her flatly, "It's not Donald, it's an old female bear." Yet as Cynthia walks away Flower does "an eerie little dance and chant" (277). She recognizes Cynthia's skepticism about spirits of humans inhabiting animals yet senses her inability to dismiss the idea completely, teasing her by intimating that a bear is not just a bear after all.

Cynthia never questioned Donald about his religious beliefs in life and continues to maintain that they are not her business, yet she reads the bear material that Coughlin has brought from Chicago and finds herself unable to banish bears from her imagination. In one of the vivid dreams she has in the hospital when she is recovering from pneumonia she recalls a time camping when she and Donald heard a baby bear crying and realizes that Donald looks too hairy in her dream. David has a recurrent dream of a baby bear playing by his bird feeder, which he senses is being watched by Donald in the form of the invisible mother bear. He must insist to himself: "Donald wasn't a bear. Donald was Donald. Why was my mind imagining a fresh mythology? Of course in Donald's tribe men had become bears but that was Donald's tribe not mine" (200). David becomes sure enough of his own identity and his feelings that he resolves to seek out Vera, the daughter of his father's Mexican helper, Jesse, and the baby bear of his dream, after having been held back for years by the knowledge that his father had raped her when she was a teenager. He can override whatever subconscious reservations about Donald's disapproval and his protectiveness of Vera the dream may represent and begin a relationship with her. Cynthia finds her own way of embracing a different future by agreeing to teach at Lame Deer on the Cheyenne Reservation in Montana, although she is influenced in her choice by a dream in which she sees herself living with Donald there, in a place that he had loved when they visited Lame Deer on a family trip. Her choice frees her to resume her teaching career, in a landscape without the associations of her past life with Donald but one in which she can imagine him.

By the end of the novel Clare, David, and Cynthia have all managed to begin new lives, with their grief for Donald and their reactions to his belief in a world of *manitos* having subsided to the point where they can move on. Harrison chose to conclude with Clare and Cynthia observing the anniversary of Donald's death by hiking to a grove of poplar and birch in a depression in the Grand Sable Dunes to which his nephew K. had guided Donald in the late stages of his illness. In an earlier scene in the grove Donald sees a bear on a hillside grazing on beach peas and wild strawberries before he lies back on a low birch limb and feels his body relax to the point where he can sleep: "[T]here was a spirit in the place that gave my body some peace" (17). A dream that reminds him of his visions on the hillside in Canada is populated by bears with wings, one of them with a face resembling his, surrounded by ravens. In the later scene Clare, sitting with her mother on the same large branch where Donald slept, sees a flock of ravens and persuades her mother to walk with her toward them, convinced that they must be following a bear. When the two peep over the top of a dune and see a large bear in the beach peas and wild strawberries, the bear stands up and woofs, staring at them. The scene prompts the same unspoken questions in both: "*Is that him? Is that him? Is that Donald who is greeting us, saying a final good-bye?*" Harrison is too good a writer to supply answers, leaving us instead with a reverberating final line: "And then he trotted over a hill as we all must" (280).

What Harrison does in these two scenes is to invest a particular place with extraordinary meaning, by associating it with emotionally charged visits and with Donald's perception of a "spirit" in the place that he believes accounts for its effect on him. And of course by having bears appear on both occasions, events that can be explained easily enough by bears' attraction to a favorite food source but that take on an aura of mystery in the context of the novel.[10] We learn from Donald that he has visited the grove before with David and that both David and Flower through their years in the woods know such special places, which "seem to carry a weight of their own." Caputo, like Harrison, suggests that there are special places associated with revelatory moments, notably the ridge where Chris encounters the grove of white pines that escaped the axes of the lumberjacks and Louis's camp on an obscure lake, both deep in the wilderness of the Huron Mountains. Chris's encounter with the old-growth pines enables him to reimagine "primeval" forest that covered the upper Midwest and much of Ontario. His experience of Louis's camp, especially when he awakens after his restorative sleep to a foggy morning that gives the forested landscape an air of unreality, suggests another kind of possibility, that of a spirit-haunted world to which he finds himself drawn. Chris has become a capable woodsman during his time in the Upper Peninsula, a "good man in the woods" in the vernacular, but by the end of the novel he feels a deeper connection with the forest, one that depends less on his skills than on a sense of its mysterious presence.

With their fictions Harrison and Caputo suggest how landscapes can come alive through their linkages with human events and also through their participation in natural rhythms that have more to do with cyclical time than with the linear time of history. Both use dreams to suggest the possibility of dissolving the boundary between the physical and spiritual worlds, relying on their sense of how dreams can connect one with the invisible world of *manitos* in Ojibwa culture. By invoking Ojibwa myths and practices and suggesting that they can have redemptive power, at least for some, they call attention to the possibility that older ways of imagining our relationship with the forest and its creatures can restore a sense of harmony with the natural world we inhabit. Neither writer offers answers to questions about whether the spirit world of Ojibwa mythology is real, but they give us characters and stories that suggest its persistence in the imagination and dramatize ways in which belief in this world, or the temptation to believe in it, can mirror human longing.

Notes

INTRODUCTION

1. In fact, the Ojibwa and Menominee, among others, continue to share the stewardship of the "northland."

2. I am indebted to Eric D. Olmanson's discussion of the pageant, with quotations from the program, in the epilogue of *The Future City on the Inland Sea* (Athens: Ohio University Press, 2007).

3. See Robert Dale Parker's commentary on "To the Pine Tree" in his pioneering edition of the poetry of Jane Johnston Schoolcraft, *The Sound the Stars Make Rushing through the Sky* (Philadelphia: University of Pennsylvania Press, 2007), 52–54.

4. Jim Harrison, *True North* (New York: Grove Press, 2004), 163.

5. For a summary account of the major fires in this period, see Donald I. Dickmann and Larry A. Leefers, *The Forests of Michigan* (Ann Arbor: University of Michigan Press, 2003), chap. 7.

6. The setting of the story is actually the Fox River, which flows through Seney and the Kingston Plains. The Two Hearted River, which Hemingway seems to have chosen for the name, is located farther east.

7. See Dickmann and Leefers, *The Forests of Michigan,* 21 (and chap. 1 generally).

8. Michael Wigglesworth, *God's Controversy with New England* (1662), in *The Poems of Michael Wigglesworth,* edited by Ronald A. Bosco (New York: University Press of America, 1989), 90.

9. See William Cronon, *Changes in the Land: Indians, Colonists, and the Ecology of New England* (New York: Hill and Wang, 1983).

10. On received views of the sublime and picturesque, see Edmund Burke, *A Philosophical Inquiry into the Origins of Our Ideas of the Sublime and the Beautiful,* edited by J. T. Boulton (London: Routledge Classics, [1757] 2008); William Gilpin, *Three Essays,* 2nd ed. (London: R. Blamire, 1784); and Uvedale Price, *An Essay on the Picturesque* (London: J. Robson, 1796).

11. Henry David Thoreau, "Walking," in *Wild Apples and Other Natural History Essays by Henry D. Thoreau,* edited by William J. Rossi (Athens: University of Georgia Press, 2002), 78.

12. Ibid., 76.

13. See Edward Abbey, *Desert Solitaire* (New York: Ballantine, 1968); and Gary Snyder, *The Practice of the Wild* (San Francisco: North Point Press, 1990).

14. See Robert Pogue Harrison, *Forests: The Shadow of Civilization* (Chicago: University of Chicago Press, 1992), 177ff., for a discussion of the origins and symbolism of the sacred forest. Simon Schama, in *Landscape and Memory* (New York: Random House, 1995), chap. 4, discusses the association of crosses with vegetation (the "verdant cross") and crosses and churches with woodland settings in the paintings of Thomas Cole and Caspar David Friedrich.

15. Michael Pollan describes this debate in *Second Nature* (New York: Atlantic Monthly Press, 1991), chap. 10. John Gatta places "A Forest Hymn" in a nineteenth-century tradition of romantic religion, characterizing it as "quasi-pantheistic." See his *Making Nature Sacred: Literature, Religion, and Environment in America from the Puritans to the Present* (Oxford: Oxford University Press, 2004), 74–76.

16. See especially the Sabbath poems collected in Wendell Berry, *A Timbered Choir* (Washington, D.C.: Counterpoint, 1998).

17. Henry D. Thoreau, *The Maine Woods,* edited by Joseph J. Moldenhauer (Princeton: Princeton University Press, 1972), 121–22.

18. The Organic Act of 1897 had established the purposes of the forest reserves and provided the legal basis for managing national forests until it was superseded by the 1960 act. In Michigan multiple use was defined in the Conservation Department report for 1945–46 as encompassing game management and recreation, including camping, as well as timber production. William D. Botti and Michael D. Moore, *Michigan's State Forests: A Century of Stewardship* (East Lansing: Michigan State University Press, 2006), 74–75.

19. Aldo Leopold, *A Sand County Almanac* (New York: Oxford University Press, 1949), vii, 203–5.

CHAPTER 1

1. Mentor L. Williams, ed., *Schoolcraft's Narrative Journal of Travels* (East Lansing: Michigan State University Press, 1992). The expedition traveled into Minnesota searching for the source of the Mississippi River. Schoolcraft and others proceeded down the western shore of Lake Michigan on their return journey. Peter Fritzell characterizes Schoolcraft's reactions to what he saw, as well as those of other early explorers and the Jesuits who preceded them, in his comprehensive "Changing Conceptions of the Great Lakes Forest: Jacques Cartier to Sigurd Olson," in *The Great Lakes Forest: An Environmental and Social History,* edited by Susan Flader (Minneapolis: University of Minnesota Press, 1983), 274–94.

2. Richard G. Bremer, *Indian Agent and Wilderness Scholar: The Life of Henry Rowe Schoolcraft* (Mount Pleasant: Central Michigan University Press, 1987), chap. 2.

3. Making a similar journey twenty years later as a member of the Houghton expedition, Bela Hubbard saw the half-buried pines that he encountered in the Grand Sable Dunes as resembling "the time-worn columns of some antique temple" and invoked the ruins of Persepolis. He found pillars and arches, and a graceful curve reminiscent of antique sculpture, in the Pictured Rocks. Bernard C. Peters, ed., *Lake Superior Journal: Bela Hubbard's Account of the 1840 Houghton Expedition* (Marquette: Northern Michigan University Press, 1983), 29, 32.

4. Indian petroglyphs offered another kind of historical record, one largely invisible to the early explorers.

5. Sydney W. Jackman and John F. Freeman, eds., *American Voyageur: The Journal of David Bates Douglass* (Marquette: Northern Michigan University Press, 1969).

6. Peters, *Lake Superior Journal,* 66.

7. Charles Whittlesey, "Two Months in the Copper Country," in *Fugitive Essays* (Hudson, Ohio: Sawyer, Ingersoll, 1952), 316.

8. See, for example, Daniel B. Botkin, *Discordant Harmonies: A New Ecology for the Twenty-first Century* (New York: Oxford University Press, 1990), especially chap. 4.

9. Lee E. Frelich, *Forest Dynamics and Disturbance Regimes: Studies from Temperate Evergreen-deciduous Forests* (Cambridge: Cambridge University Press, 2002), 15–16. Frelich argues that at shorter time scales, decades to centuries, forests exhibit periods of relative stability.

10. See Alan Trachtenberg, *Shades of Hiawatha: Staging Indians, Making Americans* (New York: Hill and Wang, 2004), chap. 1, on the reception of the poem and Longfellow's construction of Hiawatha as a "white man's Indian."

11. J. D. McClatchy, ed., *Henry Wadsworth Longfellow: Poems and Other Writings* (New York: Library of America, 1984), 57.

12. Helen Carr, *Inventing the American Primitive: Politics, Gender, and the Representation of Native American Literary Traditions, 1789–1936* (New York: New York University Press, 1996), 135–38, describes Longfellow's debt to John Heckewelder's account of the Delaware, John Tanner's captivity narrative, and George Copway's history of the Ojibwa nation. See Christoph Irmscher, *Longfellow Redux* (Urbana: University of Illinois Press, 2006), on Longfellow's sources and his sanitizing of the Ojibwa legends that he knew through Schoolcraft's versions and on his transformation of the figure of Manabozho.

13. See Robert F. Berkhofer Jr., *The White Man's Indian: Images of the American Indian from Columbus to the Present* (New York: Alfred A. Knopf, 1978), 86–96, on nineteenth-century assumptions about "the tragedy of the dying Indian" and the inevitability of the social progress that would displace him.

14. See Frank Bohn, "This Was the Forest Primeval," *Michigan History* 21 (1937): 21–38, for a reminiscence of the life of a physician in "Hiawatha land" at the beginning of the logging era.

15. *The Hiawathan: Michigan's Upper Peninsula Magazine,* 1948–; *Upper*

Peninsula of Michigan (Auto Club of Michigan, 1940); *Land of Hiawatha: Michigan's Upper Peninsula* (Upper Peninsula Development Bureau, 1935).

16. In Anishnabeg mythology Mudjekeewis was the older brother of Manabozho (Longfellow's Hiawatha). Mondamin became the spirit of corn.

17. Donald A. Dickmann and Larry A. Leefers, *The Forests of Michigan* (Ann Arbor: University of Michigan Press, 2003), chap. 5.

18. See Michael E. Soule, "The Social Siege of Nature," in Michael E. Soule and Gary Lease, *Reinventing Nature?: Responses to Postmodern Deconstruction* (Washington, D.C.: Island Press, 1995), 155.

19. See James C. Scott, *Seeing Like a State: How Certain Schemes to Improve the Human Condition Have Failed* (New Haven: Yale University Press, 1998), chap. 1. Scott uses the term *legible* primarily to refer to the replacement of old-growth forest by forests regularized and simplified through the application of principles of scientific forestry.

20. Dennis A. Albert and Patrick J. Comer, eds., *Atlas of Early Michigan's Forests, Grasslands, and Wetlands* (Lansing: Michigan State University Press, 2008).

21. For tables enumerating these uses, see Dickmann and Leefers, *The Forests of Michigan*, 76–78, 86. For details about the daily lives and beliefs of the Ojibwa, see Edmund Jefferson Danziger Jr., *The Chippewas of Lake Superior* (Norman: University of Oklahoma Press, 1979); James A. Clifton, George L. Cornell, and James M. McClurken, *People of the Three Fires: The Ottawa, Potawatomi, and Ojibway of Michigan* (Grand Rapids: Michigan Indian Press Grand Rapids Inter-tribal Council, 1986); and Charles E. Cleland, *Rites of Conquest: The History and Culture of Michigan's Native Americans* (Ann Arbor: University of Michigan Press, 1992).

22. Ignatia Broker, *Night Flying Woman: An Ojibway Narrative* (St. Paul: Minnesota Historical Society, 1983), 33.

23. Ibid., 32–33, 35, 131.

24. On the nature of *manitos* and relationships with them, see Basil Johnston, *The Manitous: The Spiritual Ways of the Ojibway* (St. Paul: Minnesota Historical Society Press, [1995] 2001), 2–3.

25. On Anishnabeg beliefs and ritual practices, see Cleland, *Rites of Conquest*, 65–72; and Basil Johnston, *Ojibway Heritage* (Lincoln: University of Nebraska Press, [1976] 1990).

26. Quoted in Charles C. Calhoun, *Longfellow* (Boston: Beacon Press, 2004), 208.

27. See Richard White, *The Middle Ground: Indians, Empires, and Republics in the Great Lakes Region, 1650–1815* (New York: Cambridge University Press, 1991), for an account of the complex interactions of Algonquian tribes with French, British, and Americans in the period from initial contact to the early nineteenth century, as well as of their struggles with the Iroquois. Carr, in chapter 3 of *The American Primitive*, writes about the ahistoricism of *The Song of Hiawatha* and the nature of its appeal to Longfellow's audience.

28. Trachtenberg, *Shades of Hiawatha*, 78.

29. For an analysis of the effects of contact with Europeans on the customary ways of Algonquian tribes, see White, *The Middle Ground,* especially chap. 11.

30. Clifton, Cornell, and McClurken, *People of the Three Fires,* 58–59.

31. Danziger, in *The Chippewas of Lake Superior,* 27, cites tribal tradition in claiming that the Chippewa (Ojibwa) occupied the area as early as the fifteenth century.

CHAPTER 2

1. J. P. Mayer, ed., *Alexis de Tocqueville: Journey to America,* translated by George Lawrence (New Haven: Yale University Press, 1960). See especially the chapter "A Fortnight in the Wilds" (354). The comparison of seemingly endless forest with an ocean became a common one in nineteenth-century American writing. See, for example, James Fenimore Cooper, *The Pathfinder* (New York: Signet, [1840] 1980), 11.

2. See Roderick Nash, *Wilderness and the American Mind,* 3rd ed. (New Haven: Yale University Press, 1982), chap. 3, for a discussion of the rise of romantic views of wilderness in Europe and America.

3. Roselynn Ederer, *On the Banks of the Beautiful Saugenah* (Saginaw, Mich.: Thomaston Publishing, 1999), 3.

4. Bela Hubbard, *Memorials of a Half-Century* (New York: G. P. Putnam's Sons, 1887), 72–73.

5. I owe the phrase "ecological nostalgia" to David Lowenthal. See his "The Pioneer Landscape: An American Dream," *Great Plains Quarterly* 2 (1982): 5–19.

6. Francis Parkman, *History of the Conspiracy of Pontiac* (Boston: Little, Brown, 1855), 39.

7. James Hall, *Legends of the West* (Cincinnati: Robert Clarke, [1833] 1885), 135.

8. William Nowlin, *The Bark Covered House; or, Back in the Woods Again* (Ann Arbor: University Microfilms, [1876] 1966), 45.

9. R. C. Kedzie, "The St. Joes," *Michigan Pioneer and Historic Collections* 28 (1900): 414.

10. Quoted in Robert E. Grese, "The Prairie Gardens of O. C. Simonds and Jens Jensen," in *Regional Garden Design in the United States,* edited by Therese O'Malley and Marc Treib (Washington, D.C.: Dumbarton Oaks Research Library and Collection, 1995), 99–123.

11. Kedzie, "The St. Joes," 415.

12. B. M. McCutcheon, "Log Cabin Times and Log Cabin People," *Michigan Pioneer and Historical Collections* 29 (1901): 609–24.

13. William Bradford, *Of Plymouth Plantation* (New York: Random House, 1952), 62; Isaiah 51:3.

14. Henry Little, "Fifty Years Ago," *Michigan Pioneer and Historical Collections* 3 (1881): 511.

15. L. D. Watkins, "Destruction of the Forests of Southern Michigan," *Michigan Pioneer and Historical Collections* 28 (1900): 150.

16. William Barillas, "Michigan's Pioneers and the Destruction of the Hardwood Forest," *Michigan Historical Review* 15 (1989): 12–15; Michael Williams, *Americans and Their Forests* (Cambridge: Cambridge University Press, 1989), 74–75.

17. Williams, *Americans and Their Forests,* 56.

18. Donald I. Dickmann and Larry A. Leefers, *The Forests of Michigan* (Ann Arbor: University of Michigan Press, 2003), 107–8; Eugene Davenport, *Timberland Times* (Urbana: University of Illinois Press, 1950), 16–17. Davenport re-creates a sense of the early-nineteenth-century landscape of the Grand River valley of southwestern lower Michigan.

19. Davenport insists that the settlers were at home in the forest and did not find it forbidding or terrifying but rather a source of abundance. *Timberland Times,* 19–25.

20. Caroline Kirkland, *Forest Life,* 2 vols. (New York: C. S. Francis, 1844), 1:176–81.

21. For a modern edition with a good critical and biographical introduction, see Caroline M. Kirkland, *A New Home, Who'll Follow,* edited by Sandra A. Zagarell, 2 vols. (New Brunswick, N.J.: Rutgers University Press, 1990). Quotations are taken from this edition. William S. Osborne, *Caroline M. Kirkland* (New York: Twayne Publishers, 1972), provides a useful overview of Kirkland's life and work. For an assessment of her originality and her influence on the development of American literary realism, see Annette Kolodny's chapter on Kirkland in *The Land Before Her* (Chapel Hill: University of North Carolina Press, 1984), 131–58.

22. Kirland, *A New Home,* 6.

23. Kirkland, *Forest Life,* 1:43.

24. Charles Lanman, *Essays for Summer Hours* (Boston: James Munroe, 1843), 82–94.

25. Ibid., 47–49.

26. Ibid., 13.

27. Caroline Kirkland, *Western Clearings* (New York: John Wiley, 1848), 94.

28. Kirkland, *Forest Life,* 1:129.

29. Ibid., 1:130–31. Lanman quotes a friend who praises Michigan's forests as much better than the famous ones of Vallombrosa in Tuscany. *Essays for Summer Hours,* 61–62.

30. Biologists now think of prairie and savanna as part of a continuum that ends with closed-canopy forest, with frequency of trees per acre determining the classification. By one definition, a savanna has more than one tree per acre but less than 50 percent tree canopy. See John T. Curtis, *The Vegetation of Wisconsin* (Madison: University of Wisconsin Press, 1959), 330. For a more recent discussion of savanna types, see Roger C. Anderson and Marlin L. Bowles, "Deep-Soil Savannas and Barrens of the Midwestern United States," in *Savannas, Barrens, and Rock Outcrop Plant Communities of North America,* edited by Roger C. Anderson, James

S. Fralish, and Jerry M. Baskin (Cambridge: Cambridge University Press, 1999), 155–67. Steve Packard describes the process by means of which he reconstructed the flora of the oak savanna in "Just a Few Oddball Species: Restoration and the Rediscovery of the Tallgrass Savanna," *Restoration and Management Notes* 6 (1988): 13–22.

31. For the story of restoration efforts in the Chicago area through 1993 with an emphasis on the role of Steve Packard, see William K. Stevens, *Miracle under the Oaks* (New York: Pocket Books, 1995). A website maintained by the Green Ribbon Initiative (www.oakopen.org) describes restoration efforts in Ohio, which include the Oak Openings Preserve Metropark, the Nature Conservancy's Kitty Todd Preserve, and three natural areas managed by Ohio's Department of Natural Resources.

32. *The Emigrant's Guide to the State of Michigan* (New York: E. H. Thomson, 1849), 11.

33. Bernard C. Peters, "Early Perception of a High Plain in Michigan," *Annals of the Association of American Geographers* 62 (1972): 57–60.

34. *Michigan Journal, 1836*. George S. May and Douglas H. Gordon, eds., *Michigan History* 43 (1959): 263.

35. Michael Pollan discusses the importance of planting orchards to settlers, who had to set out at least fifty apple or pear trees as a condition of a land grant in the Northwest Territory. See his *The Botany of Desire* (New York: Random House, 2001), 16.

36. Charles Fenno Hoffman, *A Winter in the West*, 2 vols. (New York: Harper and Brothers, 1835), 1:143. Prince Puckler-Muskau had contributed to the vogue for English parks through a series of letters to his wife from England (1826–29) in which he delighted in views that included ancient trees and carpets of grass, which he found in his visits to country houses and castles. See Flora Brenner, ed., *Puckler's Progress* (London: Collins, 1987).

37. Hoffman, *A Winter in the West*, 1:183.

38. James Fenimore Cooper, *The Oak Openings* (New York: Townsend, 1860), 11.

39. Daniel Peck, whose reading of *The Oak Openings* remains one of the most astute, notes the influence of neoclassical aesthetics, citing Joseph Addison on "The Pleasures of the Imagination": "[W]e find the works of Nature still more pleasant, the more they resemble those of Art." Quoted in H. Daniel Peck, *A World by Itself: The Pastoral Moment in Cooper's Fiction* (New Haven: Yale University Press, 1977), 46.

40. Blake Nevius, *Cooper's Landscapes: An Essay on the Picturesque Vision* (Berkeley: University of California Press, 1976), 96–98, 100, 107. See chapter 2 for a concise account of these aesthetic categories and how Cooper responded to them, especially during his European stay. On Cooper's landscapes and visual sense, see also James T. Callow, *Kindred Spirits: Knickerbocker Writers and American Artists, 1805–1855* (Chapel Hill: University of North Carolina Press, 1967); Donald A. Ringe, *The Pictorial Mode: Space and Time in the Art of Bryant, Irving, and Cooper* (Lexington: University of Kentucky Press, 1971); and Peck, *A World by Itself.*

41. Peck, *A World by Itself,* 56–57.

42. Blake Nevius makes this point, comparing Cooper's use of clearings in his forest romances (e.g., *The Deerslayer*) to settings for theatrical episodes. *Cooper's Landscapes,* 98–100.

43. Peck, *A World by Itself,* 49–55.

44. Wayne Franklin has described the tendency of Cooper's plots to force the mythic into history and to disturb the mood of "discovery" associated with the wonder "evoked by an archetypal new world," seeing wonder and violence as linked in his work. *The New World of James Fenimore Cooper* (Chicago: University of Chicago Press, 1982), 107, 6–7.

45. See, for example, John P. McWilliams, *Political Justice in a Republic: James Fenimore Cooper's America* (Berkeley: University of California Press, 1972), 291–97.

46. Peck, *A World by Itself,* 72; McWilliams, *Political Justice in a Republic,* 295–96, 193.

47. John James Audubon, *Ornithological Biography,* 5 vols. (Edinburgh: Adam and Charles Black, 1831–39), 1:32.

CHAPTER 3

1. See Dave Dempsey, *Ruin and Recovery* (Ann Arbor: University of Michigan Press, 2001), 46–48, 62–64.

2. William B. Mershon, "Lumberman's Memorial Dedicated, July 16, 1932: Address by William B. Mershon," Bentley Historical Library, University of Michigan.

3. Theodore J. Karamanski, *Deep Woods Frontier: A History of Logging in Northern Michigan* (Detroit: Wayne State University Press, 1989), 83–84, 186.

4. Ibid., 57, 59–64.

5. Rolland H. Maybee, *Michigan's White Pine Era* (Lansing: Michigan Historical Commission, 1960), 43; Donald I. Dickmann and Larry A. Leefers, *The Forests of Michigan* (Ann Arbor: University of Michigan Press, 2003), 157, 160, 169.

6. See William Cronon, *Nature's Metropolis: Chicago and the Great West* (New York: W. W. Norton, 1991), chap. 4, for an excellent analysis of the functioning of the wholesale lumber market in Chicago and its relationship to the logging of white pine in western Michigan and eastern Wisconsin. For a recent history of the spread of commercial logging across the country in the nineteenth century, see Thomas R. Cox, *The Lumberman's Frontier: Three Centuries of Land Use, Society, and Change in America's Forests* (Corvallis: Oregon State University Press, 2010).

7. Robert W. Wells, *Daylight in the Swamp* (New York: Doubleday, 1978), 110–11; Dickmann and Leefers, *The Forests of Michigan,* 127–28.

8. Earl Clifton Beck, *Lore of the Lumber Camps* (Ann Arbor: University of Michigan Press, 1948), 29–32.

9. Quoted in John S. Springer, *Forest Life and Forest Trees* (New York: Harper and Brothers, 1851), 132–33.

10. John Greenleaf Whittier, "The Lumbermen," in *The Complete Poetical Works of John Greenleaf Whittier* (Boston: Houghton Mifflin, 1894), 359–61.

11. Beck, *Lore of the Lumber Camps*, 33–34.

12. Ibid., 194–97.

13. Daniel G. Hoffman makes this connection in *Paul Bunyan: Last of the Frontier Demigods* (Philadelphia: University of Pennsylvania Press for Temple University Publications, 1952), 15–17.

14. For a summary of the oral tradition based on these recollections, see Bernice K. Stewart and Homer A. Watt, "Legends of Paul Bunyan, Lumberjack," *Transactions of the Wisconsin Academy of Sciences, Arts, and Letters* 18, no. 2 (1916): 639–51.

15. See Hoffman, *Paul Bunyan*, 29–31, for commentary on the significance of the Bunyan stories for the lumberjacks.

16. George Angus Belding, "By the Banks of the Manistee," quoted in Beck, *Lore of the Lumber Camps*, 85–86.

17. John W. Fitzmaurice, *"The Shanty Boy"; or, Life in a Lumber Camp* (Upper Saddle River, New Jersey: Gregg Press, [1889] 1970).

18. "Ghost Wail," foreword to George Angus Belding, *Tales from the Presque Isle Woods* (New York: Exposition Press, 1946), 21.

19. See, for example, Robert I. Thompson, *Newaygo White Pine Heritage* (Newaygo, Mich.: Newaygo City Bicentennial Committee, 1976), on the impact of logging along the Muskegon River; Matthew J. Friday, *Among the Sturdy Pioneers: The Birth of the Cheboygan Area as a Lumbering Community, 1778–1935* (Victoria, B.C.: Trafford Publishing, 2006); Forrest B. Meek, *Michigan's Timber Battle Ground: A History of Clare County, 1674–1900* (Clare County, Mich.: Clare County Bicentennial Commission, 1976); and James K. Jamison, "Pine," in *This Ontonagon Country* (Ontonagon, Mich.: Ontonagon Herald, 1939) (pamphlet).

20. See Fred C. Burke, *Logs on the Menominee* (Menasha, Wis.: George Banta, 1946), on the workings of the Menominee River Boom Company.

21. "The grayling is gone forever—gone with the pines and the [passenger] pigeons and the Michigan that used to be." Hazen L. Miller, *The Old Au Sable* (Grand Rapids, Mich.: William B. Eerdmans, 1964), 105–6. William B. Mershon figures in this history as an avid defender of the grayling and the health of the Au Sable.

22. Irene M. Hargreaves and Harold M. Foehl, *The Story of Logging the White Pine in the Saginaw Valley* (Bay City, Mich.: Red Keg Press, 1964).

23. Ibid., 39, 46.

24. William S. Crowe, *Lumberjack: Inside an Era in the Upper Peninsula of Michigan*, edited by Lynn McGlothlin Emerick and Ann McGlothlin Weller (Skandia, Mich.: North Country Publishing, 2002).

25. Ibid., 2.

26. Ibid., 10–11.

27. Walker D. Wyman, *The Lumberjack Frontier* (Lincoln: University of Nebraska Press, 1969), 48, 80.

28. See, for example, Wells, *Daylight in the Swamp*, 224–25.

29. Helen Longyear Paul, ed., *Landlooker in the Upper Peninsula of Michigan* (Marquette, Mich.: Longyear Research Library, 1983), 71.

30. Isaac Stephenson, *Recollections of a Long Life, 1829–1915* (Chicago: Privately printed, 1915).

31. George W. Hotchkiss, *History of the Lumber and Forest Industry of the Northwest* (Chicago: George W. Hotchkiss, 1898), 305.

32. John Emmett Nelligan, as told to Charles M. Sheridan, *The Life of a Lumberman* (N.p., 1929), 201–2.

33. Ibid., 37–38.

34. Stewart Holbrook, *Holy Old Mackinaw: A Natural History of the American Lumberjack* (New York: Macmillan, 1938), vii–viii.

35. Ibid., 16.

36. For a collection of anecdotes about Seney, see Louis C. Reimann, *Incredible Seney* (Ann Arbor: Northwoods Publishers, 1953).

37. Jim Carter, "Crossroads at the Fox River," in *A Most Superior Land,* edited by David M. Frimodig and Susan Newhof Pile (Lansing: Michigan Natural Resources Magazine, 1983), 67–75.

38. Holbrook, *Holy Old Mackinaw,* 255, 248.

39. John Bartlow Martin, *Call It North Country* (New York: Alfred A. Knopf, 1944), 138.

40. Herbert Nolan, *Logging the Tittabawassee* (Tawas City, Mich.: Printer's Devil Press, 2005), 46.

41. Crowe, *Lumberjack,* 69–70. Matthew J. Friday, in *Among the Sturdy Pioneers,* 86–87, debunks reports of widespread carousing in Cheboygan, observing that most of the lumberjacks went home to resume their work on farms.

42. William Davenport Hulbert, *White Pine Days on the Taquamenon,* edited by Richard Hulbert (Lansing: Historical Society of Michigan, 1949).

43. William Davenport Hulbert, *Forest Neighbors: Life Stories of Wild Animals* (London: Limpus, Baker, 1903). John Burroughs praised Hulbert's animal stories for not crossing the line between fact and fiction, as he condemned the work of Ernest Thompson Seton and William J. Long for doing: "The sketches are sympathetically done, and the writer's invention is called into play without the reader's credulity ever being taxed." "Real and Sham Natural History" (1903), reprinted in *The Wild Animal Story,* edited by Ralph H. Lutts (Philadelphia: Temple University Press, 1998), 129–43, 132. Lutts discusses contemporary debates over animal psychology in his introduction and the final essay of the collection on the "Nature Fakers" controversy (268–90).

44. J. D. McClatchy, ed., *Poems of Henry Wadsworth Longfellow* (New York: Library of America, 2000), 154.

45. Ibid., 255.

46. Thompson, *Newaygo White Pine Heritage*, 11. For other examples of the life story of a pine, see the version in Thomas Hubbell's 1908 address to the Boy's Club of Manistee in Dickmann and Leefers, *The Forests of Michigan*, 174–75; and Nelligan, *The Life of a Lumberman* , 66–72.

47. "Point of View," reproduced in Burke, *Logs on the Menominee*, 81.

CHAPTER 4

1. John Emmett Nelligan, *The Life of a Lumberman* (N.p., 1929), 93–94.

2. Edna Rosemary Butte, "Stewart Edward White: His Life and Literary Work," PhD diss., University of Southern California, 1960. See also Judy Alter, *Stewart Edward White* (Boise: Boise State University Press, 1975).

3. Other contemporary writers in this vein included Rex Beach, Zane Grey, and James Oliver Curwood, who spent most of his adult life in Michigan but based his fiction primarily on his experiences in the Canadian wilderness.

4. For recent accounts of this literary movement, see Nancy Glazener, *Reading for Realism: The History of a U.S. Literary Institution, 1850–1910* (Durham: Duke University Press, 1997), especially chap. 4; and T. J. Jackson Lears, *No Place of Grace: Antimodernism and the Transformation of American Culture* (New York: Pantheon, 1981), chap. 3.

5. Lears, *No Place of Grace*, 103.

6. White describes reading Cooper when growing up, along with Scott's *Ivanhoe* and a version of Malory's *Morte d'Arthur*. Charles C. Baldwin, *The Men Who Make Our Novels* (New York: Dodd, Mead, 1925), 550.

7. The manuscript of *The Blazed Trail* includes the subtitle "A Story of Strong Men," dropped in publication. The handwritten manuscript can be found in the Special Collections of the University of Michigan Library.

8. Frederick Jackson Turner, *The Frontier in American History* (New York: H. Holt, 1920). For a discussion of the American wilderness cult that developed in the late nineteenth and early twentieth centuries, see Roderick Nash, *Wilderness and the American Mind,* 3rd ed. (New Haven: Yale University Press, 1982), 141–60. Roosevelt articulated the ideal of the "strenuous life" in a speech in Chicago in 1899.

9. Roosevelt referred to his time with White in a letter to John Hay describing the highlights of his western trip: "Stewart Edward White, the author of *The Blazed Trail*, which among recent novels I like next to *The Virginian*, was also with me for a fortnight." Elting Morison, ed., *The Letters of Theodore Roosevelt*, 4 vols. (Cambridge: Harvard University Press, 1951), 3:548. Roosevelt listed White with other writers he praised for portraying nature truthfully, after John Burroughs and John Muir, in his essay "Nature Fakers," *Everybody's Magazine* 17 (September 1907): 427–30.

10. Theodore Roosevelt, *An Autobiography* (New York: Charles Scribner's Sons, 1920), 31.

11. Theodore Roosevelt, *The Works of Theodore Roosevelt,* 24 vols. (New York: Charles Scribner's Sons, 1923), 2:xii.

12. Richard Slotkin, in *Gunfighter Nation: The Myth of the Frontier in Twentieth-Century America* (New York: Atheneum, 1992), writes at length about the frontier as mythic space and the evolution of popular fiction that exploits masculine virtues associated with an evolving understanding of the frontier experience.

13. See Henry Nash Smith, *Virgin Land: The American West as Symbol and Myth* (New York: Random House, 1950), on the development of the cowboy and other types of western hero in dime novels and on the evolution of thinking about the frontier.

14. Stewart Edward White, *The Blazed Trail* (New York: Grosset and Dunlap, 1902), 188.

15. Stewart Edward White, *The Riverman* (New York: Doubleday, Page, 1909), 310.

16. Stewart Edward White, "The Great Log Jam," *Frank Leslie's Popular Monthly,* July 1901, 210–23. For a more extensive account, see Ronald E. Kuiper, *Crisis on the Grand: The Log Jam of 1883* (Spring Lake, Mich.: River Road Publications, 1983).

17. White comments in the article, "The excitement was intense. Men who have served in the war tell me that the intoxication of battle was nothing to it. In this combined the elements of desperation and the spirit of the American pioneer bent on victory." "The Great Log Jam," 218.

18. Stewart Edward White, *Blazed Trail Stories* (New York: McClure, Phillips, 1904), 58.

19. Stewart Edward White, *The Forest* (New York: The Outlook Company, 1903), 5.

20. Baldwin, *The Men Who Make Our Novels,* 551.

21. Stewart Edward White, *The Silent Places* (Garden City, N.J.: Doubleday, Page, 1904), 109.

22. "The Ballinger Case: A Study in Official Fitness," *American Magazine,* March 1910; "The Case against Ballinger—Cleared Up," *American Magazine,* September 1910. White praised the whistle-blower who exposed Ballinger's dealings and characterized Ballinger's defense of his actions in a subsequent congressional investigation as "reluctant, insincere, and evasive," deploring Taft's continuing support of him.

23. Quoted in Butte, *Stewart Edward White,* 240. Yard, who would go on to become one of the founding members of the Wilderness Society and later its executive director, made his comment in 1924.

24. Quoted in ibid., 142.

25. *The Rules of the Game* is part of a trilogy of novels about the Orde family. The last to be published, *The Adventures of Bobby Orde* (1911), is a story about Bob Orde's boyhood in Michigan intended for young readers.

26. Quoted in Slotkin, *Gunfighter Nation,* 40.

27. White's Hilda Farnam has affinities with the heroine of a novel that had appeared the year before *The Blazed Trail,* Elia W. Peattie's *The Beleaguered Forest*

(1901). Peattie's heroine and narrator, Regina Grey, having impulsively married a lumberman who isolates himself in his lumber camp and sinks into a drug-induced depression, finds solace and even ecstasy in the scent and sound of pines (their "hymn") and peace sitting under a tree she calls "the King of Pines" and her "Altar Tree." Peattie draws a sharp contrast between desolate scenes of charred stumps and the "beleagured" forest with which Regina empathizes. She talks to the trees and says of a Norway pine that she sees fall: "[I]t had been a poem: it became a log" (264). Unlike White, Peattie makes the artistic sensibility of her heroine (who plays the flute, writes poetry, and paints) the moral center of the novel. Logging is simply a form of destruction, with corrosive effects on those who practice it.

28. John D. Guthrie, *The Forest Ranger and Other Verse* (Boston: Gotham Press, 1919), 13, 21, 68, 74, 115.

29. "Women in the Forest Service," www.fs.fed.us. The first female chief, Abigail R. Kimball, was appointed in 2007.

30. Hamlin Garland, *Cavanagh, Forest Ranger: A Romance of the Mountain West* (New York: Harper and Brothers, 1910). Also in 1910, Zane Grey published *The Young Forester* (New York: Harper and Brothers), a boy's adventure story set in the Arizona mountains in which the villain is a "timber shark" illegally clear-cutting pines in a national forest. Grey's young protagonist, an aspiring forest ranger, rouses the actual forest rangers to reclaim the forest and establish a regimen of selective cutting based on a knowledge of forestry.

31. See Jean Holloway, *Hamlin Garland* (Austin: University of Texas Press, 1960), 178–79.

32. Hamlin Garland, *A Daughter of the Middle Border* (New York: Grosset and Dunlap, 1921), 342–44.

33. Garland went on to write another novel dealing with the Forest Service, *The Forester's Daughter* (New York: Harper and Brothers, 1914), which pits an exemplary ranger and his supervisor against a "slovenly, lawless mountain town" (72). The central drama in this novel involves the romance of the supervisor's supremely capable daughter and an easterner who has come west to recover his health and escape a future of working for his father, a timber baron who helped "devastate" Michigan.

34. Stewart Edward White, *The Rules of the Game* (New York: Doubleday, Page, 1910), 451.

35. See Nancy Langston, *Forest Dreams, Forest Nightmares: The Paradox of Old Growth in the Inland West* (Seattle: University of Washington Press, 1995), 157–59, on the Forest Service's early efforts to establish a market for its timber.

36. See Leo Marx, *The Machine in the Garden* (London and New York: Oxford University Press, 1964), 13–16.

37. The group of signers included western writers Hal Evarts and Bill Irwin, Albert Payson Terhune, and Harold Titus of Michigan.

38. A copy of the letter can be found in the Harold Titus Papers, Bentley Historical Library, University of Michigan, box 5.

39. On the origins and persistence of the image of Alaska as the last frontier, see Susan Kollin, *Nature's State: Imagining Alaska as the Last Frontier* (Chapel Hill: University of North Carolina Press, 2001).

40. Stewart Edward White, *Wild Geese Calling* (New York: Country Life Press, 1940), vi.

41. Earlier White had treated hand logging at greater length in his novel *Skookum Chuck* (1925), a chapter of which focuses on the prolonged, finally successful effort of a reclusive and self-sufficient hand logger on the British Columbia coast to skid a giant log ("The Transcendental Hand Logger").

CHAPTER 5

1. Mildred Walker, *Fireweed* (New York: Harcourt, Brace, 1934), 287. The University of Nebraska Press reprinted *Fireweed* in 1994 with an introduction by Annick Smith.

2. Lewis C. Reimann, *When Pine Was King* (Ann Arbor: Edwards Brothers, 1952), 18; Theodore J. Karamanski, *Deep Woods Frontier* (Detroit: Wayne State University Press, 1989), 203.

3. Edna Ferber, *A Peculiar Treasure* (New York: Doubleday, Doran, 1939), 371–72.

4. Edna Ferber, *Come and Get It* (Garden City, N.Y.: Doubleday, Doran, 1936), 102.

5. Ferber, *A Peculiar Treasure*, 372.

6. Wyler replaced Howard Hawks, who was fired by Goldwyn after filming a few scenes. The cast of the film version includes Edward Arnold as Barney, Frances Farmer playing both Lottas, Walter Brennan as Swan Bostrum, and Joel McRae as Barney's son (renamed Richard).

7. Ferber, *A Peculiar Treasure*, 372.

8. James Kates, *Planning a Wilderness: Regenerating the Great Lakes Cutover Region* (Minneapolis: University of Minnesota Press, 2001), 46–48.

9. Jeff Alexander, *The Muskegon: The Majesty and Tragedy of Michigan's Rarest River* (East Lansing: Michigan State University Press, 2006), especially 8–9, 24–26; David Cassuto, *Cold Running River* (Ann Arbor: University of Michigan Press, 1994), 2.

10. Kates, *Planning a Wilderness*, xv.

11. Susan N. Pyle, ed., *A Most Superior Land* (Lansing: Michigan Natural Resources Magazine, 1983), 84–91. The Isaac Stephenson Company published a promotional booklet, *The Story of Cloverland* (1910), which traded on Stephenson's reputation in an effort to sell four hundred thousand acres in the vicinity of the Escanaba River: "[H]e foresaw this country, cleared of timber, transformed into broad, rich fields and meadows upon which would be grazing countless thousands of livestock" (15). A booklet published in 1911 by the Upper Peninsula Development Bureau, *Seven Million Fertile Acres in the Upper Peninsula of Michigan,*

emphasizes the abundance of wild clover on cutover lands in the course of making an enthusiastic case for the suitability of the Upper Peninsula for farming of virtually any kind: "Get out on God's acres! Buy a farm!" (46).

12. Alvah H. Sawyer, "The Forests of the Upper Peninsula and Their Place in History," *Michigan History* 3 (1919): 367–83. Leo Alilunas describes the promotion of cutover lands in western lower Michigan in "Michigan's Cut-over 'Canaan,'" *Michigan History* 26 (1942): 188–201.

13. See Norman J. Schmaltz, "The Land Nobody Wanted: The Dilemma of Michigan's Cutover Lands," *Michigan History* 67 (1983), 32–40.

14. Kates, *Planning a Wilderness,* chap. 3. Lovejoy resigned his position as a professor in the University of Michigan's School of Forestry in 1920 to argue his views to a wider audience and subsequently worked for the Michigan Department of Conservation.

15. Harold Titus to E. G. Rich, March 2, 1922, Harold Titus Papers, Bentley Historical Library, University of Michigan, box 1.

16. See Stephen J. Pyne, *Fire in America: A Cultural History of Wildland and Rural Fire* (Princeton: Princeton University Press, 1982), 24–29, for an account of the behavior of mass fires, and pages 203–6 for a description of the Wisconsin fires of 1871. Denise Gess and William Lutz, in *Firestorm at Peshtigo: A Town, Its People, and the Deadliest Fire in American History* (New York: Henry Holt, 2002), tell the story of the Peshtigo fire and its aftermath.

17. Franklin B. Hough, *Report on Forestry* (Washington, D.C.: Government Printing Office, 1892), 239.

18. Pyne, *Fire in America,* 205–6.

19. For accounts of these and subsequent Michigan wildfires, see Stewart H. Holbrook, *Burning an Empire* (New York: Macmillan, 1943), chap. 9; and Donald I. Dickmann and Larry A. Leefers, *The Forests of Michigan* (Ann Arbor: University of Michigan Press, 2003), chap. 7.

20. Quoted in Hough, *Report on Forestry,* 242.

21. James H. Lincoln and James L. Donahue, *Fiery Trial* (Ann Arbor: Historical Society of Michigan, 1984).

22. Earl Clifton Beck, *Lore of the Lumber Camps* (Ann Arbor: University of Michigan Press, 1948), 241–43.

23. George Angus Belding, *Tales from the Presque Isle Woods* (New York: Exposition Press, 1946), 115–16.

24. Hough, *Report on Forestry,* 233.

25. Pyne, *Fire in America,* 204–5.

26. Rudolph Anderson to Harold Titus, March 5, 1921, Harold Titus Papers, Bentley Historical Library, University of Michigan, box 1.

27. Ben East, "Titus Prophet of Conservation for Michigan's Wilds," undated newspaper article [1935?], Harold Titus Papers, Bentley Historical Library, University of Michigan, box 5.

28. Clarence Andrews, *Michigan in Literature* (Detroit: Wayne State University Press, 1992), 89, citing a contemporary review in *Variety.*

29. Dave Dempsey, *Ruin and Recovery: Michigan's Rise as a Conservation Leader* (Ann Arbor: University of Michigan Press, 2001), 111–12. See Kates, *Planning a Wilderness*, chap. 7, for a fuller discussion of Titus's career as a popular writer and conservation activist and of the debates over the use of the cutover lands in the 1920s. See pages 128–30 for an analysis of Titus's use of the persona of the Old Warden.

30. Harold Titus, "The Old Warden on the CCC," *Field and Stream*, October 1933, 64.

31. Harold Titus, *Timber* (Boston: Small, Maynard, 1922), 27–28.

32. In her study of the Forest Service's management of the forests of the Blue Mountains of eastern Oregon, Nancy Langston describes the ideal of European silviculture as "a waste-free, productive stand: nature perfected by human efficiency." She argues that intensive management in the Blue Mountains, including the suppression of even light fires, had the unintended consequence of displacing the dominant ponderosa pines in favor of thickets of firs that were highly susceptible to insect epidemics. See her *Forest Dreams, Forest Nightmares: The Paradox of Old Growth in the Inland West* (Seattle: University of Washington Press, 1995), especially the introduction.

33. Kates argues that Titus either didn't recognize or chose to ignore the loss of local autonomy as the management of forest resources became bureaucratized. See *Planning a Wilderness*, 127–28.

34. A prior novel in the series, *Connie Morgan in the Lumber Camps* (New York: G. P. Putnam's Sons, 1919), portrays a winter in the lumber camps of Minnesota and the subsequent spring drive, with a plot that turns on Connie's ability to outsmart caricatured villains representing the Industrial Workers of the World (IWW) and the German-run syndicate that dominates logging in the area.

35. James B. Hendryx, *Connie Morgan and the Forest Rangers* (New York: G. P. Putnam's Sons, 1925), 40.

36. See Harold Titus, *Flame in the Forest* (New York and Chicago: A. L. Burt, 1932–33); and "The Picture that Walked," *American Forestry* 28 (December 1922): 715–19. The central action of the novel takes place on a tract of northern hardwood forest intended for sale to hunting and fishing clubs that would retain the right to log it selectively, "the new idea in forest management" (42). In the story a forester points the way to reviving the town by planting trees along the river and opening an inn that paves the way for summer cottages.

CHAPTER 6

1. See William B. Botti and Michael D. Moore, *Michigan's State Forests: A Century of Stewardship* (East Lansing: Michigan State University Press, 2006).

2. Quoted in Paul W. Hirt, *A Conspiracy of Optimism: Management of the National Forests Since World War Two* (Lincoln: University of Nebraska Press, 1994), 35.

3. The Department of Natural Resources replaced the Department of Conservation in 1969.

4. Botti and Moore, *Michigan's State Forests,* 93–94.

5. *Northwoods Call,* August 12, 2009.

6. Theodore Roosevelt, *The Wilderness Hunter* (New York: Charles Scribner's Sons, 1923), 7.

7. J. Hector St. John de Crèvecoeur, "What Is an American," in *Letters from an American Farmer,* edited by Albert E. Stone (New York: Penguin, [1782] 1963), 76. For an account of the early opposition between agrarianism and hunting and the transformation of the image of the hunter in the nineteenth century, see Daniel Justin Herman, *Hunting and the American Imagination* (Washington, D.C.: Smithsonian Institution Press, 2001), especially chaps. 3 and 6.

8. William Nowlin, *The Bark Covered House, or Back in the Woods Again* (Ann Arbor: University Microfilms, [1876] 1966).

9. John E. Howard, ed., *Hunting Expeditions of Oliver Hazard Perry* (Deforest, Wis.: St. Hubert's Press, [1899] 1994), 188.

10. W. Mackay Laffan, "Deer-Hunting on the Au Sable," *Scribner's Monthly,* April 1878, 753–67.

11. Edwin C. Nichols, "A Sketch of the Nichols Deer Hunting Camps," in William B. Mershon, *Recollections of My Fifty Years Hunting and Fishing* (Boston: Stratford, 1923), 89–97.

12. Herman, *Hunting and the American Imagination,* 174–76.

13. Paul Russell Cutright, *Theodore Roosevelt the Naturalist* (New York: Harper and Brothers, 1956).

14. George Bird Grinnell and Theodore Roosevelt, eds., *Trail and Camp-Fire* (New York: Forest and Stream Publications, 1897), 343. For a discussion of the implications of the ideal of the sportsman for conservation, see John F. Reiger, *American Sportsmen and the Origins of Conservation,* 3rd ed. (Corvallis: Oregon State University Press, 2001). James B. Trefethen, *An American Crusade for Wildlife* (New York: Winchester Press and the Boone and Crockett Club, 1975), offers a more reliable account of the early history of the conservation movement.

15. Theodore Roosevelt, *The Wilderness Hunter* (Charles Scribner's Sons, 1923), xxxi.

16. On the influence of the Boone and Crockett Club in particular, see Trefethen, *An American Crusade,* and Daniel J. Philippon, *Conserving Words: How American Nature Writers Shaped the Environmental Movement* (Athens: University of Georgia Press, 2004), chap. 1.

17. Trefethen, *An American Crusade,* 122, 155–56.

18. On Mershon's career as a conservation activist, see Dave Dempsey, *Ruin and Recovery* (Ann Arbor: University of Michigan Press, 2001), especially 40–42, 46–48.

19. Mershon, *Recollections,* iv.

20. Stewart Edward White, *The Adventures of Bobby Orde* (Garden City, N.Y.: Doubleday, Page, 1911).

21. W. B. Mershon, *The Passenger Pigeon* (New York: Outing Publishing, 1907), chap. 1.

22. Mershon, *Recollections,* iii, 128.

23. Eugene T. Peterson, *Hunter's Heritage: A History of Hunting in Michigan* (Lansing: Michigan United Conservation Clubs, 1979), 28.

24. A. D. Shaffmaster, *Hunting in the Land of Hiawatha* (Chicago: M. A. Donohue, 1904), 181.

25. Peterson, *Hunter's Heritage,* 49.

26. John G. Mitchell, "Bitter Harvest: Hunting in America (Book One: The Guns of Gaylord)," *Audubon* 81 (1979): 54–83.

27. The Fish and Wildlife Division of the DNR promotes fair chase principles and also a code of ethics promulgated by the Boone and Crockett Club: "Fair chase principles address the sporting, lawful pursuit of free-ranging wild game animals and extend beyond the hunt itself, as an attitude and a way of life based in a deep-seated respect for wildlife, for the environment, and for other individuals who share the bounty of this state's natural resources." Draft Deer Management Plan, 22. www.mich.gov/dnr. What such efforts must contend with is the transformation of firearms hunting into a high-tech enterprise and the influx of hunters with widely varying experience, expectations, and attitudes toward hunting.

28. Hans Huth, *Nature and the American: Three Centuries of Changing Attitudes* (Berkeley: University of California Press, 1957), chap. 7.

29. Charles E. Cleland, *Rites of Conquest: The History and Culture of Michigan's Native Americans* (Ann Arbor: University of Michigan Press, 1992), 258; Mary L. Ploor, "Along the Shores of Gitche Gumee," *Michigan History* 91 (2007): 26–30.

30. Charles Hallock, *Vacation Rambles in Northern Michigan* (N.p.: Passenger Department, Grand Rapids and Indiana Railroad, 1878), 24, 27.

31. Anon., *My Rambles in the Enchanted Summer Land of the Great Northwest* (Chicago: Chicago and Northwestern Railway, 1882), 9.

32. *Michigan Summer Resorts, Including the Michigan East Coast Resorts* (Detroit: Pere Marquette Railroad, 1913).

33. *Health and Pleasure Resorts* (Bay City, Mich.: Detroit and Mackinac Railway, 1917), 6, 17, 12.

34. James O'Donnell Bennett, *West Michigan's Flaming Forests* (Grand Rapids: West Michigan Tourist and Resort Association, 1935).

35. Warren James Belasco, *Americans on the Road: From Autocamp to Motel, 1910–1945* (Cambridge: MIT Press, 1979), 7, 74.

36. For a comprehensive survey of this movement, see Peter J. Schmitt, *Back to Nature: The Arcadian Myth in Urban America* (Baltimore: Johns Hopkins University Press, 1969).

37. J. C. Long and John D. Long, *Motor Camping* (New York: Dodd, Mead, 1923).

38. F. E. Brimmer, *Autocamping* (Cincinnati: Stewart Kidd, 1923), 17–19.

39. In 1917 the Forest Service commissioned a report that surveyed current

recreational uses of the national forests and made a strong case for recreation as a use comparable to such traditional ones as timber production, grazing, and watershed protection. Frank A. Waugh, *Recreation Uses in the National Forests* (Washington, D.C.: U.S. Department of Agriculture, 1918).

40. Harold K. Steen, *The U.S. Forest Service: A History* (Seattle: University of Washington Press, [1976] 2004), 118–22, 157–58, 209–12; Samuel P. Hays, *The American People and the National Forests: The First Century of the U.S. Forest Service* (Pittsburgh: University of Pittsburgh Press, 2009), 73–74, 84, 123, 138.

41. Hays, *The American People and the National Forests,* 83–85.

42. James E. Scott, "Forests as National Playgrounds," *American Forests and Forest Life* 31 (1925): 25–28, 52, 54.

43. Schmitt, *Back to Nature,* 159–61.

44. *The Parks of the People* (Lansing: Michigan Department of Conservation, 192–?), 6.

45. Helen Foster, *1921–1946: Twenty-five Years of Conservation in Michigan* (Lansing: Michigan Department of Conservation, 1960), 83–84.

46. Long and Long, *Motor Camping,* 34–37, 46–53, 80–85; Belasco, *Americans on the Road,* 71.

47. Leon F. Kneipp, "Forest Recreation Comes of Age," *American Forests and Forest Life* 36 (1930): 415–18.

48. Paul S. Sutter, *Driven Wild: How the Fight Against Automobiles Launched the Modern Wilderness Movement* (Seattle: University of Washington Press, 2002), 87–88. Kneipp changed the designation "wilderness area" to "primitive area" on the grounds that many of the areas had been altered by human uses such as grazing or logging.

49. John C. Miles, in *Wilderness in National Parks: Playground or Preserve* (Seattle: University of Washington Press, 2009), 30–31, argues that tension between use and preservation is inherent in the language of the act establishing the Park Service.

50. The editorials appeared in the June and September 1928 issues, 195–98, 232. See also Irving Brant, "America Invades the Wilderness," *American Forests and Forest Life* 35 (1929); and John C. Phillips, "The Passing of the Maine Wilderness," *American Forests and Forest Life* 34 (1928).

51. Sutter, *Driven Wild,* 83, 96.

52. Aldo Leopold, "Conservation Esthetic," in *A Sand County Almanac* (New York: Oxford University Press, 1949), 165–66.

53. Robert Marshall, "The Problem of the Wilderness," *Scientific Monthly* 30 (1930): 142.

54. Robert Marshall, *The People's Forests* (New York: Harrison Smith and Robert Haas, 1933).

55. See Sutter, *Driven Wild,* chap. 6, on the evolution of Marshall's thinking about wilderness.

56. Marshall, *The People's Forests,* 68–76.

57. See Marshall's chapter on the forests of the Selkirk Mountains, "A Bio-

logical Interlude," in *The People's Forests*. Marshall was a trained forester who played an active role in shaping federal forestry policy as head of the Forestry Division of the Bureau of Indian Affairs and then, until his untimely death, as the first head of the Division of Recreation and Lands for the Forest Service.

58. William H. H. Murray, *Adventures in the Wilderness; or, Camp-Life in the Adirondacks* (Boston: Fields, Osgood, 1869). A facsimile edition, with an introduction by Warder H. Cadbury, was published by Syracuse University Press for the Adirondack Museum in 1970.

59. Ibid., 12–14.

60. William H. H. Murray, "Sabbath in the Woods," in *Adventures in the Wilderness,* 196–97.

61. John Muir, *The Mountains of California,* edited by Edward Hoagland (New York: Viking Penguin, [1894] 1985), 40.

62. Douglas Brinkley, *The Wilderness Warrior: Theodore Roosevelt and the Crusade for America* (New York: HarperCollins, 2009), 178–79.

63. Theodore Roosevelt, *Hunting Trips of a Ranchman* (New York: G. P. Putnam's Sons, 1885), 206.

64. See Roderick Nash, *Wilderness and the American Mind,* 3rd ed. (New Haven: Yale University Press, 1982), 149–51.

65. Stewart Edward White, *Camp and Trail* (New York: Outing Publishing, 1907), 30.

66. Stewart Edward White, *The Forest* (New York: The Outlook Company, 1903), 5.

67. See "The Long Trail," in Rudyard Kipling, *The Complete Verse* (London: Kyle Cathie, 2002), 131–33. Kipling understood the Long Trail as involving a sea journey, in response to "the beat of the off-shore wind." The refrain of the poem rings changes on the appeal of the Long Trail, for example, "And life runs large on the Long Trail—the trail that is always new."

68. In the same year in which he published *The Forest* and a year before *The Silent Places,* White offered a version of the "Long Trail" for boys in *The Magic Forest* (New York: Macmillan, 1903), a liberally illustrated "modern fairy tale" popular enough to be reprinted six times. White uses the plot device of a nine-year-old boy separated from his parents on a train trip across Ontario and then rescued by a band of Ojibwa, who take him north with them by canoe to a place where they set up their summer camp. The narrative shows him progressively learning the ways of his Ojibwa benefactors and loving his summer adventure of living the life of an Ojibwa boy before being reunited with his parents.

69. I am indebted to Philip J. Deloria's excellent chapter on Seton and the evolution of the scouting movement in *Playing Indian* (New Haven: Yale University Press, 1998).

70. Ernest Thompson Seton, *The Book of Woodcraft and Indian Lore* (Garden City, N.Y.: Doubleday, Page, 1912), 3.

71. Ernest Thompson Seton, *Boy Scouts of America: A Handbook of Woodcraft, Scouting, and Life-Craft* (New York: Doubleday, Page, 1910), ix. Seton notes

on the title page that the handbook incorporates Baden-Powell's *Scouting for Boys.* He had previously accused Baden-Powell of copying many of his own ideas for the English handbook.

72. See Kevin C. Armitage, *The Nature Study Movement: The Forgotten Popularizer of America's Conservation Ethic* (Lawrence: University Press of Kansas, 2009), chap. 3. Armitage discusses the educational theory, derived in large part from psychologist G. Stanley Hall, on which Seton based his view that encouraging primitive instincts embodied in Indian life as he understood it would prepare children for the adult world.

73. Seton, *The Book of Woodcraft,* 13–41.

74. See Deloria, *Playing Indian,* chap. 4, for an analysis of the conflict between Seton and Beard and an account of the emergence of the Order of the Arrow.

75. *Camp Hayo-Went-Ha,* 1917, Library of Michigan, Lansing; Benjamin Hathaway, *The League of the Iroquois and Other Legends* (Chicago: S. C. Griggs, 1882). In his narrative poem Hathaway makes Hayo-Went-Ha into a legendary figure comparable to Manabozho, the model for Longfellow's Hiawatha.

76. See James Morton Turner's excellent analysis of the evolution of camping and its implications in "From Woodcraft to 'Leave No Trace,'" *Environmental History* 7 (2002): 462–84. The article is reprinted in Michael P. Nelson and J. Baird Callicott, eds., *The Wilderness Debate Rages On* (Athens: University of Georgia Press, 2009).

77. A recent study commissioned by the U.S. Fish and Wildlife Service shows hunting licenses declining nationally from approximately 16,750,000 in 1982 to just over 14,500,000 in 2006. Mark Damian Duda, *The Future of Hunting and the Shooting Sports* (Washington, D.C.: United States Fish and Wildlife Service, 2009), 15.

78. Armitage, *The Nature Study Movement,* 162–63.

79. Long and Long, *Motor Camping,* 157–67.

80. Modern commentators have tended to contrast Burroughs with his friend and rival Muir. See Bill McKibben's introduction to *Birch Browsings: A John Burroughs Reader* (New York: Penguin, 1992); and James Perrin Warren, *John Burroughs and the Place of Nature* (Athens: University of Georgia Press, 2006), a pioneering critical study of the writings of Burroughs in relation to those of Emerson, Thoreau, Whitman, and Theodore Roosevelt, as well as Muir.

81. John Burroughs, "English Woods: A Contrast," in *Fresh Fields* (Boston: Houghton Mifflin, 1902), 36–37.

82. McKibbin, *Birch Browsings,* 1–26.

83. Ibid., 115.

84. Bill McKibben, "The Art of Seeing," in *Birch Browsings,* 121, 123.

85. See Stephen Mercier, "John Burroughs and the Sentimental: Revaluing the Literary Naturalist," *Interdisciplinary Studies in Literature and the Environment* 17 (2010): 526–40, on the emotive and domestic character of much of Burroughs's writing.

86. The list of winners is available on the website of the John Burroughs Association (www.jbnhs.org), along with winners of a parallel award for an outstanding natural history essay given annually since 1993.

87. O. B. Eustis, *Notes from the North Country* (Ann Arbor: University of Michigan Press, 1983); Lon L. Emerick, *The Superior Peninsula: Seasons in the Upper Peninsula of Michigan* (Skandia, MI: North Country Publishing, 2002 [1996]).

88. See David Backes, *A Wilderness Within: The Life of Sigurd F. Olson* (Minneapolis: University of Minnesota Press, 1997), 70.

89. See Sigurd Olson, "Why Wilderness," in *The Meaning of Wilderness,* edited by David Backes (Minneapolis: University of Minnesota Press, 2001), 42.

90. Sigurd Olson, *Listening Point* (New York: Alfred A. Knopf, 1958), chap. 6; Sigurd Olson, *The Singing Wilderness* (New York: Alfred A. Knopf, 1956), 161–62.

91. Olson, *Listening Point,* 241–42.

92. Olson, "We Need Wilderness," in *The Meaning of Wilderness,* 61.

93. Olson, *Listening Point,* 73, 75.

94. See Finis Dunaway's excellent analysis of the impact and the implications of the Sierra Club's Exhibit Format Series in *Natural Visions: The Power of Images in American Environmental Reform* (Chicago: University of Chicago Press, 2005), chaps. 5–7.

95. See ibid., especially 134–43, 146–47, 163–64, 195–96.

96. Ansel Adams, "The Artist and the Ideals of Wilderness," 49–59; William O. Douglas, "Wilderness and Human Rights," 5–15; Joseph Wood Krutch, "Human Life in the Context of Nature," 67–73; all in *Wilderness: America's Living Heritage,* edited by David Brower (San Francisco: Sierra Club, 1961).

97. Wendell Berry, *The Unforeseen Wilderness* (San Francisco: North Point Press, 1991).

98. Stephen Trimble and Terry Tempest Williams, *Testimony: Writers in the West Speak on Behalf of Utah Wildlands* (Minneapolis: Milkweed Editions, 1996); Hank Lentfer and Carolyn Servid, eds., *Arctic Refuge: A Circle of Testimony* (Minneapolis: Milkweed Editions, 2001).

99. John Knott, ed., *Michigan: Our Land, Our Water, Our Heritage* (Ann Arbor: University of Michigan Press for The Nature Conservancy, 2008); Dave Dempsey and David Lubbers, *The Waters of Michigan* (East Lansing: Michigan State University Press, 2008); Ron Leonetti and Christopher Jordan, *Of Woods and Waters: A Photographic Journey across Michigan* (Bloomington: Indiana University Press, 2008).

100. Quotations and model names are taken from *ATV* 14, nos. 1 and 4 (2010).

101. *100 Years of Conservation . . . for the Greatest Good* (Washington, D.C.: U.S. Department of Agriculture, 2005), 8. The Forest Service estimates that OHV users in national forests grew "from about 5 million in 1972 to almost 36 million in 2000—a 600-percent increase."

102. See Hirt, *A Conspiracy of Optimism,* especially the introduction and chap. 8.

103. Ibid., xli. For tables on timber production see pages xliv–xlv.

CHAPTER 7

1. See Samuel P. Hays, *Beauty, Health, and Permanence: Environmental Politics in the U.S., 1955–85* (Cambridge: Cambridge University Press, 1987), for an analysis of the development of the environmental movement and resistance to it in the period from midcentury to the early 1980s. Donald Worster, in *Nature's Economy: A History of Ecological Ideas* (Cambridge: Cambridge University Press, 1977), traces the emergence of what he labels the Age of Ecology.

2. Roger A. Sedjo, ed., *A Vision for the U.S. Forest Service: Goals for its Next Century* (Washington, D.C.: Resources for the Future, 2000), 177, 218, 222–23.

3. Samuel P. Hays, *Wars in the Woods: The Rise of Ecological Forestry in America* (Pittsburgh: University of Pittsburgh Press, 2007). Hays offers a comprehensive account of the factors contributing to the emergence of ecological forestry and to subsequent controversies over forest policy.

4. The term *New Forestry* was associated with Jerry Franklin and those who collaborated with him on pioneering studies of forest ecosystems based on research conducted in the Andrews Experimental Forest, part of the Willamette National Forest in the Oregon Cascades. For an account of the development of this research and the controversies it precipitated, see Jon R. Luoma, *The Hidden Forest: The Biography of an Ecosystem* (New York: Henry Holt, 1999).

5. Hays, *Wars in the Woods,* 174–78.

6. Harold K. Steen, *The U.S. Forest Service,* centennial ed. (Seattle: University of Washington Press for the Forest History Society, [1976] 2004), xi–xii.

7. T. C. Boyle, *A Friend of the Earth* (New York: Viking Penguin, 2001), 168.

8. For definitions, see, among others, Eric Yencey, *Virgin Forest: Meditations on History, Ecology, and Culture* (Athens: University of Georgia Press, 1998), 118; and Elliott A. Norse, *Ancient Forests of the Pacific Northwest* (Washington, D.C.: Island Press, 1990), 56–61, 158–59 (table comparing characteristics of ancient forests and plantations). For a discussion of the continuing difficulty of reaching agreement on a definition of old growth, see Thomas A. Spies and Sally L. Duncan, eds., *Old Growth in a New World: A Pacific Northwest Icon Reexamined* (Washington, D.C.: Island Press, 2008), 313–16.

9. William Dietrich, *The Final Forest: The Battle for the Last Great Trees of the Pacific Northwest* (New York: Simon and Schuster, 1992), 105.

10. Langston, *Forest Dreams, Forest Nightmares,* 155.

11. Ibid., 306.

12. For an economical summary that contextualizes the dispute, see E. Norman Johnson and Frederick J. Swanson, "Historical Context of Old-Growth Forests in the Pacific Northwest: Policies, Practices, and Competing Worldviews," in *Old Growth in a New World,* edited by Thomas A. Spies and Sally L. Duncan (Washington, D.C.: Island Press, 2008), 12–28.

13. Dietrich, *The Final Forest,* 29.

14. The final two essays in Spies and Duncan, *Old Growth in a New World,* 303–26, summarize recent discussions of forest policy, insofar as they are repre-

sented by the range of contributors to the book, and offer prescriptions for the future management of Northwest forests.

15. See Brent S. Steel, "Common Sense versus Symbolism: The Case for Public Involvement in the Old-Growth Debate," in *Old Growth in a New World*, edited by Thomas A. Spies and Sally L. Duncan (Washington, D.C.: Island Press, 2008), 116–26. Hays, in *Wars in the Woods*, 174–86, discusses the controversy over the Healthy Forests Initiative as another battle in the ongoing war between commodity and ecological forestry.

16. James R. Strittholt, "After the Smoke Clears: Ecological Impacts of Salvage Logging," in *Wildfire: A Century of Failed Forest Policy*, edited by George Wuerthner (Washington, D.C.: Island Press, 2006), 185–89; J. E. Franklin, "Comments Submitted to the U.S. Forest Service on Its Draft Environmental Impact Statement for the Biscuit Recovery Project," quoted in Gary Snyder, *Back on the Fire* (Emeryville, Calif.: Avalon Publishing Group, 2007), 88.

17. For accounts of the court decisions, see www.earthjustice.org.

18. These are described by Dominick DellaSalla, chief scientist for the National Center for Conservation Science and Policy (Ashland, Oregon), in an article summarizing recent disputes over owl policy and the protection of old growth. *Seattle Post-Intelligencer*, September 26, 2008.

19. William Dietrich, "Who Won the Spotted Owl War?" *Forest Magazine* (winter 2004).

20. Norse, *Ancient Forests of the Pacific Northwest*, 273.

21. Robert G. Lee, "Sacred Trees," in *Old Growth in a New World*, edited by Thomas A. Spies and Sally L. Duncan (Washington, D.C.: Island Press, 2008), 96–97.

22. The Wilderness Act of 1964, reprinted in J. Baird Callicott and Michael P. Nelson, eds., *The Great New Wilderness Debate* (Athens: University of Georgia Press, 1998), 120–30.

23. Federal wilderness areas in Alaska deviate from the norm in allowing for "inhabited" wilderness and activities related to subsistence living. See John C. Miles, *Wilderness in National Parks: Playground or Preserve* (Seattle: University of Washington Press, 2009), chap. 11.

24. See especially William Cronon's influential "The Trouble with Wilderness; or, Getting Back to the Wrong Nature," in *Uncommon Ground: Toward Reinventing Nature*, edited by William Cronon (New York: W. W. Norton, 1995), 69–90.

25. Char Miller, *Gifford Pinchot and the Making of Modern Environmentalism* (Washington, D.C.: Island Press, 2001), 155, 407n.

26. John Muir, *Our National Parks* (Boston: Houghton Mifflin, 1901), 336–37.

27. For a discussion of the Hetch Hetchy dispute and its significance see Roderick Nash, *Wilderness and the American Mind*, 3rd ed. (New Haven: Yale University Press, 1982), 161–80.

28. William Rossi, ed., *Wild Apples and Other Natural History Essays by Henry D. Thoreau* (Athens: University of Georgia Press, 2002), 62–63.

29. John Muir, *My First Summer in the Sierra* (New York: Viking, [1911] 1987), 52.

30. John Muir, "God's First Temples," *Sacramento Daily Union,* February 5, 1876, cited by Daniel J. Philippon, *Conserving Words* (Athens: University of Georgia Press, 2004), 136.

31. John Muir, *The Mountains of California,* edited by Edward Hoagland (New York: Viking, [1894] 1985), 124.

32. I discuss Muir's sense of the vitality and dynamic flow of the natural world at length in *Imagining Wild America* (Ann Arbor: University of Michigan Press, 2002), chap. 3.

33. In *A Passion for Nature: A Life of John Muir* (New York: Oxford, 2008), Donald Worster discusses the nature and growth of this influence in his biography and asserts that Muir's "passion for nature had ignited a conservation movement across the country that was political, religious, aesthetic and moral in scope" (451).

34. Peter C. List, ed., *Environmental Ethics and Forestry: A Reader* (Philadelphia: Temple University Press, 2000), 180–83.

35. Aldo Leopold, *A Sand County Almanac* (New York: Oxford University Press, 1949), 201–26. On the evolution of Leopold's ideas about a land ethic and land health, see especially Susan Flader, *Thinking Like a Mountain: Aldo Leopold and the Evolution of an Ecological Attitude toward Deer, Wolves, and Forests* (Madison: University of Wisconsin Press, 1994); and Julianne Lutz Newton, *Aldo Leopold's Odyssey* (Washington, D.C.: Island Press, 2006).

36. I am indebted to Julianne Lutz Newton's discussion of how these terms functioned for Leopold. *Aldo Leopold's Odyssey,* 338–43.

37. On Leopold's linking of science and aesthetics, see Alan G. McQuillan, "Cabbages and Kings: The Ethics and Aesthetics of New Forestry," in *Environmental Ethics and Forestry: A Reader,* edited by Peter C. List (Philadelphia: Temple University Press, 2000), 293–318.

38. Aldo Leopold, "The Wilderness and Its Place in Forest Recreational Policy" (1921), in *The River of the Mother of God and Other Essays by Aldo Leopold,* edited by Susan L. Flader and J. Baird Callicott (Madison: University of Wisconsin Press, 1991), 79. For a discussion of the evolution of Leopold's thinking about wilderness and his involvement in the Wilderness Society, see Philippon, *Conserving Words,* chap. 4.

39. See Curt Meine, *Aldo Leopold: His Life and Work* (Madison: University of Wisconsin Press, 1988), 16, 128. Meine notes that White's work was among Leopold's favorite boyhood reading and that he reread White's *The Cabin* when he was convalescing from an attack of nephritis that he suffered while working for the Forest Service in New Mexico.

40. Aldo Leopold, "Wildlife in American Culture," in *A Sand County Almanac* (New York: Oxford University Press, 1949), 179. Leopold regarded Roosevelt as a great sportsman because he expressed this tradition "in words any schoolboy could understand" while crediting White with offering a "more subtle and accurate expression" of it.

41. See Aldo Leopold, "Conserving the Covered Wagon" (1925) and "Wilderness as a Form of Land Use" (1925), in *The River of the Mother of God and Other*

Essays by Aldo Leopold, edited by Susan L. Flader and J. Baird Callicott (Madison: University of Wisconsin Press, 1991), 128–32, 134–42.

42. Aldo Leopold, "The River of the Mother of God," in *The River of the Mother of God and Other Essays by Aldo Leopold,* edited by Susan L. Flader and J. Baird Callicott (Madison: University of Wisconsin Press, 1991), 127. This essay was previously unpublished.

43. Aldo Leopold, "Deer and Dauerwald in Germany," parts 1 and 2, *Journal of Forestry* 34 (April 1936): 336–75 and 34 (May 1936): 460–66. See Meine, *Aldo Leopold,* 353–60; and Flader, *Thinking Like a Mountain,* 139–44, for accounts of Leopold's German experience and its effect on his views of forestry and game management.

44. Aldo Leopold, "Wilderness" (draft of a speech, 1935), in *The River of the Mother of God and Other Essays by Aldo Leopold,* edited by Susan L. Flader and J. Baird Callicott (Madison: University of Wisconsin Press, 1991), 226. Leopold comments, "I think it was Stewart Edward White who said that the existence of one grizzly conferred a flavor to a whole county" (228) and notes that this flavor had vanished from the German hills.

45. "Report on the Huron Mountain Club" (1938), reprinted in "Huron Mountain Wildlife Foundation Report, 1955–1966," 1967, 40–57, Bentley Historical Library, University of Michigan. Meine describes Leopold's visits to the Huron Mountain Club and characterizes his recommendations in *Aldo Leopold,* 385–86. Flader discusses the context of Leopold's report and efforts that he made to ensure its implementation in *Thinking Like a Mountain,* 159–63. For a history of the club, with commentary on its internal politics, see Arthur Mayer, *Huron Mountain Club: The First Hundred Years* (Huron Mountain Club, Mich.: The Club, 1988).

46. See Ethan Carr, *Wilderness by Design: Landscape Architecture in the National Park Service* (Lincoln: University of Nebraska Press), 240–41, on the origins of the system of land-use zoning in the master plan for Mount Rainier National Park developed by landscape architect Thomas Vint.

47. Aldo Leopold, "The Last Stand," in *The River of the Mother of God and Other Essays by Aldo Leopold,* edited by Susan L. Flader and J. Baird Callicott (Madison: University of Wisconsin Press, 1991), 290.

48. Ibid., 292–93. Leopold returned to the example of the Spessart in the "Conservation" section of his posthumously published *Round River,* using it to illustrate his oft-cited maxim "To keep every cog and wheel is the first precaution of intelligent tinkering." Aldo Leopold, *Round River,* edited by Luna B. Leopold (New York: Oxford University Press, 1953), 147.

49. Jack Van Coevering Papers, Bentley Historical Library, University of Michigan, box 13.

50. Raymond Dick, "Going, Going, the Forest of the Porcupines," *National Parks Magazine,* September, 1943, 11–14.

51. Ben East, "The Mountains of Michigan," *Grand Rapids Press,* August 6, 1943.

52. Ben East, "Trail Talk," *Grand Rapids Press,* February 26, 1944.

53. Aldo Leopold, "Wilderness as a Land Laboratory," in *The River of the Mother of God and Other Essays by Aldo Leopold,* edited by Susan L. Flader and J. Baird Callicott (Madison: University of Wisconsin Press, 1991), 288.

54. Ibid., 289.

55. Quoted in Meine, *Aldo Leopold,* 361.

56. On the early opposition to aesthetic objectives by foresters, see Samuel P. Hays, *The American People and the National Forests: The First Century of the U.S. Forest Service* (Pittsburgh: University of Pittsburgh Press, 2009), 41–45.

57. See J. Baird Callicott, "The Land Aesthetic," in *Companion to "A Sand County Almanac,"* edited by J. Baird Callicott (Madison: University of Wisconsin Press, 1987), 157–71. I am indebted to Callicott's analysis of Leopold's contributions to a natural aesthetic.

58. Aldo Leopold, "Marshland Elegy," in *A Sand County Almanac,* 96.

59. Aldo Leopold, "Conservation Esthetic," in *A Sand County Almanac,* 174.

60. Leopold, "Marshland Elegy," 101.

61. Ecological forestry has been called "thoroughly Leopoldian." McQuillan, "Cabbages and Kings," 301.

62. Another popular writer of the same period, Helen Hoover, also contributed to the image of the "north woods" of the upper Midwest with a series of books about her experiences living with her husband in a cabin on the edge of Minnesota's Superior National Forest, the best known of which is *The Long-Shadowed Forest* (New York: W. W. Norton, 1963).

63. On Olson's role as a conservation activist, see David Backes, *The Wilderness Within* (Minneapolis: University of Minnesota Press, 1997), especially chaps. 13 and 14.

64. Henry David Thoreau, *Walden,* edited by J. Lyndon Shanley (Princeton: Princeton University Press, [1854] 1971), 317; Sigurd Olson, "We Need Wilderness," in *The Meaning of Wilderness,* edited by David Backes (Minneapolis: University of Minnesota Press), 68.

65. Sigurd Olson, "What Is Wilderness," in *The Meaning of Wilderness,* edited by David Backes (Minneapolis: University of Minnesota Press), 153.

66. Sigurd Olson, *The Singing Wilderness* (New York: Alfred A. Knopf, 1956), 129–34.

67. Gordon Hempton and John Grossman, *One Square Inch of Silence: One Man's Search for Natural Silence in a Noisy World* (New York: Free Press, 2009).

68. Sigurd Olson, "The Preservation of Wilderness," in *The Meaning of Wilderness,* edited by David Backes (Minneapolis: University of Minnesota Press), 70. In his introduction Backes addresses criticisms of Olson's defense of wilderness (xxvii–xxxiii).

69. Kathleen Dean Moore, "In the Shadow of the Cedars: Spiritual Values of Old-Growth Forests in the Pacific Northwest," in *Old Growth in a New World,* edited by Thomas A. Spies and Sally L. Duncan (Washington, D.C.: Island Press, 2008), 168–75.

70. Donald M. Waller, "Getting Back to the Right Nature," in *The Great New*

Wilderness Debate, edited by J. Baird Callicott and Michael P. Nelson (Athens: University of Georgia Press, 1998), 559, 561. For Cronon's essay, see pages 471–99.

CHAPTER 8

1. Samuel P. Hays, *Wars in the Woods: The Rise of Ecological Forestry in America* (Pittsburgh: University of Pittsburgh Press, 2007), 156. Hays discusses the resistance to the vocabulary of ecological forestry among advocates of commodity forestry (128).

2. Duncan A. Harkin, "The Significance of the Menominee Experience in the Forest History of the Great Lakes Region," in *The Great Lakes Forest: An Environmental and Social History,* edited by Susan Flader (Minneapolis: University of Minnesota Press, 1983), 96; Thomas Davis, *Sustaining the Forest, the People, and the Spirit* (Albany: State University of New York Press, 2000), 14–18. The Menominee Forest has been managed by the tribe since its reservation was established in 1854, for much of that time under federal supervision. The Nicolet National Forest has been managed by the Forest Service since it was constituted in 1930, jointly with the Chequamegon National Forest since 1993.

3. See William S. Alverson, Walter Kuhlmann, and Donald M. Waller, *Wild Forests: Conservation Biology and Public Policy* (Washington, D.C.: Island Press, 1994), chap. 13 and postscript (257).

4. John J. Berger, *Forests Forever: Their Ecology, Restoration, and Protection* (Chicago: Center for American Places, 2008), 136, summarizing research by Hans Burkhardt.

5. *Menominee Tribal Enterprises Forest Plan, 1996–2005,* quoted in Davis, *Sustaining the Forest,* 48.

6. Ignatia Broker, *Night Flying Woman: An Ojibway Narrative* (St. Paul: Minnesota Historical Society Press, 1983), 56.

7. William B. Botti and Michael D. Moore, *Michigan's State Forests: A Century of Stewardship* (East Lansing: Michigan State University Press, 2006), 151–52.

8. Anne Woiwode, *A New Way of Thinking: Biological Diversity and Forestry Policy in the Northwoods of the Great Lakes States* (Sierra Club, 1994). See especially chapter 3, "An Example of a Place."

9. Donald I. Dickmann and Larry A. Leefers, *The Forests of Michigan* (Ann Arbor: University of Michigan Press, 2003), 236. Burt Barnes, Professor Emeritus of the School of Natural Resources and Environment of the University of Michigan, recalls assisting Forest Service employees in identifying acreage for inclusion, using the new ecosystem classification system, and persuading them to regard some timber-growing units that they were reluctant to include as "aspiring old growth" (personal communication).

10. Botti and Moore, *Michigan's State Forests,* 151–52, 160. See the 2001 DNR report, "Proposed Old Growth and Biodiversity," the 2002 Public Advisory Team

report to the DNR, and the 2005 report of the DNR's Conservation Commission at www.mich.gov/dnr.

11. Department of Natural Resources, *Wildlife Action Plan* (2005); *Within-Stand Retention Guidelines* (2006). www.mich.gov/dnr.

12. Department of Natural Resources, "Michigan State Forest Management Plan" (April 2008), www.mich.gov/dnr.

13. See www.fscus.org for U.S. standards and ongoing FSC activities in the United States. A watchdog site, www.fsc-watch.org, monitors FSC activities worldwide. The SFI, which was founded by the timber industry, has been more sharply criticized by environmental organizations for the practices it allows.

14. Botti and Moore, *Michigan's State Forests,* 156–58.

15. "Michigan State Forest Management Plan," April 2008, 7, 29.

16. Ibid., 259, 262.

17. Ibid., 259.

18. Craig Howard, "Project Summary: The Lake Superior State Forest Sustainable Forest Management Pilot Project" (1999), www.mich.gov/dnr.

19. Anne Hayes, Tom Clark, and Craig Howard, "Workshop 1 Summary: Values and Indicators of the Lake Superior State Forest" (1998), www.mich.gov/dnr. A comparable summary of the second workshop report reflects further discussion of appropriate values and indicators.

20. "Hiawatha National Forest Record of Decision," U.S. Department of Agriculture, Forest Service, 2006, ii, www.fs.fed.us.

21. See "Travel Management; Designated Routes and Areas for Motor Vehicle Use; Final Rule" (U.S. Department of Agriculture, Forest Service, 2005), www.fs.fed.us.

22. "Hiawatha Record of Decision," 26, 27.

23. Philip Cafaro, "Teaching Disrespect: The Ethics of Off-Road Vehicle Use on America's Public Lands," in *Thrillcraft: The Environmental Consequences of Motorized Recreation,* edited by George Wuerthner (White River Junction, Vt.: Chelsea Green, 2007), 31–35.

24. David G. Havlick, *No Place Distant: Roads and Motorized Recreation on America's Public Lands* (Washington, D.C.: Island Press, 2002), 107–8.

25. "Deer Management Plan," Michigan Department of Natural Resources and Environment, 2010, 9, www.mich.gov/dnr.

26. S. D. Cote, T. P. Rooney, J.-P. Tremblay, C. Dussault, and D. M. Waller, "Ecological Impacts of Deer Overabundance," *Annual Review of Ecological Evaluation Systems* 35 (2004): 113–47.

27. Dickmann and Leefers, *The Forests of Michigan,* 45, 193–94.

28. Ibid., 7–8.

29. "Summary of Public Comments and DNR Responses to Draft Michigan State Forest Management Plan (General Comments)," 4, www.mich.gov/dnr.

30. "Vegetation Management Comments," 8, www.mich.gov/dnr.

31. "Hiawatha Record of Decision," 34.

32. *A Critique of the Ottawa National Forest Plan* (Washington, D.C.: Wilderness Society, 1986).

33. "2006 Land and Resource Management Plan," Ottawa National Forest, 1–9, www.fs.fed.us.

34. "Final Environmental Impact Statement," Huron-Manistee National Forests, 2006, J-38, www.fs.fed.us.

35. "Final Environmental Impact Statement," Ottawa National Forest, 2006, J-65, www.fs.fed.us.

36. Some of the early research in Oregon's Andrews Forest that informed the New Forestry demonstrated the role of natural processes of decay in regenerating a forest. For a narrative account of this research, see Jon R. Luoma, *The Hidden Forest: The Biography of an Ecosystem* (New York: Henry Holt, 1999), especially chap. 5.

37. John Muir, "A Wind-Storm in the Forests," in John Muir, *The Mountains of California,* edited by Edward Hoagland (New York: Penguin, [1894] 1985), 171–72.

38. "Fiscal Year 2008 Monitoring and Evaluation Report," Hiawatha National Forest; "Fiscal Year 2009 Monitoring and Evaluation Report," Hiawatha National Forest, both at www.fs.fed.us.

39. *Anglers of the Au Sable v. United States Forest Service,* 590 F. Supp. 2d. 877 (E.D. Mich. 2008).

40. "Goliath, meet Rusty Gates," *Michigan Environmental Report,* winter 2009, www.environmentalcouncil.org. *EJ Magazine* (Knight Center for Environmental Journalism, Michigan State University), spring 2004, www.ejmagazine .com.

41. See Emily M. Slaten, "'We Don't Fish in Their Oil Wells, and They Shouldn't Drill in Our Rivers': Considering Public Opposition under NEPA and the Highly Controversial Regulatory Factor," *Indiana Law Review* 43 (2010): 1319–49, for a summary of literature arguing that narrow judicial interpretation of NEPA subverts its intent. Slaten uses the Mason Tract case as an illustration of the tendency to devalue public opinion by restricting the meaning of "highly controversial," a factor discounted by the district court judge in his ruling on this case.

42. *Kurt Meister v. Sec. of United States Dept. of Agriculture et al.,* 07-CV-13008-DT (E.D. Mich. 2009).

43. *Kurt Meister v. United States Dept. of Agriculture et al.,* 09-1712 (E.D. Mich. 2010).

44. *Habitat Education Center v. U.S. Forest Service et al.,* 363 F. Supp. 2d 1070 (E.D. Wis. 2005). See also *Habitat Education Center v. U.S. Forest Service et al.,* 363 F. Supp. 2d 1090 (E.D. Wis. 2005); and *Habitat Education Center v. U.S. Forest Service et al.,* 381 F. Supp. 2d 842 (E.D. Wis. 2005).

45. Personal communication from Kathrine Dixon, litigator for the Environmental Law and Policy Center. See Douglas Bevington, *The Rebirth of Environmentalism: Grassroots Activism from the Spotted Owl to the Polar Bear* (Washington, D.C.: Island Press, 2009), especially chap. 5, for a discussion of the success of

smaller, "grassroots" environmental groups in forcing the modification or cancellation of timber cuts through aggressive litigation. Bevington focuses particularly on the winning record of the Center for Biological Diversity and its strategy of using alleged violations of the ESA as the basis for court challenges to proposed timber cuts and other management practices in the Southwest and elsewhere.

46. Broker, *Night Flying Woman,* 8, 54–57.

47. Karen C. Danielson, "The Cultural Importance, Status, and Ecology of Giizhik (Northern White Cedar) in the Ceded Territories" (2002), www.glifwc.org.

48. Chief Tom Tidwell, "Restoring America's Forests through Landscape-Scale Conservation," speech delivered to the annual convention of the Society of American Foresters," November 2, 2009. See also the notice of intent to prepare an environmental impact statement in connection with developing a new planning rule to establish a framework for managing national forests and grasslands, December 18, 2009, www.fs.fed.us.

49. Alverson, Kuhlmann, and Waller, *Wild Forests,* 234. See pages 251–54 for a cogent statement of this position.

50. Klaus J. Puettmann, K. David Coates, and Christian Messier, *A Critique of Silviculture: Managing for Complexity* (Washington, D.C.: Island Press, 2009), 110, 117.

51. Dickmann and Leefers, in *The Forests of Michigan,* 263–66, suggest that "By 2050 white pine may once again be poised to retake the throne as king" (277).

52. On northern Wisconsin forests comparable to those in Michigan, see, for example, Thomas P. Rooney and Donald M. Waller, "Plant Species and Diversity in the Once and Future Northwoods," in *The Vanishing Present: Wisconsin's Changing Lands, Waters, and Wildlife,* edited by Donald M. Waller and Thomas P. Rooney (Chicago: University of Chicago Press, 2008), 75–90.

53. Botti and Moore, *Michigan State Forests,* 141–42; *North Woods Call,* January 27, 2010 (on moose restoration).

54. Objectives include expanding hemlocks by twelve thousand acres and white pines by twenty-one thousand. *A Process for Implementing Mesic Conifer Restoration on State Land, Western Upper Peninsula, Michigan* (Lansing: Michigan Department of Natural Resources, 2004), www.mich.gov/dnr.

55. "Two-Hearted River Forest Reserve Management Plan," September 2009, www.nature.org. *Wavelengths,* spring 2009, 1–2. *Wavelengths* is a newsletter published by The Nature Conservancy in Lansing, Michigan.

56. Personal communication from Brian Carlson of The Nature Conservancy.

57. Mary Lauritsen and Norma Jean Lauritsen, *Sylvania: Where Man Is a Visitor* (Rhinelander, Wis.: Jensmarie Publishing, 2006), chap. 2.

58. Henry David Thoreau, *Walden,* edited by J. Lyndon Shanley (Princeton: Princeton University Press, [1854] 1971), 318.

59. The Arthur Carhart National Wilderness Training Center was estab-

lished at the University of Montana in 1993 as a joint project of the Forest Service, the Park Service, the Bureau of Land Management, and the Fish and Wildlife Service to train wilderness managers and develop educational resources for the public. In a booklet titled *Wilderness Quotes* issued by the Center, Muir is the most frequently quoted author, followed by Leopold and then Thoreau.

60. I am indebted to Katherine Strong's valuable thesis, "The Conceptualization and Implementation of the Wilderness Idea in the Porcupine Mountains," written to satisfy the requirements for a master of science in environmental policy degree, Michigan Technological University, 2005.

61. Dave Dempsey, *Ruin and Recovery: Michigan's Rise as a Conservation Leader* (Ann Arbor: University of Michigan Press, 2001), 197–99.

62. Samuel T. Dana, "The Porcupines: Time of Decision," *Outdoor America,* January 1959, 11–13.

63. Quoted in Strong, "The Conceptualization and Implementation of the Wilderness Idea," 59.

64. It is unclear who gave the falls their Ojibwa names, although it is known that a village existed at the mouth of the Presque Isle River. Michael Rafferty and Robert Sprague, *Porcupine Mountains Companion,* 2nd ed. (Houghton, Mich.: Neqauaket Natural History Associates, 1993), 15, 139.

65. Personal communication from Robert Evans, retired Forest Service employee.

66. *Porcupine Mountains Wilderness State Park Master Plan* (Lansing: Natural Resources Commission, 1972), 9, 16–17.

67. Strong, "The Conceptualization and Implementation of the Wilderness Idea," 89–90.

68. Personal communication from Robert Sprague, park administrator.

69. Tidwell, "Restoring America's Forests."

70. Lee E. Frelich, *Forest Dynamics and Disturbance Regimes: Studies from Temperate Evergreen-deciduous Forests* (Cambridge: Cambridge University Press, 2002), 21. Frelich discusses changing disturbance patterns in the northern forests of the Lake States, including the possibility of larger blowdowns than those shown in the historical record due to more severe thunderstorms.

CODA

1. The present version of the Midewiwin includes both male and female leaders and members not training to become shamans.

2. The archetypal Upper Peninsula experience of getting lost in the woods is a favorite motif in Harrison's writing about Michigan. See, for example, his first novel, *Wolf* (New York: Simon and Schuster, 1971). Harrison speculates on what it means to get lost in his essay "Passacaglia on Getting Lost": "The shock of being lost as a metaphor is the discovery that you've never been 'found' in any meaning-

ful sense. When you're lost you know who you are. You're the only one out there." *Just Before Dark* (Livingston, Mont.: Clark City Press, 1991), 264.

3. Jim Harrison, *Off to the Side* (New York: Atlantic Monthly Press, 2002), 157. Brown Dog, a favorite character in several of Harrison's novellas through whom he explores the tragicomedy of life below the poverty line in the Upper Peninsula, declares, "My favorite thing is just plain walking in the woods." Jim Harrison, *The Woman Lit by Fireflies* (Boston: Houghton Mifflin, 1990), 48.

4. Jim Harrison, *Returning to Earth* (New York: Grove Press, 2007), 162.

5. Vieux Desert is based on the Lac Vieux Desert reservation (near Watersmeet), which Caputo relocates for the purposes of the novel.

6. Philip Caputo, *Indian Country* (New York: Random House, [1987] 2004), 162–63.

7. The Windigo was a giant, ravenous cannibal who roamed the winter woods and embodied the spirit of excess. Belief in *windigos* was related to the threat of starvation in winter.

8. For a recent discussion of research on the Midewiwin, the rise and decline of the society in different Ojibwa communities, and the contemporary revival of interest in Mide teachings and ceremonies, see Michael Angel, *Preserving the Sacred: Historical Perspectives on the Ojibwa Midewiwin* (Winnipeg: University of Manitoba Press, 2002).

9. Harrison, *Off to the Side,* 268.

10. Basil Johnston comments on the Ojibwa belief that places have spirit and possess "a mood which reflects the state of being of that place." *Ojibway Heritage* (Lincoln: University of Nebraska Press, [1976] 1990), 34.

Index

Page numbers in boldface refer to illustrations.